Contents

Acknowledgements   v

Prologue   1

1   WALKING SIDEWAYS   3

2   EARLY YEARS   10

3   SCHOOL DAYS   15

4   AN ARMFUL OF BOXCAR   30

5   PENNED IN   42

6   GETTING BY   48

7   WAR   52

8   LOVE AND WAR   56

9   THE HOME FRONT   64

10   TORONTO   69

11   FRUSTRATION   74

12   SUCCESS   79

13   SECOND TIME LUCKY   85

14   PARTNERS   92

15   CAUGHT   104

16   THE DON   115

17   CELLMATES   124

18   GONE   141

19   HIDING OUT   152

20   THE BOYD GANG   159

21   GOIN' SOUTH   168

22   ON THE LAM   172

23   POLITICS AND INTRIGUE   184

24   IN COLD BLOOD   192

25   AMBUSH   206

26   A REAL PAYNE   226

27   ANSWERED PRAYERS   242

28   KEYED UP   255

29   FALLOUT   272

30   MANHUNT   283

31   TRAPPED   294

32   ON TRIAL   310

33   DEAD MEN WALKING   321

34   KINGSTON   335

Epilogue   347

Notes   356

Sources   359

Index   361

For Nancy

Acknowledgements

I would like to thank Edwin Alonzo Boyd for agreeing to be interviewed, with no conditions, for this book and for two CBC *"fifth estate"* items that preceded it. I would also like to thank Boyd's wife, Marjorie, and their friend Pearl, whose cheerful disposition in spite of chronic disabilities was an inspiration.

Special thanks also to Jack Webster, historian with the Metropolitan Toronto Police Museum and Discovery Centre, for all his help and guidance; retired Kingston police chief Bill Hackett for his help in the early stages; Hartley Stewart for allowing me access to the *Toronto Sun* library with its invaluable *Toronto Telegram*; the *Sun's* Chief Librarian, Julie Kirsh, and her resourceful staff, including Susan Dugas and Catherine Flannery; John Honderich, Peter Taylor, and Jean Bradshaw for access to photos and headlines from the *Toronto Star*; the Toronto Arts Council for timely financial assistance that helped me complete my research; my publisher Don Sedgwick for keeping the faith when I fell behind schedule; Christine Innes and Janine Laporte at Doubleday; editors Matthew Kudelka and Anne Holloway; Doug Bassett; and Norman Boyd, Dorreen Boyd, Michael Jackson, Jocko Thomas, Helen Payne, Frank Cater, John Clement, John Sanderson, Allan Lamport, Maurice Richardson, and Mike Filey, for their insights and recollections.

Regrettably, John "Jack" Gillespie, the fearless and decent former Toronto policeman who played a key role in the story, died suddenly, two weeks before the manuscript was completed. His input added rich detail to this account and I was shocked and saddened by his death. I express my condolences to his family.

Finally, I wish to thank my old friend Doug Bradford, whose scowling self-portrait hanging over my desk seemed to be urging me to finish the book so that we could go fishing on Lake Lauzon.

*Thieves respect property; they
merely wish the property to
become their property that they
may perfectly respect it.*
— **G.K. Chesterton**

*I know I shouldn't say this, but
geez I loved robbing banks.*
– Edwin Alonzo Boyd

Prologue

Toronto in the late 1940s and early 1950s was considered a bastion of provincial conservatism. This perception would change with the gradual scrapping of "blue laws" and the influx of immigrants, which together helped transform Toronto into one of North America's most progressive, cosmopolitan cities. But even back then, beneath the veneer, *Toronto the Good* – "the city of churches" – boasted a wild cast of characters and an underbelly that made it a rollicking and sometimes dangerous place. In the background raged a fierce newspaper war between the *Toronto Daily Star* and the *Toronto Telegram* that fostered headlines which easily rivalled those of today's most brazen tabloids.

It was also the dawning of the television age, which saw the birth of the CBC and the emergence of Lorne Greene, "the voice of doom," who brought the news headlines to life. Crime, scandal, and political peccadillos were the grist – all provided by flamboyant politicians, journalists, lawyers, and, most importantly, the crooks and the tough cops who chased them.

The United States had seen the era of Al Capone, John Dillinger, Pretty Boy Floyd, and Baby-Face Nelson. Now the bad guys were being played on the silver screen by James Cagney, George Raft, and Edward G. Robinson. And some of the violent images in those movies were becoming a reality on the streets of Toronto as it was hit with an epidemic of bank robberies. The bankers, the politicians, and the police blamed each other. The banks armed their tellers and managers, who were expected to protect the money. The bullets often flew, but the robberies continued.

It was a time of bookies, bootleggers, tommy guns, gangster's girls, shoot-outs, and police manhunts. And at the infamous Don Jail, the hangman stood ready at the trapdoor.

It was not surprising that in this environment even moderately successful criminals became larger than life, and had their exploits blown out of proportion. It was indeed an exciting time – the time of the Polka Dot Gang, the Numbers Mob, and, most famous of all, the notorious Boyd Gang, which for three years dominated the headlines, until its leader, Edwin Alonzo Boyd, became somewhat of a folk hero.

1

Walking Sideways

The knot in his stomach wasn't exactly unfamiliar. He'd felt it often in the war. It wasn't fear really, more a nervous excitement. He was convinced nothing could go wrong. The meticulous planning would see to that. Still, he had brought along something to calm his nerves.

On the seat beside him, in his parked panel truck, was a quart of Irish whisky in a brown paper bag from the liquor store. He broke the seal with a firm twist of the cap and tipped the bottle to his lips, gulping the whisky like water. He wasn't much of a drinker and it burned all the way down. In England he had discovered scrumpy, a dangerous Devon cider. He'd liked the taste, but it had quickly made him drunk. A few sips of it would have been enough on this day, but there hadn't been any in the liquor store and now he was counting on the whisky.

It was mid-morning, September 9, 1949, a Friday. The rain of the day before had been pushed out by dry air from the west. It was perfect sunny weather with the temperature in the low sixties and climbing. Near the Toronto waterfront people were already streaming into the grounds of the Canadian National Exhibition – the "Ex" – where a dairy display and the morning session of the Canadian Checkers Championships were under way. In the afternoon there would be aerobatics by the air arm of the Royal Canadian Navy, and eager couples would fill the dance tent, where Guy Lombardo and his Royal Canadians were performing.

But now, in a weathered rented garage on a laneway behind a quiet residential street in north Toronto, the man waited in his truck. Sunlight flooded through the lone window, high on the east wall of the sagging frame building, providing enough light for him to check his appearance in the rearview mirror. He was satisfied it wasn't anybody he knew. Wads of absorbent cotton were stuffed into his cheeks, upper and lower lips, and both nostrils, forcing him to breathe through his mouth. Black mascara had broadened and darkened his eyebrows; his cheeks were rouged; and he had recently grown a moustache. He seldom wore a hat, but he liked the look of his dark fedora, tilted at a jaunty angle. He tugged firmly on the brim and sat back in the seat, waiting for the effects of the whisky. After several minutes he took another long swig, and then another.

Nothing was happening. The bottle was nearly half-empty and he couldn't wait any longer. Opening the glove compartment, he removed the white cotton sugar sack and the Luger he'd taken from a dead German on his way through France. He shoved the whisky into the glove compartment and got out of the truck. He neatly folded the white sack and slipped it into the right pocket of his dark-blue suit jacket, then tucked the Luger under his belt on the left.

There was no one in the laneway when he left the garage on foot, padlocking the doors behind him. The whisky perplexed him. If it had been scrumpy, he was certain, he would be walking sideways by now. He headed west to Elm Road, north for several blocks, and then west again on Old Orchard Grove until he reached Avenue Road.

Continuing north, he felt the first effects of the whisky, and when he tripped on a curb, three blocks from his destination, he knew he *was* walking sideways. This wasn't in the plan, but it was too late to back out.

The Armour Heights branch of the Bank of Montreal on the east side of Avenue Road had been open just over an hour when he walked through the door shortly after 11 a.m. The usual Friday rush was an hour away and, other than manager George Elwood and three of his staff, there was no one in the bank. From behind the desk in his small office, Elwood glanced up from his paperwork. The lone customer was dressed well enough, with a suit and tie, but there was something unsettling about him – perhaps the unnatural facial swelling, especially around the mouth.

Elwood thought the man looked suspicious and decided to attend him himself. There was no one in the teller's cage closest to the front door. The man was headed toward Joyce Empey, a young teller in the second cage, when Elwood intercepted him at the counter.

"Can I help you?" he asked.

The man handed him a folded cheque drawn on a downtown branch of the Bank of Montreal. Through habit, Elwood checked to see if it was endorsed. Instead of a signature there was a handwritten message in pencil. It said "HOLD-UP" in large print, and below, in smaller print, "If you don't want to be a dead hero, fill this sack with money." The man pushed the white bag across the counter towards Elwood.

"Are you kidding?" he asked.

The man pulled aside his suit jacket, revealing the Luger. The banker could see his eyes below the brim of the fedora. He would describe them later as "real *inward* eyes." Elwood quickly passed the note and the bag to Empey in the teller's cage. As she read the note, the robber pulled out the Luger and levelled it at the manager's chest.

"What ... what will I do?" asked Empey.

"We have no choice, give him the money," said Elwood, staring at the Luger. He was thinking of the bank-issue revolver in his office drawer and, even closer, the fully loaded, .38 calibre Ivor Johnson revolver in Empey's drawer. The gun was within Empey's reach, but the robber was too close and, the teller worried, too unpredictable.

As Empey began transferring money from her cash drawer to the sugar sack, she pressed the silent alarm with her foot. There was more than $2,000, in denominations no larger than twenties. Instead of stuffing the bills into the bag by the handful, she slipped them in one or two at a time, hoping the police would soon arrive.

The man had a grip on his gun, but the whisky now had a grip on him. Everything was blurry. He knew he was supposed to be holding up the bank, but he blacked out two or three times as he stood there. Attempting to steady himself, he held the Luger with both hands, arms outstretched, adopting the shooting stance that twenty-five years later would be taught in police colleges and imitated a thousand times in movie and television police dramas. Empey wasn't impressed. The man reeked of liquor, and the way he was holding the gun convinced her he was an amateur.

While the cash was slowly piling up in the sugar sack, salesman William Cranfield was across the street at Tom Graham's Hardware,[1] closing a deal to supply the store with skis for the coming season. After exchanging pleasantries with the sales clerks, Cranfield left the store and crossed the street to his blue sedan, which was parked near the bank.

Meanwhile the robber, like a driver coming to a clear stretch of road after a succession of fog patches, realized that the teller was stalling and that he had been in the bank far too long – well beyond the three-minute limit he had set for himself.

"There are going to be a lot of dead people around here if you don't hurry up," he said, waving his gun. "And don't press any alarm." He hadn't spoken loudly, but it was enough to attract the attention of a clerk sitting at a desk beyond the counter. She glanced up to see Elwood and the teller looking pale and nervous, their attention focused on the slight man in front of them. Realizing it was a robbery, she too pressed her silent alarm.

Empey quickly put the rest of the money in the bag and pushed it towards the robber, whose attention had shifted to the large steel door behind Elwood.

"What about the money in the safe?" he demanded.

"You have it all," said Elwood. "On Fridays, everything we have in the bank is in sight." It wasn't true, but the bank stood to lose thousands more if the safe were cleaned out.

Fearing another blackout and the arrival of the police, the robber decided to leave – he would settle for whatever was in the sack. Grabbing it from the counter, he backed towards the front door, his gun still aimed at Elwood and the teller. On his way out, he passed the clerk's desk. "I was afraid to look at him, but I did," she said later. "I can still see those terrible eyes, jet-black and wicked, staring at me." In fact, the robber's eyes were blue.

"Don't press any alarm!" he warned again as he went out the door. As soon as he was out of sight, Elwood grabbed Empey's revolver and went after him.

"Call the police!" he shouted to his accountant on the way out.

Cranfield's car was parked, facing north, just over a car's length from the bank. He was behind the wheel and about to start the engine when a man appeared at the door on the passenger's side. He tried frantically to open it, but it was locked. Running around the front of the car, he yanked Cranfield's door open.

"Get out!" he ordered, waving his gun and grabbing the key. They exchanged places, and the man stuffed the Luger under his belt, inserted the key in the ignition, and jabbed repeatedly at the floorboard with his foot – too drunk to realize that the starter button was on the dashboard.

"Get away from here!" he shouted at Cranfield, who was still standing beside the driver's door. The salesman was moving reluctantly to the rear of the car when Elwood charged out of the bank, revolver in hand. He fired. The bullet whizzed by Cranfield and pierced the trunk of the car.

"What the hell are you doing?" Cranfield yelled.

"It's a hold-up!" Elwood yelled back.

Cranfield ran for cover behind a nearby store as Elwood continued firing. The robber, unable to start the engine, jumped from the car with bullets flying around him. Elwood emptied the five-shot revolver, but all the bullets missed.

Clutching the sugar sack, the robber ran north along Avenue Road past several small shops. At ROBERTSON 5¢ TO $1⁰⁰ STORE, he turned east on Dunblaine Avenue, a residential street. Elwood, meanwhile, was also running – back into the bank for his own revolver, then back out to the street to resume the chase. But the robber was gone.

In front of a house on Dunblaine the escaping man stumbled and fell, spilling some of the cash on the lawn. He scrambled to stuff the bills back into the sack and then disappeared between two houses. Now he was heading south, doubling back behind the bank through a maze of houses, lanes, and garages.

He vaulted a fence, landing in a flower garden behind another house. He slowed when he reached Haddington Avenue, where a woman was at a window checking on her child, who was in a playpen on the lawn. "And while I was looking out, I saw this man walking across the road. He had what looked like a sugar bag in his hand and he didn't seem to be in any hurry. He walked up my driveway and I thought he was a peddler so I went to my back door in case he knocked, but he must have started running because by the time I got to the back door, he was nowhere in sight."

The robber had jumped over her rear fence, this time landing in the backyard of a house on Felbrigg Avenue. His presence startled two women who were talking over a side fence.

"Hey! What are you doing there?" asked one of them.

"I'm just taking a short cut," the man replied calmly.

"Well don't take any short cuts through our property!"

"I'm looking for a friend of mine who is supposed to be washing windows somewhere around here."

"I don't care who you're looking for, it's not your property."

The man shrugged and continued through the yard. He didn't appear to be in a hurry, but when he reached Felbrigg he picked up his pace, heading east towards Elm Road. One of the women told her thirteen-year-old son to follow him on his bicycle. The surveillance ended at a nearby bus stop when the robber turned and glared at the boy, who quickly turned his bicycle around and pedalled home.

As he retraced the route to his truck, the man removed his jacket and tie. He dropped the tie and the Luger into the sack, covering both with his jacket, and then tucked the sack under his arm. He spit the wads of cotton from his mouth and opened the neck of his shirt. He was calmer now, and looked like a man out for a stroll on a sunny day. A couple of police cars, their telltale rear aerials bending and bobbing, sped past him on their way to the bank.

While he was continuing south, police from North York, Toronto, and the Ontario Provincial Police were converging on the bank. When they arrived, Cranfield, Elwood and his staff, and other witnesses described to them what they had seen and heard. They would have to go through it all again for the reporters and photographers from the three Toronto newspapers, who were already rushing to the scene.

As police dusted Cranfield's car for fingerprints, the owner proudly pointed out the bullet hole in the trunk and talked about the unexpected present he had found on the front seat – a $20 bill left behind by the bandit.

The consensus of the witnesses was that the robber was five foot seven or eight, forty to fifty years old, and slight of build, with a thin black moustache and a ruddy complexion. They agreed he was wearing a dark-brown fedora, blue suit, blue-striped shirt, and dark tie.

Scores of police officers fanned out from the bank on motorcycles, in patrol cars, and on foot, in a street-by-street search. Shortly before 1 p.m. a suspect was picked up on Felbrigg Avenue, but he was quickly released. Police also searched buses and streetcars and set up roadblocks to check all vehicles heading north out of Toronto. Within two hours of the robbery, a hitchhiker on Highway 11 had been questioned and released and five other suspects – one taken off a bus and one from a streetcar – had been picked up and paraded before Elwood and his staff for identification. They too were soon released. Police said later they believed the bandit escaped by boarding a bus and mingling with the passengers.

In fact, after scrambling through the neighbourhood around the bank, the robber had casually walked to the garage and his waiting truck. He considered himself lucky, because he was still feeling sluggish from the whisky. He slept for an hour.

He had brought along a damp cloth and a razor. After he had woken up and his head had cleared, he wiped off the rouge and mascara, shaved his moustache, and changed his shirt. Only then did he count the money – $2,256. It wasn't as much as he had expected but, everything considered, it was a good day's work. The more he thought about it, the better he felt: he could actually rob a bank and get away with it.

Early Years

East of Lake Huron's Georgian Bay, two or three hours' drive north of Toronto, is Muskoka, a rugged land of rivers, lakes, and forested islands on the southernmost edge of the Precambrian Shield. Before it became Ontario's premier cottage country, it was a preserve of the wealthy, who stayed in the exclusive resort hotels that had sprung up after the railway was pushed through in 1875. One hundred years later there would be four hundred tourist hotels and resorts and more than twenty thousand cottages.

Until early in the twentieth century, there was also a thriving lumber industry, with sawmills in Muskoka's three main towns – Gravenhurst, Huntsville, and Bracebridge. And there was some farming, but it was a struggle because arable land was scarce, with rock and thin soil predominating.

Edwin Alonzo Boyd's roots were in Muskoka. His middle name came from his grandfather, Alonzo Boyd, an early pioneer who worked at logging and farming and who was known as Lon. Lon was short, sported a handlebar moustache, and chewed tobacco. He was married and had three sons, one of whom died in childhood. In his later years Lon worked in the lumber camps as a cook's helper and handyman. He was well known as "a kind of a character" who could do just about anything.

Lon's eldest son, Edwin Glover Boyd, was born in Kilworthy, near Gravenhurst, on July 1, 1892, and spent his early years there. The family lived in a farmhouse "sitting on a pile of rocks with just enough soil to grow a few vegetables," as one relative described it.

Glover Boyd's mother died young, and he followed his father to the lumber camps, where for a time he was a teamster, using horses to haul logs out of the woods. But he soon gave that up and moved to Toronto before the First World War. He was an accomplished electrician and was hired by Eaton's department store. Family history has it that he installed the light over the statue of Timothy Eaton at the main Yonge Street entrance of the old Queen Street store.

It was at Eaton's that Glover Boyd met Eleanor McCallum, a slim, dark-haired clerk several years his senior. They soon fell in love and made plans to marry. She told him she was raising her young brother, eight-year-old Harold, because her mother was a widow with health problems. And Harold would be coming to live with them. That wasn't a problem, said Glover. He learned later that Harold was not Eleanor's brother, but her son, born out of wedlock.

Edwin grew up thinking Harold was his uncle. "But he was really my half-brother. And I don't think my dad knew until a month or two after they married. I don't know if he would have married if he had known about it before." Harold's true identity would remain a secret to everyone else in the family for almost three decades.

Edwin Alonzo Boyd was born on April 2, 1914. He would be known simply as Ed to family and friends, but the name Alonzo had an appeal that years later the media would be unable to resist. It was always "Edwin Alonzo Boyd" or "Alonzo Boyd," never Ed, which simply wasn't flashy enough.

Four months after Ed was born, the British Empire, of which Canada was part, went to war with Germany. Glover Boyd joined the army in August 1915. Edwin was seventeen months old when his father went overseas. It would be almost four years before he returned.

In the war, Glover served in France with the Royal Field Artillery. For a time he was transferred – probably because of his skills as an electrician – to the Canadian Squadron of the Royal Air Force. He spent six weeks in two different hospitals with a severe elbow fracture and was once given a severe reprimand for driving a military vehicle without permission. He left the army with the rank of sergeant.

During the war, Ed lived with his mother and Harold in a walk-up apartment in a house on Marchmount Road near Davenport and Ossington. The second-floor apartment was small, and the family that owned the house lived downstairs. Harold had his own room, and Ed slept in his mother's bed. During the day, Eleanor Boyd worked at an ammunition factory and Harold looked after Ed.

Those early years were largely uneventful and not unpleasant for young Ed. Eleanor was a doting mother and Harold was always helpful and treated him kindly. "I don't remember having a lot of other children to play with. But Harold took me places and always found things to do. He was supposed to keep an eye on me when my mother was at work and he did a good job of it."

Ed was short-changed when it came to grandparents. His paternal grandmother and maternal grandfather both died before he was born, and he had no memory of Lon Boyd until after the war. His maternal grandmother, a large woman with chronic health problems, visited from time to time. There were also visits from his three aunts, Eleanor's sisters, who lived in Toronto, and from his Uncle Oswald, his father's younger brother.

While Glover Boyd was fighting the war overseas, Eleanor was facing her own ordeal at the ammunition factory. She was burned on one side from her knee to above her hip when she was struck by a wayward artillery shell casing on the assembly line. The heavy, plant-issue coveralls she was wearing saved her from even more serious injury. She recovered, but for the rest of her life she kept the scar covered.

Young Ed had his own close call while playing in front of the house one day. While being chased by other children, he ran into the path of an oncoming car. The car was halfway over him when it stopped, and he crawled out from under it. He wasn't hurt, but horrified onlookers rushed to his side. "They were all shook up and they picked me up and asked me if I was all right." Ed liked all the attention and never forgot it.

Glover Boyd had joined the Salvation Army before he went overseas, and when he returned home they sent a uniformed band to give him a rousing welcome on the front lawn. Afterwards everyone crowded into the apartment for tea and cake. Eleanor had often showed her son a photo of his father holding him in his arms. But the boy had no memory of him, and when Glover walked through the door after the war there was no resemblance to the clean-shaven young man in the photo. The stranger was a tough, seasoned army sergeant with a walrus moustache. He had served three years and ten months overseas. Now he was home and he wanted to share his wife's bed.

Five-year-old Ed saw his parents whispering in the kitchen, his father somewhat glum. It was near the boy's bedtime when his mother came out and told him there would be new sleeping arrangements that night.

"Your father wants to sleep in my bed," she said.

"But that's where I sleep," pleaded Ed.

"Well, tonight I want you to sleep on the trunk. I'll make it nice and comfortable for you."

More than seventy-five years later, Edwin Alonzo Boyd still remembers how he felt that night. "We had a big steamer trunk and I slept on that. She said it would be just for one night, but I was never in her bed again. That was my place, not his. And I didn't know him – he was just a big stranger. I felt really rejected – mother didn't want me anymore. I guess it kind of stuck in my subconscious."

Now that Glover Boyd had returned the apartment was obviously too small, and they soon moved to a duplex on Bee Street[2] in Todmorden, an area beyond the Don Valley, in East York.

To support his family, Glover Boyd decided to return to the Muskoka woods to work in logging and lumbering. For almost two years he travelled back and forth between his job and his family in Toronto. When Eleanor gave birth to another son, Gordon, in the spring of 1920, Glover intensified his search for work closer to home.

Eleanor was pregnant again when he answered a recruiting ad for the Toronto Police Department. He was a fraction under the height requirement, but that was overlooked because he was a veteran with overseas service. He was twenty-nine years old and five feet nine and three quarter inches, and his weight was one hundred sixty pounds. He said he was an electrician by trade. His application was accepted, and he would remain on the force as a constable for the next twenty-five years. Three months after he was hired, Eleanor presented him with a third son, Norman. Their last child, Irene, would soon follow.

Young Ed's relationship with his father was tentative at best; but even with the expanding family, the love he felt for his mother endured. It was understandable: he knew her better, and she indulged him, while his father, who was deeply religious and had a military bearing, was the authoritarian figure. But even Eleanor had her limits. The few times she was truly angry with him, he knew he'd done something to justify it.

Such was the case at a family reunion in Kilworthy, with relatives from Muskoka and Toronto attending. Ed was crouched by the porch at the front door of the farmhouse, and whenever a woman or girl walked above him, "I would stick my hand under her dress. I thought it was lots of fun, but I wasn't looking at who I was doing it to."

The game ended when his hand went under his mother's skirt. "She slapped me across the face. She was really mad. I was a little kid and I didn't think they were making a big deal out of it, but they were." The slap was warranted, he decided later.

3
School Days

Edwin Alonzo Boyd was on his own by the age of sixteen, his world view and his moral code already shaped. He did not get to go to high school or college, so his early experiences at home and church and in school had an inordinate influence on how he turned out as an adult. There would be no other structured authority in his life until he joined the army.

There was a lot of upheaval in those first years. His family moved four times and switched churches three times, and he went to four different elementary schools – one of them twice.

Ed didn't start school until he was seven years old – a year later than most children. With a new baby in the house, and his father travelling back and forth to Muskoka, his parents had simply forgotten to enrol him in the fall of 1920. And two weeks after Ed turned seven, in April 1921, his father had begun his new job with the police department. In July, Norman was born, leaving Eleanor occupied with two small children.

Ed might well have missed the 1921–22 school year but for a conversation with his mother shortly after school started that September. She noticed him moping around the house.

"Why don't you go out to play?" she suggested.

"There's nobody to play with, mom."

"What do you mean?"

"They're all back at school."

"Well, don't you want to go back to school?"

"I don't know, I was never there yet."

The next day she enrolled him in a school a couple of blocks from home. He had been at school only a few days when he was traumatized by an incident that caused him to miss several more weeks. One day he was desperate to go to the bathroom, but the teacher ignored him. "I put my hand up but she didn't take any notice, so I shit my pants," he recalls bitterly. With the other students making faces and complaining about the odour, the teacher took the boy into the hall and ordered him to the bathroom, and then home. "I couldn't wash myself very well and I didn't know what to do, so I went outside the school and finished what I started."

A teacher from another class happened to glance out the window, and Ed was mortified when he looked up, trousers around his ankles, and saw her watching him. "That was the last time I went to school for a long time."

For whatever reason, his absence wasn't noticed for several weeks. Eventually his mother was notified and she alerted his father. It was just after a heavy rainfall, and Glover found his son playing in a large puddle.

"What's the matter with you?" he demanded. "You haven't been to school in weeks."

"Is that right?" replied the boy, sheepishly. "Is that how long?"

As Glover flushed with anger, Ed ran off. Father chased son down the street. The boy was too fast, but inevitably had to face his father at home. "He marched me down the basement and gave me a damn good whack with a hockey stick."

Before he finished his first year of school, the family moved again, this time to 1 Harris Avenue, a short walk to No. 10 Police Station – Glover Boyd's first posting – at Main Street and Swanwick Avenue in Toronto's east end. The house was a block north of Danforth Avenue, just around the corner from Gledhill Public School, which Ed transferred to with just a few weeks left in the school year.

What young Ed liked best about the Harris Avenue house was a hideaway under the back porch – a closed-in storage area with its own tiny hinged door. He called it his fort. And it was in his fort, when he was nine, that a female cousin and her older girlfriend introduced him to sex. "The older girl was the instigator. There was no intercourse, but we did a lot of other things. I didn't like it much, but I went ahead and did it anyway."

One of his younger brothers, about three or four at the time, was posted as a lookout. He heard everything that went on, including excessive use of the word "fuck."

The next day, while attempting to describe to his mother what he had seen in the hideout, the boy blurted out: "Ed fucked Dorothy! Ed fucked Dorothy!" When Eleanor related the story to Glover, he was bemused rather than angry.

In September 1923, just over a week after Ed started third grade at Gledhill, Glover moved the family several blocks north to 160 Chisholm Avenue, and the boy transferred to nearby Secord Public School. Until then, his grades had been poor, and although his performance improved in several subjects, he was transferred back to Gledhill Public School for fourth grade in September 1924. He doesn't remember why the switch was made.

Religion was important to Eleanor and Glover Boyd. The children had baths on Saturday night, and on Sunday they dressed up for church and Sunday School. Ed had a strong tenor voice and when he sang at church, people noticed. "They all knew about my singing, and that made me feel good."

The Boyd family worshipped for a time at the Salvation Army centre[3] on Cedarvale Avenue, where Ed joined the Boy Scouts. Later, they crossed the street and joined the Faith Tabernacle, an evangelical church focusing on scripture study, which suited Glover Boyd, who wanted to be more proficient in Bible language. The church boasted its own resident faith healer, Oliver E. Crockford, who later became reeve of Scarborough.

Crockford's skills were sought when young Ed smashed his wrist while walking a spiked steel fence. "I was stepping between the spikes showing off to some other kids, and I missed my footing." His chest struck one of the spikes, but it wasn't punctured because his wrist took the brunt of the fall. The wrist was never X-rayed, but Ed insists it was broken in three places. "You didn't need an X-ray to tell it was broken, because it was twisted like an S."

Crockford was summoned to pray over the boy, and within a day or two he could do handsprings and back-flips. Glover Boyd called it a miracle. "My mother and dad were real honoured to think the Lord had healed me." The knuckle on Ed's injured wrist retracted as a result of the accident. "It's in there somewhere, but you can't see it."

The Boyds soon moved again, this time nine blocks west to 31 Glebemount Avenue. This small, two-storey brick house, a block north of Danforth, would be young Ed's last permanent residence for many years. The move meant a transfer to yet another school. This time it was the new Earl Beatty Public School. It was at Earl Beatty that Edwin Alonzo Boyd came into his own. He would always be slight and wiry, but now he began to fill out a bit. With that came increased self-confidence. He disdained traditional school subjects but excelled at sports and music. "I was always looking for something that made me stand out, and I couldn't get it by schooling because I didn't give a damn about reading and writing and all the rest of it."

The home front, meanwhile, had stabilized. Glover Boyd was into his fourth year on the police force, and with the birth of their daughter, Irene, he and Eleanor were now raising four children. Harold, now in his twenties, continued to live with the family, his presence causing no apparent tension between Eleanor and Glover. "They both knew the truth," says Ed, "but my mother always talked about him as her brother and we didn't know any different, nor did Harold – he thought he was my uncle."

By now, Harold had a job as a milkman, delivering milk door to door with a horse-drawn wagon. Harold had mastered the harmonica and he taught Ed how to play. Ed was soon considered the best player at Earl Beatty, where one of the teachers encouraged him to join the school's mouth organ band. Later he would be picked to join a YMCA band, which won honours at the CNE and often performed in school auditoriums and church basements in and around Toronto. "We had about forty guys," Ed recalls, "dressed in light blue capes, with red silk lining, white trousers and shirts, and blue tams pulled down on one side."

The YMCA band had one member who did all the singing, and who began each performance with the band's trademark introductory tune. Edwin Boyd, in his eighties, can still belt out a lusty rendition:

"We're the Danforth 'Y' Boys / Rough and ready we / Happy go lucky as you wish to see / Here to entertain you / Chase the blues away / So it's hip hooray for the Danforth boys / Of the Danforth Y–M–C–A."

J.D. Walker, who co-ordinated the band's appearances for the YMCA, didn't know Ed could sing until the day they were in the same car on the way to a performance in the town of Streetsville. Walker and another adult were in front. Ed and three other boys were in back. When the boys started singing old favourites, Ed joined in and Walker took notice. He was impressed.

One day soon after, the regular singer was late for a performance. Walker approached Ed and told him he would have to sing the opening number. This was the break he'd been waiting for. "But I'd never sung in front of a big audience like that before. I got about two or three words out and I lost my voice – I messed it all up. J.D. Walker wouldn't talk to me after that. He thought I did it deliberately."

Ed got into trouble at school, but he wasn't a serious troublemaker. He had a vibrant imagination. And he didn't like other people's rules, and would skirt them or break them whenever he thought he could get away with it. Because he was such a fast runner, he often created situations for which fleet footwork turned out to be necessary.

But he wasn't quite fast enough to escape the boot of a Roman Catholic priest from St. Brigid's Church, which was just up the street from the Boyd house on Glebemount. The priest always wore a long black robe, and Ed thought he was a bit odd. The boy called him names and taunted him. The priest suffered the insults in silence until one day he decided he'd had enough, and was close enough to surprise Ed. "He chased after me, and managed to give me a good kick in the ass."

Ed also learned not to insult the girl who lived in the corner house down the street. She was taller and heavier than he was, but because she was a girl, he didn't think it was a problem. Like the priest, she was usually silent when he called her names. But one day was different.

"Look, I've had enough from you," she said. "I'm going to beat your head in."

Ed decided not to test her. "I thought, 'Jeez, maybe she's good at this stuff,' so I decided to run. She started to run after me. She couldn't catch me, but I didn't call her any more names."

Because Ed's father was a Toronto policeman, any kind of rebellious act he engaged in impressed his friends, and was probably somewhat magnified in their minds.

Like the Harris Avenue house, the house on Glebemount had a back porch with an enclosed cubbyhole beneath, except there was no tiny door providing access to Ed. He solved the problem by digging a tunnel large enough for him to squirm under the wall. He liked it under there because he could listen to conversations in the house without being detected. And sometimes he and his friends smoked in the hide-out. "We used to go down to Danforth and pick up cigarette butts where the guys had thrown them before they got on the streetcars."

By the time he was thirteen, with an indulgent mother busy with three young children, and a father on shift work, Ed was spending most of his spare time playing school sports or roaming downtown Toronto. There were also his outings with the YMCA band, and the violin lessons (short-lived) that his parents signed him up for. He wanted to take guitar lessons instead, so that he could sing while he played, but they insisted on the violin. "The reason they did that was because dad had always wanted to play the fiddle, so he thought it would be good for me. He never thought in terms of whether I would like it."

Despite his reluctance, Ed was doing well with the violin, so well that he won prizes and was moved to an advanced level – a level he wasn't ready for. The music was too complicated for him to read. "I don't know why they did that. I should have asked for some answers." The lessons were taught above a shop at Woodbine and Danforth, and when he realized he couldn't keep up with the others, he simply stopped going. He didn't tell his parents he had quit the lessons. He would hide the violin and go downtown and roam around Eaton's or Simpson's, spending the dollar that it cost for the lessons on jelly beans or peanuts.

A.G. Walter, one of Ed's teachers at Earl Beatty, had competed internationally for Canada as a runner. "He didn't like me at all because I was fast and limber, and he thought I should go into training to become a competitive runner or gymnast. But I wasn't interested in that." Walter thought Ed was squandering his natural athletic talents.

But young Ed didn't think so. He used his talents to show off at every opportunity. For a time he found a Saturday job delivering meat for a butcher on Danforth. It wasn't uncommon for other merchants to see him walking past their stores on his hands or doing forward or backward flips. He did the same on his way to and from Earl Beatty school. "I used to go everywhere on my hands. Sometimes I'd do flips for a whole block. Many of them didn't know my name, but they were acquainted with the silly things I did to get attention."

That kind of athletic vanity wasn't what Walter had in mind, and Ed believes the teacher was out to get him. One day Walter called for quiet in his class just as Ed was closing his inkwell, which slipped and made a slight noise. The teacher raced down the aisle, grabbed Ed by the collar, and hauled him out to the hallway, where another teacher held him while he gave Ed a brutal strapping.

Ed was hurt that the other teacher, one of his favourites, would participate in such severe and unwarranted punishment. "It really broke my heart. I was the best player in his mouth organ band and he holds my hands out while Walter really lays it on me with the strap. They were black and blue for a couple of weeks."

Despite the problems, Ed was satisfied — his athletic ability, his antics, and his membership in the school and YMCA mouth organ bands were bringing him some of the attention he craved. He was also the goalkeeper for the school's successful soccer team, and a good skater, although too small to play on the hockey team. His definition of success may have been considered questionable by others, but at least he was being noticed, and that was important to him.

One of those who noticed him was the attractive Jean Phillips, who lived a block east of Ed. She introduced herself to him one night at the school's outdoor skating rink. After a short conversation she announced, "You're my boyfriend now."

"I am?"

"Yes you are."

Ed liked Jean, and they began spending a lot of time together, but the relationship didn't last. One day he took some money from his mother's purse and was proud of himself for getting away with it. When he boasted of it to Jean, she wasn't at all impressed. "She wouldn't have anything to do with me after that." It was only then that Ed realized stealing money might be morally wrong. Jean's reaction reminded him of how his mother had slapped him years before, when he stuck his hand under her dress.

Ed always liked the movies, and when he didn't have the money he would sneak in the back door of the neighbourhood theatre, usually by himself but sometimes with one or two of his friends. Policemen often came into the theatre for a few minutes when they were on foot patrol.

Ed was sitting in a row near the front after sneaking in one day when a policeman came in and stood just to the side in front of him. "I didn't look at him, but a few minutes later the light from the screen got brighter and I realized it was my old man. He was on the beat, just filling in a little time. He didn't see me, and I didn't dare say anything."

Young Ed loved the summers during his school years in Toronto. Two or three times he attended YMCA camps, where he always won the running races. "When I went up there I always shaved my hair right off – so I was 'Baldy.' " And when he was in the city there was always the Toronto Transit Commission's "swimming car," which took youngsters to the Don Valley. "The streetcar would take us to Broadview Avenue and we'd walk down the hill to a little bridge below and swim down there for a couple of hours, then the streetcar would come along again and take us home."

During the summer of 1928, fourteen-year-old Edwin Alonzo Boyd decided to join the Foreign Legion. He had read about it in the library and he thought it would be the life for him – high adventure and travel to exotic places. He reasoned that if his parents had their say, he wouldn't be going anywhere. To pull it off, they would have to think he was dead.

He made careful plans, and one day, at first light, he rode an old bicycle down to the beach at the foot of Woodbine Avenue on Lake Ontario. He carried with him an old pair of trousers, an old shirt, and a pair of worn-out running shoes. His name was on a slip of paper in the pocket of the shirt. At the beach he put the bicycle down, placed the old clothes and shoes on top, and walked back to Danforth and then east to Kingston Road, which becomes Highway 2.

His plan was to make it as far as Oshawa on the first day. By dusk he had covered about twenty miles and was in Whitby, just west of his destination. But he was tired, hungry, and homesick. Thoughts of a hot meal and a comfortable bed buried his dreams of the Foreign Legion as quickly as a Sahara sandstorm can fill in a foxhole. "I turned around and started walking home along the railroad tracks. There was no moon and it got black dark, so I went back down to the highway."

Ed was wondering if he would ever make it home when two raucous couples pulled up in a car. They were headed for Toronto and offered him a ride. He couldn't believe his good fortune. "It was a Tin Lizzy with curtains on the windows. It didn't go very fast and it made a lot of noise, but they drove me all the way home. When they found out I was hungry, they got me a hot dog and a Coke. They said anything else you want, just ask for it, so I got some jelly beans and some popcorn."

It was near midnight when they dropped Ed off on Danforth at the foot of his street. Afraid to go into the house, he crawled into his hideout under the rear sunroom and fell fast asleep. In the morning he was ravenous and thought he might sneak into the house for some food. Just then he heard his mother crying and the front door slamming. Looking out the crawl hole, he saw his family getting into the minister's car. "I thought, well that leaves the coast clear, I'll go in and cut a hunk of bread or something."

The door was unlocked, and Ed entered quietly and went to the kitchen. There on the table was a large layer cake with white icing.

He cut off a large slab and was about to devour it when he heard
movement above in Harold's room, and then footsteps on the stairs.
The boy ran to the basement and hid behind the coal furnace with
its maze of large pipes. But Harold followed him.

"Anybody there?" asked Harold in a loud voice, peering into the
dim basement.

Ed didn't answer. He was busy stuffing cake into his mouth.

Squinting and feeling his way, Harold came closer, until he was
within a foot or two of the boy.

"Is there anybody there?" he repeated.

Suddenly, Ed stepped out, his face covered in white icing. Harold
shrieked, fainted, and fell to the floor. Ed didn't know what to do, but
Harold quickly revived.

"Ed! What are you doing here? You're supposed to have drowned.
They're dragging the lake for you down at the foot of Woodbine."

The boy related his failed plan to join the Foreign Legion. Harold
ran upstairs to phone the police or the lifeguard office at the beach.
Ed's relieved parents rushed home, and after his mother calmed
down she warned him not to go to the beach anytime soon.

"Why not?" he asked.

"The lifeguards said if they ever catch you down there, they'll throw
you in the water and sit on you."

The story was all over Earl Beatty when Ed returned to school in
the fall. He was lectured by some of the teachers and was even called
before the stern principal. "He gave me proper hell. All the teachers
would look at me and shake their heads." Almost seventy years later
he still relishes the story and feels no regret. Once again, Ed Boyd
had been noticed.

He remembers that after the incident his father was very angry.
"He was going to beat the hell out of me, but mother talked him out
of it. She said, Don't hit him, he's had enough trouble for one day."

Ed considered his father a strict disciplinarian, though he probably enjoyed more freedom to go his own way than most boys of his
age. And Glover no doubt was proud of his son's athletic and musical abilities. When friends or neighbours visited, he often encouraged
Ed to entertain them with the mouth organ or violin. "He showed

me off, you see. He would get a certain amount of approval from the people because I was talented."

Because he was the oldest of the four children, Ed was expected to set a good example for the others, and when he didn't, he was disciplined. He says there was no psychological intimidation, such as "grounding" or "go to your room." "He used violence to resolve things. He was religious, and as far as he was concerned the Bible said give your kids a good going over so they wouldn't end up as bad people.

"He had a temper, and whenever he got mad he would take me down the basement and pick up a hockey stick or a broom handle, whatever was handy, and give me a few good swats. I used to put on a big act that it hurt more than it really did, because it would bother him and he would stop."

Ed's view of his father is disputed by his brother Norm, who says Glover Boyd was no different from most fathers of that era. "All they were trying to do is to keep their kids on the straight and narrow, and I don't think he was any worse than anybody else. I think in a lot of cases, Gord's opinion and my opinion are quite different from Ed's opinion."

The relationship between Ed and his father would make an interesting psychological case study, given Glover Boyd's early absence during the war, and the child's resentment when he was banished from the warmth and security of his mother's bed.

Ed remains adamant that his father bullied him and treated him unfairly. "I don't know how he was with the other kids, because right after my mother died, I was kicked out to a farm."

Of sixteen possible health problems listed on Ed's elementary school record, only one was checked off. It was No. 8 – defective teeth – an incongruous finding given the Hollywood smile that would be flashed across the front pages of Canada's newspapers thirty years later.

The problem with his teeth was related to nutrition, which Ed says his mother knew nothing about. "She was always thin and didn't eat properly. Often when I came home from school at noon all I had was a couple of pieces of toast with tea. I don't remember drinking much milk." He does remember drinking a lot of Coke and eating junk food, including his beloved jelly beans. He also ate a lot of peanuts, often passing them around at school, which earned him the nickname "Peanuts."

Whatever his feelings for his father, Ed looked forward to Sunday dinners, when Glover usually did the cooking. "He liked to eat, and whenever he was off he would make a big dinner with potatoes and roast or steak."

Poor nutrition and dental problems aside, Ed's health was always excellent. The exceptions were the usual childhood diseases, including chicken pox and mumps. He remembers his grandfather, Lon, coming down from Muskoka to sit with him when he was restricted to his bedroom with German measles. The blinds were always drawn to keep the room darkened, and his grandfather sat with him for hours, telling him stories of the Muskoka woods and his early days in the lumber camps.

In early 1930 Gord and Norm contracted scarlet fever, a more deadly disease. As was the practice in those days, the house was quarantined, and a sign to that effect was hung on the front door. Ed didn't catch the disease, but he was confined to the house. Eleanor Boyd was looking after the boys when she became sick herself. Ed believes she was susceptible to illness because she was frail and didn't eat properly.

In March of the same year Ed heard his mother calling to him in a distressed voice. He went to her and she asked him to help her get to the bathroom upstairs. "She needed help to get on the toilet. I'd never done anything like that, so it was kind of a shock to me."

Just then, Glover Boyd came home. "He kicked me out of there. He took mother to the hospital and that was the last we saw of her." Eleanor Boyd, in her late forties, was dead.

Her coffin had a sealed glass top because of the scarlet fever, and Ed and the other children weren't allowed to go to the funeral. "Dad said she looked all right in the coffin." Glover went to the mortuary with Eleanor's sisters and Harold, who was unaware that it was his mother and not his sister who had died.

Norm Boyd was just eight and a half when his mother died. "It was quite a shock," Norm says now, "but it probably had more of an effect on Ed because he was older and he knew her longer than we did."

Glover Boyd told friends that Eleanor's death had a devastating effect on his oldest son: "And he got so you couldn't talk to him. He wouldn't let anyone into his confidence. He may have been emotionally confused with it all."[4]

Shortly after Eleanor's death, the quarantine sign came down and an Irish immigrant woman was sent by the church to help with the children. Her name was Minerva – nicknamed Minnie – and eventually she and Glover Boyd would marry.

Ed turned sixteen less than a month after his mother's death. He had shown no interest in school for some time, and now he was free to quit. He was repeating his final year, and had spent so little time there that his official school record shows no marks for any subjects after seventh grade. He was, however, interested in continuing his education at a technical school where he could pick up a useful trade. His father agreed it was a good idea and promised to send him to one.

Despite his poor grades in most subjects, Ed was strong in spelling, earning marks of 89, 73, and 77 in the last three years for which there is a record. His next-best subject was reading, and in his last year and a half at Earl Beatty he probably spent more time in the local library than he did in the classroom. "Most of what I learned was from my own reading and experience."

Ed doesn't remember his parents ever reading to him or encouraging him to read. But he discovered the public library and would spend hours reading fairy tales. "And when I got too old for that, I started reading cowboy stories." Then it was action and adventure tales. One of his early favourite fictional characters was Jack Harkaway, the hero of several illustrated English stories that were popular with young readers back then. In his later travels, Ed would sometimes use Harkaway's name as an alias.

Minnie had a male friend, also from Ireland, who was an expert at karate and judo, which he taught to Ed with Glover Boyd's encouragement. "He was pretty good, and I learned a lot from him, especially judo."

Ed believes that the relationship between Minnie and her Irish friend was more than platonic. "I think she wanted to marry him, but my old man got in there and that was it." With romance budding between Glover and Minnie, Ed says they didn't want him around, and his father soon forgot his promise to send him to a technical school. Instead, he arranged for Ed to work on a farm north of Toronto, near Thornton. "I would have had a trade, but he got wound up with this damned woman that took my mother's place, and that was it."

When Earl Beatty School was informed that Ed was going off to work, he was recorded as having passed eighth grade and was officially graduated. The date was June 26, 1930.

Ed's resentment over having to miss technical school and leave home was tempered by the excitement of doing something new and different. It was an adventure. The 120-acre farm was owned and operated by a twenty-two-year-old nephew of one of Glover Boyd's cousins. "His name was Milt, and he was a real go-getter who knew what he was doing. He had a lot of cows and chickens and a half-dozen horses. I did some of the work, but I didn't get paid anything. He let me live there to learn how everything operated."

Milt had a brother who also worked on the farm, and two sisters who lived with their parents two farms over. The sisters, Bertha, seventeen, and Irene, in her twenties, worked hard on the family farm, but often found time to come over and cook for their brothers and Ed. The newcomer was the nearest male around, and both sisters found him attractive.

At the time, Ed's sexual experience was limited to the groping he'd done with his cousin and her friend under the back porch of the Chisholm Avenue house. But that was soon to change. It began the day Ed and Bertha were alone in the house and she began tickling him.

"You know what you're going to get if you keep tickling me?"

"Yes, I know."

It was in the cold of winter and Bertha was wearing long-johns under her dress. "By the time I got through the underwear, I almost lost my desire to go any further. Anyway, I got her half-naked but we heard somebody outside, and that was as far as we got. We didn't get another chance."

But he did get a chance with the older sister in a furtive encounter at the main house. "I kind of talked her into taking her pants off, and we had intercourse, but I didn't know much about what I was supposed to do, and right away I went off and spoiled the whole thing. I just didn't have the experience."

After almost two years on the farm, Ed was bored and decided to move back to Toronto. He hitchhiked home, but after a month decided Glover and Minnie didn't really want him around. "You feel that you're not part of the family anymore, so you leave." Ed might have felt unwanted but he was also bored, because he had nothing to do.

It was the summer of 1932. The country was in the grip of the Great Depression, with 30 percent of the labour force – more than one million people – out of work, and one in five Canadians dependent on government relief for survival.

Eighteen-year-old Ed decided to join the vast army of rootless men riding out the Depression on trains. He went down to the Don Valley and caught a freight train heading north. "And when I got on the boxcar, it was full of men from other countries. A lot of them were smoking hand-rolled cigarettes, which were horrible to smell. And you could smell garlic everywhere. That was my first time away on my own."

4
An Armful of Boxcar

Edwin Alonzo Boyd's first train ride took him as far as North Bay, Ontario. Shortly after he arrived at the railway yards, a policeman grabbed him.

"You're pretty young," said the officer. "What are you doing here?"

"I'm going out west."

"What's your name."

"Ed Boyd."

"I seem to know you."

"Well, my father's a policeman in Toronto."

"He is, eh? Don't you think you should go home and be a good son instead of riding the rods?"

Ed shrugged.

"If you want, I'll put you on a passenger train and you can go back to Toronto and get a fresh start."

Ed was quickly swayed and was headed back to Toronto on the next train. He stayed for a few weeks, but knew it wasn't working out. He went back to the marshalling yards in the Don Valley and jumped another freight train. "Only this time when I got to North Bay, I didn't stop – I just kept right on going."

He got as far as Port Arthur before police pulled him and four others off the train and took them to jail. They weren't charged, but they spent forty-eight hours in the cells. They were fed watery porridge for breakfast, watery soup for lunch, and in the evening a small portion of meat with a piece of hard, stale bread. At night they were given blankets, but had to sleep on the floor, which they were used to from boxcar living. "It was kind of a novel experience, and I didn't mind it at all, except for the food."

As soon as they were released, Ed jumped another freight train and continued west. In his chosen boxcar he met freckle-faced Jake Dunn,[5] about his own age. Jake was a heavy smoker, and soon they were sharing cigarettes. They had no money, but Jake was an experienced panhandler and taught Ed how to go door to door for handouts. Nervously he knocked on his first house. A woman answered.

"I'm sorry to trouble you, but I'm looking for enough to get a bed for the night," he said. "I haven't got any money and I need food. Could you give me twenty-five cents to help out?"

To his amazement, the women dug a quarter from her purse and handed it to him. "I just kept going from house to house, up one side of a street and down the other, and after about an hour I had seven dollars. At that time you could get a bed for twenty-five cents a night at the YMCA."

Ed had no moral qualms about bumming from house to house. He'd heard enough about the Bible at church and at home, and the only religion he was exposed to now was at the Salvation Army, where he and Jake went for free meals. "I just laughed at the religious part, I thought it was a lot of baloney then, but it came in handy, because there were so many women involved in religion that you could get a free meal by just shining up to them."

Bumming came easy to Ed, and he and Jake kept it up in town after town all the way to Winnipeg. "If the train stopped in a small town at night and we saw a lot of lights, we would get off and go bum a few houses. I would ask for food, but they would usually give me money instead. And I thought, gee, this is better than working." To this day he finds it remarkable that so many people took pity on him and gave him money.

When they arrived in Winnipeg, it was not exactly a hospitable environment. The Depression had hit the four western provinces the hardest. Their export-driven economies had collapsed, there were crop failures, and the price of wheat was at its lowest in recorded history. In Saskatchewan, 66 percent of the rural population had been forced onto relief, and the other western provinces were technically bankrupt after 1932.

Ed and Jake spent some time in Winnipeg before moving on to

Edmonton, where their panhandling didn't go over as well. They each took one side of a street, but a man at the second or third house Ed went to turned him away and threatened to call the police. They switched to another street, but their luck wasn't any better. "The police starting scouting up and down the streets until they saw me coming down from a veranda and they grabbed me."

"What are you up to?" asked one of the officers.

"I'm just knocking on people's doors to see if they can help me get a bed for the night."

"So you're panhandling, eh?"

"Not really, I just need a place to stay."

"I'm going to let you go this time, but if you knock on any more doors, we're going to have to put you in jail."

Luck ran out for Ed and Jake in November 1933, when they were arrested and charged with vagrancy. Each was fined $20 and costs. Neither could pay, and they were sentenced to six weeks in jail. But Edwin Alonzo Boyd was not the name on the RCMP books: he had no wallet or identification on him and said his name was John Wilson Harkaway, after his fictional hero Jack Harkaway. "You could only use that name every so often, because a lot of people recognized it from the books."

Ed and Jake were sent to the Fort Saskatchewan provincial jail about eighteen miles northeast of Edmonton on the banks of the North Saskatchewan River. They were released on Christmas Eve along with two war veterans, who took them down to the local Legion Hall and filled them with beer. Ed had never drunk beer and he ended up vomiting all over the sidewalk outside. "I went to the drugstore where the guy gave me some stuff to make me vomit more, and I got rid of it all." He vowed never to drink again.

They returned to Edmonton and found rooms for a dollar each per week. They paid for two weeks in advance, but as soon as they started panhandling again, the police chased them. "This time we weren't going to hang around. We grabbed an armful of boxcar and kept going until we got to Calgary." To find shelter and keep out of the clutches of the police, they decided in January 1934 to go to a government relief camp west of Calgary.

Unemployment relief camps had been set up by the federal government in 1932 to provide work and shelter for single, homeless men. They were operated by the Department of Defence but staffed by civilians. The camps were voluntary, although "sometimes the Mounties shoved you into the camps to get you off the railroads." Homeless men were provided a bunkhouse bed, three meals a day, work clothes, and medical care. They worked forty-four hours a week clearing bush, building roads, planting trees, or constructing public buildings. The pay was twenty cents a day. The camps were sprinkled across the country, and about 170,000 men had gone through them by the time they closed in June 1936.

Ed and Jake worked on the Trans-Canada Highway, which was being pushed through to British Columbia. But after only a few weeks, there was a communist-inspired strike and they ended up back in Calgary. They arrived in town too late to check into the Salvation Army, but Ed was pleasantly surprised when a chinook wind brought in summer weather. "I'd never seen anything like that. I just slept there right on the sidewalk, and I did that every night the chinook was on."

Soon after, Ed became ill and was looked after for three weeks by the Salvation Army. He thinks it may have been an especially severe case of flu. He spent the whole time on a cot in a cubbyhole. Jake proved to be a loyal friend and waited for him to get well.

For a while they hung around Calgary, where Ed spent a lot of time reading in the library. Then they decided to hop a freight train for Toronto, and perhaps continue to the east coast. As it turned out, Jake lined up a job at a mill in Kitchener and Ed decided to stay home in Toronto for a while. Glover Boyd told his son that there was always room for him, but Ed didn't feel comfortable. "He put up with me, and he never criticized me or anything I did. I don't know what it was."

After a short stay, Ed was ready to move again. This time he headed northwest to a relief camp near Nipigon, Ontario, where again he found himself working on the Trans-Canada Highway. It was still winter and working outside in the cold was tough, but Ed found it bracing.

It was at the Nipigon camp that he met Duke O'Kane, an Englishman of Irish ancestry with a very proper public-school accent. Duke was in his late thirties, a thin, sharp-featured man about Ed's height. He was a loner, a "remittance man" who was sent a monthly stipend by his family on the condition that he stay away from England. It wasn't a lot of money, but enough to live on. He never told Ed why his family had shipped him over to Canada.

Duke walked with a swagger and was known for his large penis in whorehouses in Northern Ontario and the West. Ed describes it as "a real weapon." One of Duke's favourite haunts was Old Mag's in Port Arthur (now part of Thunder Bay). Mag was a large, husky woman with a booming voice. Everybody knew her, and purportedly she ran most of Northern Ontario's prostitution and the bootlegging that went with it. "When you met somebody and told them you'd been through Port Arthur, they'd always ask you, 'How's Old Mag doin'?' "

Ed and Duke decided to leave the camp in early May 1934, a month after Ed's twentieth birthday. They hopped a freight and leisurely made their way west to Kelvington, Saskatchewan, arriving at night in late August. They went to sleep in a barn at the end of the main street. When they awoke in the morning they were covered in lice. They were desperate to boil their clothes and kill the lice, and the local barber came to their aid. He invited them to build a fire in the field behind his house and provided a large washtub, in which they boiled their clothes and had a bath. Duke and Ed were grateful to the barber and asked if there was any work they could do for him as payment.

"I don't have anything," he said, "but if you fellahs want to stay around and look for work you can sleep in my car." He pointed to an old Dodge near the house. They accepted his offer, but the weather was mild and they slept outdoors, using the car only when it rained. The barber had a lovely wife and a beautiful fifteen-year-old daughter. "The daughter looked like a movie star," recalls Ed. "I think Duke wanted to get into her pants, but her mother had warned her about people like him."

Ed and Duke found work as stookers with local wheat farmers. Horse-drawn binders cut and tied the wheat into sheaves, which were dropped to the ground in batches of six or eight. Stookers gathered the bundles and arranged them in tight formations with the grain kernels facing up. It was heavy work that paid three or four dollars a day.

Duke wasn't fond of such strenuous exertion. "He would stook for a couple of days, and then he would quit and hang around in town." The workers were paid at the end of each day, and when Ed arrived in town with his earnings, Duke would borrow much of it to play snooker. He always promised to pay it back, but he never did.

They stayed in Kelvington, sleeping in the barber's car, for three or four weeks before heading to Winnipeg. Even with Duke tapping his resources, Ed had been able to save thirty dollars. "It kept me going for two or three months. Things were so cheap in those days, you could get a meal for twenty-five cents, including coffee, ham and eggs, potatoes, and dessert."

They were especially fond of Chinese restaurants, which usually had generous portions of bread or crackers in bowls on the table. "When we were hungry and didn't have a lot of money, we'd go in, order a cup of coffee, and eat half the bread, or order soup and fill it with crackers until we were full."

With so many single men riding the rails, especially in the West, prostitution flourished. In most towns and cities the police didn't interfere as long as certain unwritten rules were followed. The prostitutes had to stay in designated areas, usually on out-of-the-way streets or on the edge of an industrial district. In smaller towns there would be a single whorehouse; in the larger cities and towns there were "lines" – rows of houses from which the women offered their services. The other requirement was the weekly checkup by a doctor, usually on a Monday. If there was any sign of venereal disease, the prostitute was ordered to leave town until she was healthy again. If she refused, the police persuaded her to leave, or arrested her.

Duke knew the location of all the brothels in Winnipeg, and when they arrived there he headed straight for the one with his favourite hooker, whom he saw on a regular basis. Ed sometimes went along, but didn't participate. His only other experience with whorehouses was the time he happened upon a short street in Lethbridge, Alberta. There were lines on both sides of the street with prostitutes of all sizes and colours sitting on verandas, some of them with their crotches exposed.

"Hey, white boy," shouted a black woman. "Come on over here and I'll show you how to do it." Ed turned and fled.

Ed and Duke left Winnipeg, bumming in all the little towns along the way, and parted company when they reached Calgary. "That was the last time I saw him," says Ed. "He was more or less a loner and he went his own way."

One of the more bizarre characters Ed met while riding the rods was Red the Barber, a former wrestler. It was an appropriate moniker, since he was also a real barber and had red hair and a red beard. He carried the tools of his trade with him, and fellow hobos could get their hair cut for a nickel. Red was a loud, burly man who engaged in sexual teasing with the younger hobos.

"Come on, you know you want to sleep with me tonight," he would say.

Ed never knew if Red was a homosexual or if it was all an act. "He never pulled that crap with me, but he would always say it to the younger ones who were just starting out."

Wherever Red went, he was recognized, and there were always half a dozen to two dozen men travelling with him. "He was like a magnet because he knew the best way to move around, and you always ate well when you travelled with him."

When it came to gathering and preparing food, Red was like the commandant of a small guerrilla band. He would set up operations under a railway bridge or in a gully, and his troops would fan out with orders to bring back specific food items. One man would be responsible for corn, another for potatoes, and so on. "And if there was a chicken or a small pig running around, he'd have us bring that back too."

When all the ingredients were in hand and cleaned, Red would cook them over a bonfire. In his journeys back and forth across the West he had plotted the best places to stop for food. "He didn't mind robbing farms and gardens, but I never saw him rob a house. He knew all about panhandling and the best places in the West to stop for food. Travelling with Red was a good way to learn the ropes." As with Duke O'Kane, Ed last saw Red the Barber in Calgary.

Friendships for the hobos riding the freight trains were often fleeting, and the names and faces of many of the men Ed travelled with are as blurred as a video on fast-forward. It was one of those now faceless men who helped him steal a Model-T Ford in Medicine Hat. It was a crank-start, so they didn't need keys. "I'd never driven a car before and I had to learn after we swiped it. We cranked it up, got it going, and took off."

Around midnight, they pulled into a closed gas station and managed to fill the tank without being detected. There were no locks on the hoses in those days. They ditched the car in Calgary and immediately hopped a freight and kept going. "I didn't bother with cars after that. The freight trains were always going in the direction you wanted to go."

The possibility of jail was an accepted risk for those riding the freights, and in February 1935, fifteen months after his six-week stint in jail, Ed was again caught begging, this time in Saskatoon. He was fined $3, plus $1.75 in costs. Again he couldn't pay, and was sentenced to two months in the Moosomin jail in southeast Saskatchewan, ten miles from the Manitoba border. And again he was incarcerated under a name other than his own. This time he said he was John Gerald Adams.

Ed's stay at Moosomin wasn't all that unpleasant. The jail included a farm, and he drove a team of horses with a sled and worked in the barn part of the time. It was there that he practised front and back somersaults from the loft into the hay. "I used to practise when nobody was watching me. I'd disappear for an hour or so and do back-flips off the beams into the hay. It helped me later in the banks when I could leap over the counters with no strain at all." His body was so limber and flexible he was able to bend over backwards and touch his nose to the floor.

Ed was released in April. By the early summer of 1935 he was again back in Toronto, ready for another odyssey. Gord, the oldest of his two brothers, was out of high school for the summer. He didn't have a job, and Ed invited him to join him on the road. Glover Boyd didn't object, and Gord decided to go.

They travelled west to Saskatchewan and Alberta and on their way back east went to a government relief camp in the wilderness north of Sioux Lookout. It was a logging camp on Lac Seul, and men and equipment were brought in by scow. Ed was hired as a night watchman and Gord worked in the kitchen. "All we were doing was eating, sleeping, and working," recalls Ed. "You could leave any time you wanted."

At the camp there were often boxing matches in the evenings to help pass the time. One of the men had boxing training and was better than the others. He was always looking for someone to fight. One day Ed asked him if he would teach him to box. They put the gloves on and went behind the huts. "The way he taught me was to treat me as if I had been boxing for years. He broke my nose. He wasn't playing around. He nearly knocked my head right off my shoulders, so after a couple of rounds I quit."

Another man, a quiet, tough street fighter, saw what happened and didn't like it. Later he challenged Ed's antagonist. "Come on, show me what you can do," he said. The centre of the dining room was cleared, and when the boxer threw a punch, Ed's defender flattened him. "He must have hit him about a hundred times in two or three minutes. God he could hit hard."

Ed was soon bored in the isolated bush camp and figured it was time to move on, but Gord decided to stay. While Ed was heading to Toronto, the police picked him up in Capreol just outside Sudbury. "They didn't want people riding the freights so they put me on a passenger train and sent me home. That was fine with me."

He arrived in Toronto just in time to get caught up in the On to Ottawa Trek – a movement that began in April 1935, when 1,500 men in British Columbia relief camps went on strike. The camps, contended critics, had been set up by the government in lieu of a proper program of work and wages.

The B.C. strikers went by train and truck to Vancouver, where there were sit-ins at the museum, the library, and the Hudson's Bay store. These actions were followed by a march on Stanley Park by 20,000 strikers and their supporters.

When there was no response from government, the organizers decided to take their protest to Ottawa, and the On to Ottawa Trek was born. More than a thousand strikers commandeered freight trains and made it as far as Regina, where their numbers doubled. Eight of their leaders went to Ottawa to present their case to Prime Minister R.B. Bennett, while the others remained behind in the Regina Exhibition Grounds. When the talks broke down, the leaders returned to Regina. On July 1, the police moved in, provoking an all-day riot that left one policeman dead, scores of police and rioters injured, and 130 strikers arrested. That part of the drama was over, but in Ontario a much smaller group was continuing the trek.

"They were just walking through Toronto from Niagara Falls when I joined them," recalls Ed. "They had about twenty women and a couple of hundred men and boys, and we walked all the way to Ottawa. I wore my shoes out."

An advance party would inform residents in towns and villages along the route that the strikers were approaching, and bags and boxes of food would appear. The marchers made it to Ottawa and camped out in a municipal park, but the leaders were rebuffed in their attempts to meet with the prime minister and were ordered out of town. City police raided the park and ripped down the shacks and lean-tos the marchers had erected. Ed and the others were told to leave Ottawa immediately. "They told us they'd put us away for a long time if we ever returned." He hitchhiked to Toronto and within days was back riding the rods. But this time it wasn't the usual aimless journey: he had a plan.

Ed always loved the movies, and even in the darkest days of riding the rods, he escaped to the cinema whenever he could scrape together enough money. The old theatres were dark: cool in the summer, and cozy in the winter. They were magical places where his imagination could soar. He liked westerns and gangster movies, but musicals were his favourite. He never forgot the musical comedy *The Golddiggers of 1933*, a Depression period piece in which Ginger Rogers, in a costume of large coins, sings – in pig latin – the hit song "We're in the Money."[6]

Now, Ed decided, he would travel to Hollywood and try his luck as an actor. "I had feelings at one time that I'd like to be a James Cagney or somebody like that."

He made it to Winnipeg and then took a freight south to a lightly travelled border crossing point. At two o'clock on a November morning, with the customs office locked and in darkness, he walked across the U.S. border into Minnesota. He marvelled at his good fortune – nobody there, and the highway stretched out before him.

Ed covered about ten miles before he saw the lights of a car. Now if he could get a ride, it would really be a special day. He waved the car down, and to his delight it pulled over and stopped.

"Hi, do you want a lift?" said the male driver, who was alone.

"That would be great," said Ed, jumping into the front.

"Where are you going?" asked the driver, pulling away.

"South."

"Do you live around here?"

"Yeah, just over there, the second farm over."

"Oh? What's the family name?"

"Johnson."

The driver, who was stocky and fit, glanced at Ed, studying his face. "I don't think that's the right name," he said finally. "I think I'd better investigate you." It was then that he told his passenger he was an off-duty border patrol officer. He drove Ed to Fergus Falls, Minnesota. The next morning, under the name Herbert John Hardley, Ed was found guilty of violating U.S. immigration laws. His sentence was twenty-four hours in custody, but he was ordered transferred to a deportation centre at St. Paul, Minnesota. It would be two months before the train carrying deportees would be ready to depart for Canada. Ed boarded with the others and was delivered to the border at Niagara Falls, where he was put on another train bound for Toronto.

Undeterred, he went right back to riding the rods. In the West he met up with his friend Jake Dunn, and they slipped effortlessly into their old pattern of bumming door to door. And if they didn't get enough for food, they would simply order meals in a restaurant and afterwards admit they had no money to pay the bill. "We got away with that often in Calgary, Saskatoon, and other places. Most of them would say, 'Oh well, turn them loose – just don't do it again.' "

In a Calgary restaurant in August 1936, the trick might have worked again except that they pushed their luck, ordering extravagant desserts after a full meal. For Jake it was a banana split, for Ed a Rainbow Special loaded with scoops of ice cream and fancy toppings. The angry proprietor refused their offer to work off their debt and called the police. In court it was the desserts that riled the judge.

"I can understand – you're hungry and you want something to eat," he told the two accused. "Everybody needs to eat – but a banana split and a Rainbow Special? I have to do something about this."

Ed and Jake didn't know what to say. "So he gave us some time." It was only three days in the Calgary jail, but it was a portent for what was to come: that conviction was the first ever under the name Edwin Alonzo Boyd.

5

Penned In

Less than three weeks after Jake and Ed were released from the Calgary jail, they jumped from a freight train a mile or two south of Saskatoon. They had decided to walk into town from that direction. It was after midnight, and as they walked along they noticed a gas station with no lights on and no houses nearby.

Approaching the building, they peered through the front windows, wondering if there might be money in the cash drawer inside. They walked around back and discovered a locked washroom window. Jake leaned against the wall, and Ed climbed his back, smashed the glass, unlocked the window, and crawled through.

Less than a minute later, a police car pulled up on routine patrol. Jake, standing watch at the back of the garage, saw the car in time and was able to duck out of sight. Ed saw the policeman through the front window and hid under a large desk.

The officer was carrying a flashlight and discovered the broken window in back. Ed could hear him grunting as he pulled himself through the window. "I should have broken out one of the front windows and got out of there." He opted to stay under the desk, thinking the officer would take a cursory look around and leave.

Instead, the officer sat at the desk, opened one of the drawers, and removed a pack of cigarettes and a lighter. Ed watched him light the cigarette and slip the lighter, and other items from the desk, into his pocket. Then he picked up the telephone and called the owner or manager of the gas station.

"There's been a break-in," he said. "They came in through the back window. You better get over here, or send somebody, because I'll be leaving pretty soon."

Ed, meanwhile, was scrunched beneath the desk, a pair of rubber
boots held against him for cover. "I put them over my hip and he
put his foot on them. I guess he figured that's what was under
there."

The officer had his flashlight in hand and flicked it on and off
every few seconds. When he happened to play the beam under the
desk, he saw two eyes staring up at him. The chair he was sitting on
was a three-legged swivel type and Ed thought of grabbing his foot
and flipping him over backwards, but decided against it. The officer
jumped up.

"Get out from under there," he ordered.

Much of what happened later remains somewhat of a blur for Ed.
He was taken to jail and then transferred to Edmonton, where he
appeared in court on September 3, 1936. He thought he was plead-
ing guilty to the service station break-in because he had been caught
red-handed. He didn't think it was that serious until he heard the
sentence – three-and-a-half years in the penitentiary. This was the
second conviction registered under the name Edwin Alonzo Boyd.

Reading about himself in the newspapers years later, he realized
the police had tacked on several other charges. "I didn't have a lawyer,
and I didn't know what I was doing. They laid all these other charges
against me that I didn't know about. I guess they were clearing off
their books." Clearing off indeed. His rap sheet for that court appearance lists convictions for twenty separate offences, mostly break,
enter, and theft.

Days before the gas station break-in, while passing through
Edmonton, Ed and Jake had paid two weeks in advance for a room
in a boarding house on 101st Street, near the Salvation Army. When
no one showed up to claim the room, the proprietor contacted the
police and gave them two names. One of them was Edwin Alonzo
Boyd – and he was in custody. The police decided to put the room
under surveillance. A day or two later they were waiting when Jake
Dunn appeared. He had used a phony name with the proprietor and
did the same with the police.

"Are you a buddy of Edwin Alonzo Boyd?"

"Nope, never heard of him."

"You don't sound very truthful. We're going to take you in."

Jake was eventually convicted in the gas station robbery and of several other offences similar to Ed's.

After his conviction, Ed, in handcuffs and with an RCMP escort, boarded a train in Edmonton for the 175-mile ride to Saskatchewan Penitentiary at Prince Albert, on the south shore of the North Saskatchewan River in the centre of the province. He and the Mountie sat in facing seats. The Mountie seemed uninterested and settled in to read a newspaper. Ed, who had learned to pick the lock on his father's handcuffs, always carried watch springs stuck in his pants behind the belt buckle. His system wouldn't work if the cuffs were double-locked, but on this day there had been only one turn of the key, and he was able to open the lock without the Mountie noticing.

"You know these cuffs won't stay on," he said, as if discussing nothing more than the weather. The startled Mountie looked over and saw the open cuffs in Ed's hand. He grabbed them and put them back on, this time double-locking them. Ed still regrets that he didn't try to escape. "I was too stupid. Instead of trying to run away when the train stopped, I had to show off."

At the train station in Prince Albert, Ed's escort signed him over to the prison officials. He was loaded into a car, and as they neared the prison Ed could see the forbidding, fortresslike building looming before him. He wasn't frightened, but felt a sense of unease and wondered what lay before him.

He was given the usual strip search and issued prison clothes – heavy denim jacket and pants, heavy wool socks and boots, and a peaked cap. His friend Jake, also convicted in the gas station robbery and several break-ins, showed up a couple of weeks later, but they were in different parts of the prison and didn't see much of each other.

Of the Saskatchewan Penitentiary, Ed remembers the profound boredom more than anything else. For the most part, prisoners were assigned meaningless, repetitive tasks. He spent most of his first year shining cell bars with a piece of emery cloth attached to two sticks. He held the sticks and moved the cloth back and forth to buff the bars. "You kept moving up until you had the bar completely shined, and then you moved to the next bar."

The only relief from that job was when he was assigned to sweep or mop the long corridors in front of the cells.

Ed's situation improved after nine months when he was transferred to the kitchen, where he was in charge of making tea in huge electric vats. He would fill the vats with water, add three pails of loose tea, and stir it with a large wooden paddle. "It was pretty lousy tea, but they put a lot of chicory into it."

He worked in the kitchen through the summer and fall of 1937. It was considered a cushy job, and he was glad to be there when the first snow signalled the arrival of the cold western winter. But it wasn't to last. A fellow inmate, self-appointed boss in the kitchen, accused Ed of not doing his job properly. "I got mad and smashed him one, and he ran to the guard."

Ed was moved out of the kitchen and isolated in a cell at the end of an empty cell block. When no one was around, he would burst into song, his voice carrying well in that setting. More than once the chief keeper came to the door of his cell.

"You're not supposed to sing," he grumbled.

Ed would sit silently until the keeper walked away, then start singing again. After two or three weeks, he was transferred to a work detail outside the walls. It was a cold winter, with temperatures often dipping to thirty below zero. Keeping warm was impossible.

The work involved digging up stumps with grub hoes a half-mile or so beyond the prison walls. With the cold, the stumps were like cement.

The inmates had their own small shack with a wood stove, but against the severe cold it didn't throw much heat, and they were forced to huddle together to keep warm. A bonfire kept the guards comfortable on the coldest of days. Warming their hands over the fire, they would sometimes taunt the inmates.

"Come on!" they would shout. "Get to work! It's not that cold out here."

Among the dozens of inmates outside the walls, friendships formed, and friends usually worked in small separate groups. Ed's group included a Native Canadian and two other men. "We liked each other and kind of hung around together." All of them hated working outside in the cold, and after three or four weeks Ed came up with a plan to get them back inside.

In the prison there was a drop box where inmates could leave notes for the administration. Ed wrote an unsigned note, purportedly from one of the outside workers, stating that four inmates had been overheard plotting an imminent escape. As the culprits, he listed his own name and those of his friends. "An hour later the four of us were working inside with brooms. They never said a word, but the warden was a retired army officer and he didn't wait any time at all."

The only other event of note during Ed's stay in the penitentiary was the loss of four front teeth from years of neglect. The prison dentist, who had his own practice in Prince Albert, would make periodic visits to look after the inmates' dental needs. Besides losing his four front teeth, Ed suffered through numerous fillings, all of them done without freezing. "He butchered me. He kept hitting the nerves and the pain was awful."

With the loss of his top four front teeth, Ed had trouble speaking properly, and his fellow inmates made fun of him. It wasn't until he returned to Toronto after his release that he was fitted for the partial plate that would restore and improve his trademark smile.

While his son was serving time in penitentiary, Glover Boyd, a respected police officer with fifteen years on the Toronto force, was working to get him released on parole. He wrote to the warden stating that he had found a job for Ed, and that upon his release he could live at home with the family.

His efforts paid off, and on March 15, 1939 – three weeks before his twenty-fifth birthday – Edwin Alonzo Boyd was released on parole[7] from Saskatchewan Penitentiary after serving two-and-a-half years.

He had experienced a lot in the nine years since he first left home to work on a farm, but his progression to adult maturity had been stunted. His formal education had ended in eighth grade; he had spent almost three years in jails and prison; and although he rode the rods almost continuously for four years, his travel was largely restricted to Ontario and the three prairie provinces. And other than furtive encounters with the opposite sex – as a boy under the back porch, and as a teenager on the farm – he'd had no meaningful relationship with a woman.

Ed was quite aware of his deficiencies. "I roamed back and forth across Canada, but I didn't get to Vancouver – I didn't even get past Calgary. I really hadn't been anywhere until I went overseas."

And the few women he'd met riding the rods were prostitutes or were travelling with someone else. "I wasn't somebody that they'd bother with anyway, because I was just travelling and didn't care one way or another."

If Ed had a blind spot, it was his unresolved conflict with his father: his emotions would forever be tainted by the early death of his mother. "He thought my going through the penitentiary system would make a big difference in my life, but all it did was teach me how to handle myself under authority."

The warden provided Ed with a train ticket to Toronto and a ten-dollar bill. He was also given a stiff, ill-fitting suit and a new pair of shoes – modified army boots that continually slipped off his heels. He was driven to the train station in Saskatoon. There was a lengthy wait for his train, so he took in a movie next to the station. It was *Typhoon*, set in the South Seas and starring Dorothy Lamour, wearing her trademark sarong as she wooed Robert Preston.

A few weeks after Ed was settled in Toronto, his friend Jake was released from the penitentiary and stopped to see him on his way to Nova Scotia, his home province. Ed suggested they resume their hobo life.

"No," said Jake. "Going to jail finished me. I'm going home to get a job."

The two men never saw each other again. "He said he would write," says Ed, "but he never did."

Getting By

A lot had happened in the Boyd family since Ed left for the farm in 1930. Glover Boyd had changed postings since his first one at No. 10 Station on Main Street, and the family had moved twice, first to 24 Yarmouth Gardens and then to 141 Roxborough Street West. Glover and Minnie had married, and first Gord and then Norm had gone to England and signed on with the Royal Air Force (RAF). Harold had long since moved out on his own. Only Ed's youngest sibling, Irene, was still at home when he arrived from the penitentiary.

Roxborough was a pleasant, leafy street between Avenue Road and Yonge, north of Bloor. The Boyd house was on the south side, where it backed onto sprawling Ramsden Park. Kitty-corner from them was evangelist Charles Templeton's[8] church. A few years later, Templeton would introduce the Youth For Christ movement to Canada. The Boyds attended Templeton's church, and Glover and Minnie were deeply involved in Bible study, having signed on for a course through a Pentecostal school.

Living at home gave Ed a chance to get to know his sister Irene, who was now a serious teenager studying to become a missionary. One day, returning from one of his runs downtown and back, Ed noticed her sitting by herself in the front room. "She was looking kind of lonesome, so I bought a brick of ice cream and we polished it off together. We sat and talked for a long time. For some reason she never forgot that." Irene would later spend years as a missionary in rural Haiti, where she lived in considerable hardship. Ed says his sister had the necessary perseverance for that kind of life, but he felt she wasn't strong enough physically. She became very ill and was sent back to Canada. She married but had no children, and Ed believes her health problems in Haiti led to her early death in the 1970s.

The job Glover Boyd had arranged for Ed was at Caulfield's Dairy on Howard Park Avenue. It was owned by Samuel Caulfield, who had been overseas in Glover's regiment in the First World War. At first, Ed was enthusiastic about the job, which paid $18 a week and involved off-loading cases of empty milk bottles to a conveyor, then stacking cases once the bottles were filled. There were eight quarts in each case. "They had to be stacked eight cases high, so I must have been in good shape because they were heavy, and I had to throw the last one up over my head to get it on top."

He liked the work because it was a day job, and because it was physically demanding, which kept him fit. The Roxborough house was three miles from the dairy, and he always walked to work – both ways.

Life got even better for Ed when Bill Underwood, an expert in unarmed combat, invited him to do some instructing at his judo studio in the evenings. The studio was on the second floor of a building on King Street a couple of blocks west of Yonge. Underwood ran judo classes during the day and in the evenings. He had several instructors and called on Ed whenever he needed him. Ed liked the studio and began showing up after work and on his days off. Besides helping out as an instructor, he was learning more advanced techniques. He was also doing weight training to improve his strength and muscle tone.

Ed and one or two other part-time instructors often laughed about Underwood's promises to pay them. "I never got a damn cent, and I don't think the other guys did either. I didn't mind at all, because I liked the exercise."

On any given night there might be four instructors and twenty or so students at the studio. Many of the students had won six- or eight-week courses from various competitions, including the Miss Toronto contest. Ed had fun teaching them. "The only trouble was, I didn't get to throw them, they always threw me." Through his training he knew how to fall without getting hurt, no matter what hold was put on him.

At that point in his life, Ed was health-conscious in the extreme and read anything he could find about physical fitness and nutrition. Besides walking to and from work at the dairy, he would run from home to the judo studio and back in the evenings.

Things began to go wrong for Ed when his boss at the dairy assigned him to a different job – on the night shift. Now, instead of hoisting milk cases, he was cleaning the large vats that held the milk before it was funnelled into the quart bottles. "It was a dirty job. The vats would be scummy from the milk and they had to be cleaned with lye and boiling water and sprayed with a hose. The lye was pretty potent stuff. I don't know if it was dangerous for me or not."

His main complaint about the new job was that it provided much less exercise. Also, working nights reduced his time at the judo studio. "I should have gone to the boss and asked him to put me back piling cases, but I didn't. I didn't have the confidence to do that." Ed worked at the new job for a month and then quit. A few days later, Glover approached him at the house.

"How's the job going?" he asked.

"I don't know. I quit."

"What! That was a good job."

"I know it was, but the minute I got good at it, they moved me to something else. Something I hated. I stayed as long as I could, and then I quit."

Ed saw his experience at the dairy as analogous to the violin lessons he took as a child. "I was playing the violin and winning all the prizes, and all of a sudden the teacher decided the other kids were not getting enough awards so she moved me to this advanced class, and I was sunk. I couldn't handle it – I couldn't even read the notes. And this guy was doing the same thing with the dairy. I was doing a good job, and it was good exercise, but he puts me on this bloody thing with the milk."

The loss of the dairy job would soon be forgotten: world events were about to overtake Ed's life. War was in the air, and his brothers were already overseas. He was bored and didn't want to miss out.

To break the monotony, he had bought himself an AJS motorcycle. He liked the sense of freedom it gave him and he took to it naturally. He didn't know it yet, but his ability to handle a motorcycle, and his judo and karate experience, would be valuable assets in the next stage of his life.

7
War

With all the talk of war, and time on his hands after quitting the dairy, Boyd decided to join the Queen's York Rangers militia, which met twice a week down at the Exhibition grounds. He signed up August 26, 1939, and enjoyed the marching, the precision drills, and a short stint spent guarding the Welland Canal after rumours that foreign agents planned to blow it up.

In September 1939, six months after Boyd's release from the penitentiary, Germany attacked Poland. Soon after, Canada was at war. His militia unit was dissolved, and most of its members scrambled to join the Canadian Army.

He was recruited by the prestigious Permanent Force, Royal Canadian Regiment (RCR), and signed up on November 12 at the Horse Palace on the Exhibition grounds. He was twenty-five and was joining thousands of others of his generation, many of them homeless and desperate and seeking an escape from the country's crushing unemployment.

Boyd lied on his application, claiming he had completed Grade 10 at Oakwood Collegiate in Toronto and had been to Riverdale Technical School (which in his youth he had hoped to attend to learn a trade). He also stated that he was a motorcycle mechanic. "I wanted them to think I was better qualified than I was. I know that I lied sometimes when I was riding the rods and bumming houses, but I never lied about anything important, because I always figured once you started lying, you just kept on lying until nobody would trust you."

Within two weeks of signing up, Boyd was sent to Valcartier, the military camp near Quebec City. When he told them he knew motorcycles, the authorities decided that would be the focus of his training

– he would be a dispatch rider. At first, however, there were no motor-cycles. "When they finally arrived, they were all English Nortons. I learned to ride them and pretty soon they had me teaching others."

For the freshly uniformed recruits, Valcartier was like one big summer camp – even more so for Boyd. His role as a motorcycle instructor wasn't structured. He wasn't included in roll call, and he wasn't called for meals. "I was just a forgotten man. So I used to get on the bus and go down into Quebec City and mooch around there all day. I'd come back and nobody had missed me, so I went into my barracks and went to sleep."

There were morning parades, but the name Edwin Alonzo Boyd was never called. "I thought, jeez, I'm really well off here."

On one of his forays to Quebec City he met an attractive, dark-haired young woman with a strong French-Canadian accent. Boyd was shy, and when they ran out of small talk he offered to buy her a milk shake. Then they went for a walk, and when the silences grew longer, it was time for another milk shake, and then another, and another. "Finally, she didn't want any more, so she walked out and left me. I had all these milk shakes in front of me – five or six of them. It took about an hour to drink them all, and I went back to my barracks, and again nobody had missed me."

But he wasn't overlooked when it came time to go overseas. "They marched me right out of my bed and onto the train for Halifax with all the rest of them." From there, they boarded a ship for Britain.

The North Atlantic seas were rough, as they usually are in December, when Ed Boyd shipped to England in 1939. He spent most of the voyage in a hammock below decks. To add to his misery, his bunk was at the front of the ship, "where the bow curves together." He was sick much of the time, but managed to twice read the Dale Carnegie book *How to Win Friends and Influence People*. "I did a lot of thinking about it, and I was pretty confident that now I knew how to get along with other people, because I'd been a loner all my life up to then." The book apparently instilled enough self-confidence in Boyd that within the next six months he would ask three women to marry him. The first was a Canadian teacher on an exchange program; the romance ended when she returned to Canada. The second proposal was to a teacher from Guildford. "She said yes, and then this guy came back, and she changed her mind." "This guy" happened to be her fiancé, back from a tour of duty with the British Army in Tunisia.

Boyd's regiment was posted to Aldershot, southwest of London. By the time he arrived there, his brother Gord, then nineteen, had been in England for more than two years. And Norm, eighteen, had been there for over a year. Both had signed on with the Royal Air Force (RAF) for six years. Neither brother knew that Ed had been in penitentiary until after his release. The three Boyd brothers were able to spend Christmas of 1939 together and had their photo taken to mark the occasion.

In Ed's Aldershot barracks, posted on the bulletin board, was a notice from a London couple inviting Canadian soldiers to stay at their home in Clapping Common during leave or on weekend passes. Ed thinks he was the only soldier who took them up on the offer. He visited sometimes, and sometimes brought his brothers along. "It was exciting walking around London. Every time we went down there, the air raid sirens were going and you could hear the bombs dropping."

The couple, Olive and Bill Prior, not much older than Ed, were generous and interesting. Bill was a machinist who made all kinds of marvellous things with metal. In his spare time he created interlocking metal puzzles that were almost impossible to solve. Olive was a professional pianist who for years had played for the ballet. It was at the Priors' house that Gordon Boyd met his future wife, a young Austrian woman who had been stranded in London when the war broke out.

There is a great deal of myth surrounding Edwin Alonzo Boyd, including the claim that he was a commando in the Second World War. The word "commando" conjures images of a soldier efficiently slitting throats behind enemy lines as his team tries to blow up a strategic target. There is no doubt that Boyd had commando training and was an expert in unarmed combat – so good that he was called on to teach others. But nowhere in his military record does "commando" appear. And he has never claimed to be a commando. He qualified as a Class III motorcycle driver and was a dispatch rider during his time with the Royal Canadian Regiment's First Division. After that he was in the Provost Corps.

The one foray Boyd's outfit made into Europe before D-Day was a fiasco. On June 13, 1940, ten days after Dunkirk, with the Germans in control of much of France, they crossed the English Channel from Plymouth, landing the next day in Brest. They had moved inland about sixty miles when they were told that the Germans had broken through and were about to overrun them. "We were ordered to get out as fast as we could. I was on my motorcycle and we drove into this big, vacant field. They began smashing up the vehicles and there was gas all over. Somebody tossed a match in, and the next thing you know, there was thick black smoke rising everywhere. The Germans could have seen us a hundred miles away."

The soldiers piled into trucks and roared back to the Channel. It was a small-scale replay of Dunkirk, up the French coast, where 340,000 Allied troops had been evacuated to England by a flotilla consisting mostly of small boats. But there were no boats waiting for the Canadians at Brest, and they had to linger on the beach with several retreating Permanent Force English units. In their haste many of the Canadians had thrown away their weapons, and the Brits, their rifles and packs in place, eyed them with disdain. Boyd's motorcycle was gone, but he had kept his service revolver.

The Canadians discovered several barrels of wine on the wharf and broke them open. "The soldiers were very undisciplined," says Boyd. "Half of them were drunk, and the other half were holding them up. Some of them even threw their weapons into the water. The English were very stiff, and never left their weapons. The Canadians didn't give a shit."

Back in Aldershot, the commanders did give a shit. The troops had been away less than four days, but most of their equipment was lost. They were confined to barracks, and it was weeks before they were outfitted with new weapons and vehicles.

Until then, Boyd had been driving Nortons. The replacements were Harley Davidsons. They were much heavier machines, but Ed soon mastered them and was instructing others. He was still a private, but he was enjoying himself and feeling successful.

8

Love and War

Not long after the foray into France, Boyd's regiment moved from Aldershot to an encampment on the outskirts of Reigate, south of London. It was a largely residential town with many parks and an ancient Norman church.

On a rainy November night in 1940, Boyd had delivered a dispatch and was returning to the Reigate base. He stopped for a cup of coffee and a sweet roll at the military canteen just off the town's main square. As he was walking back to his motorcycle, he noticed a young woman standing on the street corner. She was dark-haired and pretty but, in the rain, "kind of bedraggled, as if she was lost or something." He approached her, introduced himself, and invited her to a small movie theatre around the corner to get out of the rain. Then they went to a restaurant.

"It's getting late, I have to leave now," she said after their meal.

"Where do you live?"

"Oh, I'm staying at the canteen."

"The canteen?"

"They let me sleep in the back room at night."

"Is that safe?"

"Oh yes."

"Do you want me to walk with you?"

"Oh no, I know my way."

The woman was Dorreen Mary Thompson, from York in the north of England, and she was twenty years old. Her father was a gunner in the present war, as he had been in the First World War. Between the wars he had worked as a coal miner near Newcastle. Dorreen had been raised by her maternal grandparents. She had a twin sister; at the time of their birth, their mother was gravely ill and didn't feel strong enough to raise both girls. The grandparents, Kate and John Hunter, had agreed to take one of them.

"They're both so much alike, which one will we take?" asked Kate.

"Take the first one that smiles at you," said John.

Dorreen had smiled first, and was taken by her grandparents when she was seven days old. She loved her grandparents and was deeply saddened when her grandfather died of cancer when she was ten. John, a railway engineer, was a tall and slim and for years had driven trains between the north and south of England.

Dorreen's eyes still mist over when she remembers the years before her grandfather died. They lived at 69½ Goodramgate in York, and on Saturdays, from the age of six until John Hunter died, she would take an empty white china jug to the local pub and have it filled with beer, "half a pint of mild, and half a pint of bitter – mixed."

She couldn't see the top of the bar, but would reach up and plunk down the empty jug. It became a game for the bartender. He would lean forward and look down at her.

"Oh, I wondered who that was."

"It's just me," the tiny girl would respond.

"I knew the jug came from somewhere," he smiled.

"No froth, please," she said, following her grandfather's instructions.

Next, Dorreen would go to the butcher shop for six-penny worth of cooked ham and one small meat pie. The last stop was for ginger ale at another shop. "And that's what we'd have. I'd have the meat pie with HP sauce, my grandparents would have the ham, and we'd all have a shandy – made with the beer and the ginger ale."

She remembers John Hunter smoking five-pack Woodbine cigarettes, which came in colourful paper envelopes. "So the men could put the five in their shirt pocket without the tobacco making a mess."

Her grandfather's cancer started as a pea-sized tumour in his neck but grew to the extent that "it just looked like somebody had shoved their fist from inside right out there."

Kate was a tall woman, sturdy, strong-willed, and kindly. After her husband died she was able to provide for herself and Dorreen, aided by John's railway pension. Kate was an accomplished "tailoress" and earned a modest income making red huntsman jackets and the black velvet jockey caps that went with them. Dorreen could ride the railway for half-fare, and her grandmother took her to the seaside for a week in the summers, renting a cottage near Scarborough.

Her grandparents were church-going Catholics, and she went to a Catholic elementary school. When her father gave up coal mining for bricklaying, the family moved to York and Dorreen was able to go to school with her siblings. Besides her twin, Joan, there was a brother and a younger sister. Dorreen often visited the family on Sundays.

Dorreen completed elementary school when she was thirteen. She loved animals and wanted to become a veterinarian, but her grandmother didn't have the resources to pay for the necessary apprentice period as a "kennel maid." Instead, at fourteen, she went to work at the Rowntree chocolate factory.

Her grandparents had never adopted her, and as soon as she began to earn an income her parents wanted her to move home with the rest of the family. Neither Dorreen nor her grandmother wanted her to leave, and there was a nasty confrontation when Dorreen's father, spurred on by her mother, came to the house.

"We want her home right now," he demanded.

"You want her home, do you?" said Kate sharply.

"Yes we do."

"Then pay me for fourteen years of maintenance."

Dorreen says her grandmother was extremely upset. "She brought me up out of the goodness in her heart. But it went on and on, and my mother became very spiteful. She couldn't have me, and didn't want her mother to have me. It was awful."

The upshot was that her mother went to the courts, had Dorreen declared "incorrigible," and had her confined to a Catholic convent for delinquent girls. She would remain there for four years. "I'll never forgive my mother – to this day – because she hurt me and she hurt my granny so much."

The convent was on the outskirts of Leeds, a substantial distance for Kate Thompson, who visited once a month. It was run by nuns of the Good Shepherd order, who wore cream-coloured habits and starched white wimples. When Boyd visited the convent many years later, it reminded him strongly of a prison: barred windows, locked doors, and nuns walking around with large rings of keys dangling from their waists. They reminded him of the keepers in the penitentiary.

"I remember, if you broke the slightest rule, you had to go and knock on the Mother Superior's door and say 'blessed be God'," says Dorreen. "Then you'd open the door and kneel and kiss the floor – kneel and kiss the floor ... oh, I hated it. It was four years of hell." Dorreen was put off religion from then on, although she still considers herself a Roman Catholic.

When the war began, most of the girls were transferred from the convent to work for government agencies. Another of the Boyd Gang myths is that Dorreen once worked as a parlour maid for Lord Louis Mountbatten. She says it isn't true. She ended up in London as maid and cleaner at a house, behind the Parliament buildings, for government employees – mostly young attorneys. "Then the bombs started falling and I was sent back to my gran in York."

After their first meeting in Reigate, Ed and Dorreen dated four or five times over the next week. He asked her to marry him, and she agreed, and on November 21, before a Justice of the Peace at the local courthouse, with Ed in his uniform and Dorreen in a pink dress, they became husband and wife. They would have been married sooner, but because Dorreen wasn't twenty-one she had to get written permission from her father, who was with the British Army in Africa.

After the wedding they spent a week in London on their honeymoon. Before they married, Boyd found a large bright front room on the ground floor of a house in Red Hill, "spitting distance from Reigate." It was perfect for him. He was riding dispatch for the RCR's headquarters company, and the major in charge lived in a house about two blocks from the Boyds' place. "I let him know where I was and he could find me whenever he wanted me. They liked me, and they liked the way I worked."

He had to be at headquarters every morning, but instead of sleeping in a tent at the Reigate camp, he spent most nights in his cozy room with Dorreen. "There was a little wall at the front of the house where the room was, and I always kept the motorcycle parked inside there, ready to go. If they wanted me at night, they sent a messenger down to get me."

On a typical day Boyd would run a message from headquarters down to Brighton on the Channel; wait for a response; deliver it to headquarters; check in with his unit at the Reigate camp; and return to Dorreen in Red Hill. "I was quite contented that I finally found someone I could love," he says.

Dorreen had a short, attractive girlfriend, Rose Marie, who shared their room for a while. Boyd didn't mind at all. "I jumped into bed with them, but Dorreen made sure that she was always between me and the other girl." Rose Marie and Dorreen also shared a dark secret, as Boyd would soon discover.

The room at Red Hill was considered temporary, and Dorreen soon found a proper apartment in a building on the main street of Red Hill. Rose Marie had moved away. The Boyds had been living in their new apartment for several weeks when Boyd returned one morning after riding dispatch all night. He walked into the apartment to find Dorreen sitting on the couch holding a baby, about six months old.

"Gee, where'd you get the nice baby?" he asked.

Dorreen burst into tears.

"What's the matter?" he asked.

"You're going to hate me," she sobbed.

"What are you talking about?"

"It's *my* baby."

Boyd was in shock. "I nearly fell off the stairway."

While in London, before moving back to York to live with her grandmother, Dorreen had often gone to Buckingham Palace on her days off. It was there she had caught the eye of tall, handsome, Billy Reardon, a member of the Coldstream Guards, standing proudly in his red uniform and tall black busby. They dated a few times and Dorreen got pregnant. She returned to York with the baby, and after a few weeks left it with her grandmother. Reardon was later killed in the war.

Dorreen couldn't bring herself to tell Ed about the baby, fearing she would lose him. Afterwards she reasoned, "If he loves me, he will love my son." She had reasoned correctly. Boyd was disappointed that Dorreen hadn't told him about the baby – in effect, she had lied to him – but when the army paymaster told Boyd he could get the marriage annulled, he demurred: "I wouldn't want to hurt the baby – it's not his fault – and I love the girl I'm married to, so I'll just raise him as mine." He later adopted Anthony, and except for the paymaster, the other soldiers accepted that he was the father.

"He turned out to be quite a nice kid," says Boyd. "I never kept it a secret. And when he was old enough to understand, I told him that I wasn't his father. It didn't seem to bother him."

On August 20, 1941, almost nine months to the day after Ed and Dorreen married, she gave birth to a son, Edwin Alonzo Boyd, Jr. The baby was born in hospital in York, with Dorreen's grandmother present. Ed was granted a week's leave and was there the day of the birth.

The baby was two days old when the air raid sirens sounded. A nurse gathered up six babies from the nursery – three under each arm – and headed for the hospital shelter. As she whisked through the doorway, baby Edwin's head hit the door jamb.

"It was a beautiful baby," says Dorreen. "And after the all-clear, I kept asking for him. It wasn't until my gran got after them that they finally brought him to me. He was all black and blue down one side of his head. It was a cerebral haemorrhage. If he had lived he would have been a vegetable. They didn't want to say what happened, but one of the nurses finally told me."

The baby died a few days later and was buried in a York cemetery on August 30. The usual hospital stay after a delivery was two weeks, but with her baby dead, Dorreen wanted out of there. "I left about the sixth or seventh day. My gran was upset with me because I wanted to walk along the river."

Fifty-six years later, Boyd doesn't have much to say about the death of his son. When asked about it, his words are matter-of-fact, but his jaw tightens and his intense blue eyes stare wistfully into the distance.

But not long after the baby's death, responding to a letter from

Dorreen, he wrote: "... Your words tell me of your precious love for me and all about the heartbreak of having our baby son snatched away. However, darling, it was better that we hadn't a chance to get to know him as we know Anthony, because it would have been harder that way. We still have our very deep love for each other."[9]

Dorreen had wanted desperately to join the army and drive trucks. In early 1941 she returned to York and joined the Army Territorial Service (ATS), but at five feet, two-and-a-half inches she was too short to drive trucks – she could barely see over the dash. But she wasn't too short for motorcycles. In York the ATS had decided to start training women as motorcycle dispatch riders. "That suited me to a T," she says. "Thirty-six of us went into training and twelve finished. I was one of the dirty dozen."

Dorreen drove Nortons, Triumphs, and Indians, but couldn't manage the Harleys, which were too big and heavy. Now there were two dispatch riders in the family. After once riding behind Dorreen on the same motorcycle, Ed decided, "Never again – I was hanging on for dear life."

About a year after they were married, Ed and Dorreen went to York to get married again – this time in the vestry of the Roman Catholic church. Dorreen's mother wasn't invited.

Kate Hunter liked Boyd, but didn't like the idea of her granddaughter being married in a registry office and felt strongly that Anthony should be brought up Roman Catholic.

Boyd had no objection to getting married again. But he believed it was all meaningless. "So far as her family was concerned, we were properly married, but it didn't matter to me or Dorreen. She was a Catholic by birth, but she wasn't a Catholic by actions."

In March 1942, on another visit to Kate Hunter's in York, Dorreen convinced Ed to stay an extra couple of days before returning to Reigate. He thought it wouldn't be a problem because he got along well with his senior officers, sometimes delivering messages to their girlfriends or wives. His immediate superior, Colonel Snow, often borrowed his motorcycle for his own use. "And he'd send me all over the blasted country with messages for this girlfriend or that girlfriend."

But when Boyd's sergeant-major reported to Snow that he had overstayed his leave, the colonel wasn't pleased, and summoned him to his office. Boyd stood silently during the ensuing harangue, which was mostly about him leaving his post in time of war. "He said he was going to make an example of me, and he put me on latrine duty for a while – digging holes for the shit." He was also docked twenty-two days' pay.

The Home Front

few weeks after Boyd was disciplined for being absent without leave, he read a notice that the army was looking for volunteers for the Provost Corps – the military police. Boyd was unhappy with the RCR and decided to apply. His application was approved, and he transferred to the Provosts on July 27, 1942.

At five-foot-seven and 150 pounds, Boyd was one of the smallest men in his unit. Even so, he excelled at self-defence and unarmed combat. He was noticed yet again and was soon teaching others. He completed a ten-week training course that involved a lot of drilling as well as classes in law and law enforcement. Now he and his father had something in common – they were both policemen.

As a member of the Provost Corps, Boyd was automatically promoted to lance-corporal, but six months later, in February 1943, the unexpected happened. His sergeant-major, a career army man, approached him on the drill square. "I want you to take the guys out there and show me what you can do."

Boyd was stunned, but he didn't hesitate. In a booming voice, he shouted commands across the square, and to his amazement the men responded in unison. Perhaps he was releasing pent-up resentment from all the years that he had been on the receiving end of orders – at home, in school, in the penitentiary, in the RCR.... Now, as if born to it, he was giving the orders.

"Have you done this before?" asked the sergeant-major when the drill was over.

"No, I haven't."

"Well, where did you learn to do that?"

"I don't know."

Several times over the next days and weeks, Boyd was called on to drill the men. He performed flawlessly each time.

"You're all right," said the sergeant-major. "You're doing well. I'm going to put in a recommendation for you."

Boyd thought he might get a minor promotion. "But a week later I had two stripes, and the week after that I had three stripes." Now he was a sergeant. It all happened in a flash, and he was so excited he invited Dorreen down to watch him perform. Dorreen shakes her head at the memory. "His voice was like thunder. He sure could yell – you wouldn't think it was him at all."

With his new job and increased pay, Ed and Dorreen were able to move into a large, two-storey house in Aldershot. And in the spring of 1943, Dorreen discovered she was pregnant again. This time it was twins, a boy and a girl, born December 21 – "Christmas babies," she called them. Dorreen didn't want to go near a hospital, and the twins were born at home with the aid of a midwife and Kate Hunter, who came down from York. The bed was moved down from upstairs, and the front room was set up for the delivery.

It was an emotional time for Ed Boyd. About a week before the twins were born, he had been admonished under Section 15(1) of the Army Act, demoted from sergeant to private, fined two days' pay, and kicked out of the Provosts. His crime – getting drunk and failing to report for duty. If he had been in any unit other than the Provosts, it would have been treated as a minor offence, but he was a policeman and was expected to set a good example. "It was my own fault. Because you're a sergeant doesn't mean you can overstay your leave two or three days. If I had a couple of drinks, I would almost forget I had to be back in camp. I shouldn't have put myself in that position. I lost everything I had – no more stripes or anything."

Boyd was transferred to the army's 3rd Division, which was made up largely of newcomers from Canada. "They decided to send me to the first unit that would be going into France. So I was just a sitting duck waiting to be plucked."

But after three months in exile, it was the Provost Corps that plucked him, recalling him to duty at the end of March 1944. He was promoted to lance-corporal, the usual Provost rank.

Boyd was with the 11th Company of the Canadian Provost Corps when it was sent to Dover on the English Channel a few days before D-Day. Because the German resistance was stronger than expected, that company wasn't sent into France until July 26, 1944, seven weeks after the invasion.

While waiting in Dover, the Canadians had to keep close watch on their equipment. "The Americans were awful thieves," Boyd says. "They were always stealing our motorcycles and jeeps. Six of us shared a jeep in our unit and one night it vanished. We knew who took it but we couldn't prove it. The Americans would steal a jeep, run into London or somewhere, and ditch it on the way back. We retaliated by stealing *their* jeeps. It was one hell of way to run a war."

In the Canadian and British section of Normandy, the key Axis stronghold was the town of Caen. German resistance was ferocious, and it was not until late July, after weeks of bombing raids and frontal assaults that killed thousands of infantry and civilians, that the Germans were driven out. And it was only then that Ed Boyd's 11th Provost Company was brought in.

"There were Canadian, British, and German soldiers lying dead in the fields around Caen," he says. "There were bodies everywhere, and nothing was being done about them at first because everybody was trying to move ahead."

The Provosts' job was to keep the roads open for troops heading to the front line. They would set up in a town or its outskirts and keep the stream of men and equipment flowing as smoothly as possible. "Whenever you went into a town that was all shot up and the buildings flattened, there were always snipers shooting from church towers or whatever. Sometimes we were the only Canadians in sight. We expected to be shot down at any time. But we were lucky, I guess. I had a few bullets whiz by, but I was never hit." He would have more bullets whiz by him on the streets of Toronto a few years later.

His unit within the Provosts had just a half-dozen men with a single jeep and a motorcycle. His sergeant, from Timmins, Ontario, was easygoing and handsome and often slipped women into his bed at night. Nobody seemed to mind. When he didn't have a woman with him, he would tell jokes and stories in the darkness. "He had us laughing all the time," says Boyd.

In October 1944, Boyd's outfit was nearing the German border when a troubling letter arrived for him at divisional headquarters. The letter was from a Canadian soldier at Aldershot. "He said don't worry about your wife and children, I'm looking after them, and all this crap. I don't know if he was trying to ingratiate himself with me, or what." Ed concluded that Dorreen was having an affair.

His sergeant-major was concerned because the soldier was known to army command as a troublemaker and womanizer. He urged Ed to return to England as soon as possible. Ed was furious and left immediately, loading his .45 and slamming it into his holster. The English Channel was rougher than usual and he vomited most of the way across.

He went to their house in Aldershot and knocked on the door, but there was no answer. He assumed, rightly, that the children were in York with Dorreen's grandmother. He waited at the house for about half an hour, until his wife's twin, Joan, arrived.

"Where did you come from?" she said, her surprise obvious.

"We were up near Germany when I got sent back here to find out if Dorreen is living with some guy. Is it true?"

"She's my sister. I don't want to tell you right out, but I have to say *yes*. You're going to find out anyway." Dorreen was expected momentarily. Joan and Ed agreed that he would hide under the dining room table while she asked her sister about the affair. "They sat and talked for a while," says Ed, "and her sister asked her leading questions, trying to draw Dorreen out. And Dorreen admitted that she had been seeing this guy, but he had gone back to Canada."

"Are you going to tell Ed about it?" asked Joan.

"Oh, I couldn't tell him that."

"But he will probably find out, and that will make it worse."

"I can't tell him, he'd never forgive me."

Joan went upstairs, and Boyd came out from under the table. "Dorreen had the awfullest look on her, shaking like anything. Of course she started crying like she always did, and she made up some cock-and-bull story. She always said she was sorry. I guess because she was brought up in the Roman Catholic Church, she thought that was all you had to do – say you're sorry and let it go at that."

When asked about that incident more than fifty years later, Dorreen laughed. "Oh, he remembered that, did he? Those were the days, my friend. It's true, it's true, but crumbs … I wasn't seventy-six like I am now."

She says that even though Ed was never a violent man, he was so angry on that occasion that he slapped her. Ed denies that. "I wasn't the slapping kind. I never, ever, slapped her. That's just her guilt talking."

Dorreen's lover had been shipped back to Canada two days before Boyd arrived in Aldershot. "I had it in my head that I was going to shoot the guy right there. But I'm not sure what I would have done." He pauses for a moment, then: "Ten to one I would have put a bullet through his head."

Ed forgave Dorreen, and they were able to salvage their marriage, but he says he never felt the same about her after that. Eighteen days later, on November 6, 1944, he was back in France, but there was no one there to meet him. He had no transport and, like his days riding the rods, he had to bum his way back to the German border, inquiring as he went if anyone knew the whereabouts of the Provost Corps. "I finally found them up at the German border. The sergeant-major hadn't expected to see me again."

Two months after the confrontation in Aldershot, Dorreen was packing up the three children to sail to Canada with hundreds of other war brides. Kate Hunter accompanied her granddaughter and great-grandchildren to Liverpool, where the troop ship *Mauritania* was waiting to take them to Canada.

The *Mauritania* landed in Halifax on December 17, 1944. "All I could see were housetops and snow," remembers Dorreen. "It was one of the worst snowstorms ever. They had to dig the train out all the way to Toronto." It would be nine more days before she and the children arrived at Union Station.

Toronto

Glover Boyd was at Union Station to meet Dorreen and the children. It was a week before Christmas, and four days before the twins' first birthday. Glover and Minnie, both devout evangelical Christians, now had their own son, Howard, and had moved into a grand, three-storey house at 53 Chestnut Park Road in Toronto's exclusive Rosedale neighbourhood. Glover was providing a large room at the front for Dorreen and the children. Dorreen's impression of Glover was favourable, although she found him somewhat "gruff and rough." Her positive impression of Glover didn't extend to his wife and their nine-year-old son. She thought Minnie was snobbish, and considered Howard a monster (he sometimes spat at her).

Boyd was posted back to England from the front on January 25, 1945. Three weeks later he was headed home to Canada. His assigned ship was carrying war brides as well as returning troops. Boyd was placed in charge of policing the troops on board. "I guess they figured they could trust me to keep them away from the women. I was married and most of the other guys weren't."

In Boyd's duffle bag, carefully wrapped in clothing, were a torn-down Thompson sub-machine-gun and a Luger he had taken from a dead German in France. "The guy was upside down on a two-seater wagon that should have had a horse in front of it. The horse was dead, about ten feet away. The Luger was right there where I could see it, so I just took it and put it in my pack. The tommy gun was American – service issue. Somebody got killed, and a guy offered it to me, so I took it."

Since he was in charge of the security detail, there was no problem bringing his duffle bag and the guns on board, where he kept them safely stowed. "I was able to get away with it, and I'm sure a lot of others did the same."

When Boyd arrived at Union Station on February 17, 1945, his father met him and took him to the house.

Glover was proud that his son had turned his life around and served his country well. And although it was never discussed, he probably felt a special pride that Ed too was now a policeman, albeit a military policeman. But Ed had not volunteered for the Provosts out of a love for police work. He saw it simply as an opportunity get out the Royal Canadian Regiment, which he believed had treated him unfairly.

After a thirty-day leave with Dorreen and the children at Glover's house, Ed reported to the huge military de-mustering encampment on the grounds of the Canadian National Exhibition. The CNE had been cancelled since 1939, because of the war, and the grounds had been transformed into the No. 2 District Depot. All of the permanent buildings were now military offices or barracks for thousands of soldiers, sailors, and airmen, as well as the women's army corps.

Bunk beds had been installed in the Horse Palace, and two servicemen had been assigned to each stall. The stalls had been thoroughly cleaned out, but the smell of horses lingered. One of the buildings, near the Dufferin Gate, housed Webb Hall, the largest mess hall in the British Empire. It could feed three thousand at one sitting. The Navy had taken over the Automotive Building near the Princess Gate, and at the Flower Building the only beds were for the troops. It was the same at the Pure Food Building and all of the others.

Boyd presented his leave documents at the long reception table and was assigned a bunk in the Horse Palace. It would be almost two months before he was officially discharged from the army.

By the time Glover Boyd met his son at the train station he had been with the Toronto police for twenty-four years, and was a year away from retirement. Although he had never been promoted, he was a respected constable working out of No. 6 Station at Cowan and Queen in Parkdale. In June 1945, Jack Webster[10] joined the force fresh out of the army, just as Glover Boyd had done twenty-four years earlier, and was partnered with the older policeman. "He was assigned to show me the ropes," says Webster, "and we walked the beat together many times."

It didn't take Webster long to realize that Glover was a very religious man. "I called him Mr. Boyd, and he was always very kind to me." Webster didn't have a car, and after work, Glover would go out of his way to drop him off near his parents' home at Shaw and Dupont. On one of those rides, Glover bragged about his son Edwin, who had been in the army overseas since the beginning of the war.

In July 1945, Glover and his protégé were on duty at Sunnyside, the waterfront amusement park and beach that between June and September attracted people from across Toronto and beyond. Gasoline and tires were both rationed at the time, and streetcars were the preferred mode of transportation. The Lakeshore line ran right through the middle of Sunnyside.

Besides the beach there was an imposing outdoor swimming pool, known simply as "the tank" to Parkdale locals; the famous, all-wood roller-coaster, "the Flyer"; two merry-go-rounds; and a Ferris wheel. Concession booths offered Sunnyside red-hots, ice cream waffles, Honey Dew, and Vernor's ginger ale. There were restaurants, games of chance, a rifle range, bumper cars, and miniature golf – called Tom Thumb Golf. You could even have your weight guessed or record your voice on a paper disk.

On Sunday nights crowds sat on benches outdoors while Art Hallman's orchestra provided the music for the People's Credit Jewellers' sing-along concerts, which were broadcast over CFRB radio. There was also dancing outdoors at the Seabreeze, or indoors at the Palais Royale or the Palace Pier.

In the last summer of the war the Sunnyside crowds were swelled by the thousands of military personnel at the nearby Exhibition grounds. The enlisted men had their own canteen – in reality a huge beer hall, where draft beer sold at ten cents a glass. One soldier described it as "ankle-deep in suds." And for senior ranks there was the officers' mess.

The servicemen often spilled out of the Exhibition grounds into

the pubs and hotels along King Street West, or into other soldiers'
hang-outs like the Edgewater Hotel at Roncesvalles and Queen.
The combination of beer and postwar euphoria created a surreal,
carnival atmosphere that intensified as they made their way towards
Sunnyside, with its music and bright lights.

Glover Boyd and Jack Webster were patrolling Sunnyside in the
uniform of the day – which included the traditional bobby helmet –
when a man ran up to them.

"You'd better get over to the weight-guessing stand," he said.
"There's a fight."

The policemen were there quickly to find a uniformed airman
shouting obscenities at the weight guesser. Two of the airman's
buddies, also in uniform, stood quietly watching.

"Cut that stuff out now," said PC Boyd in his deep, measured voice.

"Who's gonna make me? You, Pop?"

Glover, who was fifty-two, tried calmly to coax the airman into
settling down, but instead he became nastier.

"Come on, Mr. Webster, take hold of his arm," said Glover, who
reached for the other arm.

The airman became violent, and in the struggle that followed, both
police helmets went flying. "Those old helmets were always the first
thing that came off when you were in a fight," says Webster. They
managed to handcuff the airman, and took him to No. 6 Station,
where he was later turned over to the Military Police.

Webster says Glover Boyd held his own in the fight. "He was a
strong guy, sort of chunky, with high cheekbones and a ruddy face."
It was Webster's first fight as a policeman, and they talked about it
over lunch.

"Gee, that was quite a scrap we had, Mr. Boyd."

"Son, if you intend to stay in this job, that'll be the first of many
you'll be in."

Glover Boyd would retire from the police force on September 7,
1946, after twenty-five years on the job.

Dorreen and Ed's stay at Chestnut Park Road was to be temporary.
They had been assigned a wartime house across from the streetcar

barns on Eglinton Avenue near Yonge Street. The house was under construction and would be ready in a few weeks.

Ed had been back in Canada a month when Dorreen received news from England that Kate Hunter, her beloved "granny," had died. It was before the days of insulin, and Kate was a diabetic who hadn't watched her diet as strictly as her doctors advised. "She had a wonderful garden outside her house," says Dorreen, "and one day she cut her foot on a spade and, because of the diabetes, gangrene set in. They told her they would have to amputate her foot, but she said, 'A woman of my size? I'm not going around on crutches the rest of my life.' She wouldn't let them amputate and she died."

In August 1945, Ed and Dorreen moved with the children into their house at 44 Eglinton Avenue West. The rent was $90 a month.

Many of the soldiers returning from overseas were being allowed to work in civilian jobs while waiting to be discharged from the army. They would spend their nights at the Exhibition grounds, sign out in the morning, and go to work. Boyd found a job at Canada Packers, filling sacks with fertilizer. At the same time, he applied to the Toronto Transit Commission for work. The TTC investigated potential employees carefully, and knew he had been in prison out West. They decided that his early troubles with the law were precipitated by the Depression and his youth, and that he had redeemed himself with his five-and-a-half years in the army. He was officially discharged on May 24, 1945, two-and-a-half weeks after the war ended in Europe. Eleven days later he was hired by the TTC.

Boyd was thirty-one when he left the military. That part of his life was over: he put away his medals and his souvenir tommy gun and forgot about them. But he kept his German Luger close at hand.

Three days before he left the army, he attended an interview at the Exhibition grounds with Captain W.G. Porter. The interview was required discharge procedure. Afterwards, Porter wrote of Boyd: "Looks like a man who should be able to take care of his own affairs and have few rehabilitation problems."

11
Frustration

The TTC trained Boyd as a streetcar motorman and conductor, and he was soon working the Yonge Street line. Because he had been overseas, he was granted an extra year of seniority for every year he worked. If he had stayed with the TTC he would have been one of the first to drive the new subway trains when the Yonge line was completed in 1954.

Boyd's job with the TTC was soon a family affair: both Norm and Gord signed on after they left the air force. Each had been in the military since the age of seventeen; neither had any adult experience with, or knowledge of, civilian life. Both felt the TTC was a good place to begin re-entering society. From there they would decide what to do with their lives.

In those days every main streetcar had a trailer car, and sometimes all three Boyds worked together at the same time on the same cars. "Sometimes you would be driving the streetcar," recalls Norm, "and other times you would be a conductor, depending on what shift you were on. You could be driver for part of a day and conductor for part of a day. It was whatever they assigned you."

With the streetcar barns across the street from their new house on Eglinton, it took Ed just minutes to get to and from work. The house itself was a small, solid bungalow with an elevated front lawn facing Eglinton Avenue, and had a front porch and two bedrooms. The kitchen stove was coal-fired, and the rest of the house was heated with an oil-burning stove. The coal was stored in a back shed, where there was also an icebox, for which ice blocks were delivered twice a week. Ed built a fence around the backyard, and a sand-box with a small roof for the children. On the front lawn he built a double play-pen for the twins, who had great fun tossing their toys out to the street, where passers-by would toss them back.

The Boyds lived just down the street from Miss Wickson's ballet studio; next to it was a real estate office that Dorreen cleaned for $47 a month. She received another $50 a month for cleaning Wickson's studio and doing her laundry.

Ed helped Dorreen with the dishes at home and with her outside cleaning work. On Wednesday nights they would wash and wax the floor of the ballet studio, using a heavy electrical polisher. Dorreen also did laundry, which Ed picked up and delivered, for several people in the upscale Forest Hill neighbourhood. "It was hard work," she remembers. "I just had my one washing machine and my iron. It was word-of-mouth business."

Ed would mind the children when Dorreen's cleaning work took her out of the house, and she would mind them while he was at work. For times when they both worked the cleaning jobs, the children had a baby-sitter.

The TTC job was steady and paid well, and Ed didn't mind the unpredictable hours (he was normally on call). With Dorreen also working and looking after six-year-old Anthony and the twins, they had little time for a social life. "If I wasn't washing and ironing, I was doing something else," she says. "And Friday was my day to clean our house. For all the laundry, mine and others', all I had was a Bendix wringer-washer. There was no dryer or anything. Ed put up a clothes-line, and that's where I dried everything – outdoors."

When Minnie became quite ill, Dorreen went back to Glover's for two weeks to help nurse her and look after the house. Ed, with the help of baby-sitters, looked after the children while Dorreen was away. It was only two weeks, but Ed missed her, and wrote her this short note: "There must be something wrong with my brain to let you go away. Coming home is like walking into a morgue. I went to a movie, even if you did keep intruding on my thoughts. We love you very much."[11]

When Dorreen returned home she was surprised at how neat and tidy the house was – until she looked in the closets. "Everything was in there," she laughs, "and I thought, oh brother."

Ed cared deeply about Dorreen, but believes, in retrospect, that the feeling wasn't mutual. He says she was constantly nagging at him to push the TTC for a regular route. But he knew such demands weren't feasible until he had more seniority. "She had a habit of putting me down because I wasn't getting ahead as quickly as some others." They often quarrelled bitterly, and a prison counsellor would report years later: "His wife would, on occasion, scream out that the twins were not his, and she named their father. Boyd had occasion to meet the alleged father and was disappointed to see how much the twins looked like him."

Boyd alleviated his growing frustration by working out at the same judo school that he had frequented before the war. There he became friends with Frank Lamb, another nonsmoking, nondrinking judo enthusiast. Lamb's wife, Flo, and Dorreen would remain friends for fifty years. Underwood sometimes enlisted Boyd and Lamb to train others. Once again, Boyd was paid in promises. For him, the workout was more important than the money.

Boyd usually kept his emotions to himself, but was in constant turmoil over Dorreen harping at him. "One thing I couldn't stand was people telling me what to do. I'd had enough of that in the penitentiary and in the army. I enjoyed working at the TTC and I could have had a good career there, but I got tired of listening to Dorreen. She wanted to run my life – so I quit."

When he informed his superiors, he was summoned to the TTC head office and was told that although he had a good military record, if he left he could not be rehired because of his criminal record. His mind was made up, he replied. He left in March 1946, after eight months on the job.

Dorreen denies badgering Ed about getting ahead at the TTC and says she couldn't understand it when he quit – but didn't complain. "It was a good job," she says. "And I was always working. We had the house and we were doing all right. I don't know why he quit."

Both Norm and Gord also quit the TTC. Norm decided to go back to school, and Gord bought a piece of land near Lindsay, Ontario, under the Veterans Land Act. Norm studied engineering and business in university, but dropped out after two years because of financial difficulties. He got a good job and never did go back.

After leaving the TTC, Ed Boyd worked for several months at a bakery and pastry shop a few blocks west of their home on Eglinton. He left the bakery and worked at a series of odd jobs, including one as a night watchman and janitor at a plumbing supply store. While reading a magazine one night he read a slogan that appealed to him, and he copied it onto the wall of the storage room at the back of the store. "I don't remember what it was now, but the boss saw it and told me to find another job."

His next job was at a grocery store three blocks north of Eglinton on Yonge Street. The owner had recently purchased the store but lacked practical business experience. "He was always asking me what he should do next," says Boyd. "It got so I was doing the deliveries and looking after the store while he'd be out cruising around looking for girls."

Boyd delivered groceries in an old panel truck. Sometimes he had to fill orders off the shelves from a list and then make the delivery. He loaded the orders into the truck and made three or four delivery runs a day. When he noticed that no one checked the boxes after they were put into the truck, he saw a way to help feed his family. "Somebody would phone in an order with fifteen or twenty different things, and if they were items I liked, I would duplicate the whole thing – fill two boxes instead of one. I'd shove them in the truck, and when I got to my place, I'd deliver my order." Boyd stayed at the grocery store for nearly a year.

By the fall of 1948, feeling desperate, Boyd began searching the want ads. He answered a job for a window-washer and was hired immediately. Boyd thought his employer had a good thing going, and in the spring decided to go into the business himself. He even purchased a vehicle, a maroon panel truck that looked like a modified hearse, with a rear door that swung out to the side. He built a rack for his ladders on top and had his name stencilled on the driver's door in small print. He was bringing in over $100 a week, except in the winter months when business trailed off dramatically. He wanted to expand his business with a modest advertising campaign and perhaps even hire one or two employees. His reputation had been solid with his bank since the war, and he asked for a $1,500 loan, suggesting as collateral the business that was so secure in the summer. The bank turned him down. Boyd was angry and resentful. Unless he could expand his business, it would never be lucrative enough to support his family.

He decided to become a taxi driver. There was work available, but he needed to apply for a licence through the Toronto Police Department. His application was turned down because of his criminal record. Boyd became angry and despondent, and as summer waned in 1949 his frustration and inner turmoil grew. He was feeling inadequate – in his mind, letting down both himself and his family. He had turned thirty-five that April but had no real prospects. He was a loner who didn't seem to fit in. He daydreamed about being an entertainer – a Hollywood actor – and had even gone to Lorne Greene's acting academy to see about enrolling. The woman he talked to seemed uninterested and was heading off to lunch. He said he would return later, but didn't bother.

If only he hadn't been held back at every turn, he thought. If only his father had kept his promise and sent him to technical school, where he could have learned a trade. If only he had stayed with the TTC. If only....

Then, in late summer, Boyd was reading the newspaper when an article caught his eye. A mentally handicapped teenager had walked into a bank at Church and Dundas streets, demanded money, and walked out with $69,000. He had sauntered up the street about three blocks before the police picked him up. The money was returned to the bank, and the youth was released soon after. Boyd couldn't believe it. "He didn't even show a gun. He just told the teller it was a holdup and they gave him the money. Right away, that sparks a thought in my mind – if it's so easy to rob a bank, what the hell am I working for? Why slave for somebody for a pittance, once a week or once a month, when I could just walk into a bank and get $69,000?"

Success

dwin Alonzo Boyd decided to rob banks not for the thrill – although that became a part of it – but because he believed he was eminently qualified. It was something – finally – that he could succeed at. He thought that with his ability and training, and with proper planning, he wouldn't get caught and it wouldn't even be that dangerous. "What it came down to, was that they had the money and I wanted it."

There was nothing spur of the moment about his first robbery. Two or three weeks of planning went into it, starting when he rented a garage (at $5 a month) well south of his target, which was the Armour Heights branch of the Bank of Montreal. He liked the interior layout of the bank and mapped out several escape routes in his head. He never once considered the Thompson sub-machine-gun hidden away in his duffle bag. "I wouldn't think of having something that big. It would just get in the way." He would never assemble the Thompson, and he eventually threw it out in bits and pieces, or simply "left it behind somewhere." The Luger would be his weapon of choice.

When Dorreen was out working or shopping and the children were asleep, Ed practised using make-up in front of a mirror. He also started a moustache. And two days before the robbery, he tested his disguise. With the rouge, mascara, and cotton batting stuffed into his nostrils and cheeks and behind his lips, he intentionally met Dorreen as she was returning from shopping. "I came walking around the corner and I looked her straight in the face, and she looked at me and didn't recognize me. And I thought, if she didn't recognize me, nobody would."

Boyd went into the bank two or three times to get a close look at how it operated. "I went in when there were line-ups. That gave me more time. I think I changed a ten-dollar bill or something."

After reading about the mentally handicapped teenager and his haul of $69,000, Boyd was somewhat disappointed at his take on his first job. "I didn't realize that you don't always get sixty-nine thousand. Sometimes you only get a thousand, or two thousand." Still, he had pulled it off, and knew he could do better if there was a next time.

His escape had been sheer luck, and as he drove home from the rented garage in his truck, he played the robbery over in his mind. Logistically, it had been a disaster, nothing like the precision military-style operation he had envisioned. He analysed his mistakes. Overshadowing all others was the whisky. That would never happen again. It had left him in a stupor and kept him in the bank long after his allotted time. It was plain stupid, he thought. The second major mistake was not having his own getaway car at the ready. "I figured the first car that came along, I would just jump in and drive away, but it didn't work like that." He couldn't depend on grabbing a stranger's car at gunpoint – it was too dangerous and unpredictable. But he already had a plan to remedy that.

That evening at home, as he was reading in the papers that the bank manager had emptied a pistol in his direction, Boyd added a third mistake to his list: he hadn't known that tellers and managers had guns and were prepared to use them. What the newspapers didn't tell him about was the secret downtown firing range in the basement of the old Bank of Toronto building where all the tellers and managers were sent for target shooting – a practice that would end in the late 1950s after a bank employee was killed by a manager's ricocheting bullet meant for a robber.[12]

Boyd decided that if he did rob another bank, he would have to neutralize the threat of being shot by the tellers or the manager. Robbing banks had turned out to be a lot more dangerous than he expected. What if that manager had been a good shot? From now on he would think as if he were still in the army, and face the possibility that he could be shot. "You had to decide if it was feasible and worth taking a chance."

When Boyd arrived home, he hid the money and didn't tell Dorreen what he'd been up to. At least now, he thought, she couldn't accuse him of not providing for the family, and the kids would have a good Christmas.

When he first looked at the newspapers early that evening he was dumbfounded. Both the *Toronto Daily Star* and the *Telegram* had huge, front-page headlines and photographs describing the robbery. And the next day even *The Globe and Mail*, the most staid of the three major dailies, ran a front-page story with a total of seven photos on the front and inside pages.

Boyd found it fascinating that he had created all this fuss. He – the loner – was the only one in the whole world who knew the person they were writing about. All those pictures and words had been inspired by *his* few minutes of action. He was anonymous, but even so, this was clear recognition of what he had accomplished – or what he had *succeeded* at.

Boyd knew nothing about the circulation war that had been ongoing between the *Star* and the *Telegram* for almost sixty years, since 1892 when the *Star* was founded by two dozen striking printers from the *Telegram*. The traditionally conservative *Telegram* considered the upstart *Star* and its owner, Joseph E. "Holy Joe" Atkinson, to be not only liberal but even Bolshevik.[13]

By the late 1940s the *Star* had a circulation of about 400,000, double that of the *Telegram*. The much despised Harry C. Hindmarsh, Atkinson's son-in-law, was a powerful force at the *Star*. Hindmarsh, heavy-set, over six feet, with short-cropped hair, was brutal with his reporters, especially if they showed talent and independence. Ernest Hemingway, who was a reporter at the *Star* in the early 1920s when

Hindmarsh was city editor, described his boss as "a son-of-a-bitch and a liar" and quit after less than four months.[14] Fifty years later, another reporter on quitting the *Star* would tack up this note: "Ernest Hemingway once worked here. Later, he blew his head off with a shotgun."

Gwyn "Jocko" Thomas, the *Star's* legendary crime reporter, started at the paper as a copy boy six years after Hemingway quit. In his memoirs, *From Police Headquarters*, he recounts how Hindmarsh visited his wrath on reporters who missed a story. "If they were away from their posts or were otherwise careless and got scooped, they were fired.... This cloud was always with us, and together with natural combativeness it often drove us to almost comic-opera frenzies of effort to beat the *Telegram*."

At the time Edwin Alonzo Boyd robbed his first bank, Atkinson was dead and Hindmarsh was president of the *Star*. His policies continued to prevail, tempered only by the Newspaper Guild, which had finally won a foothold and begun to improve conditions for reporters. In 1949 the war between the two papers was in something of a lull, but that was soon to change.

George McCullagh, wealthy owner of *The Globe and Mail*, entered the fray when he purchased the *Telegram* for slightly more than $3 million. McCullagh didn't mince words about his intentions. Addressing *Telegram* employees the day after he bought the paper, he said, "The outstanding thing that brought me into the evening newspaper field was to knock off the *Star*. The *Star* has done enough to the profession of journalism that we ought to go in and teach it a lesson.... I'm going to knock that shit-rag right off its pedestal."[15]

Jocko Thomas says Hindmarsh and McCullagh absolutely hated each other. McCullagh once told *Time* magazine, "That fellow Hindmarsh is so ugly that if he ever bit himself he'd get hydrophobia."

McCullagh brought in his friend John Bassett to run the paper, which adopted Hindmarsh's tactic of sending flying squads of reporters and photographers to blanket a crime scene or any other breaking news event. The *Telegram's* new aggressiveness soon paid off, and in the first six months under McCullagh, circulation increased by sixty thousand. The war raged again, and would continue until the *Telegram* finally folded in October 1971.

The *Star*'s coverage of Ed Boyd's first bank robbery included a banner headline across all eight columns, with four large photos directly beneath. The right-hand photo showed a policeman studying Cranfield's car for fingerprints. Under it began the story, which continued onto page 2, where there were two more photos, including a four-column shot of the bank. The *Telegram* refused to be outdone: its headline, BANK BANDIT ESCAPES 6 SHOTS, GETS $2,000, also ran across the full eight columns of page 1. (The *Telegram* headline was slightly inaccurate – the bank's Ivor Johnson pistol could only fire five shots.)

Thomas recalls that gunpoint bank robberies were unusual in Toronto until Boyd's time, and his use of a note was unheard of. "Prior to that, we didn't have any *note-jobs*. They came in later when the banks filled their staffs with women and told them if they received a note, to hand over the money so they wouldn't be hurt."

Thomas says it was no surprise that both the *Star* and the *Telegram* led with the bank robbery story in their afternoon home editions. Both papers produced seven or eight editions a day, and in those days "they thought nothing of stopping the presses and re-plating the papers."

Thomas worked out of the small press office at the old police headquarters at 149 College Street. When a call came in about a serious crime he would take a cab or his own car to the scene. The reporters and photographers would get there almost as quickly as the police, and in those days they enjoyed free rein to interview witnesses and take all the photos they wanted as soon as the police completed their inquiries. "You had to get the pictures and interview the bank staff. Interviewing them on the spot was the name of the game. Nowadays the cops close the doors and you don't even get the names of the bank staff."

Once the reporters had their facts they would call them into the newspapers. "The *Star* used to insist that you dictate the story from the scene. There was no rewrite desk, like they had later, where you just give the facts to some guy who puts it in shape. You had to dictate off the top of your head and you got used to that."

Thomas says Boyd was smart, or lucky, in choosing the Armour Heights bank for his first robbery. "That section of North York didn't get much patrolling in those days. It was right near the Toronto boundary and they would have quite a ways to go to get there. And some of those North York divisions were pretty stripped of men in the mornings when they had to go to court to testify in cases they were involved in."

When Boyd read the stories about the robbery, he realized just how lucky he had been. Not only had the bank manager missed him with all five shots, but he had eluded the police by a matter of minutes. One of those policemen was Maurice "Moe" Richardson, then a detective-sergeant with the North York force. He and his partner, Bert Trotter, had been patrolling in Willowdale just north of the bank in their 1949 Mercury. Police cars were unmarked in those days, distinguishable only by the big aerial in back.

"We weren't too far away that day," recalls Richardson. "We came down Avenue Road and when we got to the bank everything was in chaos. We should have got him, but he slipped away through the backyards. He was lucky the bank manager was a poor shot." It wasn't the last time Moe Richardson would cross paths with Edwin Alonzo Boyd.

13
Second Time Lucky

oyd wasn't sure if he would ever rob another bank, but he knew that if he did, he would have to be certain his disguise was effective. A few days after the first robbery, he dressed neatly and returned to the Armour Heights bank. Shortly before noon he walked up to Joyce Empey's wicket and with a friendly smile asked her to change a twenty-dollar bill. She cheerfully completed the transaction without any hint that she recognized him.

With the robbery proceeds Boyd paid off a few bills and helped with household expenses. He was also able to buy decent gifts for Dorreen and the children at Christmas. Dorreen never asked about the money, but she knew he didn't have a regular job and wondered where it came from. By the New Year of 1950 his cache was all but depleted. It didn't take much for him to convince himself that it was time to rob another bank. He enjoyed having cash at hand – it made him feel worthwhile. He convinced himself the next robbery would go much more smoothly – he wouldn't need luck to bail him out.

Many years later, when he was seeking to understand what had driven him to rob banks, Boyd linked it to a compulsion to succeed. However sloppy the first bank job had been, he had still pulled it off. "I enjoyed planning a bank robbery, especially when I was doing it myself. Most important, it was knowing I could be successful. And I think it was also that my dad had been a policeman, and that nobody knew who was doing these things."

By mid-December, a month before his second robbery attempt, Boyd was breaking the law again. He had also started another moustache. He practised stealing cars, and he rented two more garages. "The garages were only $5 a month, and every one was rented under a different name. Eventually I had so many of them I had to keep books on them. I always put my own padlocks on the doors. It was like having a little home right close." (Perhaps they were larger versions of the cubbyhole he called his "fort" below the back porch of his childhood home.)

Boyd used the garages to store junk or equipment from the house, including – until he lost track of it – his disassembled tommy gun. He would also use the garages to house stolen cars before a robbery. "A lot of the city streets had back lanes with garages in those days. It was just made for robbing banks."

The first car he stole in Toronto was in front of a busy drugstore, where drivers would stop on their way home for a pack of cigarettes or some other last-minute item. "Usually they left the motor running because it was chilly. I waited until a guy jumped out and ran across the road, and I just got in and drove away."

Some nights he merely observed, picking up drivers' patterns of behaviour. He concluded that the best time to steal a car was at ten or eleven at night, when people were in a hurry to get home and would leave their keys in the ignition while they ran into a store.

It was cold at ten in the evening of January 16, 1950, as salesman Fred Care locked the doors of the used cars on the Cedarvale Motors lot at 979 Eglinton Avenue West. Before locking up the office, he started his own car in front of the dealership, to warm it up. When he came out of the building minutes later, he saw someone else driving his blue 1949 Meteor along Eglinton.

"I remember it like it was yesterday," says Care, who is now eighty. "The car was brand-new. I used it as a demonstrator, and it only had seven hundred miles on it." Care ran back inside and telephoned the police.

"Which way was he headed?" asked the dispatcher.

"East," replied Care. "You can't help but get him – he's right about at Eglinton and Bathurst by now. I'll sit in the office and wait for you."

But Edwin Alonzo Boyd was gone, and the Meteor was soon locked away safely in one of his rented garages. Care waited more than an hour and then borrowed a used car off the lot and drove home. "It's lucky I didn't wait any longer," he says. "I would have been sitting there for three days."

Two days later, on Wednesday, January 18, Boyd parked the Meteor on Sandra Road, immediately west of the new Canadian Bank of Commerce on the north side of O'Connor Drive at St. Clair Avenue East. He was in full disguise, with shabby clothes and his face puffed out and reddened. From several days of reconnaissance, he knew that at exactly 12:30 p.m. the manager returned to his apartment above the bank to have lunch.

On this day there were no customers in the bank when the manager left. Five minutes later, Boyd entered the bank. Georgina Black was in the teller's cage, and accountant William Church was at his desk next to her. The two were separated by a partition of frosted glass. Church was talking to his wife on the telephone. The teller heard Boyd enter the bank but did not look up until he reached her cage. He handed her a Bank of Commerce cheque. She examined it and saw printed on it in pencil: THIS IS A HOLD-UP. A black handgun was aimed at her through the bars of the wicket.

"Mr. Church!" she called, her voice cracking. The accountant stood up, peered over the glass partition, and saw what was happening. Twenty-nine-year-old Church had been a lieutenant in Canada's 48th Highlanders in the Second World War, and he knew by the gun's shape that it was a German Luger.

"Hang up the phone and get over here," ordered Boyd, pointing the gun at Church, who placed the receiver on his desk and moved behind Georgina Black. Church's wife had heard the twenty-one-year-old teller's voice over the phone. "I thought it was just a mouse had scared her or something. I heard a man raise his voice and I thought it was my husband speaking to her. We were having a little argument over something when he left the phone. I hung on for a while, didn't hear anything, and then hung up." Boyd's puffy, rouged face led Church to believe the gunman was "hopped-up with dope" – a detail the newspapers would exploit later in the day.

Boyd pushed his white cloth sugar bag towards the teller.

"Fill it up," he ordered, thrusting the Luger at her. "And hurry up." She quickly began emptying bills into the bag from her cash drawer.

"Where's your gun?" asked Boyd.

"I ... I don't have one," she lied.

When the drawer was empty of cash, Boyd reached over for the bag. Waving his gun, he ordered the accountant and the teller into the open bank vault. Church closed the vault door behind them, waited a few seconds, and then came out. Boyd was gone. The accountant grabbed a bank-issue revolver from his desk and ran out onto the street in time to see Boyd pulling out from Sandra Road in the blue Meteor. Church was prepared to fire as the car turned west on O'Connor but he was afraid of hitting passers-by. Instead, he ran to his own car in the bank lot. But he had trouble starting it. "By the time I pulled out onto O'Connor Drive, the bandit had about a hundred-yard head start," Church told reporters later. "I was able to jot down the licence number, but in the chase in and out of traffic, I lost him." When he reached Donlands Avenue and O'Connor, he realized the robber had given him the slip, and turned around and returned to the bank.

On being informed of the robbery, L.E. Miller, the forty-year-old bank manager, had rushed down from his apartment. It wasn't a new experience for him: ten years earlier he had been held up at gunpoint at a sub-branch of the Bank of Commerce in Baden, Ontario. And ten days after that he and his wife had been confronted by a masked gunman in their apartment above the same bank. His wife was tied up, and he was forced to enter the bank, where he foiled a robbery by convincing the gunman there was a time lock on the vault. Now his latest bank, open just eight months, had also been hit.

Boyd had realized he was being pursued and was able to lose Church by turning sharply onto Don Mills Road and heading north. He was aided by the weather, which had turned nasty that morning, with strong winds and driving snow, and was worsening by the minute. Certain that Church could give a good description of the Meteor, and probably the licence number, Boyd looked for a spot to abandon the car. About five hundred yards north of O'Connor, he pulled onto a sideroad leading to the East York disposal plant.

Meanwhile, police radios across Greater Toronto were crackling with news of the armed hold-up and descriptions of the robber.

Witnesses said he was slight, about five-foot-seven, and that his face had been "puffed out" with cotton batting or paraffin wax and reddened with rouge or lipstick. He had "an unusually heavy moustache" and was wearing a ski cap and a dark windbreaker.

One of the first police officers to join the chase was East York Constable Cecil Caskie, who by chance checked Don Mills Road and noticed the blue Meteor on the sideroad. He arrived less than a minute after Boyd abandoned the vehicle. "I found the engine of this car very warm and the keys in the ignition were still swinging." The police were certain the bandit had fled into the heavy brush of the adjoining swampy ravine, near what is now Taylor Creek Park and the Don Valley. By 2 p.m., in a swirling snowstorm, about seventy-five uniformed officers and detectives from East York, Toronto, and surrounding departments were combing the six-square-mile area from four different directions. They were soon bolstered by reinforcements from the Ontario Provincial Police. Roadblocks had been set up on all streets leading in and out of the ravine, and police were canvassing nearby homes along Don Mills Road, O'Connor Drive, and St. Clair Avenue. They were also stopping and searching freight trains on the CNR line running through the ravine.

The police dragnet was for nothing. Boyd had been in the bush only long enough to spit the cotton from his mouth and wipe off his make-up. His windbreaker was reversible, and he turned the dark side in, removed his ski cap, and walked quickly to O'Connor Drive. From there he walked a few blocks south to a rented garage where his panel truck was waiting. By the time most of the police search team arrived, he had already left the area.

The abandoned Meteor was taken to East York police headquarters and checked for fingerprints, but none were found – Boyd had worn gloves. There was no damage to the car, but Fred Care still wasn't pleased when police returned it to him. "There were only a few more miles on it," he says, "but they sure left a hell of a mess with their fingerprinting." Powder residue and smudges were everywhere. The first thing most car thieves do is adjust the rearview mirror to see if they are being followed. Police had removed the mirror, dusted it for prints, and left it lying on the front seat.

Boyd counted his loot before returning home in mid-afternoon. It was slightly more than his first robbery, but not as much as he had hoped for. The snowstorm was getting worse when he parked his truck behind the house on Eglinton. Unaware of how close he had come to being caught, he was feeling elated.

Once again the *Star* and the *Telegram* gave the robbery massive coverage, even though it was competing for space with a major American story – the Brinks Robbery, which had taken place in Boston the night before. Nine bandits wearing Halloween masks had broken into the company's main vault and walked out with $1.5 million – at that time the largest cash robbery in American history. Edwin Alonzo Boyd's take was a mere $2,862, but newspaper readers could be forgiven if they thought the amounts had somehow been reversed. Although both stories made the page 1, it was the Bank of Commerce heist that got the banner headlines. HUNT DOPE-CRAZED BANK BANDIT, screamed the *Star*. Across the top of the *Telegram*'s page 1 was BANK BANDIT ELUDES POSSE IN BUSH CHASE. There were two photos on page 1, and on page 2 a five-column map and five more photos. Flush against a page 1 photo of Fred Care's abandoned Meteor, near the ravine, was the headline SCARFACED GUNMAN / LOOKING 'HOPPED UP' / GETS $1,000 IN LOOT. (The bank didn't provide the correct amount of its loss until days later.)

Dorreen had wondered about the source of Ed's income, but had never questioned him. It certainly hadn't occurred to her that her husband was a bank robber. But if he was supposed to be working at odd jobs, as he said he was, how did he manage to look so neat at the end of the day? "He used to go out in the morning nice and clean and shaved, and then he'd come back the same way – as if he should have an attaché case. I got suspicious."

Dorreen had heard about the Bank of Commerce robbery on the radio, and when Ed returned home later that afternoon, she picked up on the elation he was feeling. When he gave her a handful of new twenty-dollar bills, she suddenly knew there were no odd jobs – her husband robbed banks.

"It was you, wasn't it?" she asked.

"What?"

"You robbed that bank."

The truth was out, and Ed's dammed up emotions spilled over. He was "like an excited kid," Dorreen says. He couldn't wait to tell her the details and show her the rest of the money. Now he wasn't the only one in the world who knew – and he didn't mind at all. "Less than three minutes flat!" he told her. "That's how quickly I was in and out of there." Most of the bills from the robbery were new, and Ed decided he and Dorreen should wash them to make them look used. He half-filled the kitchen sink with water, and she soaked the bills.

"Don't use soap," he instructed.

After the bills were soaked and the water drained off, Ed put them in the coal-fired oven to dry. "I think he opened it two or three times to make sure they weren't cooked," Dorreen remembers.

Later, when Boyd read about the robbery in the newspapers, he realized it had been another close call. He began to think an accomplice – a partner – might be the answer. One could control the customers and staff while the other grabbed the cash; that way, more cash drawers could be emptied in the same amount of time. "I had learned that you couldn't walk into a bank by yourself and be out in less than three minutes with any significant amount of money."

14
Partners

About 11:15 p.m. on Monday, July 3, 1950, Mary Helen Guinane parked her new green Ford convertible in the Dominion Store parking lot at 2300 Yonge Street. When she returned half an hour later, the car was gone. It was already in one of Edwin Alonzo Boyd's rented garages.

With a wife and three kids to support, and no full-time work, Boyd was nearly broke again by the Dominion Day holiday. He decided to rob another bank, this time with a partner. The identity of the man he chose has never been revealed. All that is known about him is the description witnesses gave to police. He was about twenty-five, which was ten years younger than Boyd at the time, and stout (one witness used the word "fat").

Boyd didn't wait long to introduce his new partner to the world of bank robbing. The day after they stole the convertible, they parked it with the motor running on Glencairn Avenue near Dufferin Street, around the corner from the Dominion Bank. It was 2:30 p.m. Boyd, in his usual make-up and thick moustache, was wearing a blue suit, straw hat, and gloves. His partner wore a peaked cap and dark clothing. Neither had shaved for several days.

There were six employees in the bank, but only one customer, when the two men came through the door with guns drawn. Teller Richard Barry was working at his desk when he looked up and saw Boyd's Luger aimed at his chest.

"Don't press any alarm!" shouted Boyd, leaping up on the counter. "Everybody get to the back against the wall!" Jumping down behind the teller's cage, he herded the hostages down a narrow stairway to the basement. The bank's acting manager, Alfred Brown, had been working behind the counter when the men came in. "It was all done very quickly," he said later. "Within a matter of seconds they had us in the basement and the door was locked." The cash drawers were quickly rifled, and the gunmen were on their way out of the bank in less than two minutes. They didn't know it, but one of the employees had managed to press an alarm button. But instead of alerting a police station, it was rigged to ring in the grocery store next door.

Store owner John Miskiw heard the alarm but didn't call the police immediately because the alarm often malfunctioned, sounding on its own. He sent his delivery boy, fifteen-year-old Tom Morris, to check the bank.

"It's empty," said the boy on his return. "There's nobody in there." Miskiw immediately called the police.

As Boyd was rushing from the bank with his partner he nearly knocked over a sixty-three-year-old woman entering the bank. She was angry and chased after them. As they rounded the corner on Glencairn, sixty-six-year-old Carl Rudge was peering into their car, suspicious as to why they had left it running in front of his house. When he looked up, he saw the two men running towards him, one of them (Boyd) carrying a white cloth bag.

"Stop those men!" shouted the woman behind them.

"What have you two been up to?" asked Rudge as the men jumped into the car. Boyd, in the passenger seat, shoved his Luger into the man's ribs.

"Scram!" shouted Boyd, shoving him. Rudge lost his balance and fell to the ground.

"They're going to shoot me!" he shouted. His two married daughters, in the house at the time, heard their father and ran out to the street just as the convertible pulled away. One of the daughters, Irene McGregor, recently released from hospital, fainted from the excitement.

Across the street, taxi dispatcher Colin McCallum saw the incident from his office and called the police. Taxi driver Fred Gipp jumped into his cab to chase the bandits, who had headed east on Glencairn. He soon lost them in the heavy mid-afternoon traffic. "I didn't have a chance – they were miles ahead of me," he told police later. The

convertible turned north on Bathurst Street and east again on
Lawrence. Boyd was crouched down in the front seat to make it look
like the driver was alone. "The other chap was driving," he remembers,
"and he hit a hole in the road which threw me right up to the roof."

They abandoned the car in a swamp near Saguenay Avenue, south off
Lawrence Avenue. The car's location caused police to speculate that
one or both bandits might have been involved in an unsolved double-
murder eleven months earlier. The victims' car had been found in the
same swamp. But Boyd and his partner had just been looking for a
place to ditch the car without attracting too much attention. Afterwards, they walked east to Avenue Road and Boyd's waiting truck.

Back at the bank, the employees and their customer had been
locked in the basement for fifteen minutes by the time Miskiw found
them and opened the door. The police converged on the bank, but the
only physical evidence they found was a footprint on the counter.
The bank had been robbed of $7,800 three years earlier. This time
only $1,954 had been taken, along with the bank's .38 calibre Smith
& Wesson revolver.

Boyd was not happy with the take from the robbery. Having a partner was supposed to have dramatically increased the amount of cash
taken; instead, after the cut, the job was his least successful. On the
positive side, except for the irritations outside the bank the operation had gone smoothly – fast and clean, the way he liked it. The
next day *The Globe and Mail* even referred to them as "a pair of busi-
ness-like gunmen."

All three Toronto dailies gave in-depth coverage to the robbery, but
this time the banner headlines were given to the widening Korean
War. Both the *Telegram* and the *Star* had correspondents in Seoul. On
the day of Boyd's third robbery American troops were pouring into
Korea, and the Russians were demanding that the United Nations put
an end to American involvement.

Although proceeds from the robbery were less than Boyd had antic-
ipated, at least he had money in his pocket again. Anthony was now
ten and the twins six, and he could treat them to a fine dinner at a
restaurant and perhaps have an evening out with Dorreen. He doesn't

remember what the family did in the days following the robbery, but there were plenty of options in Toronto that week. The movies cost as little as fifty cents for adults, and there was a wide choice. Westerns were popular: *Winchester '73* with James Stewart was playing at Loew's, while Gregory Peck was in *The Gunfighter* at the Imperial. In a lighter vein, *Tight Little Island* – billed as "the comedy that kept Toronto in stitches for 9 hilarious weeks" – was back again at the Danforth, Fairlawn, and Humber Theatres, and in its fourth week at the Hyland was *Kind Hearts and Coronets*, with Alec Guinness.

If they wanted the kids to see live animals, the Ringling Brothers and Barnum & Bailey Circus was at the Woodbine Golf Course. If Ed and Dorreen decided to get a baby-sitter one evening, there was dancing at the air-conditioned Tempo Room at the Embassy, or at the El Mocambo they could catch The Gay Cavalleros, featuring Francine Dey, "singing star of New York Night Clubs."

Three months after the Dominion Bank robbery, Boyd was again broke. He reasoned that the money would have lasted twice as long if he had been on his own. There were benefits to having a partner, but his had moved on, so he decided to go it alone once more.

His target this time was the Imperial Bank at Fairlawn and Avenue Road in North York, a few blocks south of the first bank he had robbed. For whatever reason, he didn't prepare and plan as well as he usually did. It was almost as if he was doing it on impulse. He didn't take the time to study the layout, or to determine the best hour to hit the bank. He stole a car from the lot behind the Capitol Theatre, but instead of driving it to one of his rented garages, he went straight to the bank, parking one street over near the Glendale Theatre.

There were no customers in the bank when Boyd entered at noon. The only person he saw was a teller, William Harry Boyce.

"This is a hold-up!" Boyd shouted, going directly to the teller's cage with his Luger out. "Give me everything in the cash drawer." But he didn't realize there was another person in the bank: the manager, W.H.G. Smith, was sitting at his desk at the rear of the bank, his office partitioned by a large glass window. When he heard the shouting and looked out and saw the pistol, he stood and leaned out.

"What's going on!" he said sharply.

The voice startled Boyd, who looked back and saw the manager. "Get out from there!" he ordered, motioning with the Luger. Smith didn't budge, and when the gunman repeated his demand, he ran to his desk and grabbed his bank-issue revolver.

Boyd's version of what happened next is probably the more reliable, simply because he was used to guns, wasn't known to panic, and had been in tight situations before.

Smith's version is that Boyd fired three shots at him and that he fired once in return. Boyd says the manager fired first and he fired twice in return, purposely aiming high. "I didn't try to hit him, I only wanted to scare him," he would tell police a year later. Whatever the sequence of shots, Boyd's idea of robbing a bank did not include shoot-outs. He fled empty-handed to the next street, where he had parked the stolen car. From there he drove back to the lot at the rear of the Capitol Theatre, where he left the car in almost exactly the same spot he had found it. "I don't think the person even knew that their car had been taken."

When Detective-Sergeant George Wilson of the North York police investigated immediately after the robbery, he found only two slugs fired by the bandit, and the one fired by the manager was so deeply embedded in the north wall of the bank that he couldn't dig it out.

Discussing that shoot-out years later, Boyd says he could feel the manager's bullet whizzing by his head. "He was shooting from a cubbyhole on one side of the bank, and I fired back to scare him." When he was shown police photos of the incident, he realized that one of his shots had missed the manager's head by inches.

"I thought I was aiming higher than that," he says, shaking his head. "I guess I came pretty near to getting the wrong end of the stick."

Boyd always tried to be ready for any eventuality when he was robbing banks. "Once in a while I got caught off balance, but I would never shoot. I was brought up in a policeman's home, I would never shoot a policeman. And the people working in the banks were good people. I didn't want to shoot anybody, I just wanted to scare them enough to get the money. Usually it worked out all right. Once in a while they'd shoot at me and I'd take off."

In the army, Boyd was trained not to shoot, to hold his fire until it was absolutely necessary. "My gun was usually always uncocked, so I didn't have to worry about it too much. I was very careful because it's such an easy thing to pull the trigger. And I always had the triggers filed down to the very finest, so that it didn't take more than a deep breath and it would go off."

The shoot-out dampened his enthusiasm for robbing banks, but by the fall of 1950 it was becoming apparent to Boyd that he would have to find a well-paying permanent job or improve the proceeds from the bank heists so that one or two more would provide him with a substantial stake to get into something legitimate. The plan he liked best was to get enough cash to purchase a small apartment house that he could live in and manage. He didn't need any more lessons in how dangerous robbing banks could be, and he took a long time deciding whether to rob another one.

In the meantime, he continued working at odd jobs while searching for something permanent. In November 1950 he found a temporary job with the City of Toronto filling potholes with asphalt. It paid just over a dollar an hour. Working on a street-repair crew wasn't the same as driving for the TTC, and the city wasn't interested in his criminal record. The job, raking and smoothing hot asphalt, was tedious and dirty, with the acrid smoke of the asphalt burner swirling around him.

He was still on the job through Christmas and the New Year. Then, as spring approached in 1951, he began to plan another robbery. This time it would be a repeat performance: he would go back to the Armour Heights branch of the Bank of Montreal – except this time he would be sober. And this time George Ellwood, the manager who had emptied his revolver at him eighteen months before, was off sick.

Once again Boyd dispensed with the rented garage, stole a black Chevrolet from a theatre lot, and drove directly to the bank, which was on Avenue Road in North York. He had disguised his face, as he had for his first robbery, and wore what witnesses would later call "an engineer's cap."

As Boyd entered the bank shortly after noon on March 19, Audrey Head, who worked there as a clerk, passed him on her way out for lunch. Once again there were no customers in the bank and young Joyce Empey was the teller. She was astonished to see him enter the bank and point the same pistol at her. Acting manager Ervin H. Leigh was in a back office with bank clerk D.A. Dempsey, who stood petrified as the robber waved his gun around. Leigh later told police that the bandit "was dressed in shabby clothing, had a moustache, and his cheeks were puffed out as though padded."

This time there was no note. "This is a hold-up!" Boyd shouted. "Don't touch the alarm! Raise your hands and step back from the counter, or I shoot!" He leaped up on the counter, stepped down into the tellers' cage, and cleaned out the contents of Empey's cash drawer, stuffing the bills into his pockets. Then he vaulted the counter and was gone. Leigh said the robber "went over the counter like a rabbit. I pushed the alarm but it was all over in less than a minute-and-a-half and there wasn't anything more I could do." Police put up roadblocks within minutes of the hold-up, but the last anyone saw of the bandit, he was driving south on Avenue Road at a high rate of speed.

Boyd returned the stolen Chev to the Odeon parking lot, once again certain that the owner was unaware the car had been taken. When he counted the money later, the total was $3,021 – his best pay-day yet. He was somewhat chagrined when the *Toronto Daily Star*, in a banner page 1 headline, announced that $6,000 had been taken. For many years Boyd thought that Empey had kept $3,000 for herself, and let on that he had stolen it. "I figured the money was missing, and I didn't have it. She was the only one handling the money, so I figured she had it all ready and just tossed it into her purse." He thought it was a wonderful plan and wanted to ask her about it until he discovered that the error was at the newspaper, not at the bank.

The newspapers played up the "repeat robber" theme after police said they were certain he was the same "puffy-faced" man who had held up Empey in September 1949, and the Canadian Bank of Commerce on January 18, 1950, and who had bungled the Imperial Bank job on October 11, 1950.

NORTH YORK BANDIT GETS $6,000

TORONTO DAILY STAR

THE WEATHER

MONDAY, MARCH 19, 1951—56 PAGES

3c PER COPY, 18c PER WEEK

MOUTH FULL OF COTTON
LONE 'REPEAT' GUNMAN
FLEES INTO CITY AT 70

HOME AND SPORT EDITION

Find Nine Dead as Prairies Dig Out of 2-Day Blizzard

McCallum On Milk Bd. – Act To Avert Strike

THE TELEGRAM Night

TORONTO, MONDAY, MARCH 19, 1961

Time To Fight Tax
Is Right At Start
Or Opposition Dies

ROBS BANK 2ND TIME ADDS $5,000 TO LOOT

Boyd was always careful to keep a low profile after a robbery. He would not make any large-item purchases without waiting a few weeks. He stayed on the job filling potholes for the city, and eventually purchased a used car. His decision to work for the city would be a fateful one, for while on that job he met Howard Gault.

Howard Ferguson Gault, at forty-two, was six years older than Boyd, not in as good physical shape, and – as Boyd gradually came to realize – a heavy drinker. Gault had been something of a drifter, and years before had walked out on his wife and two children. This wasn't exactly Boyd's idea of a dream partner. On the plus side, Gault had once been a guard at the provincial prison farm at Burwash, south of Sudbury, so he knew about guns. Boyd wasn't looking for a rocket scientist – just somebody who would follow orders.

Gault was already a petty thief of sorts, and one day walking with

Boyd after work he revealed his secret. "You know," he said, "you can make a lot of money doing something else on the side."

"Like what?" asked Boyd.

"Well, you may not think too much of this, but I go around stealing from people's cars at night. It pays for my beer and a few other things."

"Well, I've got a far better way to make money," said Boyd.

"You do?"

"Yeah, I'll show you."

Boyd drove Gault to the Lansing branch of the Dominion Bank at 189 Sheppard Avenue East, which he had been thinking about robbing for some time.

"See that bank over there," said Boyd.

"Yeah."

"Well, we're going to rob it."

"We can't do that!"

"Yeah, we can. While you've been robbing cars, I've been robbing banks. It's just as easy, only you get a lot more money from a bank. We'll plan it well, and I'll show you what to do. After you've thought about it, you won't have any problem."

"I don't know," Gault frowned.

"Look, there's nothing to it. I've been in the army – I know the score. All we have to do is carry out the thing as if it were an army operation. We'll be in there three minutes or less, just long enough to grab what we can out of the till." Gault agreed to go along.

Boyd then decided to increase the odds of success by adding a third partner. It took a lot of persuading, but he was finally able to convince his youngest brother, Norm, to help with the robbery. It was the only robbery he would go on with his brother. Norm, whose life has been exemplary since the end of the Boyd Gang saga forty-five years ago, is understandably reluctant to talk about it.

On Saturday, September 1, 1951, the three men drove in Boyd's panel truck to a theatre parking lot on north Yonge Street just inside the city limits. They stole a 1950 Mercury from the lot and drove it to the Lansing branch of the Dominion Bank. It was near closing time, and they sat in the car waiting for the last customers to leave. But a bank employee came to the door and locked it. The men thought about leaving, but then they noticed that a man and a woman were still in the bank talking with the manager in his office. Just then, an eighteen-year-old junior clerk, Helen Butler, left the bank, relocking the door. She went to a nearby shop and returned with her key moments later. As she was unlocking the door, Boyd saw his chance.

"Let's go," he said, and the three of them rushed for the bank door. "This is a hold-up," he said, grabbing her by the shoulder and pushing her ahead of them into the bank. The sleeve of her blouse tore as he pushed her, and he apologized. "I felt sorry for doing that. You don't expect these things to happen, but you never know. I never tried to be violent at any time. I always tried to keep a revolver between me and them and that usually worked."

Butler later described Boyd to reporters as "a very dirty-looking man who looked like he might have been unloading coal earlier."

Boyd shouted "Hold-up!" and ordered Butler and senior clerk Ruth Davidson to the rear office of the acting manager, William Lepper, who was still with his two customers. Another employee, Ruby Richardson, was in the teller's cage at the front facing the window. She fainted and slumped to the floor when she saw Boyd enter with a gun. Richardson had just returned to work after recovering from a nervous breakdown.

Boyd herded the staff and customers into the bank vault. There he held his Luger on them while Gault cleaned out the cash drawers and Norm Boyd stood guard at front. By this time passers-by were stopping to watch the action through the window.

Boyd covered the staff and customers with the Luger as he backed out of the bank behind his brother and Gault. They jumped into the Mercury parked in front of the bank. They later abandoned the car on north Yonge Street and walked south to Boyd's truck at the theatre parking lot.

It was banner headlines all around again. Once again the *Star* got the amount was wrong, but this time in Boyd's favour – the take was actually $8,029.

TORONTO DAILY STAR

59TH YEAR   SATURDAY, SEPTEMBER 1, 1951   18 PAGES   3c PER COPY, 18c PER WEEK

3 ROB LANSING BANK OF $5,000

FORCE GIRL CLERK BACK   HOME AND   Sight Smoke, Said Best
INTO BANK, LOOT $5,000   SPORT EDITION   Tip Yet in Barilko Hunt
BANDIT 'DIRTY LOOKING'   TWO CHILDREN ORPHANED AS YOUNG PARENTS KILLED IN LEVEL CROSSING CRASH NEAR OWEN SOUND

Ed Boyd now regrets having talked Norm into participating. "I know my reputation has probably hurt him over the years. It was just one bank, but he was scared to death. He just walked up and down and didn't know what to do with himself. He was in a daze and wishing he was somewhere else."

Now that he was a full-fledged, relatively successful bank robber, Boyd decided "things were getting too hot" for him to continue living in the war-time house on Eglinton Avenue West. Most of the banks he had robbed were not that far north of where he lived, and he worried that somebody might spot him, or that a curious neighbour might hear or see something. "I started scouting around and checking the newspaper for some place where we could get away from everybody else," he says.

The place he settled on was a rough, cinder-block building on a desolate lot on Old Rose Bank Road in the town of Pickering, just east of Toronto. The place didn't even have running water, and Boyd had to drill a well and install a pump. "There were other people not too far away, but we didn't have much to do with them."

Dorreen didn't say much at the time, but she was not at all happy to be leaving their comfortable house in downtown Toronto for the isolation of Pickering. "We only lived in it a few months. If we had kept it we could have sold it for the bloomin' Pickering airport.[16] When we first went there it wasn't really a house, just big cement blocks and a roof and doors. It was in the middle of a meadow."

With money in his pocket, Boyd spent most of the summer of 1951 working to make the place liveable for his family. Dorreen says he was handy at everything, from mechanics to woodworking and even plumbing. His brother Norm helped him put in bedrooms for the children. As the heat of the summer waned, as the air turned crisper in the evenings, and as his supply of cash dwindled, Boyd's thoughts inevitably drifted to the drawers full of money just waiting for him in banks not far away.

15
Caught

Boyd was not happy with his erstwhile partner, Howard Gault. After their first robbery together, Gault had developed an inflated ego, and he wanted to rush out and purchase a good used car. Boyd objected strongly – don't do anything to attract attention until the heat was off, was his credo – and Gault reluctantly agreed to wait until Boyd gave him the go-ahead. But when Boyd went to see Gault at his house a few days after the robbery, he was just pulling up in a shiny used car.

"Where'd you get the car?" asked Boyd.

"Oh, I needed a new one, so I bought it."

"I told you not to do that, because it's dangerous."

"Oh well…" he shrugged.

Boyd could smell alcohol on Gault's breath and suspected he was trying to impress his latest girlfriend with the car. "When he drank he became so confident in his own abilities, he wasn't thinking right. I could see I was going to have trouble with him. He drank too much and that was more of a danger than I realized. And he lied to me. The minute I turned my back, he went out and bought that car." Boyd decided he would use Gault only as a last resort.

Those were Boyd's feelings before the mellow summer and early fall he spent working on the Pickering house. He didn't see much of Gault in that time. But now that he was ready for another influx of cash, he pushed Gault's negatives to the back of his mind. He needed a partner on his next robbery, and Gault, if nothing else, had experience.

The weekend before Boyd attempted his seventh robbery, Toronto was hosting the young Princess Elizabeth and her husband, Prince

Philip, the Duke of Edinburgh, on their first Royal Tour to Canada. The future Queen was filling in for her ailing father, George VI, who would die four months later. Being a largely Anglo-Saxon city at the time, Toronto went all out to give the future Queen a rousing welcome. The city was in a frenzy; at every public appearance the crowds were massive, and at every parade the adoring public stood a dozen deep.

Dorreen and the children, stranded in Pickering, didn't get to see the Princess and Prince. And Ed had other things on his mind. Around the time the royals were arriving in Montreal, he and Gault had met and decided to rob a bank. This time there would be none of the usual long-term planning. They would meet a week later, drive around until they decided on a target, and then just do it.

By noon on Tuesday, October 16, they were sitting in Boyd's maroon panel truck on north Yonge Street. Boyd had his Luger and Gault a .38 Smith & Wesson that Boyd had taken from a bank in an earlier robbery. They drove around for a few minutes, looking for a suitable target. Then Boyd thought of the perfect bank, and the one he was most familiar with – the Armour Heights branch of the Bank of Montreal. Remembering the fuss the newspapers had made when he robbed it the second time, he wondered what the reaction would be if he hit it a third time. Gault too thought it was a great idea.

First they needed a getaway vehicle. As was now the usual procedure, they would steal a car from a parking lot. Boyd drove to a lot across the street from the Fairlawn Theatre on Yonge Street, a few blocks north of Lawrence Avenue. He was in his usual disguise, his face smudged with lipstick and cotton stuffed into his cheeks and nostrils. Gault was wearing work clothes and a hunting cap with the peak pulled low. Both men also wore dark glasses. To enhance his disguise, Gault removed his false teeth, wrapping them in a soiled handkerchief and leaving them on the front seat of the truck.

They left the truck and hot-wired a black 1948 Chevrolet sedan in the same lot, then drove west on Fairlawn Avenue and north on Avenue Road. As they approached Haddington Avenue and the Armour Heights bank just before 12:30 p.m., Boyd slowed down to look inside.

Bank manager W.W. Keeler was out for lunch, and his second officer, Ervin Leigh, was engaged with a customer, Mrs. James W. Stephenson, who had her two children in tow. As he stood behind the counter, which faced the street, Leigh noticed the black Chev moving north slowly past the bank. He could see the two male occupants, both wearing dark glasses, staring intently at the bank.

"I don't like the look of those two," said Leigh, who had been in the bank when it was robbed in September 1949 and again in March 1951. Mrs. Stephenson turned to look towards the street, but the car had moved past the window.

Leigh continued to glance out the window as he talked to Mrs. Stephenson. A few minutes later he noticed the same car driving slowly south with both occupants again peering into the bank.

"There they are again," he told Mrs. Stephenson. "I think they might attempt a hold-up. Excuse me, I'm going to call the police." Leigh went to the phone and talked to George Wilson of the North York Police Department. Wilson was the same detective who had dug Boyd's bullet out of a bank wall after his bungled robbery attempt a year earlier. A patrol car would be sent immediately, said Wilson. Seconds after the phone call, Leigh looked out to see the black Chev pull up in front of the bank and stop. "The men did not get out of the car, but kept looking the bank over – making a reconnaissance," he told police later.

Leigh left the counter and walked to the front of the bank and stared out at Boyd and Gault. Startled, they turned away so they wouldn't be recognized and quickly drove off. Leigh ran out the door hoping to get the licence number, but by the time he got to the street, the car had disappeared. Just then the police car arrived, and he told the officers what had happened.

Boyd realized they had been spotted, and instinct told him he should drive to his truck and go home to Pickering. There would be other days, other banks. But Gault, feeling self-assured with the .38 in his pocket, argued that they should try another bank. Boyd thought for a moment, drove south to Lawrence and Yonge, and parked near the Dominion Bank. This time they simply got out of the car and went in with guns drawn. Had they looked in first, they might have hesitated.

The only customer was a hairdresser, Dawn Foster, who was cashing a cheque, but there were also eleven employees. Boyd, fearless as always, leaped effortlessly to the counter.

"Don't move!" he shouted. "This is a stick-up!"

Foster said the bandit had "beady eyes" and with the cotton batting stuffed into his nostrils he looked like a monster. "Quit staring at me!" he ordered, waving his gun.

As Gault climbed over the counter and began emptying the cash from the teller's cages into a shopping bag, Boyd jumped to the floor, went to the centre of the bank, and ordered everyone to the rear near the vault. He didn't see bank secretary Adelene Jamieson pull the alarm switch under the accounting desk on her way to the back. Jamieson, whose late husband had been a bank manager, told a reporter later: "Frankly, I just didn't like the idea of a couple of hoodlums coming in here and walking out with a lot of money that doesn't belong to them." The alarm sounded at No. 12 Division in north Toronto.

Boyd now suspects that Gault had been drinking on the day of the robbery. He didn't smell beer on him but wonders if it could have been vodka or some other alcohol with an undetectable odour. Gault seemed calm enough while they were driving around in the truck, but once inside the bank his behaviour became erratic. Perhaps he was simply intoxicated at the sight of so much cash. For whatever reason, he grew excited as he shovelled the money from the cash drawers into the shopping bag. "Look at all this!" he cried, admiring the stacks of bills.

"Hurry up!" said Boyd, agitated. But Gault continued to comment on their good fortune as their stay went beyond Boyd's three-minute limit. Now Gault was flipping stacks of cash in the air, exclaiming, "Boy, we really got a pile here."

"Let's go!" said Boyd, backing out of the bank.

Constables Walter McLean and Frank Skelly from No. 12 Station were on patrol in their scout car about four blocks away when the dispatcher directed them to a robbery in progress at the Dominion Bank at Avenue Road and Lawrence. Motorcycle policeman Donald Stewart saw his fellow officers speed by and followed to offer assistance.

As Boyd came out of the bank and ran for the getaway car, parked facing west on the north side of Lawrence, the police car pulled up and McLean went after him. The two arrived at the Chev about the same time. "I reached in the open window and threw the door against him and it knocked him off his feet," says Boyd, who didn't draw his gun. He jumped in the car and drove off.

McLean pulled out his revolver and started shooting. "I fired at the car in an effort to stop it," he said. One shot hit the trunk of the Chev. Two others missed. Behind the wheel, Boyd bobbed from side to side to avoid the gunfire. He had always told Gault that if they were being pursued, Gault was to run in the opposite direction and Boyd would come around the block and pick him up. But Gault didn't have a chance. He had been followed out of the bank by accountant John Goodfellow, who was armed with a bank revolver and had joined the chase.

When Stewart saw Skelly chasing the puffing Gault in a laneway at the rear of the bank, he ran north from Lawrence through a vacant lot and cut off the bandit in a used car lot. Gault was carrying his revolver in one hand and the shopping bag full of cash in the other. "Stop or I'll shoot!" yelled Stewart, firing two or three warning shots into the air. Gault, now out of breath, dropped the gun and the bag and stopped running. Stewart checked Gault's .38 and found it fully loaded. He then checked Gault's pockets and found extra rounds of ammunition. Gault was taken to No. 12 Station at Montgomery and Yonge, where the money was counted by accountant John Goodfellow and an inspector from the Dominion Bank's head office. The total was $12,234.

TORONTO DAILY STAR

THE WEATHER

TUESDAY, OCTOBER 16, 1951—34 PAGES   3c PER COPY, 18c PER WEEK

YONGE ST. BANK HELD UP, NAB ONE

RECOVER LARGE SUM
HUNT 2ND BANDIT IN
NORTH TORONTO HOLDUP

HOME AND SPORT EDITION
MAKING CHILDREN HAPPY ONE GOAL OF COMMUNITY CHEST

BRITISH REINFORCEMENTS
RUSHED IN TO SUPPORT
60,000 HOLDING SUEZ

NAB 2, REGAIN $12,800 IN CITY BANK HOLDUP

While Stewart and Skelly were chasing down Gault, McLean was in his cruiser in hot pursuit of Boyd. He lost sight of the Chev for a few moments and then saw it abandoned, partly on the sidewalk, at the Yonge and Fairlawn parking lot. Witnesses said they had seen the bandit drive off in a panel truck and gave the officer a description.

Boyd had spit the cotton from his mouth and wiped off his make-up. He now made a cursory run past the bank, but there was no sign of Gault. He was certain the police had him, and he was just as certain Gault wouldn't keep his mouth shut.

At the police station, Gault, still missing his teeth, was placed in a cell for a time and then moved to an adjoining room, where Detective Richard Gibson cautioned him and informed him of his rights. Gault then gave a statement; they had him red-handed, and the revolver in his possession linked him to the Dominion Bank hold-up of July 4, 1950. But, he told them, he didn't even know Boyd then. He said Boyd had given him the gun to use in the September 1 robbery of the Sheppard Avenue Dominion Bank, which he freely admitted to. In his statement, Gault gave the police Boyd's name and a description of the truck. He also told them that Boyd had robbed other banks.

Auto squad detectives Barry Lorimer and Frank Cater were at the courthouse in downtown Toronto when they were told of the bank robbery at Yonge and Lawrence. "We jumped in our car and went up to patrol the area northeast of there," recalls Cater, who is now eighty and lives in Burlington, Ontario.[17] "As we were getting up there, the licence number and a description of the truck came over the radio." They had circled the eastern limits and were heading back west along

York Mills Road, admiring several large new homes, when Boyd passed them in the opposite direction. Boyd had decided to drive to Pickering and, if Gault had talked, to wait for the inevitable.

"Christ, Barry!" said Cater. "There's the god-damned truck."

"What do you mean? Where?"

"We just passed him. He's behind us."

Traffic was light, and Cater pulled into a driveway and turned around. "At that time the auto squad had souped-up pursuit cars – the only ones in the department. We could do eighty in second gear. I didn't want to zoom right up on him because we wanted to figure out what to do. We didn't want to do anything stupid." When Boyd turned north on Bayview Avenue, the detectives decided to try to pull him over. A short distance from the turnoff there was a slight hollow in the road with a guard-rail of wooden posts connected by strands of heavy wire cable. There was no oncoming traffic.

"Get ready, Barry," said Cater. "I'm going to push him right over to the side." Lorimer unholstered his .32 Colt and rolled down his window. As Cater pulled alongside the truck, Lorimer extended his arm through the open window and aimed at Boyd's head. "I kept even with the truck and then nosed him to the shoulder," says Cater. "Both cars stopped, and Barry had his gun right under Boyd's nose."

The startled Boyd had both hands on the steering wheel.

"Don't move your hands one inch off that wheel," said Lorimer. "Not an inch." Cater, who was six-foot-three and well over two hundred pounds, got out of his car with his gun drawn and kept Boyd covered while Lorimer went around to the passenger side. The Luger was tucked under Boyd's belt and, Cater says, "he was shaking – you could see he was thinking about risking it and making a grab for his gun. If he had, he would have been shot dead, but thank God it didn't happen that way."

With Cater's gun inches from his head, Boyd didn't move as Lorimer reached in and searched him. "In the waistband of the accused's trousers I found a .9mm German Luger, serial #895," he wrote in his report later. "This pistol was fully-loaded with 8 rounds of .9mm ammunition in the clip and one round in the chamber. The action was cocked and the safety catch was applied." Boyd was ordered from the truck and searched more thoroughly. He was co-operative and seemed unruffled and resigned as he was handcuffed.

"How did you get my licence number?" asked Boyd politely.

"We had a description," said Lorimer.

"Did you get my pal?" asked Boyd, but the policemen didn't respond. As they began to search his truck, Boyd told them they wouldn't find any money. "My pal got it," he said. Lorimer and Cater decided to complete their search later, and removed the truck and Boyd to No. 12 Station. Later, in a metal tool chest in the rear of the truck, they found a pair of rubber gloves, a Second World War commando knife, a holster, several lengths of cord, and a "quantity" of ammunition. Also mascara, lipstick, one towel and face cloth, a bar of soap, a blackjack, a spare clip for the Luger, and three road maps of Greater Toronto. Gault's false teeth were found in a search of the front seat; Gault wouldn't get them back until three days later, in the Don Jail.

After being questioned by detectives at No. 12 Station, Boyd was taken to Toronto police headquarters, which at that time and until the late 1970s was housed in a grand Romanesque sandstone building at 149 College Street. It later became part of the Ontario College of Art. It was in a tiny third-floor room in that building that Jocko Thomas and other crime reporters spent much of their time looking for stories. The room, with its two battered desks, was right next to the elevators where prisoners were often brought in.

In his book *From Police Headquarters*, Thomas remembers warm summer nights in the 1930s when, through the open windows, reporters could hear gunshots from nearby Queen's Park Crescent. "Trigger Payne," one of them would declare, and twenty minutes later, Constable Adolphus ("Dolph") Payne would emerge from the elevator with yet another car thief.[18] Payne was on the auto squad, and he had memorized the licence plate numbers of dozens of stolen cars. He was a good shot, and he had earned his nickname through his knack for shooting out tires when a suspect tried to flee. "There were no restrictions on the police use of firearms then," says Thomas.

Dolph Payne was a sergeant of detectives with the auto squad when he met Edwin Alonzo Boyd in October 1951. Payne was by then one of the most respected investigators on the Toronto police. In later years, many would call him "Canada's Greatest Detective." At police headquarters on that autumn day in 1951, the curtain was about to rise on the second act of a drama that would have a lasting impact on the lives of both Payne and Boyd.

Dolph Payne, five years older than Boyd, was born and raised in farm country at Crooked Creek, a crossroads near Port Hope, east of Toronto. He was third-youngest in a farming family of eight children – four boys and four girls. The hundred-acre farm produced vegetable crops, cattle, chickens, and horses, and Dolph did his share of the chores from an early age. "They were wonderful people and he had a wonderful family life," says his widow, Helen. "They were all brought up to be ambitious kids and to work hard – none of them were loafers."

Payne had to walk three miles each way to his one-room country school. Like Boyd, he didn't go beyond the eighth grade. Eventually he left the farm and found work at a supplier plant in Bowmanville that sold rubber mats to General Motors. When it closed in the wake of the stock market crash of 1929, he moved to Toronto and joined the Toronto Police Department at $28.80 a week. The amount was considered "city pay," which all municipal employees started at. If you worked for the city it was considered lifelong employment. To the banks you were a good risk – on $28.80 a week you could buy a home and raise a family.

Even when he was a rookie cop assigned to the waterfront, where the ferries came in from the Toronto Islands, Payne's superiors took notice. He was supposed to be directing traffic, but he had a keen eye and excelled at nabbing pickpockets who mingled with the crowds waiting to catch the streetcars.

In the summer of 1934, Helen Croft, an attractive nineteen-year-old American, was visiting relatives in Toronto on her two-week vacation. One Saturday night shortly after eleven, she was alone waiting for a northbound streetcar at Yonge and King after a full day at the Sunnyside amusement park. The street was all but deserted, and she was concerned about her aunt and uncle waiting up for her at their house on Dupont Avenue. She hadn't noticed the young, six-foot policeman, wearing the traditional English bobby helmet, standing quietly in the shadows. It was Dolph Payne, and he was smitten.

Helen was a dark-haired beauty and she knew how to dress. She was from New York City, where she worked for B. Altman & Company, an exclusive department store. "I modelled for them, and when we didn't have fashion shows, I would be selling ready-to-wear clothes in the ladies' department." On this night, when Payne walked out of the shadows, she was wearing a stylish beige and white checked linen suit and a wide-brimmed white linen hat.

"He was very officious," recalls Helen. "He wanted to know why I was standing there, who I was, where I was going."

"It's too bad," he said, "I've just come on duty or I would have been glad to drive you to your aunt's place. But I'm off tomorrow and I could show you around Toronto. I have a Ford car."

"Well, if you'd like to come up tomorrow and meet my aunt and uncle and they think it's okay, why it would be very nice," she told him.

"So the next day he drove up in this shiny new Ford, and he had white slacks on and blond, beautiful hair." Helen's aunt and uncle approved, and Payne drove her to Wasaga Beach on Georgian Bay for the day. He was on the three-to-eleven shift the next night but invited her to meet his sister after work. After that, Helen and Dolph met for lunch every day until she returned to her job in New York. They continued their romance by correspondence. In November of that year, when Payne went to visit Helen in New York he brought along an engagement ring. They were married eighteen months later.

On the police force, Payne earned a reputation for doggedness, and he would often stay beyond regular work hours if he was pursuing a lead. "It annoyed me sometimes," Helen remembers, smiling. "I'd have dinner ready and there was no Dolph. He loved his work, but he wasn't much for running around with the boys. He enjoyed his home life." On the auto squad, where he tracked down car thieves, Payne would spend hours studying the classified ads in the three Toronto dailies. He made careful notes of garages for rent, and when he no longer saw them listed in the ads he would drive over and check them for stolen cars or other goods. There is a good chance that if Boyd had not been caught after the last robbery with Gault, Payne would have eventually found one of his garages. Payne's oft-stated credo was that no matter what crime was committed, there was almost always a car involved.

The Boyd case would be the most famous of Payne's long career, but there were hundreds of others that he brought to a successful conclusion through his diligence. At six feet and over two hundred pounds, Payne was an imposing presence, but he was also amiable and soft-spoken. He was a master interrogator and could be intimidating when necessary. When he met Boyd he wanted a confession that would close the books on several Toronto bank robberies. Gault had given them considerable information, but because Boyd had always used disguises, Payne thought it might be difficult to make robbery charges stick in court if he pleaded not guilty.

Boyd didn't reveal much in his interviews at No. 12 Station. He was tired when they brought him to police headquarters on College Street, but Payne and his partner, Ken Craven, would grill him continuously for several hours. When nothing worked, Payne, feigning anger, threatened Boyd while Craven played the role of "good cop."

"Come on, come on now, take it easy, Dolph," Craven would say. "This guy is a good guy, he's going to tell us everything." Boyd says his impression of Craven was that he was "a nice policeman – like my father. But the other guy – Payne – he looked like he wanted to kill me."

There were different rules in those days, and when nothing else worked, Payne backhanded Boyd across the jaw. Boyd was stunned that a policeman would do such a thing. "If you don't talk you'll get a lot more than that," said Payne. Boyd came to believe he wouldn't be left alone until he told them what they wanted to know. He was pensive for a moment. They had Gault, they had his Luger, and they had his truck with the make-up and the ammunition. He decided to talk.

"You fellahs tell me what banks have been robbed, and I'll tell you which ones I was involved in," he said finally.

Payne and Craven left the interrogation room with Boyd's signed confession admitting to six bank robberies and one attempted robbery. Edwin Alonzo Boyd was on his way to the Don Jail.

16
The Don

The Toronto Jail, more commonly known as "Don Jail" or simply "the Don," earned a mention in a 1996 annual human rights report from the U.S. State Department for its decrepit condition. Inmates, the report said, complained of inhuman conditions resulting from overcrowding and inadequate health facilities. "Conditions were described as so depressing that some inmates purportedly pleaded guilty in order to be sent to other facilities and thus avoid awaiting trial in the jail." And a study of the Don in the spring of 1996 declared that "the current conditions are inhumane for inmates, present untenable working conditions for the staff, and ultimately create hostile conditions for the larger community."

The jail they described is not the original Don Jail but an annex built in 1958. But the complaints were remarkably similar to those that ultimately led to the closing of the original jail in 1978. For half a century, grand juries, royal commissions, and other critics routinely railed against it.

The original Don, at Gerrard Street East and Broadview Avenue, was designed by prominent Toronto architect William Thomas. The building had an inauspicious beginning: it burned down in 1858 before it was completed, and it would be another seven years before it was rebuilt and opened for its first prisoners.[19] The imposing structure, of grey stone, has eighteen-foot stone walls and a four-storey centre pavilion with flanking three-storey wings. The Italian Renaissance columns along its front are tethered by evenly spaced, roughly carved stone bands that function as symbols of confinement and enforced conformity.

In *Toronto Architecture: A City Guide*, Patricia McHugh writes that

"earnest Victorians, dedicated to such humanitarian issues as impris-
onment and reform, took their prison buildings very seriously." Latter-
day critics, "appalled at the tiny cells, may not realize that correctional
philosophy of the time called for many small cells where prisoners
could solitarily *think upon* their transgressions." The classically inspired
jail sits serenely "on its rise of ground like a grand palace, entered by
one of the noblest doorways in the city."

Christopher Hume, architecture writer for the *Toronto Star*, agrees
that the jail is grand, but he also finds it "thoroughly ominous". In
an article about prison architecture he wrote of the Don: "The scale
overwhelms. The front door alone is enough to make a visitor squirm,
no matter how innocent." And he wonders if the bearded figure gaz-
ing down from the keystone above the entrance is Father Time, grimly
reminding prisoners who enter of what lies ahead.

Whatever its worth as architecture, the Don has always been under
siege from critics. When it first opened, outraged Toronto citizens
described it as "a palace for prisoners" and much too opulent for low-
life criminals. But by the turn of the century there was an about-face
– now the jail was too dungeonlike. It has been called everything from
a cesspool to a school for criminals. In 1928 a grand jury said it was
a disgrace to the city. City Council agreed, but a few days later shelved
a motion calling for a full investigation by the provincial government. Another grand jury described the Don as "an overcrowded
dungeon, somewhat like the Black Hole of Calcutta." In 1930 the
Don was condemned again in scathing terms by the Ross Royal
Commission. Once again no action was taken.

Ever since the jail's first prisoners – Irishmen from failed Fenian
Raids – arrived in shackles in 1866, inmates at the Don have sought
to escape its confines. In 1869, the year public executions were abolished (the Don had its own gallows inside the walls), Mac Spellman,
Charlie Jarvis, and George Pearce escaped. Known as the Spellman
Gang, they sawed through the bars of their cells and lowered themselves to the ground on knotted sheets. In 1908, seven men gained
temporary freedom: after spending weeks chipping away at stone and
mortar, they slid over the wall on a rope and knotted blankets.

The most sensational escape was that of young Frank McCullough, who was awaiting the hangman for the murder of a Toronto detective. He sawed his way out, thus becoming the only inmate in the Don's long history to escape from a death cell. He was captured three weeks later and was hanged at the jail on June 13, 1919.

In 1906, guards searching the cell of Norman Neal discovered five hacksaw blades and promptly moved him to another cell. Five days later he took a sixth saw from its hiding place and sawed his way to freedom. In 1930, twelve hours after he was sentenced to fifteen years for shooting a policeman, a prisoner was back on the street after cutting through his cell bars with a hacksaw blade that had been smuggled in to him. And in 1944, bank robber Allan Baldwin, beginning a nineteen-year sentence, beat and strangled guard Robert Canning after escaping from the jail hospital. Baldwin was captured almost immediately near the Humber River, and a manslaughter conviction was added to his record.

There were also many failed escape attempts. Most notable was that of the notorious Polka Dot Gang, which was active in southern Ontario and Toronto in the spring and summer of 1945, four years before Edwin Alonzo Boyd began his bank robbery spree. The gang's name derived from the polka dot handkerchiefs they used to cover their faces during robberies. They specialized in holding up businesses like Swift Canadian of Stratford and John Duff Ltd., a Hamilton packing company. The gang liked to carry machine-guns and usually left their victims trussed up. In August 1945 two of the senior members of the gang, Kenneth Green and George Constantine, were involved in a shoot-out after police caught them breaking into Urquhart Motors at Dufferin Street and Eglinton Avenue. They evaded capture, and no one was injured. Two months later the police cornered a car on Dupont Street and captured three of the gang, including Green and Constantine, who were sentenced to fourteen years in prison.

More than half a dozen of the gang and their associates were in the Don with Green and Constantine, who were awaiting transfer to Kingston Penitentiary. One afternoon in the jail's exercise yard the gang beat and tied up two guards, and then formed a human pyramid in order to hoist one another over the wall. However, the first one to the top was met by an armed guard, and the plan and the pyramid quickly collapsed.

After Frank McCullough sawed his way out of his death cell in 1919, there was an administrative shake-up at the jail and a new governor was appointed (they weren't called wardens). He was a square-shouldered military man with the unlikely name of Col. G. Hedley Basher. Basher had immigrated to Canada from England in 1913 and was invited to join the Toronto police after capturing a man who had escaped from police custody. Basher joined the force when he was twenty but took a leave of absence to enlist in the Canadian army. He went overseas in August 1914 and within a year had been commissioned with the British Army. He gained prison experience when he was appointed commandant of a detention barracks at Aldershot, and then governor of a "field" military prison in France. After the war he returned to the Toronto Police Department as a patrol sergeant. A short time later, after McCullough's escape, he was appointed governor of the Don. Basher went right to the death cell where the sawed bars had been welded back and ordered the window bricked up.

Basher was over six feet tall, solidly built, with broad features and a waxed walrus moustache. His intimidating appearance was complemented by a deep, forceful voice. He was a strict disciplinarian who during his twelve years at the Don would be feared by guards and prisoners alike. In 1931 he was transferred to the Langstaff jail farm just north of Toronto.

Basher remained at the jail farm until September 1939, when he was called up to help mobilize the Royal Regiment of Canada for overseas duty. Soon after it arrived in England, Basher was promoted and left the regiment to serve in North Africa and Italy. He had a reputation as the toughest commanding officer in the Canadian Army and received the Order of the British Empire (OBE). After being demobilized in December 1944, Basher returned to Toronto, where he was appointed by the provincial government to conduct a survey of all the province's penal institutions. After he completed that work in 1945, he was appointed superintendent of the Guelph Reformatory.

Edwin Alonzo Boyd
growing up in Toronto
during the First World War.
(Toronto Star)

Edwin Boyd on the soccer team
at Earl Beatty School.

*Eleanor Boyd, Edwin's beloved
mother, died when he was fifteen.*

*Glover Boyd, with No. 6 Division of
Toronto City Police in December 1942,
four years before his retirement.*
(Toronto Police Museum)

Boyd (front row, extreme right) *sent this picture to his wife Dorreen while he was a dispatch rider with the Royal Canadian Regiment in England.* (Toronto Star)

Edwin Boyd with his war bride, the former Dorreen Thompson, in England. (Toronto Star)

The Boyd brothers, Edwin, Norman and Gordon, get together on leave in England during the Second World War.

Toronto policeman Glover Boyd with sons Gordon (middle) and Edwin at Union Station in 1945. (Toronto Star)

Colonel Hedley Basher was twice called in to restore order and discipline following high-profile escapes from the Don Jail. (Toronto Telegram/Toronto Sun)

Adolphus Payne as a 25-year-old Toronto policeman, 1934. (Helen Payne)

Helen Croft, 20-year-old New York fashion model, with her engagement ring from Dolph Payne, 1934. (Helen Payne)

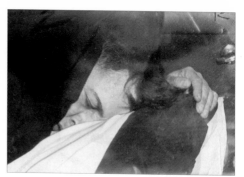

Edmund Tong, unconscious and in critical condition on stretcher at scene of the shooting. (Toronto Telegram/Toronto Sun)

Legendary Edmund "the Chinaman" Tong, Sergeant of Detectives with the Toronto Police Department.

A hacksaw blade, secreted in Lennie Jackson's artificial foot, was used to cut the bars in the first escape from the Don Jail. (Toronto Police Museum)

Intersection of Landsdowne Avenue and College Street where Toronto policemen Edmund Tong and Roy Perry were shot by Steve Suchan. (Toronto Police Museum)

*Leonard Jackson
with model
Ann Roberts.
They married in
Montreal after
his first escape
from the Don Jail.*
(Toronto Police
Museum)

*Toronto police detective
Jack Gillespie wounded
Lennie Jackson four times
in Montreal shoot-out.*
(Toronto Telegram/Toronto Sun)

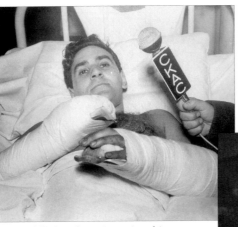

*Leonard Jackson being interviewed in
Montreal General Hospital after
wild shoot-out with police.*
(Toronto Star)

*Ann Jackson appealing for Edwin Boyd's
surrender at a Montreal radio station.*
(Toronto Telegram/Toronto Sun)

Toronto police chief John Chisholm (left), with Detectives Dolph Payne and Ken Craven, as Mayor Lamport shows off the loot after Boyd's capture on Heath Street.
(Toronto Star)

Five handguns, commando knife, ammunition, and almost $25,000 in cash found in Boyd's briefcase after capture on Heath Street.
(Toronto Telegram/Toronto Sun)

Heath Street apartment in quiet Toronto neighbourhood where Edwin Boyd was captured after his first escape from the Don Jail. (Toronto Telegram/Toronto Sun)

In the fall of 1951, Basher was still at Guelph when Edwin Alonzo Boyd arrived at the Don Jail to await a preliminary hearing on six counts of bank robbery and one count of attempted robbery. Boyd's career would soon cross paths with Basher's.

Boyd arrived at the Don handcuffed to other prisoners. They were taken through the front entrance to the "bullpen" – a holding area where prisoners were stripped, searched, and handed the coarse blue-denim prison pants and shirt. They were also issued underwear and black lace-up ankle-boots. Boyd knew about institutional life, having spent time in a penitentiary and in camps and barracks during his five years in the army. But for first-timers, some of them serving merely five days for being drunk, the experience was unnerving. The stone floors magnified every sound, and with all the traffic in and out, the jail was as loud as a busy railway station. At that time, roughly sixty-five new prisoners were processed through the Don every day of the year, and every weekday at least that many were being moved in and out on their way to and from court hearings. Fear in the bullpen was palpable, with those in for minor offences finding them-selves shoulder to shoulder with hardened criminals destined for Kingston Penitentiary. Once the prisoners had been sorted, however, the Kingston prisoners were separated from short-timers.

The jail was originally designed to accommodate no more than 231 male prisoners and 30 females, but that figure had been boosted year after year. By the time Boyd arrived on October 17, 1951, the official capacity for male prisoners was 341, but the daily average over the previous three years was 450. The cells were on three levels in the wings that flanked the central pavilion, which housed the front entrance hall, main office, governor's office, visiting room, property room, and library. On the second floor directly above the pavilion was the women's section, with a capacity of forty prisoners in cells and a small dormitory.

Boyd was one of about sixty "potential penitentiary men" awaiting a preliminary hearing or trial. Another thirty had already been sentenced to penitentiary but remained at the jail pending an appeal or awaiting a new trial. It was these "Kingston prisoners" who posed the greatest security threat.

The Don's governor, Charles Sanderson, on the job just fifteen months, was progressive, fair, and reform-minded. He carefully studied each new prisoner's charge sheet and previous record. He considered Boyd's early brushes with the law during the Depression years as trifling. Boyd had served his country well during the war, and although he had robbed banks at gunpoint, he had fired his gun on only one occasion and had never hurt anyone. He had even apologized to a bank clerk for tearing her blouse. Boyd was on the Kingston list, but in Sanderson's mind there were others who were much more dangerous and brutal.

The only precaution he took with Boyd was to keep him separate from Howard Gault. It was Sanderson's policy to keep apart prisoners who had committed crimes together, so they wouldn't be planning new ones on his watch. Gault, still missing his teeth, wasn't anxious to face Boyd after giving him up to the police.

But Boyd was more angry at himself for choosing Gault as a partner in the first place. "He was a real moron because of the drinking. He thought that he was in command of himself but he wasn't. Soon as they started threatening him he told them who I was and where I lived and everything. It was my own fault. If I had stayed on my own, kept in good physical shape, and planned the robberies properly, I don't think I would have ever been caught."

Two days after Boyd entered the Don, Dolph Payne and another detective visited Gault and returned his false teeth after he signed a statement acknowledging that he had left them in Boyd's truck prior to the Dominion Bank robbery.

Charles Sanderson had started his career as a guard at the Guelph Reformatory in 1939, but left in 1941 to enlist in the army. He went overseas to England, landed in France on D-Day, and participated in the northwestern campaign to Germany. At war's end he revived his career as a guard at Guelph. He was promoted quickly within the corrections system and by the summer of 1950 was governor of the Don Jail.

He arrived to find staff morale "the lowest of any institution I have ever been in." The main cause of this was poor pay and the lack of a pension plan or paid sick leave. There were other problems: the Don was consistently understaffed, and many of the guards were not properly qualified or trained. Some of them, Sanderson knew, had got their jobs through political patronage.

Sanderson would tell a Royal Commission in 1952 that many unsatisfactory guards "were taking care of prisoners who, in many cases, had served years and years and years in institutions. They knew far more than the guards could dream of knowing. It was not a great state of affairs and I spent many, many nights without sleeping."

Sanderson didn't believe in prisoners, especially the younger ones, sitting around with nothing to do. He thought it was an acceptable risk to have those serving short terms – a month or two – working outside. Of the thousand or so prisoners who worked outside during his tenure, only two ran off. Both were under twenty: one had eighteen days left to serve, and the other only eight. "We tried to give them decent healthy work, and it was a calculated risk," said Sanderson. The escapees, on that hot day in June 1951, were caught within half a mile of the jail. Sanderson himself and one guard gave chase and collared them.

Some accused Sanderson of mollycoddling prisoners. But he accepted the view of most North American penologists of the day – that the jail system was a disgrace, and that the idleness of prisoners was the main reason. "I have seen men lying around the corridors day after day, week after week, and month after month. It must be a terrific strain on them."

At that time more than twenty thousand prisoners passed through the Don's gates each year, most on remand and many entering jail for the first time. Sanderson believed that without counselling and recreation programs many first-timers would become habitual criminals. He introduced work projects, with inmates cleaning the brick face of the old building and improving the grounds. Residents living nearby congratulated him for the upgrades. Sanderson sent two of his officers to Guelph for training as counsellors and recreation officers. He allowed music and sporting events to be played on radios in the corridors and, improvising because of a lack of funds, set up an impressive recreation program.

He introduced five-pin bowling using short lengths of rubber hose as pins and beanbags as bowling balls. The long corridors in front of the cells were used as alleys, and regulation league bowling sheets were used to keep score. There were chess and checkers tournaments and, for card players, tournaments for bridge, cribbage, euchre, and gin rummy. In the exercise yard he introduced quoits – similar to horseshoes – using rubber hoses wired together to form small rings. The rings were tossed towards a peg imbedded in the ground.

Individual and team winners from each corridor would play off until there were champions for each sport or game. There was no money for awards or trophies, but the prisoners collected their old newspapers and sold them to buy apples or oranges as symbolic prizes. Sanderson used the recreation activities to maintain discipline by threatening to withdraw a prisoner's right to play if jail rules were contravened.

Guards liked the program because the overall mood was much improved and prisoners were much less hostile and noticeably more co-operative. Provincial inspectors praised Sanderson and suggested that money be found for equipment, such as volleyball nets and balls for the exercise yard.

Sanderson backed up his guards, but before dispensing discipline he always listened to the prisoner's side of the story. If he decided the prisoner was at fault, he had no qualms about ordering corporal punishment – the strap – which he did at least eight times while he was governor. But sometimes he sided with a prisoner. There were many first-rate guards at the Don, but the pay was so poor that Sanderson couldn't get enough of the "good, sound men" he needed. He knew about the bad apples. He had been a guard himself and had witnessed guards deliberately goading prisoners into breaching regulations so that they would receive the strap. "There are some officers who have neither the ability nor the intelligence to properly carry out their orders," he said, "and they expect the head of the institution to cover up their deficiencies by force."

One of the young guards at the Don told Sanderson he had once been assigned, with two older guards, to search three new prisoners in the bullpen. The prisoners were stripped and searched, and when they stooped over to retrieve their clothes, the two older guards kicked them in the buttocks, sending them sprawling.

"Why did you do that?" asked the young guard later.

"To put them in their place and let them know who's the boss," replied the older guards. The young guard told Sanderson he was relieved that kind of conduct was no longer tolerated.

Not one guard or inspector ever complained about the job the new governor was doing. The jail was considered so stable under his administration that when the Burwash prison farm was on the verge of a riot in the fall of 1951, twenty of the ringleaders were taken out and sent to the already overcrowded Don.

This, then, was the world that Edwin Alonzo Boyd was entering when he was led to his second-floor cell at the north end of the west wing of the Don Jail. His cell, on a corridor with eighteen others, was seven by six feet. There was a bed, blanket, and pillows. There was no plumbing in the individual cells, and prisoners were required to use a "night pan," which was stored under the bed. During the day they could use the toilets and sinks at the end of each corridor. Across the corridor from the cells, Boyd saw large windows facing north to the exercise yard. He noticed that the glass on the windows was frosted, and covered by large screens of heavy mesh that were hinged at the top and bolted on one side at the bottom and had a padlock on the other side. He figured there were probably bars over the windows behind the screens and the glass, and he was right.

17

Cellmates

Although Edwin Alonzo Boyd had been anonymous until he was caught trying to rob his seventh bank, the publicity given his successes no doubt inspired others to try their luck. His exploits were certainly noticed by Toronto's underworld, and by the "rounders" on its fringes. It perhaps even made them envious. Sergeant of Detectives Edmund "Eddie" Tong, who had helped put away the Polka Dot Gang and many other robbers and murderers, was certainly interested. Tong was a legend within the Toronto police and in the city's underworld. He had a large network of informants in the criminal world whose identity he would never reveal, even to his partners.

Eddie Tong was born in Leeds, in Yorkshire. He immigrated to Canada in 1926 and joined the Toronto Police Department three years later at the age of twenty-four. His abilities were noticed early in his career, and by 1933 he had been transferred to the detective office at the College Street headquarters. Retired staff superintendent Jack Gillespie remembered Tong as an exceptional investigator with a wonderful sense of humour – a stocky version of Columbo, the TV detective. "He always had a nice suit and tie on but he had this awful-looking hat and old overcoat, and in the winter he never did his galoshes up. He'd walk into the office with an old satchel that was always open." The noise of the galoshes' buckles flopping against each other announced his arrival.

"Eddie, why don't you do your galoshes up?" one of his fellow officers would ask.

"What for?" he would reply. "I'm going to have to take them off eventually."

Tong drove a battered old Buick. One day somebody gave him a secondhand Buick to use for parts. He came into the detective office the next day with a big smile. "Listen, you bunch of jerks," he said. "I'm the only guy in the department who owns two Buicks."

Tong was called "the Chinaman" because of his name and his black hair, which he combed back off his forehead. "I went for the odd walk through Chinatown with Eddie," Gillespie recalled, "and all the people knew him and liked him. He made them laugh."

"I'm the mayor of Chinatown," Tong would announce, "and don't forget my name – Tong[20] – means warfare."

Tong was devoted to his wife and two children – a young son, and a daughter who suffered from a debilitating disease. Even though he couldn't afford it, he was always giving handouts to people in need. "I'd see him walk along the street and there'd be some poor old guy down on his luck," said Gillespie. "Eddie would be talking to him and the next thing you know, Eddie would slip him five dollars and say, 'Go get something to eat.' That's why he never had any money. He was broke all the time."

Tong may have been sentimental, but he could be tough when he had to be – he had been a semi-pro soccer player before coming to Canada. He was stocky – about five-foot-ten and 180 pounds – and had a ruddy complexion and noticeably red lips. Tong kept himself in good shape, Gillespie recalled. "If he was making an arrest he could handle himself, but I never, ever saw him pull his gun out or raise his hands to anybody."

Gillespie was of Irish descent, and Tong always called him "Reilly" when they worked together. During a four-month stint as full-time partners in 1949, Tong introduced Gillespie to his routine of visiting some of the taverns that had opened since the Ontario government began issuing lounge licences. Places like the Silver Rail on Yonge Street, the Holiday Tavern at Queen and Bathurst, and the Horseshoe Tavern at Queen and Spadina had become the waterholes of choice for Toronto's criminals and their hangers-on. Tong visited more often when there was a sudden, marked increase in bank robberies. "There were a lot of criminals hanging around these bars," said Gillespie. "Eddie Tong would say, 'Okay Reilly, let's go in and let them know we're around.'"

Tong was so well known to the underworld types that they would call out his name and offer to buy him a drink. Many of them had spent time in jail, and it was probably Tong who had put them there. "Eddie would just look around and smile and nod. I never saw him take a drink with them. But they sure knew who he was. When any of the big-time gangsters got out of jail, they'd have a party and send Eddie an invitation. He might show up just to see who was there, and maybe sing a song with them."

Reporter Jocko Thomas and Tong had been friends. They had been to each other's homes. "I'd been down to his place for supper when my wife was away in the States with her illness. He had this nice little house in the Don Valley area with a white picket fence. He was very, very devoted to his wife and children."

Thomas says Tong was a natural for police work. "He had a certain way about him. Stool pigeons and informants liked to give him information." One of the complaints about Tong was that he refused to share his informants with fellow officers, but Thomas understands that. "He didn't trust anybody. He didn't want them to know who his stoolies were. He wouldn't tell anybody, because it can get around, you know. A lot of those guys weren't as discreet as he was. And he also knew that – just like a newspaperman's contacts – his stoolies and informants were his bread and butter. Tong was a real good copper. He would have gone to the top, I think."

Thomas says Tong was tough when he had to be. "Those were the days when police were rough with prisoners. The police were expected to get statements. If you had your statement, your case was pretty well over. Today, statements seem to be thrown out of court, ninety percent of the time."

The Horseshoe Tavern, now over fifty years old, started out as a blacksmith's shop in 1861. By turns it was a shoe store, an apparel shop, and a "fancy goods shop", until the legendary Jack Starr purchased the property in 1947 and over the next three decades developed its foot-stomping reputation as a country music mecca.

In the late 1940s and early 1950s, most of the Horseshoe's customers, especially in the day and early evening, were merchants and workers from the garment district on nearby Spadina Avenue.

Cigar-chomping wholesalers and manufacturers, and salesmen and models were part of the mix, as were the unsavoury regulars who gathered around some of the tables at the back. Among the latter was Frank Watson, who was well known to Eddie Tong and the Toronto police and had a record dating back to 1937. Watson, who wore rimless glasses and was slight of build, looked more like a bank clerk than a criminal. Tong considered him a thug, like many of the others who drove big cars, wore flashy suits, flaunted wads of cash, and left big tips.

Leonard Jackson was a twenty-eight-year-old waiter at the Horseshoe. He was polite and friendly, and Frank Watson took a liking to him. Jackson was impressed by the cash and the cars, but he knew they were unattainable for someone slinging beer and waiting tables. Jackson wore an artificial foot as a result of an accident, and some of the regulars and his fellow workers gave him the nickname "Stubby". But soon he would earn another nickname – "Tough Lennie". For although Jackson was polite and friendly, seldom drank, and didn't smoke or use foul language, he was an intense man, bitter about his handicap, and a very good street-fighter.

Jackson was slightly under five-foot-ten, with a medium, wiry build and dark hair and eyes. According to Gillespie, Tong and Jackson became aware of each other for the first time in the summer of 1950 at the Horseshoe. A few months later Gillespie met Jackson while paying a routine visit to a petty thief who lived on McCaul Street, south of College around the corner from police headquarters.

"I was with a different partner by then," said Gillespie, "and we walked into the house to see this criminal and there was Lennie sitting in the kitchen. I didn't know him, but I got talking to him and he wasn't like a criminal at all. He was very polite, pleasant, and easy to talk to." But what Gillespie remembered most from that brief encounter was the look in Jackson's eyes. "They were dark, deep-set, and very intense."

Lennie was born Leonard Stone in Toronto on April 23, 1922, to a Jewish mother and an English father. His mother, Lillian, had two children from her first marriage and three, including Lennie, from her second. After her second husband abandoned her, Lillian kept the name Jackson and moved to Niagara Falls, where she went into the hairdressing business. The family attended the local Anglican church, and Lennie was a regular at Sunday School.

Lillian must have found it difficult to raise five children and run a business on her own. One relative says she was strict and domineering with her children, and that didn't sit well with Lennie and at least one other son. Samuel, who went by the name Sammy Stone, was charged with break-and-enter in Niagara Falls in May 1931 and sent to the Victoria Industrial School at Mimico, Ontario. (Years later, he would do time at Kingston for armed robbery.) Lennie, who was nine at the time, went his own way. After completing eighth grade in Niagara Falls, he quit school and went to work as a farm labourer, just as Ed Boyd had. Also like Boyd, he gave that up and was soon riding the rods. But instead of travelling west, Lennie headed to the United States. Four months before his sixteenth birthday, in December 1937, police arrested him in El Paso, Texas, and deported him to Canada. Undeterred, he headed right back to the United States, where he was convicted of various minor offences, similar to the vagrancy and panhandling charges Boyd had piled up during his years riding the rods.

On September 10, 1939, at the Exhibition Grounds in Toronto, Lennie Jackson joined the Royal Regiment of Canada – Col. G. Hedley Basher's reserve army, which had been activated at the start of the war. The age requirement was eighteen, but like thousands of underage recruits, Lennie lied about his age and signed up. Two months earlier, Ed Boyd had signed on with the Royal Canadian Regiment.

Col. Basher, former governor of the Don Jail, and Lennie Jackson, inmate-in-waiting, arrived in England in November 1940. Eight days later, Jackson stayed out all night and was disciplined: seven days' field parade and eight days' loss of pay for being absent without leave (AWL).

Jackson, who suffered from chronic respiratory problems – asthma, hay fever, and bronchitis – spent a month in hospital in October 1941, and again in February 1942, and was classified as unfit for duty because of his health. Two weeks after being reinstated, in May 1942, he was back in hospital once again. Shortly after his recovery he disappeared for two weeks. This time he was sentenced to fourteen days' detention and twenty-nine days' loss of pay. In May 1943, Jackson was transferred to the 48th Highlanders and promoted to lance-corporal, but a month later he was back in hospital and again classified as unfit for duty. Shortly after returning to duty in July 1943, he went AWL again for a few hours. This time he lost two days' pay and was given a severe reprimand. By November 1943 he had lost his stripe and was back with the Royal Regiment of Canada as a private.

On February 1, 1944, Jackson was rotated back to Canada and sent to the #2 District Depot at the Exhibition Grounds to await his discharge from the army. Before his official discharge, Jackson underwent three pre-discharge interviews.

"Jackson is a single youth who lived most of his life at home," the first interviewer wrote. "His parents separated when he was about nine years old and he was raised by his mother who established a hair-dressing business in order to take care of her five children. At times the family suffered privation. As a youth he was fond of mechanics but had little opportunity to pursue the development of any hobby. He cared little for study and his reading was not significant.

"This soldier impresses one as being thoroughly dissatisfied with the Army.... It is felt he should be given the opportunity to prove his worth in some task which requires little mental acumen." The interviewer's last comment, though disparaging, related to tasks that might be assigned to Jackson during his last weeks in the army, not to potential civilian employment.

The second interviewer wrote: "Jackson has apparently made arrangements to enter the employ of the Michigan Central Railway as a fireman. He is ambitious to extend his education however, and wishes to take at least six months schooling in English and Mathematics. In view of his normal school progress there should be no hesitation in granting this request in this matter as it will be of great assistance to him later on in advancing himself in the type of work he has elected."

The third interview, conducted two days before Jackson's discharge, indicated that he had no assured employment, but mentioned the railway job and the merchant navy as possibilities: "Stated he wanted to get to England, made no mention of interest in returning to school."

Finally, on June 28, 1944, three weeks after D-Day, Jackson was officially discharged. He was twenty-two years old and had been in the army four years and nine months. Jackson was restless, and when he found he couldn't get the Michigan railway job he coveted, he decided to join the merchant navy. It would allow him to travel, there would be less of the rigid discipline of army life, and the fresh sea air might provide relief from his allergies and chronic respiratory problems. On August 4, 1944, less than two months after leaving the army, he applied for and was granted a Merchant Seaman's Identity Certificate in Toronto. His fingerprints and photo were included in the application. His weight was 165 pounds, and a scar over his left eyebrow was listed as a "visible distinguishing mark."

Like many Canadian merchant seamen, Jackson decided to serve on Norwegian ships. In the last year of the war he was on three different ships, sailing to ports in Russia, Norway, England, Scotland and Italy, and to New York. Jackson's second ship, the *Idefjord*, was torpedoed by a German submarine. It stayed afloat, although Jackson and the rest of the crew abandoned ship. They later boarded again, and the ship was towed to Murmansk for repairs.

Jackson left the merchant navy in the late summer of 1945 and returned home to Niagara Falls, but he was soon bored there. He tried Toronto for a while, but he wanted adventure and was gripped by wanderlust and the lure of the unknown, and this led him once again to the rails – this time with tragic consequences. In late summer or early fall of 1946 he slipped while trying to hop a freight train at the railway yards near the Exhibition Grounds. As he fell to the ground his left foot went under a wheel and was severed. He was rushed to hospital, where doctors, unable to reattach the mangled foot, cut the leg cleanly just above the ankle.

Now twenty-four, and disillusioned and despondent, Jackson spent six months recuperating in hospital and at home in Niagara Falls. He was fitted with a prosthesis and eventually pulled himself out of his depression and began going out. One of the places he frequented was Rocco's Pool Room on Victoria Avenue at the top of Clifton Hill.

This was a low-income neighbourhood of small shops and restaurants that the locals referred to as Niagara Falls Centre.

John Clement was a law student from Niagara Falls and would later serve as a provincial cabinet minister. "We used to gravitate to the pool rooms when we were home for the summers," he recalls. "Rocco's was one of them, and I think I was nineteen or twenty the first time I saw Lennie. He was a pool shark, but he wasn't a punk who hung around there all the time. He would just come in for a Coke and a game of snooker. The street I lived on was in sort of the posh area of town and you were proud of yourself for knowing somebody like Lennie – from the other end of town. He was five or six years older than us and we considered him very *cool*. He was a nice guy – never loud or pushy. He'd been overseas, and he'd been hurt – he was cool."

Lennie decided he needed a career to support himself. He took a six-month course in hairdressing and started his new career working in his mother's shop. He stayed at hairdressing for several months, but was soon bored, and the long hours standing on his artificial foot were painful. This wasn't how he wanted to spend his life. He moved to Toronto once again, and this time found work at the Horseshoe Tavern.

Jackson's sister, Mary Mitchell, was separated from her husband and working as a model and part-time hostess at the Holiday Tavern a few blocks west of the Horseshoe. While working a modelling job in Windsor, Ontario, she met another model, a young Englishwoman named Ann Roberts. Ann was from the north of England and had immigrated to Canada with her husband at the end of 1947. They settled in Toronto, where their marriage soon ran into trouble. In June 1948, when she was twenty-one, they legally separated, with Kenneth Roberts suing for divorce on grounds of adultery. She did not contest the divorce, and it was granted in May 1951.

Lennie was shy around women, and Mary suggested she could introduce him to Ann. "I'll choose my own girl," he snapped. Then, in May 1950, Ann happened to be walking along Queen Street West when she bumped into Mary and Lennie near the Horseshoe. "I fell in love with him that first day," she would say later. At five-foot-nine, Ann was almost as tall as Lennie. She was soft-spoken, and he was captivated by her English accent and quiet charm. He asked her out the next night, and they kept steady company for the next four months.

Lennie had mastered his artificial foot and was comfortable going out in public. "Don't believe the stories of witnesses who claim they could recognize Leonard by his limp," said Ann. "It just wasn't so. I went out with him for two weeks before I found out about his wooden foot. And then it was only because his sister told me."

By September 1950 Lennie and Ann were living together in an apartment on Sackville Street in downtown Toronto. She worked as a model, and he continued working at the Horseshoe. But it wasn't long before Lennie Jackson decided he wanted some of the better things in life, and that the way to get them was not by waiting on tables in a bar, but by robbing banks. To line up accomplices, he didn't have to look any farther than big-tipping Frank Watson.

On February 27, 1951, two men entered the Canadian Bank of Commerce in the village of Pickering, just east of Toronto, a few minutes before closing time. There were no customers in the bank. The men were carrying brown paper bags with revolvers inside. They rattled the bags to get the attention of the six bank employees, including the manager, Neil R. Shortreed, who had his back to the door when the bandits came in. "I looked around and saw one of the men taking a gun out of a bag. He pushed it into one of the girl's faces and demanded money."

The junior clerk, Helen Butt, and senior clerk, Mary Riley, were standing behind the counter towards the rear of the bank, as was Shortreed. They saw that both men carried handguns. One of the men entered the manager's office and came out a side door behind the counter. Crouching, he pointed his gun at the bank employees.

"Get down on the floor," he ordered. Helen Butt complied, but Shortreed noticed that the floor was dirty. "I had my good suit on," he told police later, "so I sort of backed into an area below a table where there was a shelf, and sat on that, facing out into the bank."

He watched as the man who had come behind the counter entered the teller's cage and emptied the cash drawer into a large, heavy canvas bag he had with him. "I saw him take the bills, and even the silver." The robber also took a bank-issue .38-calibre Ivor Johnson revolver. He then walked back to the vault and motioned to Shortreed to join him. On his way to the vault, the manager stepped on the floor alarm.

"Open it!" ordered the robber, his gun at the manager's back. Shortreed fiddled with the dial of the combination lock, stalling for time. Seconds later the phone rang, and when he reached around the vault to answer it, he saw that both men were gone. Helen Butt and Mary Riley both got a good look at the man giving the orders – the apparent leader. "I would never forget his eyes," said Riley. Later she and Helen Butt would pick him out of a police line-up. The man they pointed to was Leonard "Tough Lennie" Jackson. The eyes, said Riley, were unmistakable.

Two weeks after the robbery, Ann Roberts and Lennie Jackson moved into an apartment on Lumsden Avenue in the Danforth-Woodbine area, a few blocks north of where Ed Boyd grew up.

On March 27, 1951, three men, one armed with a shotgun and the others with revolvers, entered the Canadian Bank of Commerce in Colborne, eighty miles east of Toronto, just before closing time and walked out with about $5,000. A fourth man was waiting in a getaway car parked in front. The Haldimand Township clerk, Max Rutherford, one of ten customers in the bank, refused to lie on the floor with the others and grabbed the barrel of the shotgun. The robber wrenched it free and struck Rutherford over the head. When the bank's manager, R.J. Virgin, told another of the bandits that he didn't have the keys for the vault, he was struck on the head with a revolver, suffering a two-inch gash. The robbers escaped in a late-model car with stolen licence plates and eluded roadblocks that the OPP had set up on all the main roads around Colborne.

That robbery came just a week after Edwin Alonzo Boyd robbed the Armour Heights branch of the Bank of Montreal for the second time. The Colborne robbery made the front pages of the Toronto dailies, but the robbers didn't get the headlines that Boyd was getting. That would soon change when Boyd took the summer off to work on his Pickering house.

Six weeks later, on May 10, 1951, three armed men held up the

Royal Bank at Woodbridge, just northwest of Toronto, escaping with about $4,000. Adopting Ed Boyd's tactics, one of the bandits vaulted the counter to rifle the teller cages. Two customers followed the robbers out of the bank hollering "Hold-up! Hold-up!" and had to dive for cover when they were fired at as they tried to get close enough to read the licence number of the getaway car. The police set up roadblocks at the western entrances to Toronto, but once again the robbers escaped.

The roadblocks went up again two weeks later when two gunmen held up the Mitchell branch of the Canadian Bank of Commerce, thirteen miles northwest of Stratford, escaping with $8,000. Both men carried .45 calibre revolvers. On their way out with the cash, they also stole one of the bank's guns. The manager, A.G. MacDougall, said he knew it was a hold-up the moment he saw the two men enter the bank. "I went into the vault and closed the inner door and they didn't see me," he said later. "They were young fellows, one wearing dark glasses and one a bandanna. They cleared out the cash drawers of three of the tills." This time the Toronto dailies gave the robbers their full attention with headlines rivalling those of Boyd's early robberies.

By this time Lennie Jackson had quit his job at the Horseshoe. He had also traded in his old car for a black Pontiac with all the extras. "I did not know how he was making his money," Ann Roberts would tell the police later. "But he always had enough for our regular needs, and always had an automobile." Soon after, Jackson traded in the Pontiac for a metallic-blue 1949 Oldsmobile Rocket, which he proudly drove over to his old workplace. Now *he* was the big tipper with the flashy car and the wad of cash. He was doing so well that Ann was able to quit modelling. On July 2, 1951, they moved again, this time to a cottage at Musselman Lake, northeast of Toronto.

Eight days later, four gunmen hit the Woodbridge Royal Bank for the second time in two months, this time taking $10,000. The *Telegram* called it a "return engagement." The robbers would have taken a lot more, but even with a gun at his head, bank manager Glen Newans refused to open the vault. Soon after the robbery the police found the getaway car abandoned on a country road outside Woodbridge.

A farmer told the police that two young blonde women had been parked for some time in the same location where the getaway car was found later. Descriptions of the women and the car were broadcast to police forces across the province, and that night the headlines told the story.

Three days after the Woodbridge robbery, four Thompson sub-machine-guns and several revolvers were stolen from the army base at Camp Borden, along with a large quantity of ammunition.

On the afternoon of July 24, a green 1951 Buick driven by Valent "Val" Lesso pulled up at the Musselman Lake cottage. Lesso was six years younger than Lennie, who introduced him to Ann and told her they were good friends. The two men spent much of the three hours Lesso was at the cottage huddled in private conversation.

Two days later, on a sultry afternoon in the Holland Marsh farming village of Bradford, thirty miles north of Toronto, off-duty OPP constable Reg Wilson noticed a suspicious man near a late-model black Ford in front of the Bank of Commerce on the main street. Wilson lived in the apartment above the bank. Without attracting attention, he walked to the side of the building and quickly up the outside stairway to his apartment. While he was loading his service revolver, three robbers, one of them carrying a tommy gun, left the bank with $4,200. The robber with the tommy gun threw it into the back seat as Wilson appeared at the corner of the building and opened fire, hitting the car four times, and perhaps, he thought, one of the gunmen. The robbers replied with a hail of bullets from inside the car. Wilson dropped to the pavement when one the shots smashed into the wall a few inches from his chest.

"If he [Wilson] had fired any sooner, he might have been cut down by the machine-gun," said Harry Barron, who had witnessed the shoot-out from his hardware store across the street. The car, which had been stolen in Toronto earlier that day, was found abandoned on a side road four miles away. A small army of policemen set up road-blocks and searched fruitlessly for the gunmen. That night and the next day there were more sensational headlines in the newspapers.

Within an hour of the robbery, Lennie Jackson and Ann Roberts had packed their bags and checked out of the Musselman Lake cottage. Taking a circuitous route, they drove north along the eastern shore of Lake Simcoe and rented a cottage at Paradise Camp, near Orillia. Three days later, leaving Ann at the cottage, Lennie returned to Toronto, where he had rented a room on the top floor of a three-storey rooming house on Roncesvalles Avenue.

There is no doubt that Lennie Jackson and Frank Watson had underworld connections, but Eddie Tong had his own contacts there. Jackson and Watson had become part of what police were calling the Numbers Mob, a loosely knit outfit that used walkie-talkies and numerical codes to signal each other, as if they were football quarter-backs calling plays at the scrimmage line. Tong had been working the case since January 22, 1951, when thieves held up the Dominion Bank at Dovercourt Road and Davenport. Through his network of inform-ers and other leads, he arrested Louis Stavroff and Tony Brunet in a Queen Street West cocktail lounge within three hours of the robbery. In Stavroff's home, police found nine revolvers, five hundred rounds of ammunition, and enough dynamite "to blow up a city block." Stavroff and Brunet were sentenced to fifteen years at Kingston.

The robberies continued, but so did Tong, who was pressing his informants and watching to see who was driving the new cars and flashing the cash rolls. He showed up at Musselman Lake the day after Lennie Jackson and Ann Roberts moved on. On July 28, two days after the robbery, he picked up two more suspects on Jarvis Street. In their rooming house the police found plans of the Bradford Bank of Commerce and a detailed map of the area.

Acting on a tip two days later, Tong, Jack Gillespie, and two OPP officers raided Jackson's rooming house on Roncesvalles Avenue. They went to his third-floor room, but there was no sign of him. Disappointed, Gillespie left by the front while Tong went out the back ... and came face to face with Jackson, who was climbing the fire escape to his room. "Eddie grabbed him and there was a fight," recalled Gillespie. "Lennie could really handle himself, but he met his match with Eddie Tong." Jackson's forehead hit the fire escape railing, which opened a gash over his left eye where he already had a scar, but he was able to struggle free and run down a back lane, with Tong in pursuit. As they ran, Tong saw Jackson flip a small paper-wrapped bundle through the open window of a car parked in the lane. Tong gradually gained on Jackson and stopped him with a flying tackle as he reached Boustead Avenue. That night the *Telegram*'s page 1 headline incorrectly reported that police had fired five shots at Jackson as he was fleeing.

The bundle in the car in the lane contained $1,500 in cash, and if Tong hadn't noticed it the police might never have recovered it, since the owner of the car had been planning to drive to Kapuskasing that afternoon. While Jackson was being arrested by Tong and Gillespie, a second police team was capturing Frank Watson at gunpoint in a downtown rooming house.

Tong and Gillespie took Jackson to the third-floor detectives' office at College Street, where he was held on vagrancy charges, pending a line-up the next night. The evening after their arrests, Jackson and Watson were placed in what would be described as the largest line-up procedure in Toronto police history, with more than fifty bank employees, customers, and other witnesses studying ten men in the lineup room over a three-hour period. Afterwards,

Jackson and thirty-five-year-old Watson were each charged with robbing five banks.

Ann Roberts was worried. She hadn't heard from Jackson since he left the Orillia cottage in his Oldsmobile early on the morning of July 29. She learned of his arrest on a radio news broadcast the next day. He was being held without bail. Ann returned to Toronto and stayed with Jackson's sister, Mary. Tong arranged for Ann to see Jackson at police headquarters, and after that she visited him twice a week at the Don Jail. In a statement to police six months later, Ann said that up until the time of his arrest for the Bradford bank robbery, "I had never seen him with a gun, had never heard him talk about guns, and had never seen him with a large sum of money. From the time I met Leonard until the time he was arrested we did not associate with anyone. When we went out, we went out together. We did not have any visitors come to our home, and we did not receive any phone calls, although there was a phone in the house."

On August 21, 1951, Jackson was taken to the Barrie courthouse for a preliminary hearing on the Bradford robbery. He was ordered to stand trial. On the courthouse steps he saw Tong and Gillespie. "Lennie and Watson were coming out of the court in handcuffs," recalled Gillespie, "and Lennie looked at Tong and said something to him like, 'You better watch out – you're going to get it.' I don't know if that was it exactly, but I know it was sort of a threat. Eddie was used to that, he just smiled. Lennie never liked Eddie Tong. I don't think he could accept that he met his match with Eddie."

Lennie Jackson had been in the Don Jail for two and a half months when Edwin Alonzo Boyd arrived in mid-October and was assigned a cell next to his. Boyd was eight years older than Jackson, but they had more in common than they realized.

On October 25, 1951, eight days after Boyd's arrival in the northwest No. 3 Corridor, William R. "Willie" Jackson – no relation to Lennie Jackson – was assigned a cell near the other two. Willie Jackson was awaiting removal to Kingston, pending appeal of a seven-year sentence for robbery with violence. Willie was five-foot-seven and had receding curly dark hair, blue eyes, and the name "Eleanor" tattooed on his right forearm. He had grown up streetwise in Toronto's tough Cabbagetown neighbourhood and had skipped school so often that Children's Aid was monitoring him by age twelve. By thirteen, he was in reform school for stealing; at sixteen, he had run off to Montreal, where he was charged with vagrancy. By eighteen, he had graduated to car theft, and when he broke the terms of his two-year probationary sentence, he was sent to the Guelph Reformatory for ninety days.

Willie, who was then twenty-five, liked to tell jokes, and later on, when he became known as a member of the Boyd Gang, he would mug for the cameras and toss one-liners to reporters. The newspapers would nickname him "the Clown", although by the time he met Ed Boyd and Lennie Jackson in the cells at the Don Jail, there was nothing in his criminal background to laugh at.

From car theft he had graduated to robbery – usually with violence. Willie Jackson was a mugger. In the summer of 1948, after serving two years in the Manitoba Penitentiary, he returned to Toronto. He needed money to maintain the drinking habit he had developed, and he knew only one way to get it. In Allan Gardens on June 5, he robbed Turpo Coté of his wallet containing $7. Two weeks later he assaulted Russell Hardy and robbed him of a small amount of cash. And two days after that he approached Montreal businessman Gilbert Holmes, who was sitting on a bench at Queen's Park just after 11 p.m.

"Do you have a match?" asked Willie. Holmes gave him a match, and Willie sat beside him, striking up a conversation. Two of Willie's accomplices suddenly appeared behind them. One of them thrust a nickel-plated revolver into Holmes' back and ordered him into the bushes, where they took his wallet and wristwatch and the key to his Bay Street hotel room. The wallet contained $6.75. The trio then forced Holmes to accompany them along Bloor Street to Sherbourne, where they took him into the ravine below the bridge and tied him up. Willie laughed and held up the key.

"You guys watch him," he ordered. "I'm going to see what I can pick up in his hotel room."

But shortly after Willie left, the two men disappeared. Holmes quickly freed himself and ran to his hotel. In the company of the hotel detective, Holmes went up to his room where they cornered Willie and held him for the police. He was charged with three counts of robbery with violence and sentenced to three years in Kingston. He was released in early 1951. A few months later, after several drinks, he beat an elderly man unconscious with a beer bottle and robbed him of a few dollars. This time he was sentenced to seven years in Kingston and twenty strokes of the strap. Now he was in the Don waiting for a decision on his appeal of the sentence.

Willie was soon entertaining Boyd and Lennie Jackson – and the guards – with a stream of jokes. Boyd's impression was that he was not as bad as his record indicated. He believed that Willie's drinking led to a lot of his problems and would always think of him as something of a simpleton who liked to hear what a good criminal he was. "I used to praise him all the time," Boyd would say long afterwards. "He ate it right up."

In the Don Jail at the end of October 1951, Boyd and the two Jacksons were facing long prison terms, and when they weren't laughing at Willie's jokes, there was only one topic on their minds – escape. For that they needed a hacksaw, and Lennie Jackson already had that covered.

18
Gone

Edwin Alonzo Boyd, working on his house in Pickering through the summer of 1951, had not been aware that other bank robbers were grabbing the headlines in his absence. When he arrived at the Don Jail he had never heard of Lennie Jackson or the Numbers Mob. But Lennie Jackson knew all about him.

"I read about you in the paper," said Jackson after introducing himself to Boyd. He admired the way Boyd took over a bank by vaulting the counter. Jackson didn't go into specifics, but Boyd quickly realized that his new neighbour had also robbed a few banks. He was surprised to learn that Jackson had an artificial left foot, because he didn't seem to limp when he walked. Boyd says Jackson was easy to talk to, but he also noticed that the other inmates on the corridor treated Jackson with a certain deference. "He had an air about him that made all the guys in the block be careful of what they said," recalls Boyd. "I think they realized he had contacts with organized criminals on the outside." Lennie was intelligent, soft-spoken, and didn't swear or curse like many of the inmates.

Boyd noticed that four or five inmates on the corridor hung around with Lennie most of the time. Boyd kept to himself but couldn't help overhearing their conversations when there were no guards around the corridor. "He had his own group," says Boyd. "And they were discussing how they were going to rob banks and so on."

Shortly after Willie Jackson arrived, Lennie took Boyd aside. "I'm thinking of breaking out of here," he said. "Do you want to come along?"

"How do you propose to do it?" asked Boyd.

"Through that window," said Lennie, nodding towards the window directly across from Boyd's cell. Boyd knew there was about a forty-foot drop to the exercise yard below.

"You'll need a hacksaw and a rope," he said.

"I've got hacksaw blades," said Lennie.

"You do?" said Boyd, surprised.

"In here," said Lennie, tapping the leather brace that covered his left calf and held his wooden foot in place. "And we'll tie sheets together to make a rope." Boyd was impressed. So far he liked what he was hearing.

"The bars are soft," said Lennie. "It's like cutting through butter." Lennie knew what he was talking about: he had already cut through the bars in a window in an east-wing corridor, as part of a mass escape plan to coincide with the royal couple's visit to Riverdale Park on Saturday, October 13. More than fifty thousand people were expected at the park, directly north of the Don Jail, and thousands of others would be lining adjacent Broadview Avenue to view the royal motor-cade. Broadview was a stone's throw from the jail, and the plan was that as the royals passed by on their way to Riverdale, Jackson and others would go over the wall and mingle with the huge crowd. But because of the royals' pending visit, the guards were extra diligent and discovered a hacksaw blade and a screen with loosened bolts, just days before Princess Elizabeth and Prince Philip arrived. The partially sawed bars would not be discovered for several months. The police and guards had searched the prisoners and their cells thoroughly but found no other saw blades. Lennie was subsequently moved to No. 3 Corridor.

"How do we get through the screen and out the window without the guards noticing?" asked Boyd.

"We cut the bolt on the bottom hinge and bend the screen up enough to get a man in there to work on the bars," said Lennie.

"They'll see the bolt is missing."

"I'll have a replacement. They won't notice it."

Boyd had already studied the screened window, which was six feet high and three and a half feet wide. It was part of a row of windows facing into the small exercise yard below. The windows were recessed and could not be seen from the guard station on the landing at the end of Corridor No. 3. With Sanderson's new deal, inmates competed in bean-bag bowling and played cards on tables in the corridor until 8 p.m., when they were locked into their cells for the night. Sawing a bar with a soaped hacksaw blade would not be a noisy operation.

Jackson's preferred window was the third one from the farthest (northwest) corner of the corridor. The screen covering it was made of heavy woven wire, tightly meshed in a diamond pattern and about one-eighth of an inch thick. There was a half-inch metal support bar across the centre of the screen; the bar was attached to a steel frame around the perimeter. On one side were three bolted hinges holding the screen in place; on the other was an iron angle bar with a slot at the bottom end that fit into an iron staple embedded in the wall. A padlock through the staple held the bar in place. Behind the screen was the frosted glass window. The bottom half of the window was fixed in place; the upper half was on a pivot that allowed it to swivel open for ventilation. Guards and inmates usually used a broom handle to open or close the window. As long as the screen was in place, guards would have no reason to think the bars beyond it had been tampered with. To get at the bars, an inmate would have to get behind the screen and through the window.

Boyd, at five-foot-eight and 140 pounds, was about twenty-five pounds lighter than Lennie Jackson and almost two inches shorter. He quickly realized that Jackson wanted him in on the escape because he was small enough to crawl under the screen and through the window opening to get at the bars. Jackson agreed that was true, but added that he also appreciated Boyd's agility and daring. Boyd thought it over for a moment.

"We have to plan every detail," he said finally.

Jackson nodded agreement.

"Okay, I'm with you," said Boyd.

Most of the bars on the windows of the Don Jail had been in place since it was first built almost a century before. The bars were "cold-rolled," made of iron imported from Russia. A good hacksaw blade could certainly cut through them, but it wasn't as if they were being held in a vice and cut on a workbench using a hacksaw with a proper handle. Boyd would be in a cramped position without proper leverage, using a blade with no handle. He would need someone to spell him off. Lennie picked Willie Jackson, who had heard about the plan and was eager to get in on the escape. None of the other fifteen prisoners would be going with them, although Lennie expected them to help keep the guards distracted. Ed Boyd and Lennie Jackson knew that if their escape was going to succeed, they would have to study the daily routines and rhythms of the jail and use them to their advantage.

The day usually began with the inmates cleaning their cells before breakfast. Since the eighteen inmates on No. 3 Corridor were Kingston prisoners, they were never brought into the dining room at the same time as the rest of the Kingston prisoners, who were in cells on a another corridor. Sanderson believed it was too dangerous to have them all in the same room at the same time. The jail's dining hall had a seating capacity of one hundred, and there were usually three or four different sittings for each meal. The breakfast call for No. 3 Corridor could come at any time between 7:20 and 8:10 a.m.

All day long there was constant movement and bustle in the Don. After breakfast the prisoners were required to clean their corridors and other common areas, including the toilets and sinks that were found on each corridor. In other parts of the jail, those inmates who had served their time were escorted to the property room to pick up their clothing and personal belongings. They were usually released between 8:45 and 9 a.m. Other prisoners were readied for transport to the courts for appeals, remands, or preliminary hearings. There were also daily parades of prisoners going to and from their weekly shower.

The breakfast routine would be repeated at lunch and dinner. Between meals – morning and afternoon – guards would escort prisoners, in groups of fifty to eighty, to the exercise yard, where they walked in circles in the "bull ring," played quoits, or stood around talking. Also, some prisoners would be escorted to the visiting area to meet with family, friends, lawyers, or clergy.

The dinner sittings, which started at 5 p.m., were always preceded by roll call in each corridor. Boyd noticed that the guards seemed uninterested as they called out the names, usually not even bothering to look up. After dinner, the inmates returned to the corridors for bowling or cards until they were locked in their cells at 8 p.m. There were no lights in the cells, and those inmates who wished to read had to do so by the dim light from the corridor. Three nights a week, radios were allowed in each corridor from 8:30 to 10 p.m., with the prisoners deciding, by straw vote, what program or sporting event they wanted to listen to. This was another of Sanderson's popular innovations.

Lennie Jackson had heard from some of the long-time prisoners how much better conditions were under the new governor of the Don. It impressed him enough that on October 14, he wrote to Ann Roberts:

> Once again I have the pleasure of writing to you my darling, and being allowed and able to do so. It may sound funny when I write this way, but when you are in the grips of the law, and you haven't the money behind you, the privileges cease. Believe it or not, I am lucky to be in custody under supervision of a man who has the integrity and honesty to treat us as human beings, which takes the bitterness out of the inmates. I have nothing but contempt for the law enforcement of this fair city. At one of the stations, an officer whom I had served overseas with, promised to phone my lawyer for me, but neglected to carry out the promise. The reason that I'm writing this my darling is that we, myself and other inmates, are being treated in the best possible manner. Of course there are rules which have to be abided by, which I find isn't hard to do. They have a change of clothing, bed sheets, and a shower once a week and continuous hot water available, so my darling my real punishment is being kept away from you.

The letter went on to profess his love for Ann in language right out of a Hollywood melodrama:

> You can't judge a book by its cover. Meaning you my precious, you are not only beautiful to look at, but your heart

and loyalty is bigger than this cockeyed world that we live in
... A man can ask no greater reward than the warm-hearted
love of a beautiful woman. Well bunny ... I'll have to close for
now....

When Lennie was arrested, his prized Oldsmobile was seized by
the police. When they released it to Ann Roberts in September 1951,
Lennie instructed her to sell it to Orgell Motors in Toronto, where
he had purchased it. She received $1,300, of which $200 went to
Lennie's legal fees. She was living off the remainder and had about
$350 left by the end of October.

Roberts could probably have gone back to modelling if she'd had
to. Circumstances were more difficult for Dorreen Boyd. She was dis-
traught when she visited her husband at the Don. There was no
money coming in, and she had the Pickering house and three kids to
worry about. Ed told her he would figure out something.

Boyd also had a visit from his father, Glover Boyd, who had moved
with his wife and son to Wiarton, Ontario, and opened a small store
after retiring from the police force.

"What are you going to do now?" he asked his eldest son.

"I don't know. It depends on the law, doesn't it?"

"Yeah, I guess it does. You've got yourself into a jam. I don't know
how you'll ever get out of it."

Ann Roberts continued to visit Lennie Jackson twice a week, sometimes accompanied by his sister Mary, or his friend Val Lesso, who
was now calling himself Steve Suchan. Although involved with another
woman, Suchan was attracted to Mary and had begun dating her.
During a visit in late October, Jackson whispered instructions to his
sister, who was to pass them on to Suchan.

Lennie Jackson and Boyd had decided that the best time to work at
sawing their way out of the Don Jail was in the afternoon and early
evening. During their walks around the bull ring in the exercise yard,
they had studied their target window and estimated the distance to
the ground. And they had decided on the best location to scale the
eighteen-foot outside wall.

They went into action after dinner on November 2, a Friday. Willie and Lennie joined some other inmates in a lively game of bowling; still others sat at worn wooden tables and played cards. The tables were near the landing, where the guard sat at his station behind a steel grille. Beyond the guard station was a second grille that closed the landing off from the main gallery or rotunda. Everything seemed normal. But the recessed windows were not in the guard's line of vision, and a casual observer would not notice that the bolt on the bottom hinge attaching one of the window screens to the wall had been sawed through.

The bolt was removed, and the bottom corner of the screen was bent upward until Boyd was able to crawl up under it to the window sill. From there, Boyd tilted open the upper window and pulled himself through until he was in the narrow space between the frosted glass and the bars. Those behind him pulled the screen back into place and replaced the bolt. With the window in shadows, Boyd could not be seen behind the wire mesh and the glass. After rubbing the saw blade with a mixture of soap and dirt, he wrapped one end with a rag and began sawing the bar. It was tedious, difficult work, and after half an hour it was Willie's turn – and then Boyd's again.

It had been decided to cut through a single bar, once at its base and again at the top just below the crossbar. That would leave a hole about nine by fifteen inches. Boyd would conceal the cuts with softened soap mixed with dirt and crawl out of the cramped space. The screen would be forced back into place and a replacement bolt, smuggled into the jail on Lennie's instructions, would be slipped into place on the hinge. Even with close scrutiny, nothing looked amiss.

On Saturday after dinner, Boyd was back in position, hunched over and in a half-crouch position, sawing furiously at the bar. Suddenly his knee locked and gave way. As he struggled for balance, his elbow struck the lower half of the swivel window, smashing it. The sound of breaking glass startled the Jacksons and the other inmates. It was loud enough that the guard heard it.

"What's going on?" he bellowed, getting to his feet on the landing. Willie grabbed the broom near the window and began sweeping up the bits of glass that had come through the screen to the floor. He had often entertained the guard with his jokes, and as the guard approached he smiled impishly. "It's just me," he laughed. "I was trying to close the window and I put the broom handle through the glass. I'm cleaning it up." The other prisoners went back to their cards and bowling, and the guard could see the screen was in its place behind Willie. He stared for a moment and returned to his post, shaking his head. Minutes later, Boyd, his heart pounding, was back in the corridor. The next morning the padlock was opened, and the screen was swung open as maintenance staff replaced the broken glass. The guard accompanying them gave the bars a cursory visual inspection, but saw nothing unusual.

The next day, the chief turnkey, Alfred Bennett, who was in charge on the 3 to 11 shift, inspected the windows at the start of his shift and noticed nothing amiss. It was Sunday, November 4. Sometime around 3:30 p.m., while the other inmates were playing cards and bowling in the corridor, Boyd and the two Jacksons removed sheets from several cells and knotted them into a fifty-foot rope. They also tore strips from other sheets and loosely braided and knotted them into a shorter rope, which they looped at one end like a lasso. By 4:30 p.m. the screen had been unbolted and Boyd was in his familiar position between the bars and the glass window. The bar he and Willie Jackson had been working on seemed no different from the others, but it had been cut almost entirely through, top and bottom. It took Boyd less than two minutes to finish the job. The exercise yard, surrounded by eighteen-foot walls on three sides and by the jail itself on the other, was in deep shadow. The newspapers said the sun would set at 5:05, but there was no sun. It was a dull and unseasonably cold day, with the temperature below freezing and a light dusting of snow on the ground. Dressed only in his jail denims, Boyd shivered from the cold as he tied one end of the knotted sheets around another bar and dropped the other end to the exercise yard below. The smaller rope was coiled over his shoulder and around his chest. He quickly lowered himself forty feet to the ground. The two Jacksons soon followed. They moved speedily along the base of the west wall of the exercise yard to where it joined the north wall.

On No. 3 Corridor the guard had started the usual roll call prior to the 5 p.m. parade to dining hall. As prearranged, other prisoners responded "Present!" when the names of Boyd and the two Jacksons were called out. The guard didn't even look up as he marked the three as accounted for.

Outside in the exercise yard, Lennie Jackson, arms outstretched, braced himself against the north end of the west wall. Expanding the loop on the short rope, Boyd handed it to Willie and stood legs apart, leaning forward, his hands on Lennie's shoulders.

Willie clambered over the two men until he was standing, balanced, with one foot on each of their shoulders. With his arms stretched above his head, it was no more than six feet to the top of the wall. On his first attempt he lassoed the decorative Victorian cornice where the two walls came together. Tugging to tighten the loop, Willie pulled himself up the rope, hand-over-hand, to the top of the wall. Boyd followed and then Lennie. "Lennie was very determined," says Boyd. "He was quite adept and he didn't let his foot get in the way of anything."

Brushing the thin layer of snow from the top of the wall ahead of him, Boyd, flat on his stomach, worked his way into position to view the laneway and Riverdale Isolation Hospital. There was no one in sight. He signalled to the others and they moved forward. One after the other, gripping the wall, they dangled over the side and let go. "After you got hanging straight down, there was only about ten or twelve feet left to drop," says Boyd. "I was worried about Len's artificial foot, but it didn't seem to bother him at all." What did bother Lennie Jackson was that his friend Val Lesso, alias Steve Suchan, was supposed to be there in his car to pick them up on the Don Roadway, which in those days ran north to Rosedale Valley Road. But Suchan was nowhere in sight. They weren't about to wait around. They skirted Riverdale Hospital and headed towards the river.

"We went down from the hospital as fast as we could," remembers Boyd. "We followed the little roadway that ran along the river, and then we started moving north. I didn't know where I was going because I didn't know that part of the Don Valley. The only one that had a clue was Leonard Jackson." Boyd was amazed at how fast

Lennie could move – so fast he was soon out of sight. "It didn't really matter one way or the other if we stayed together, and I figured that when he got ahead of us that would be the last we saw of him, but he was waiting for us up ahead at a little graveyard."

The Don's inmates were being locked into their cells for the night as the chief turnkey, Bennett, began his final inspection of the jail on his shift. At 8:10 p.m. he checked the windows on No. 3 Corridor and discovered that the lower corner of the screen on the third window from the end had been pried upward. Training his flashlight on the bars beyond the frosted glass, he noticed that one of the lower ones was missing – sawed away – and that a sheet, tied to one of the intact bars, was hanging out the window.

Bennett immediately instructed the guards to lock the prisoners in their cells and take a count. It was discovered that three men were missing, and a more diligent roll call revealed the names of the missing inmates. Their cells were subjected to an immediate, thorough search. In front of Boyd's cell, two lengths of hacksaw blade were found hidden between the maple floorboards of the corridor and the flagstone entrance to the cell.

Bennett would tell a Royal Commission several months later that he thought Boyd and the Jacksons were model inmates. "They were good prisoners as far as I was concerned. I had no trouble with them – no suspicions." He said the jail was overcrowded and that there weren't enough guards to keep an eye on so many prisoners. "There are four hundred brains working against me, what can I do?"

The Don's governor, Charles Sanderson, was attending a Sunday evening church service and was not immediately informed of the escape. Jail officials telephoned No. 9 Police Station to check the Humberside address of Ann Roberts and Mary Mitchell, and No. 4 Station was asked to check the Winchester Avenue address of Willie Jackson.

The next day the newspapers were filled with stories and photographs of the escape. It was the first time that Boyd and the Jacksons appeared together on the front pages. It wouldn't be the last. Wanted posters with mug shots of the three men were released by the provincial police, and the province offered a $500 reward for information leading to their arrests. Photographs were sent to all police departments in Canada and to American border cities.

The police were warned to proceed with caution. Boyd and the Jacksons were considered "vicious and dangerous," and it was expected that they would arm themselves at the earliest opportunity and shoot it out if cornered. The police were told to be especially watchful of banks. According to the *Telegram*, the Toronto police feared that the three men, "in desperate straits, may rob a bank for sorely needed funds."

Hiding Out

Val Lesso was born in Czechoslovakia on St. Valentine's Day, 1928, so his parents named him Valentine, a name that he always hated, later changing it to Valent. Still later he would prefer an alias, Steve Suchan.

He was eight years old in 1936 when he and his mother, Elizabeth, came to Canada to join his father, Joseph. Suchan attended the primary grades in a rural school outside Cochrane in Northern Ontario. He was a quiet boy who became an accomplished violin player. He attended high school in Cochrane and came to Toronto on his own in 1946, with his parents following the next year. Suchan was unsettled in Toronto, moving from job to job. His first was with Crystal Glass & Plastics Company. Later he operated a punch press at the John T. Hepburn steel company, and then he went to a glass company on Spadina Avenue. He liked the job, but he was handling large glass sheets such as oversized mirrors and quit because he was still studying the violin and feared he might cut his hands.

Suchan lived with his parents and younger brother, first at 73 Marion Street and later at 27 Sorauren Avenue. After the glass company he went to work in the shipping department of Standard Chemical in Leaside.

Suchan had befriended George B. Kindness through their mutual interest in violins. Kindness made and repaired violins and bought and sold the instruments out of his shop at 96 Church Street. He had known Suchan about three years when, in July 1950, Suchan approached him and offered to sell his expensive violin for cash and the .455 Smith & Wesson revolver that Kindness kept in his shop. Kindness didn't ask him why he wanted the revolver. The gun was properly registered, and on August 5, 1949, Kindness went to the office of the Ontario Provincial Police for approval to sell it to Suchan. The permit approving the sale was signed by the OPP's Registrar of Firearms.

Suchan was authorized to own the gun, but the form stated: "This permit does not give the right to carry a pistol or revolver." But Suchan later purchased a shoulder holster, and sometimes drove to an isolated gravel pit west of Toronto for target practice. Whenever he carried the revolver, it gave him a sense of power.

On March 3, 1950, Suchan was sent to the Guelph Reformatory for three months on six fraud-related charges after he tried to pass three forged cheques totalling $664.

Suchan met Betty Huluk and Anna Bosnich on a blind date in October 1950. He and Huluk went on two dates and then he started dating Bosnich, who was six years his senior. Bosnich had married at eighteen and had an eight-year-old daughter, whom she was raising on her own. She had been separated from her husband for some time and had gone back to using her maiden name, Camero. She supported herself and her daughter first with her own hairdressing business and later as a real estate broker. She lived at 190 Wright Avenue between Roncesvalles and Sorauren, not far from Suchan's parents. Camero knew Suchan only as Val Lesso. Also living at Camero's house were her mother, a roomer, and her friend Betty Huluk, who worked at Chan's Fruit Market around the corner on Roncesvalles.

On December 30, using his real name Val Lesso, Suchan signed on to work at the exclusive King Edward Hotel as an elevator operator. Within two weeks he was promoted to doorman, where he was making $26 a week plus tips. It was while he was at the King Edward that Suchan met and became friends with Lennie Jackson. On March 24, 1951, Suchan quit his job; two days later he began robbing banks with Jackson. Their first stick-up was the Canadian Bank of Commerce in Colborne, Ontario.

By that time, Suchan and Camero had begun going steady. She still knew him only as Val Lesso. He often took her to the movies and to taverns, where she met some of this friends. "But," she complained, "he would always introduce them by their first names, and I did not get to know their last names." Suchan eventually moved in with Camero, though he would stay only a day or so at a time before going home to his parents. He bought a car and a new violin, which he sometimes played at dance recitals. He told Camero he was in the income tax business, and even had a business card to prove it.

He saw less and less of Camero after he met Lennie Jackson's sister, Mary Mitchell, following Jackson's arrest in July 1951. It was much more exciting to be around the worldly Mitchell, but Suchan had a reason for staying in touch with Camero: she had become pregnant by him in the spring of 1951.

When they were well away from the Don Jail, Lennie Jackson telephoned Steve Suchan at Anna Camero's. "Where the hell were you?" he wanted to know. "I ... I forgot," stammered Suchan. It seems more likely that Suchan hadn't shown up because he didn't think Jackson and the others would be able to escape. And since the police had not connected him to any of Jackson's bank robberies, he did not want to gamble on being picked up as part of a bungled escape. Suchan drove to a prearranged spot, met Boyd and the Jacksons, and whisked them to his second-floor room at Camero's house on Wright Avenue. He introduced Lennie Jackson to her as "Freddie," but did not introduce either Boyd or Willie Jackson. Camero was unaware that Suchan had secreted a number of guns in the house. "They had all the guns that they got when they broke into Camp Borden," says Boyd. After a couple of hushed phone calls, Boyd and the Jacksons, now armed, left with Suchan and picked up a second car around Parliament and Gerrard Streets.

Lennie then called Ann Roberts, who was at home at 211 Humberside Avenue when her landlord, George Hill, summoned her to the telephone. Roberts had known nothing of the escape plans and was surprised and elated.

"Hi, Bunny," said the familiar voice.

"Where *are* you?" she asked, barely able to contain her excitement.

"I'm out. Come down to Parliament and Gerrard. Take a streetcar and make sure you're not being followed." She met him half an hour later. He was behind the wheel of a car parked near the intersection. Boyd was beside him in the front seat.

"Leonard told me how he and Boyd had a tough time getting over the jail wall," she would tell police later. Boyd got out of the car, and Ann slipped in beside Jackson. Boyd walked back several car lengths to where Suchan and Willie Jackson were parked in the shadows. They drove to 27 Sorauren Avenue, which Suchan's parents Elizabeth and Joseph Lesso were operating as a rooming house. Suchan had arranged for Boyd and Willie Jackson to take over the second room from the front on the ground floor. The Lessos lived at the back of the house on the ground floor next to the bathroom.

Tenant Jean French and her husband, who were renting the front room and veranda on the second floor, noticed that they were treated differently after the two men arrived in early November. Included in their rent was the use of the telephone in the downstairs hallway and access to the Lessos' kitchen stove to boil water for tea. But after the two men arrived, the kitchen door was always locked. French would knock strongly on the door but "nobody bothered to open it" except, once or twice, Suchan's young brother. "I thought Mrs. Lesso was trying to get rid of us," said French, who would move out a month later. Even their access to the phone was curtailed. On one of the few occasions she was able to get to the phone, she was talking to her husband when she saw Boyd come out of his room and walk past her to the bathroom. He was wearing trousers but no shirt and had a towel over his shoulder. Boyd returned to his room, and French heard voices. "I don't know what they said, but another man came out wearing blue trousers and cleaning his ear out with a towel." She also noticed the tattoo on his arm. In a courtroom months later, French would point out Boyd and Willie Jackson as the men she had seen at the Lesso house.

While Boyd and Willie Jackson were settling in for a night's sleep in a comfortable bed, Lennie Jackson and Ann Roberts were spending the night together at a tourist camp east of Oshawa. "When we stopped outside of Oshawa on the night of his escape, I noticed that he was in possession of a long-barrelled revolver tucked in the waist band of his trousers," said Roberts. "I didn't question him as to where he got the revolver or whether or not it was loaded." They spent the night in Oshawa and didn't leave until after six the next night, when it was dark. From there, they drove to Kingston and another tourist camp. The next morning they continued to Montreal, where they found a room at Castle Tourist on Mountain Street. He went in with her to arrange the room, then left for a short time, returning without the car.

Boyd made no attempt to contact his wife or relatives in the days immediately after his escape, believing the police would likely have them under surveillance. Boyd's assumptions were correct: detectives Dolph Payne and Barry Lorimer filed a report the day after the jail break stating that the homes of Boyd's brother Norman (60 London Street), his friend Frank Lamb (360 Harbord Street), and another friend were all under observation. So was the Pickering house.

"Norman Boyd was followed in his automobile license 85-F-37 all through the downtown district and finally to his garage," said the report. "He was then taken to No. 11 Station and questioned. We believe at present he doesn't know where his brother Edwin is." The detectives added that Lamb, Boyd's friend from judo, had been out to visit Dorreen in Pickering the day before the jail break. They recommended that Lamb's home be kept under surveillance but "not be searched as it may prove to be a contact point."

Boyd says his brothers and other relatives were ready to open their doors to him "but I didn't want to put any pressure on them, so I kept away."

Payne and Lorimer also visited Howard Gault at the Don Jail. He told them he had no idea where Boyd might be, although Boyd once told him that if he did escape he would immediately "pull a quick job in Mimico, Ontario, and then clear out." On the basis of that information, the banks in Mimico were alerted and police patrols beefed up during banking hours. The detectives also suggested that Boyd's fingerprints be forwarded to Washington and Ottawa "as there is some suggestion that Boyd might attempt to join the American Army."

Dorreen Boyd remembers detectives arriving at her Pickering home the night of her husband's escape from the Don.

"Have you seen your husband?" one of them asked.

"No," she replied coldly. "I don't know where he is."

"Well, your neighbours say he's been around."

"I don't care what they say. I haven't seen him."

They turned to eleven-year-old Anthony.

"Have you seen your father?"

"I haven't seen him for a long time."

"Oh, you must have seen your father."

"I haven't seen him," answered the boy, a hint of anger in his voice.

"They kept asking until finally Anthony just shut up and didn't say a word when they spoke to him," says Dorreen. "And then they went away. They looked through the whole house."

Detective Jack Gillespie would not find out for several months, but Edwin Alonzo Boyd and Willie Jackson were hiding right under his nose. "I used to drive up Sorauren Avenue," he said. "It was a two-way street then and I'd make a U-turn and drop in to visit my aunt. She lived at number 6, just north of Queen Street, and they were just up the street at number 27."

Boyd and Willie Jackson were fairly safe hiding out with the Lessos, but Boyd was soon bored and devised a way to break the monotony. "I figured Willie and I could dress up as women and walk around after dark and nobody would bother us. I'd been going to the movies all my life and I always had tremendous admiration for people who could disguise themselves and play different roles. Willie couldn't see putting on woman's clothes, but I dressed up with a long skirt that came down enough to cover my shoes. Willie thought it was great to take me by the arm and walk down the street as a couple. I smoked a bit then, and we'd go into a store and buy cigarettes or sit in a restaurant and have a meal. The disguise was terrific. I didn't have a wig, so I just used a kerchief and put on a little lipstick."

Boyd still laughs at the memory. "I enjoyed it," he says. "When I spoke, I softened my voice and raised it a tiny bit to sound less like a man." Using make-up and disguising himself was nothing new for Boyd, but he would rather have been using those skills to rob a bank.

While Boyd was hiding out at the home of Suchan's parents, the case against forty-three-year-old Howard Gault was reaching a conclusion in the courts. He pleaded guilty to two counts of bank robbery on

November 14, and on November 20 he was sentenced to seven years at Kingston. Gault told the court he had no previous record and for eighteen months had worked for the city works department with Boyd. "I was contented, and I had a nice home," said Gault. "Boyd often wisecracked: why don't you go out and rob a bank?" Gault said he had not wanted to rob the first bank and had begged Boyd not to go through with it, but had agreed to go along after Boyd called him a coward.

Gault said that after the first robbery he often saw Boyd's truck parked outside his Madison Avenue home, and felt Boyd was watching him. He added that on the day he was caught robbing the Dominion Bank at Lawrence Avenue and Yonge Street, he had told Boyd he was ill and wanted no part of the crime.

The magistrate, F.C. Gullen, said of Gault's statement: "What the accused has said would have carried some weight had there been only one offence."

The court was told that after Boyd called Gault a coward before the first robbery, he again pressed Gault to join him, saying, "You'll find out how simple it is."

The Boyd Gang

On Tuesday, November 20, the day Howard Gault was sent off to Kingston Penitentiary, Edwin Alonzo Boyd was in a familiar place – atop a counter with a revolver in his hand, demonstrating just how simple it was to rob a bank.

The night before, a blue 1949 Ford sedan had been stolen from a lot at Vaughan Collegiate. Now, just before 10:30, Boyd, Suchan, and the two Jacksons pulled up in the same car around the corner from the Bank of Toronto at Dundas and Boustead. Seconds later they were in the bank, with Boyd shouting, "This is a hold-up!" as he leaped up on the counter.

Maynard Elroy Copes, assistant accountant, turned when he heard the shouting and saw one gunman on the counter and another pushing manager Brian Branston from his office. The manager was forced to lie on the floor with nine of his employees while the bandits rifled the teller's cages of $4,300. In the confusion, the bank employees could not be sure how many robbers there were. Most of them said three. The newspapers said five. After a thorough investigation, the Toronto police decided it was four.

The *Star's* Jocko Thomas wrote on the day of the robbery: "The gang is believed by police to have been led by Edwin Alonzo Boyd, master bank robber, who escaped with two other desperate criminals from the Don Jail two weeks ago." The robbery had been conducted with "split-second timing." The stolen car used in the robbery was recovered the next day in an enclosed industrial yard at the High Park Paving Company. No fingerprints were found on the vehicle.

Thomas says that after the escape when the robberies started, he was the first to write of the group as "the Boyd Gang." "It was because

I knew of Boyd from those earlier robberies, and the editors liked it because 'Boyd' fit the headlines better than 'Jackson'."

Boyd's initial enthusiasm over the prospect of working with a gang of bank robbers who knew what they were doing quickly waned when it became apparent that there were major personality conflicts, particularly between himself and Steve Suchan. "Suchan was very jealous of the fact that Leonard Jackson wanted me to be in the gang with them," says Boyd. "Suchan wanted to be the important one next to Len." Besides Suchan's proprietary feelings about Lennie Jackson, there was the considerable age difference between Boyd, who was then thirty-seven, and Suchan, who was twenty-three. "Lennie and Willie would listen to me, but not Suchan. He wouldn't take orders or discuss anything with me and Willie. He thought we were interlopers who just happened to break out of the Don with Lennie. Lennie was a good solid guy, but he had too many things on his mind."

Boyd decided on a pragmatic approach: he would associate with Lennie and Suchan, and if it became intolerable he would leave. "I took them as they were. I didn't try to like them or not like them. I just figured they were available if we wanted to rob a bank. They had their friends and their women, and that was plenty to keep them occupied."

Willie Jackson was the most carefree of the lot. He was elated after the Bank of Toronto robbery – his first – and was ready for more. He hadn't been the least bit nervous and had actually enjoyed himself.

Prior to the new gang's first robbery, Boyd had been able to convince Lennie that it was less dangerous to rob banks in the city and its suburbs than in outlying communities, where roadblocks and long distances came into play.

Although the Bank of Toronto robbery had gone smoothly, they were disappointed with the amount of their take. Boyd was worried about supporting himself and his wife and three children. Lennie was so broke he had had to sell his car in Montreal, although he was probably bankrolled for a time by his criminal friends, and also by Suchan, who had shared in the profits of their earlier robberies. But now Suchan too was in need of new resources: he had expensive tastes and was also trying to juggle relationships with Mary Mitchell and

Anna Camero. Only Willie Jackson seemed contented with his share of the first $4,300.

One evening nine days after the Bank of Toronto robbery, in the Beaches neighbourhood of Toronto, Boyd hot-wired another blue Ford sedan, this one a 1950 model. He removed the licence plates, replacing them with plates stolen from a junked vehicle. The Ford was kept overnight in a rented garage. The Boyd Gang would use it the next morning in the biggest bank robbery in Toronto history up to that time.

The target was the Royal Bank of Canada on Laird Drive in Leaside. Lennie Jackson had been thinking about that particular bank even before he went into the Don. It had been talked about on the street as easy and lucrative prey – if the timing was right. The right timing was Friday morning, when the bank had plenty of cash on hand to meet the payrolls of workers from the nearby industries: the CNR shops, a Frigidaire plant, and a sprinkling of smaller workplaces. Six years earlier, the bank had been robbed of $11,500 by five gunmen.

It was a pleasant, sunny day with a light wind and temperatures slightly above 40°F when the Boyd Gang entered the bank shortly after 11 a.m. Two bank customers, John Lowes and Ernest Bluethner, were talking to accountant Cecil J. Young when they heard shouting and were confronted by Boyd, who jabbed a revolver in Lowes' ribs and ordered all three men to face the wall. Boyd turned away, not noticing that Lowes and Bluethner were standing with their hands in the air. Lennie Jackson, who was standing by the front door with a Thompson sub-machine-gun, realized the men would be visible through the window and ordered them to lower their hands. "He immediately walked towards us, and struck Mr. Bluethner across the small of the back with the barrel of the gun," Lowe told police later. By this time, Boyd and Willie Jackson were vaulting the bank counter. "Willie was in good shape, and he flew over the counter just the way I did," says Boyd. There were no individual tellers' cages, only drawers behind the counter.

A bank stenographer, Mrs. Fred Bebe, was standing behind the counter when Boyd landed beside her. "Just keep quiet and you won't get hurt," he said.

"He had a soft voice, but you could tell he meant business," she told a *Telegram* reporter after it was all over. "He even smiled at me – the rat."

While Boyd and the Jacksons were taking control of the front of the bank, Suchan came through the rear entrance and into the office of the manager, Albert Hockley. A customer, George Sauriol, had just concluded an appointment with Hockley and was about to leave when the door opened in his face. He was confronted by a man with a revolver. "Get back! Get back!" shouted Suchan. "Keep your hands down – not up, and get out there against the wall with the others." Hockley later told police that the gunman was wearing "a reddish-brown top-coat and a light grey fedora." The surprise was complete, and Hockley had no chance to press the alarm on his desk. "They were very efficient and seemed to know their business."

Bette Campeau, a twenty-seven-year-old teller, was behind the counter cashing a cheque for a customer when she heard shouting and looked up to see Willie Jackson waving his hands in the air. He was wearing a grey overcoat and a grey fedora with the brim turned down all the way around. "I didn't pay any attention," said Campeau later. "I thought he was a drunken man acting crazy or something. He jumped on the counter and I looked up and he pointed a gun at me and said, 'Move back to the wall.' Then he jumped down beside me. I was just bewildered." As she stood near the wall, she glanced back and saw Boyd wearing a brown overcoat and a fedora turned down at the front. He and Willie were carrying white pillowcases, which they began filling with cash from the counter drawers. Campeau and assistant accountant John Maclean overheard the bandits conversing calmly as they worked.

"How are we doing?" asked Willie.

"Not bad," said Boyd.

"Do you think we're getting enough?"

"Yeah, quite a lot. Looks like we did all right."

There were fourteen employees in the bank and about a dozen customers, some of whom entered while the hold-up was in progress. Lennie Jackson, wearing a fawn-coloured overcoat, grey trousers, and a grey fedora, was there to greet them. "Lennie stood at the door with a machine-gun, looking like Pretty Boy Floyd," laughs Boyd. "When anybody came in, he'd put the gun right against their chest and tell them to get over in the corner. He kept them under control while we were filling the pillowcases with cash."

W.J. Knox was the last customer to enter the bank during the robbery. "The first thing I saw was this man jumping the counter carrying a white pillowcase. I couldn't understand what was happening. But then a man behind me growled out of the side of his mouth, 'Turn around and stand still.' " He caught a glimpse of Lennie Jackson's sub-machine-gun and did as he was told.

Boyd knew this was the biggest haul of his bank-robbing career. The cash drawers were empty and his three minutes were up. "Let's go!" he shouted as he and Willie vaulted the counter, their pillowcases bulging with cash.

The gunmen sped away in their stolen Ford, leaving behind a stunned and confused bank staff. When the police arrived moments later, some witnesses said there were six robbers. Others said five, and still others said four. The police settled on five, and although Boyd's brother Norman was not involved, one of the employees would later pick him out of a line-up as one of the robbers.

THE WEATHER

TORONTO DAILY STAR

FRIDAY, NOVEMBER 30, 1951—36 PAGES   3c PER COPY, 18c PER WEEK

ROB LEASIDE BANK OF $30,000

STEN-GUN FIVE STAGE
BIGGEST BANK HOLD-UP
IN HISTORY OF TORONTO

HOME AND SPORT EDITION

ONTARIO AND FEDERAL GOVERNMENTS AGREE ON SEAWAY DEVELOPMENT

*Shoot Down 11 Red Planes
In Big U.N. Jet Victory*

Soldier Vote Favors PCs In 15 Toronto, York Ridings

THE TELEGRAM

76TH YEAR   52 PAGES   TORONTO, FRIDAY, NOVEMBER 30, 1951   PRICE 5 CENTS

Night
Final Sports—Markets

20 Face Bandits' Guns

6 GET $30,000 BANK LOOT

The gang abandoned the stolen Ford on Pottery Road in the Don Valley, where they switched to another car. When the *Telegram* and the *Star* went to press that day, the bank was still trying to figure out its losses and could provide only an estimate – $30,000. The figure was used in banner headlines in both papers. The *Telegram* said there were six gunmen and the *Star* said there were five. Both papers named Edwin Alonzo Boyd as the probable leader of the gang. The *Star* again called him a "master bank robber" and said that the two men who had escaped with him from the Don Jail earlier in the month may have been accomplices. The *Telegram*, quoting a police source, said Boyd may have "imported boys from across the border" to assist in the robbery. The next morning the Royal Bank revealed the actual amount of their loss – $46,270.

Two bank robberies within ten days, one of them the largest cash haul in the city's history, set off a new round of finger-pointing among the politicians, the bankers, and the police. It was as if the city and surrounding towns had been under siege in the two years since Boyd began robbing banks. He certainly hadn't been operating in a vacuum: even before Lennie Jackson and the Numbers Mob came along in early 1951, there had been many other robberies, perhaps inspired by the newspaper accounts of Boyd's (then anonymous) heists.

In a scene reminiscent of *Bonnie and Clyde*, thirty-two-year-old Joseph H. McAuliffe of North Bay, Ontario, had walked into the Langton branch of the Imperial Bank of Commerce on June 21, 1950. He was wearing a straw fedora and dark glasses and carrying a tommy gun. He herded the bank staff and customers into a vault and walked out with $22,575 in a paper shopping bag. Two Norfolk County tobacco farmers chased the getaway car along county back roads, until McAuliffe's car ran into a ditch. He fired out the rear window, hitting his pursuers, and then casually walked to their car and fired several more shots at close range. Both men died, one with six bullets in the back, the other with two in the chest and one in the arm. After a four-day manhunt McAuliffe was captured in a shack near Staffordville, nine miles from the murder scene.

Three weeks later the Acme Farmers Dairy at Walmer Road and

MacPherson Avenue in Toronto was robbed of $21,000 by two armed men. Dairy driver Charles Tavignot jumped from his milk wagon and chased the robbers up a laneway, but gave up when they turned and fired, hitting him in the foot.

On November 29, 1950, three gunmen masked with khaki handkerchiefs and wearing shabby clothes took $9,500 from the Canadian Bank of Commerce at Roncesvalles and Wright Avenues. One of the robbers vaulted the counter in Boyd style. The *Telegram* said the bandits "dressed like yokels but worked with city-slicker smoothness."

And so it went, robbery after robbery. The newspapers thrived on it and constantly tried to out-scoop each other. "Crime always sold newspapers," says Jocko Thomas. "I knew that from my days selling newspapers at Bloor and Bathurst, when the guy who ran the corner told me, 'Kid if you want to sell papers, cry out, "Read all about the big murder!" ' And I did, even though usually there was no murder. I used to sell a lot of papers that way. And don't forget the robberies were happening during the razzle-dazzle days of Toronto journalism when the *Star* and the *Telegram* were in an unbelievably fierce competition for circulation."

Toronto writer and historian Mike Filey believes it was more than just the newspaper war that led to the banner headlines and the voracious public interest. "Toronto in the late forties and early fifties was not the Toronto it is today," he says. "It was really nothing more than a large town. And when Edwin Alonzo Boyd started wandering into banks and pointing guns, it was almost unheard of – and that's what got him the notoriety."

Filey adds that in those days life was much simpler. There was a hockey team and a baseball team, "but there weren't all the other attractions we have today. Restaurants were scarce, and if you wanted a good meal you went to a hotel. Sunnyside was the most excitement you could get during the summer, and travel to Europe was virtually unheard of for most people. So the Boyd Gang was a big-time event in a rather staid city where there was nothing going on on Sundays, and I'm not sure that people didn't look forward to reading about his exploits."

So the headlines continued stirring not only readers but also protagonists, such as the bankers and the police, who were caught in the fallout. The bankers complained that the police seemed unable to cope with the wave of robberies. The police suggested that the banks hire off-duty policemen to ensure security.

The police were also under attack for not controlling what was perceived to be a general rise in "hoodlumism." John Innes, Toronto's controller, had said a year earlier that the answer was to have more policemen pounding the beat. "I know that the force is hampered by a shortage of men and I'm not suggesting there is anything fundamentally wrong with our force, but I do believe that the trend of modern police methods has swung too far away from the 'neighbourhood cop' system." Innes wanted to see funding to hire more auxiliary officers so that the regular constables would be able to work on beat patrol instead of traffic and parking enforcement.

"Every available cop should be ordered back on the street," said Innes. "You can't protect a neighbourhood by sitting in swivel chairs, and over-emphasis on radio-equipped squad cars has left big areas of the city without beat patrolmen."

In July 1950, in the heat of a debate over the amalgamation of Toronto with some of its surrounding municipalities, Toronto's police chief, John Chisholm, urged the formation of a Metro police force under one command operating throughout the 240-square-mile area of what would soon be called Metropolitan Toronto. Lack of such a force had rendered useless some Toronto drives against crime, he said. At the amalgamation hearings at Queen's Park, he said that efficiency in police communications was moving backwards rather than forwards. "Before 1941, the Toronto force had a one-way radio system and all the suburban police were hooked into it," he said. "After 1941, Toronto installed a two-way system and so did the surrounding municipalities. Now there are thirteen police radio systems operating on thirteen different frequencies and no one force can break in on the other to flash crime news. And there is confusion, duplication and waste."

Jack Webster, now with the Toronto Police Museum, remembers as a young officer the difficulties created by so many different jurisdictions. "We didn't go into any of those other municipalities unless it was hot pursuit," he says. "You couldn't go in and make your own arrests, and that was awkward. You had little places like Weston with eleven officers, Mimico with five officers, Leaside with nine officers, and East York with thirty-two. Then you had the larger ones like North York, Etobicoke, and Scarborough with about two hundred each. It didn't change until January 1, 1957, when all the forces amalgamated into one."

The Boyd Gang had less onerous matters to worry about as they sat around a table at the Suchans' home on Sorauren Avenue after the robbery. They were almost giddy as they divided the Royal Bank's $46,270 into four piles.

21

Goin' South

Steve Suchan's parents, Joseph and Elizabeth Lesso, sat around the table with their son, the two Jacksons, and Boyd as the loot from the Royal Bank was being counted and divided. Boyd noticed that Joseph Lesso was watching the cash expectantly. From time to time he would say something in Slovak to his son, who responded curtly.

"The old man seemed to be a nice guy, and I thought he should get his share, seeing that he was hiding us out," says Boyd. "I asked Suchan about it and he said he would look after it, but I found out later he told his father he wasn't getting a thing. I don't think Suchan thought too much of the old man. Suchan's way of thinking was to hang on to the money and push everybody else out of the way."

Ann Roberts was still in Montreal, and the night of the robbery Suchan and Lennie Jackson spent the night at Anna Camero's house on Wright Avenue. Camero still knew Suchan as Val Lesso, and Jackson as his friend Freddie. This was the second time she had met Freddie. Two days later, the two men would leave for Montreal.

Boyd and Willie Jackson stayed on a few more days at the Lessos' rooming house on Sorauren Avenue. With the guns from the Camp Borden break-in, and three or four bank guns Boyd had stashed in one of his rented garages, there was plenty of firepower to go around. Willie Jackson didn't have much experience with guns and had become enamoured of the revolver Boyd had given him for the Leaside robbery. "He liked to have the gun right there where he could look at it," says Boyd. "I gave him the gun I didn't want – a big forty-five Smith & Wesson revolver – and he really liked it. The police had my

Luger and I preferred something small – I think I was carrying a nine-millimetre Browning or something."

Willie was like a kid at Christmas staring at the revolver and over and over again counting his share of the loot – $11,567. "He had never seen so much money," says Boyd. "I told him it wasn't important, that there was a lot more where that came from. But he slept with it under his pillow, with his gun right there."

The next day, Joseph Lesso took Boyd aside and said he had a secure hiding place if he and Willie wanted to safely stash their money instead of carrying it around with them. Boyd thought it was a good idea – if the police were tipped off to their whereabouts at least the money would be safe. He asked Lesso to show him the hiding place. "It was down under the floor in one of the cupboards off the hall. You lifted a couple of boards, and there it was. It thought it was terrific because I didn't want to have all that cash on me. Of course, I didn't know that Suchan hadn't given the old man anything."

Boyd kept a wad of bills that would fit in his pockets – about $3,000 – and secreted the rest under the floor of the cupboard. He tried to convince Willie Jackson to do the same.

"The old man's got a good spot," Boyd told him. "My money's in there. You should put yours in too. You don't want to be carrying all that around with you all the time. If the police came tearing in after us, at least we'd still have our money."

Willie was skeptical. "He just kind of looked sideways at me and shook his head," laughs Boyd.

"My money is staying with *me*," he declared.

Boyd reassured him, and Willie reluctantly agreed. "I hope you know what you're doing," he said.

The following day, Suchan stopped in for breakfast on his way to Montreal. His father wasn't there, and his mother seemed agitated. They were talking heatedly in Slovak when Boyd came into the kitchen.

"Where's your money?" asked Suchan.

"Your old man hid it under the cupboard floorboards in the hall."

"You better go and see if it's there."

Boyd rushed to the hiding place and discovered that all the cash – about $17,000 – was missing. He stormed back to the kitchen. "It's all gone!" he told Suchan.

"You shouldn't have listened to him," said Suchan, shaking his head. He explained that his father had mental problems, for which he had spent time in hospital. But he didn't tell Boyd his father had been enraged at being left out of the spoils from the bank robbery. Boyd's anger quickly passed. "When something like that happens, I just take it as part of life," he says. He went into the bedroom to tell Willie about their loss.

"The money's gone," he said.

"What!"

"The old man took off with our money."

Willie grabbed his .45 and ran into the kitchen, where he pushed Elizabeth Lesso to the floor, sat on her chest, and held the gun to her face. "Where's the money?" he demanded. "I'm going to jam this right down your throat if you don't tell me! Where is it? And where's your goddamned husband?"

"I ... I don't know," said the terrified woman. "He went out through the front door early this morning."

It took Boyd several minutes to get Willie calmed down. "Threatening her isn't going to help anything," he said. "She has no money. Her old man's got it all. I told you, there's more where that came from. If we don't get it back, we'll get some more."

They wouldn't get their money back. Winter was three weeks away in Toronto, and Joseph Lesso had boarded a plane for a Florida vacation that would last more than three months. On February 22, 1952, eleven weeks after his departure, he sent his wife a letter, in Slovak, from St. Petersburg. The letter read: "Well greetings from Florida, from your husband ... Are you well? I am sending greetings also to my boy Valentine and to his friends. At the present time I am well. I feel better, but nobody can help my heart. I feel sad when I see families with children, playing on the sand. I am sending three pictures. Write me a few lines ... I will be here for three more weeks, so be well and I will come to see you in a few weeks."

One of the photographs Lesso sent back was of him with the movie star Roy Rogers. "His arm was around Roy Rogers' shoulder," says Boyd, "but it turned out to be just one of those cardboard cut-outs. It looked like the real thing, though."

Boyd suggested to Suchan that since it was his father who had taken the money, what was left of the four shares should be divided among them. Suchan scoffed at the idea: "You shouldn't have put your money in there."

On the Lam

Steve Suchan, Lennie Jackson, and Lennie's sister Mary Mitchell arrived in Montreal on December 3, 1951. Suchan had purchased a new Chrysler before the trip. He dropped Lennie off at Castle Tourist, the Mountain Street rooming house where Ann Roberts was waiting for him. Suchan and Mitchell went to the Berkley Hotel, where they registered as husband and wife under the names Victor J. Lenoff and Mary Lenoff. A few days later, using the same names, they moved into unit 330 at the Croydon Apartments, 3455 Côte de Neiges. Suchan signed a one-year lease at $145 per month.

The day after Lennie Jackson arrived back in Montreal, he set out to purchase a good used car, preferably another Oldsmobile. Assisting him was Montreal taxi driver Sidney Backman, a former travelling salesman whom Ann Roberts had met while on the road modelling. They visited several car dealers before Lennie settled on a navy-blue 1950 Oldsmobile. Jackson had the car he wanted, money in his pocket, and was with the woman he loved. For now his thoughts were of romance, not banks. He felt more secure living away from Toronto, but took steps to alter his appearance by growing a moustache and wearing black, horn-rimmed prescription glasses.

Boyd and Willie Jackson, no longer enamoured of their Lesso hideout, headed for Montreal a few days after the others, also taking rooms at the Berkley Hotel under false names. Even with the theft of three-quarters of his share of the robbery proceeds, Willie Jackson still had close to $3,000, and he was ready for a good time. He wasn't interested in a fancy apartment or a new car. Restaurants and bars were another matter. It soon became obvious to Boyd that at the rate his three partners were spending money, it wouldn't be long before they would have to rob another bank. They should have been keeping lower profiles and spending a lot less. "The only reason I was robbing banks was so I wouldn't have to work for a living, but here they were throwing money around and showing off to their friends."

A week before Christmas 1951, Willie Jackson was in a nightclub on St. Lawrence Boulevard in Montreal. He was in an expansive mood, turning on the charm and wit as he wooed a woman he had met a couple of nights before. As he downed drink after drink, what few inhibitions he had vanished like the smoke from his expensive cigar. The other patrons took notice as his voice rose and he flashed his roll of bills. He was breaking one of Boyd's cardinal rules: Don't draw attention to yourself. His suit jacket was unbuttoned so that whenever he leaned back he exposed the .45 revolver that was tucked into his belt. And on a visit to the washroom, to impress a stranger he purposely flashed the revolver and bragged about his "toughness." The stranger was impressed enough to telephone the police, who swooped into the nightclub and arrested Willie, who didn't resist. The revolver was fully loaded, and twenty bullets were found in his pockets.

He gave police the name he was using at the Berkley Hotel – William Gibson – but fingerprinting revealed his true identity. Willie survived a police line-up in connection with the recent armed hold-up of a Montreal tobacconist, but was charged with carrying an offensive weapon. On December 20, a Toronto detective and two OPP officers arrived to ask Willie about Boyd and Lennie Jackson, and to return him to Toronto to face a charge of escaping from the Don Jail.

Three days after Christmas he was sentenced to two years for the escape. It would be tacked on to the seven years and twenty lashes, for robbery with violence, that he had been facing before the escape. He said he knew nothing of the whereabouts of Boyd or Lennie Jackson, and told the court he had nothing to do with the sawing of the bars at the Don Jail. "I saw the window open and I went out," he said. "The others had gone." Willie was sent directly to Kingston Penitentiary.

Boyd, Suchan, and Mary Mitchell left Montreal for Toronto the day after Willie's arrest. Lennie Jackson and Ann Roberts had been talking about getting married, but she didn't have her divorce papers, which were required under Quebec law. They decided to try their luck in the Maritimes. They made it as far as Edmundston, New Brunswick, staying in tourist cabins along the way, but returned to Montreal when they were told there would be at least a five-day waiting period. Roberts decided she would simply declare to Quebec authorities that she had never been married before. "I registered myself as a spinster, and in this way we obtained a marriage licence," she would tell police later. On the licence application, Lennie listed his name as George Jackson Jr., and his occupation as hairdresser, and used the street and number of his mother's house in Niagara Falls as his address.

Ann and Lennie spent Christmas together in Montreal and were married on January 2, 1952, at St. James the Apostle Anglican Church. Ann Roberts was now Ann Jackson. A week later they checked out of their room at Castle Tourist and drove west on a five-week honeymoon that took them as far as Swift Current, Alberta. "This journey was made in the Oldsmobile," said Ann. "All during the tour Leonard carried the long-barrel revolver."

Most of Jackson's cash was gone by the time they returned to Montreal in early February. They took a room at 1519 Bishop Street while they looked for an apartment where they could do their own cooking. A week later they moved into a $12-a-week basement apartment in a small lowrise building at 1930 Lincoln Avenue just over a block from Suchan's apartment. It was a single-room apartment with kitchen facilities available off the hall. Soon after, Ann discovered that she was pregnant. Like Suchan, Lennie was going to be a father.

A few days before Christmas, Suchan, Mary Mitchell, and Ed Boyd had checked into the Sunnyside Motor Hotel on Lakeshore Boulevard in Toronto. Mitchell, who knew the proprietors, booked and paid for adjoining rooms No. 50 and No. 48. Suchan used his Montreal alias, Victor J. Lenoff, and Boyd checked in under the name Thompson, his wife's maiden name. He would stay at the Sunnyside three or four times over the next two months. On one occasion Boyd called a taxi to pick him up at the motel and was shocked when the driver who answered the call turned out to be his half-brother, Harold. "He took one look at me and nearly shit his pants," says Boyd, laughing at the memory. "He was scared to death."

"I don't want to take you anywhere," said Harold.

"Look, all you have to do is drive me up to where the streetcars are," said Boyd. Harold reluctantly agreed and drove him to Roncesvalles and Queen. "He took every side street he could find, and when I got out he took off like a bat out of hell."

Anna Camero's pregnancy was now well into the final month, and Steve Suchan managed to slip away from Mary Mitchell long enough to have dinner with her on Christmas Eve at her Wright Avenue home. Midway through the evening, Suchan told her he had to leave for a while but would return later. Instead, he returned to the motel to spend the rest of the night with Mary. Camero would not see him again until 1:30 a.m. on January 1, when he arrived on her doorstep to wish her a Happy New Year. "I was sick at this time, due to my pregnancy, and I told him not to come back," she said later. Camero gave birth to a son at Mount Sinai Hospital on Saturday, January 12. Suchan arrived at the hospital after the birth and stayed for two hours. He visited every day and drove Camero and their baby home from the hospital on January 16. Four days later, Suchan and Mary Mitchell were back in their Montreal apartment.

On Christmas day, Dorreen and the three children joined Boyd at the Sunnyside Motor Hotel. There was no Christmas tree, but they exchanged gifts and had a turkey dinner. It had been almost two months since his escape from the Don, and Boyd felt it was safe enough to chance a visit to the house in Pickering. He was there for New Year's Eve, and he and Dorreen decided she should probably give up the house and take an apartment while he worked out a plan for the future. Soon after, the children went to stay temporarily at the home of Bill Underwood, Boyd's friend who had operated the judo school. Boyd's eldest son Anthony, then eleven, was later sent north of Toronto to a farm owned by a minister who was a friend of Boyd's father. And the eight-year-old twins were enrolled in a boarding school. "It was kind of a ticklish time," says Boyd. "I wasn't used to being on the run, and I was thinking too much about hiding out instead of using my brain to work out a plan. Looking back now, I should have left some money with Dorreen and taken a train out to Western Canada. I could have made a new life and sent for her and the children later, or just hid out on my own." Dorreen stayed for a while with their friends Frank and Flo Lamb, but eventually found a room in a house near Avenue Road and Bloor Street, where Ed sometimes stayed.

On January 9, 1952, calling himself Charles Hunter of 17 Hillcrest Avenue, Montreal, Boyd purchased a grey 1951 Nash sedan. "I got a car that I could rely on. I used it to run back and forth to Montreal several times."

By mid-January, Boyd was down to his last few dollars and Suchan was complaining that he was nearly broke. Boyd decided it was time to rob another bank. He would have preferred Lennie Jackson's advice and participation, but Lennie was still out west with his new wife. "I didn't trust Suchan," says Boyd. "But Leonard knew what he was doing. He really was astute when it came to handling guns and throwing a scare into people. It was reassuring to have him standing at the door with a machine gun. If Len Jackson and I had hooked up without the others, we probably would have been still going."

Boyd picked the Bank of Toronto at 1436 Kingston Road as his next target. After studying the layout and possible escape routes, he decided he would need at least two more accomplices to pull it off. Boyd had met Willie Jackson's brother, thirty-one-year-old Joseph, who lived in Toronto. "Joe was a more serious type than Willie, but he was just as interested in the money and it didn't take much to convince him to go along."

Next, Boyd telephoned Suchan in Montreal. "I told him I was getting the job ready and gave him the date. He said he would be in Toronto the next day, but he didn't show up. I was mad as hell." No doubt Boyd also continued to harbour animosity towards Suchan for not sharing his take from the Royal Bank after his father walked away with most of Boyd's and Willie's share. Boyd waited two days and telephoned Suchan again.

"What the hell are you doing?" he shouted into the phone. "I had this job all ready to go."

"Oh, I thought you were just fooling," was Suchan's feeble response.

"Hell, I don't fool about things like that! I've already lined up another man to help, and if you're not in, I'll get somebody to replace you." Suchan and Mary Mitchell were in Toronto the next morning.

To Boyd's surprise, Mary wanted to participate in the robbery. He thought it over and agreed.

Waldimar Weisman parked his 1950 black Ford sedan behind the College Theatre at College and Dovercourt about 11 p.m. on January 24, planning to leave it there until morning. But during the night Boyd hot-wired the car and drove it to a rented garage, where he replaced the licence plates with a set stolen from an auto wrecker.

About 11 a.m. the next morning, Boyd was whistling softly as he entered the Bank of Toronto, on Kingston Road near Warden, with Suchan and Joe Jackson. Teller Beverley Machesney was standing at the rear of the bank facing the front door when Boyd came in and walked towards her. She was about to ask, "What can I do for you?" when he produced a revolver. "It's a stick-up!" he shouted. The manager, Robert Chambers, was standing near Machesney and turned when he heard the words. Boyd ordered them and the other employees to face the wall and lie face down on the floor.

Mrs. Murray Finlay, who lived across the street from the bank, dropped in to make a deposit and was confronted by Boyd. "Get over to the wall," he said, waving his gun at her. She stood frozen. He nudged her with the barrel. "Face the wall!" he ordered. "It's a stick-up." She went to the wall but stood facing the interior of the bank, and saw Boyd leave the main cashier's cage and move to the north end of the bank to empty the cash drawers there. Then he vaulted the counter and went through the manager's office to the accountant's desk, where Mrs. Finlay watched as he pried open the drawers. "At this time he was looking directly at me and grinning," she said.

David Forgie, a Scarborough fireman, was standing in the doorway of the bank talking to a friend when the three gunmen came out of the bank, one of them carrying a cloth bag. Forgie heard someone shout that there had been a hold-up, and he started after them until Suchan turned and pointed a revolver at him. Forgie retreated to the doorway as the gunmen jumped into the stolen Ford and sped off. Forgie was able to get the licence number. The getaway car headed west on Kingston Road and then north on Cornell Avenue. They drove about four blocks to a Dominion Store parking lot, where Mary was waiting in another car. She drove through the city while they lay on the floor out of sight.

The robbery netted $10,000 and a .38 calibre Ivor Johnson revolver. The newspapers gave the story the usual dramatic play, with photos and screaming headlines, and the police had no doubt the Boyd Gang was at work again. Later, one witness would make a lukewarm identification of Joe Jackson, and charges against him would be dropped at a preliminary hearing. Several witnesses would identify Boyd and Suchan, but defence lawyers would raise enough doubts that they too were eventually acquitted.

TORONTO DAILY STAR

THE WEATHER

ROB SCARBORO BANK OF $15,000

TAKE GUN, KICK CLERK
AT KINGSTON RD. BANK
3 FLEE IN STOLEN CAR

HOME AND SPORT EDITION

2 Young Brothers, Sister
Burn to Death at Washago

RT. HON. VINCENT MASSEY, LOUIS BREITHAUPT TO ASSUME HIGH OFFICES

After the robbery, Steve Suchan and Mary Mitchell took a short working vacation to the United States. Suchan, the former King Edward Hotel doorman, had befriended Edward Allard, the doorman at their Montreal apartment building. Allard would tell the Toronto police that Suchan, whom he knew as Vic Lenoff, had several times invited him up to his third-floor apartment. The visits were short, since he could not leave his post for more than five minutes at a time. On one occasion Suchan played the violin for him. On another he demonstrated his marksmanship using an air pistol to shoot at magazine covers. On January 30, 1952, a postcard addressed to "Eddie (Doorman)" at the Croydon Apartments was sent from Syracuse, New York. The card read: "Hello Ed. Having a pleasant trip so far, will send you a card from New York." It was signed Vic and Mary Lenoff. A second card followed from New York City a few days later. The message was similar: "Hello Ed. Having a wonderful time here. See you soon." While in New York, Suchan also telephoned Anna Camero, telling her he was there on business. On their way back to

Montreal, Suchan and Mitchell stopped in Buffalo, where he placed an order for several handguns through an underworld contact. The guns would arrive in Montreal a few days later.

Lennie and Ann Jackson were back from their honeymoon by the time Suchan and Mitchell returned to Montreal in the second week of February. On Valentine's Day, Suchan's twenty-fourth birthday, he sent greetings via telegram to Anna Camero and their month-old baby. Two days later, Sunday, February 17, Suchan arrived in Toronto for a short visit, during which Camero expressed her displeasure at how he was treating both her and their son. Her displeasure would deepen a few days later when she received a letter from him asking for $200. His cut of the bank robbery loot had been just over $3,000, but his trip to New York, the weapons purchase, and his taste for expensive suits and fine restaurants had left him nearly broke again. When Camero ignored the letter, he telephoned her and was able to convince her to wire the money to him. She was at home ill, but wrote a cheque to her mother, who in turn purchased a money order and wired it to Victor J. Lenoff on February 26. That money would-n't last long, and he would soon be forced to sell his car.

Ed Boyd was disappointed in the take from the most recent bank robbery, and he was becoming disillusioned and despondent. "It was kind of difficult to be a member of a bunch of crooks and at the same time have to raise a family. I tried to do it but it wasn't possible." And he felt his gang had let him down. "I was a guy who trusted people. I thought if you were a crook – like in the James Cagney pictures – the guys backed each other up. But they didn't do that in Toronto. They always stuck with their own group. I wasn't really pulled into their company. Whenever a bank robbery was over, they were away with their buddies and their women. They never came near me. The only time they came near me was when they wanted help with a bank robbery. I was trying to make an income from robbing banks, and so I would plan one and I'd get them into it. Len Jackson wasn't around much, and Suchan didn't listen. They boasted a lot about what they were doing. I learned in Kingston some of these underworld types were narcotics peddlers and the like. If I had known that, I might just stayed away from all of them."

But Boyd planned another robbery and got the word to Suchan and Jackson in Montreal. They agreed to a date for the job but failed to show up. This time he decided to go ahead without them. And this time he would use most of the proceeds to build a future. His plan was to pay a minimum fee to whomever he recruited, and start a nest egg to purchase a small apartment building or rooming house. He would offer his new partners a share in the project. He envisioned himself living in the building, which he would manage and maintain, with the income from rentals going to support his family and pay his partners.

Boyd approached Willie Jackson's brother Joe, who quickly agreed to the proposal. He would receive $2,000 from the robbery and would be a junior partner in the rooming house scheme.

"Do you know anybody else we can get to come in on it?" asked Boyd.

"Well, there's my brother-in-law, Allister Gibson," said Jackson after a moment's thought. Both Jackson and twenty-five-year-old Gibson were living at 327 Jarvis Street.

"Gibson was just in on the one robbery," says Boyd. "We talked him into it because we needed another guy. He liked the money part, so Joe and I played that up pretty good. He saw we were living off the top of the land, so he figured he'd get in on it too."

Gibson would tell police later that he thought over Boyd's propo-sition "and decided to go into it to see if I couldn't make a better life for my wife and family, as I was sick of living in the hole I was in. I had worked steady for the past six years for the same company, with the exception of six months when I went to the tobacco fields to try and make more money. I guess I didn't realize what I was getting into."

Boyd set his plan in motion on February 28, 1952, when he stole the licence plates from a Nash coupe. Sometime before noon the same day, he stole a dark-green 1948 Chevrolet coupe from the park-ing lot behind the A&P Store at Yonge Street and Lawrence Avenue. Boyd drove the car to a garage he had rented behind a house on Euclid Avenue between College and Dundas Streets. There he switched the licence plates.

Four days later, at 12:25 p.m., Boyd parked the stolen Chev a few doors west of the Bank of Montreal on the north side of College

Street at Manning. He sat in the car while Jackson and Gibson entered the bank and mingled with the customers. Then he entered and walked to the rear of the bank, and the hold-up went into action.

Teller Margaret Smith was running some cheques on the adding machine with her back turned when she heard Boyd shout, "This is a hold-up!" She quickly turned and tried to get to the floor alarm in her cage. "But the man jumped right over the top of the cage, and right down in front of me," she told police. "He had a gun and told me to get out of there and face the wall." Smith complied, but glanced back to see the gunman scooping the money from her till into a shopping bag. The cage beside hers was locked. But "he tore the top of the cage door off and cleaned it out."

There were more than thirty customers and staff in the bank, and Gibson was petrified. "My job was to jump the counter and clean out the money in the middle tills," he said. "I did jump the counter and waved my gun and got the bank employees to face the wall, but I was too scared to touch the money." Joe Jackson was at the front of the bank holding a revolver on the customers as Boyd cleaned out the tills.

A clerk was in the basement of the bank gathering papers for a messenger when he heard a commotion upstairs and heard a voice shout, "This is a hold-up!" The clerk got halfway up the stairs before deciding it might be wiser to stay in the basement. He retreated, and flipped the alarm switch, believing it would ring at the police station. But he had not been instructed in how to use the switch and had turned it to the *off* position. Upstairs, two employees had managed to press alarm buttons, but because the system was off, the police department was not alerted.

Marie Upritchard, the manager's stenographer, was sitting on a swivel chair at her desk typing when Boyd announced the hold-up. "I was so nervous, I couldn't do anything but stare," she told police. She said Boyd kept checking his watch and shouting orders to the others. "I just couldn't turn away from the calm one … the leader. I was fascinated by him." Another witness described Boyd as "very handsome."

The *Telegram* and the *Star* ran banner headlines with wildly differing estimates of the amount taken. In the body of the *Tely*'s main story about the hold-up, it was reported that "Edwin Alonzo Boyd, suspected mastermind of many of the robberies, is still at large." The actual take from the robbery was $24,696, about $4,000 of which was in U.S. bills.

TORONTO DAILY STAR

60TH YEAR   TUESDAY, MARCH 4, 1952—40 PAGES   3c PER COPY, 18c PER WEEK

COLLEGE BANK LOOT SAID $50,000

Waiting Period Cut to Pay
Millions More to Jobless

HOME AND SPORT EDITION

City Water Fluoridation
Favored by Health Board

HEALTH BOARD ADOPTS FLUORIDATION PLAN

THE TELEGRAM

Night
Final Sports–Markets

70TH YEAR   34 PAGES   TORONTO, TUESDAY, MARCH 4, 1952   PRICE 5 CENTS

12 Banks Looted In 14 Months

ARMED 3 GRAB $24,000

The afternoon traffic was heavy. Boyd drove the getaway car west two or three blocks along College Street before cutting south and circling back to the garage on Euclid, just a couple of blocks from the bank.

In a statement to Detective Dolph Payne five weeks after the robbery, Gibson said Boyd paid him $1,000.

"Is there any of this money left?" asked Payne.

"No."

"What did you do with the thousand dollars?"

"I spent three hundred of it on a Studebaker car, gave away two hundred, took a trip to the United States, and spent the rest on clothes for my boy."

"Is there anything further you wish to say?"

"I'm glad it's off my mind, and it will never happen again."

Joe Jackson told Payne that all of the $2,000 Boyd paid him went into buying and repairing vehicles.

Boyd would explain to Payne that he kept most of the money from the robbery because "we intended to invest a large portion of it in a rooming house, the profits or income to be split between us." He also told Payne that the only reason he went back to robbing banks "was because I was up against it and needed money to support my wife and children."

Politics and Intrigue

T he escape of Edwin Alonzo Boyd and Lennie and Willie Jackson from the Don Jail, and a new surge in bank robberies around Toronto, precipitated a political and public outcry that resulted in a shake-up at the Don Jail and at City Hall.

The influence of the rigid Col. G. Hedley Basher was again felt at the Don Jail when the provincial government plucked him from the Guelph Reformatory, where he had been superintendent since February 1946, and appointed him deputy minister of the Department of Reform Institutions. His appointment took effect January 1, 1952, and by the end of the month the Don's progressive governor, Charles Sanderson, was gone. Both prisoners and guards had liked Sanderson and feared his job was in jeopardy because of the escapes. The Civil Service Association of Ontario, representing the guards, took pre-emptive action at a meeting in early November 1951, when it approved a "spontaneous vote of confidence … with reference to your administration and policy" and promised Sanderson close co-operation in the future. But such sentiment didn't stop Basher.

Sanderson left the Don Jail on January 28, 1952, after just eighteen months on the job. Basher transferred him to the Burwash prison farm and replaced him with Thomas Woodward Brand. Basher had first met Brand during a riot in Burwash in 1947. Brand had been there for two and a half years at the time and was in charge of 150 inmates in Burwash's outlying camps. "I was very much impressed with the manner in which he had this place under control and the manner in which it was operated, despite the fact there had been very serious disturbances in the main institution," Basher said later. "He had such good control of his unit there was no difficulty whatsoever."

When Basher took over the Guelph Reformatory, he had brought Brand in as assistant superintendent. Now he appointed him governor of the Don Jail. Brand liked many of the programs Sanderson had introduced, and made only a few minor changes. Overall discipline was tightened somewhat, but prisoners continued to feel that they were being treated in a civilized manner.

Meanwhile, on January 1, Allan Lamport had taken over as mayor of Toronto, following his victory at the polls in the fall election. Lamport was a feisty, flamboyant self-promoter who had pushed hard as an alderman and controller to bring taverns, Sunday sports, and lotteries to Toronto. He considered himself a crime-busting mayor and a strong supporter of the police. He was also pushing hard for amalgamation of Toronto with its neighbours. Lamport, who turned ninety-four in April 1997, remains in good health and as outspoken as ever. In his day he was a soldier, alderman, mayor, provincial Member of Parliament, and chairman of the TTC. He was awarded the Order of Canada in 1994.

In the late 1940s Lamport pushed to have taverns licensed when he saw carloads of Torontonians travelling to Buffalo to drink. He wanted them to spend their money in Toronto. "For a long time I stood alone at council on that one," he says. A 1950 magazine article stated that "Lamport was the only city politician to speak solidly in support of cocktail bars and now that they are open he is probably the only city politician who has absolutely no compunctions about visiting – or being seen in them."

Lamport was defeated in his first run for mayor in 1950 but won the next time "even with the churches and the newspapers against me." When he took office as mayor – the last mayor before amalgamation – he went on the offensive against the bankers and defended the police. He blamed the banks for having so much cash lying around with very little protection. "The bank guns weren't much good, because these crooks had more nerve than any manager or teller with a gun, and you know who'd get shot first. We had an organized gang

– the Boyd Gang – which was the toughest outside of New York City, but we had some very courageous police officers like Chief Harold Chisholm, and Payne, and Sergeant Tong. We had some great soldiers in that department."

Lamport wanted the banks to install secure, vaultlike rooms in their basements where transactions involving large sums of money would be conducted by appointment, leaving minimal amounts in the tills upstairs for day-to-day business. "They would have had to spend a little money, but that would have cleaned it up entirely."

When the bankers said the proposal wasn't feasible, Lamport threatened them with special taxes to cover the policing costs of so many robberies. "The cops were spending so much time on bank robberies we didn't have them for other things. I'm not condemning the banks, but Boyd and these other guys were prepared to do a lot of thinking and outsmarting, and they got away with it. They were breaking in right and left."

Jack Webster was a motorcycle policeman in Toronto at the time and said some bank employees were frightened to go to work. "I can remember very well when the calls would come over that there was a bank job – the Boyd Gang strikes again. If you were in that area, you would be searching back lanes and stopping cars and looking in cars. Bank staffs, the majority of them female tellers, were terrorized. The banks were being hit far and wide – the east end, North York, Bradford…. Dolph Payne told me that in conversations he had with bank managers, they didn't know how they were going to operate. Staff were frightened to come to work. And you can understand how a young woman or a young man would feel – suddenly having a gun thrust in their face – it was a frightening situation."

Lamport says the sensational newspaper coverage of the bank robberies added to the pressure on him and the police to crack down. "The papers just *snappled* on to this," he says, and the readers loved it. "A good story sent a quiver up their back and made them feel that they belonged to a big lively city."

Lamport was on the job less than a month when the Boyd Gang robbed the Bank of Toronto on Kingston Road. Five weeks later, there was the College Street robbery. Two other banks were held up by other gunmen in that same period. In those days the mayor of Toronto was also the city's chief magistrate and chairman of the police commission, and this gave Lamport all the more reason to bring the Boyd Gang and other bank robbers to heel. "This was all a big strain on me," says Lamport. "They knew we meant business. They got wise to me being pretty tough. It was my duty and I fulfilled it."

When Boyd robbed the Bank of Toronto with Suchan and Joe Jackson on January 25, they made the front pages, but Lamport grabbed the biggest headlines when he condemned "secret deals" at the CNE that were creating "midway millionaires ... at the expense of the city taxpayers." He promised to open the books and to ensure that future midway contracts were open to public tender. "I've only begun to scratch the surface," said Lamport.

John Sanderson, a retired elementary school principal in Sault Ste. Marie, recalls visiting Eddie Tong's family in Toronto. Sanderson had grown up in Harriston, a small farming community about ninety miles northwest of Toronto, and Tong and his family used to vacation at the nearby Gordon farm. "I went to high school with Lamont Gordon, whose family owned the farm," says Sanderson. "Around 1950, Lamont and I stayed with the Tong family for a couple of days while we were in Toronto. I was about seventeen or eighteen at the time. I never forgot it because the Tongs had a pet skunk, and I was a little scared of it. It had been fixed, but I think its sweat or something still had a skunky smell. Maybe I was imagining it, but I was sure I could smell it."

Sanderson says the warmth and closeness of the Tong family were obvious. "I liked Tong. He was a bear of a man. At seventeen or eighteen you're not usually impressed with *any* adult, but he impressed me a lot."

Tong took Sanderson and Lamont to the CNE. Tong would walk up to a game concession and grab a stuffed animal or toy that was being offered as a prize and hold it out to him and Lamont. "You want this?" he would laugh. "You can have anything you like."

"He was just joking, and he'd put it back," says Sanderson, "but he said nearly all of them in the booths had records and were on his sheet – they were his informants."

Eddie Tong had one informant who, in early March of 1952, would pass him information that would prove disastrous for Steve Suchan and Lennie Jackson – and for Tong himself. The informant was Jackson's own sister, Mary Mitchell. She had told her brother and the rest of the gang that she talked to Tong from time to time, but only to see if she could find out if the police were closing in on them. But all that changed when her relationship with Suchan became strained after the birth of his son. He was feeling guilty about Anna Camero, who wasn't shy about telling him he was neglecting her and the baby.

Mary Mitchell was still jealous and worked out a plan that she thought would keep Suchan away from Camero. On one of her visits with Tong, sometime in mid to late February, she gave him a description and the licence number of Camero's car and told him that underworld types were using it to transport stolen goods to Montreal. Later she would tell Suchan and her brother that she gave Tong the information only after he had burned her breasts with a lit cigarette. She even showed them the burn marks. Suchan and Jackson believed her story and were enraged.

Dolph Payne and Jack Gillespie – and eventually Ed Boyd – believed that the burns to Mary Mitchell's chest were superficial and self-inflicted. "Every time I saw her come out of Tong's office, she was smiling," said Payne. "I didn't see her every time she came out of there, naturally, but Tong would never have burned her. Mary Mitchell was a wicked woman."[21] Gillespie, who worked with Tong, said Mary Mitchell was giving information to Tong "and at the same time she was going back to the guys and saying that Eddie beat her up and did this to her and that to her – which was a bunch of bloody lies. But that made Suchan and Lennie really hostile towards Eddie. And Eddie would never do that. She was really mad at Suchan for fooling around with the other woman. You couldn't believe Mary Mitchell. Her saying that Eddie Tong burned her was all bullshit."

Boyd didn't hear until later about Mary's claims regarding Tong. "She just said that Tong had been questioning her, and that was about it. She said she never told him anything, but all the time she was telling him everything. She was a nice person to talk to but she was always on the lookout for guys who had money." Boyd lays some of the blame on Suchan "because he used to lay on the line to Mitchell that he could be trusted, but it was all crap – he was always fooling around."

Dorreen Boyd was seeing more of her husband now that she had given up the Pickering house and the children were with others. She made a couple of trips to Montreal with Boyd, staying at Suchan and Mary Mitchell's apartment, and got to observe the gang at first hand. There seemed to be mutual respect between Lennie Jackson and her husband. "Lennie was a nice guy," she says. "I liked him. He was such a doll – good looking and very well-spoken, too. He was such a gentle guy, was Lennie. And Ann was a nice girl." She says Boyd didn't like Suchan because he didn't trust him. "But could Suchan ever play the violin. Oh God, he was good. He had it with him there in Montreal." Dorreen has no kind words for Mary Mitchell, saying only, "She was a whore."

It will never be known whether Suchan eventually came to disbelieve Mitchell's story about Tong burning her, or if he took a calculated risk by continuing to stay in contact with Camero. He liked travelling with Mitchell and sharing the Montreal apartment with her, but now he was almost out of money. There would be no more travel for pleasure or expensive restaurant meals until he robbed another bank. Mitchell returned to Toronto near the end of February, knowing Suchan would soon be following.

Lennie and Ann Jackson were still in their basement apartment on Lincoln Avenue, where Jackson was passing himself off as Fred Wilson, a salesman. The building's caretakers, Laurette and Henri Côté, would see him leave the building each morning about 10 and return between 5:30 and 6 p.m., usually carrying a briefcase. "I did question him as to what he did while he was away in the daytime," said Ann, "but he accused me of nagging him and I did not question him further. He continued to carry his gun with him when he went out, with the exception of when he went to get a haircut. He would have to take his coat off and someone might see the gun."

Shortly after Mitchell left for Toronto, Lennie and Ann invited

Suchan to their apartment for dinner. The Jacksons had only two place settings, and Suchan brought his own plate and cutlery. "Why don't I drive you over to see my apartment," Suchan suggested after the meal. The three of them piled into his black Chrysler and drove to the Croydon Apartments. "The apartment was sparsely furnished with no curtains," said Ann Jackson, "and it appeared to me as if he was living alone. He said he couldn't afford to keep it any longer and he was going to move."

A few days later, Suchan was on a train back to Toronto. He telephoned Anna Camero twice on Monday, March 3, and arrived at her house shortly before midnight. "He was alone and we remained up most of the night arguing," said Camero. "I was not very satisfied with the way he had been treating me."

Camero's telephone rang the next morning about 7 a.m., and Suchan answered it. It was Lennie Jackson calling from the train station in Oshawa. He wanted Suchan to come and pick him up. Taking the train into Union Station in Toronto would be too dangerous. The call had awakened Anna Camero.

"I have to go and meet a friend," said Suchan. "Can I borrow your car?" She handed him the keys. He returned to the house about 9:30 a.m. accompanied by Lennie Jackson, whom Camero still knew only as Freddie. He had been clean-shaven the last time she saw him, but now he had a moustache. He had also gained weight and was wearing horn-rimmed glasses. Jackson went to sleep in the back room while Suchan lay down in Camero's room. Camero went into the living room with the baby. Jackson slept about an hour and then came into the living room, where he lay on the chesterfield and talked to her. Suchan slept until mid-afternoon.

Camero's friend Betty Huluk was still living at the house and when she arrived after work she brought along a newspaper. Camero was busy with the baby and passed the paper to Suchan. She noticed Suchan and Jackson huddled in hushed but animated conversation over something they saw in the newspaper. "I found out later there was a headline about a robbery," she said. "They said they were going out to get something to eat, and they returned before midnight."

What Suchan and Jackson had seen in the newspaper was an account of Boyd's heist of $24,696 from the Bank of Montreal at College and Manning. He had pulled it off without them. They met up with Boyd and Dorreen later that night.

"Suchan had run out of money completely," says Boyd. "He had sold his car and he was just kind of marking time. I told them when they didn't show up I went ahead with the robbery without them." Dorreen told Suchan he wasn't getting any of the money.

"Well I don't want it," said Suchan. "I'm not the one who robbed the bank." Boyd says Suchan wanted a cut of the loot, but was in no position to ask for it after freezing him and Willie Jackson out when Joseph Lesso went off to Florida with their money.

Anna Camero was in bed by the time Suchan and Jackson returned to her house around midnight. During the day she had noticed on the dresser in her room a textbook on pistols and revolvers and the 1952 edition of *Gun Digest*. There was also a metal target and two air pistols in a box. "What is this?" she asked Suchan when he came in.

"Oh, it's a set I got as a Christmas present," he said.

On Wednesday, March 5, Suchan and Jackson got up about 10 a.m., borrowed Camero's Monarch, and went out two or three times for short periods. In the afternoon they spent some time in Camero's basement, and when they came up, each was carrying one of the air pistols.

"Are they harmful?" asked Camero.

"No," said Suchan. "You can use darts or pellets with them. It's not harmful."

"Well what are you doing with them?"

"We were just trying them out."

"Well as long as they're not harmful. I wouldn't want them around the house because my little girl could injure herself."

A few days later she discovered that a life-size plaster "dummy head" and a papier-mâché torso, stored in the basement since her hairdressing days, had been damaged. The plaster head and the torso's chest were riddled with holes. Steve Suchan and Lennie Jackson had used both for target practice.

In Cold Blood

On the morning of Thursday, March 6, Suchan and Jackson were up about 9 a.m. Anna Camero had already left the house. She had driven to Fern Avenue School to check into complaints that her daughter had been arriving late for school. When Camero returned, Suchan asked to borrow the car. Camero took pride in her 1951 black Monarch sedan with whitewall tires. She had purchased it new from Elgin Motors, and she took good care of it. Now it had some minor scrapes and dents, and she blamed Suchan. They argued about it for a while, but as usual, she gave in to him. She couldn't find her keys and gave him a spare set from her dresser drawer. Suchan and Jackson left, but returned a short time later, handing her the keys.

Camero's friend, Betty Huluk, had the afternoon off and arrived home from work about 12:30 p.m. Her room was the first off the hallway, and on this day she left her door open. At about 12:45 she saw Suchan and Jackson go out the front door. She didn't notice that they were carrying bulging briefcases.

There has been a lot of speculation about where Suchan and Jackson were headed on that fateful day. Suchan would testify in court later that he was driving Jackson to the bus station on Bay Street for a trip to Oshawa, where he would catch the train to Montreal. But Jackson knew that the bus station was just as dangerous for him as Union Station, which he had avoided when he arrived in Toronto. He knew from his days at the Horseshoe that Tong had informants everywhere, and he knew that his picture and Boyd's were likely posted at the bus terminal. If he was planning to return to Montreal, why wouldn't Suchan simply drive him to the train station in Oshawa, where he had picked him up? On a more mundane level, since he was travelling without luggage, why would he leave his custom-tailored sports jacket hanging in Camero's house? The more likely scenario is that he and Suchan were intent on either robbing a bank that day, or casing a bank to rob later. Both of them were out of money, and they certainly weren't about to go out and look for work. Jackson's new wife was pregnant, and he may have wanted to move east or west to start a new life. If so, he couldn't do it without a stake, and the quickest, easiest way to get one was to rob a bank. They had the experience and the guns. And hadn't Boyd, just two days before, walked out of a bank with almost $25,000 for three minutes' work, using two rookie accomplices?

Whatever their plans, it is known that Suchan found Camero's car keys, and that he and Jackson drove off from Wright Avenue shortly before 1 p.m. They had failed to heed Mary Mitchell's warning that she had told Sergeant of Detectives Edmund Tong that Anna Camero's 1951 black Monarch sedan, license No. 418-A-2, was being used by unnamed criminals to transport stolen property to Montreal.

Tong and his partner, Detective-Sergeant Roy Perry, had been watching the Monarch for several days, but had yet to see anyone driving it. Tong had told Perry only that the car was owned by a woman, whom he wasn't yet ready to question. "I have information that the car is sometimes driven by someone other than the owner," he told Perry.

Perry and Tong were driving north on Roncesvalles Avenue when they saw a black Monarch pull out from Wright Avenue just ahead of them. "Get on him – that might be it," said Tong to Perry, who was driving the police cruiser.

There were several cars between them and the Monarch, and they weren't close enough to check the licence number or see who was driving. They followed as the car turned east off Roncesvalles and took several side streets before emerging on Dundas Street West. There, the officers got close enough to confirm that the licence number was the one they were looking for and that two males were in the front seat. Both cars continued east and entered College Street. As the Monarch approached the intersection at Lansdowne, Suchan began to slow as he saw cars in front of him stopping for a red light. Behind him, Perry decided to make a move and pulled beside the other car. Tong rolled down his window.

"Pull over to the curb, boys," he said.

The cars were no more than three or four feet apart. Suchan and Tong had never met and didn't know each other. Whether Jackson recognized Tong's voice or caught a glimpse of him will never be known. Nor is there any way of knowing whether Tong could see Lennie on the other side of Suchan. And even if he could, would he have recognized him with the moustache and glasses? Suchan must have known, however, that it was a police car. Who else would be pulling him over? And he quickly realized that if he stopped, his world would completely unravel. Both he and Jackson were armed. He was harbouring an escaped fugitive. He had harboured Edwin Alonzo Boyd, who was on the RCMP's most-wanted list. And he had participated in several bank robberies. There were plenty of witnesses. He could be picked out of a police line-up. All of these thoughts must have been tumbling through Suchan's mind as he slowly eased the Monarch to the curb. The police car was still beside him, but it had stopped and its hood was adjacent to the Monarch's rear fender. By now the light had turned green and the cars behind were moving around them and through the intersection. Suchan gripped his .455 Smith & Wesson revolver.

Tong got out and approached the Monarch. When he was within three or four feet, he seemed to hesitate and twist his body in a half-turn to the right. Perry heard a shot at the same time and saw Tong fall heavily, face down, to the pavement. The bullet had entered his chest slightly below the left nipple, passing through his lung, severing his spinal cord, and lodging under his right shoulder-blade. As Perry yanked at the emergency brake, a bullet ripped through the right-hand side of the windshield past his ear. Instinctively, he threw up his right arm to protect his head. He saw a flash as the driver fired again. More shots followed as he tried to get out of the cruiser. Suddenly he felt a sharp pain and his right arm went numb as a bullet struck him between the wrist and the elbow. If his arm hadn't been raised he likely would have been shot in the head.

Jackson would testify later that when he saw a figure approaching the car "through the corner of my left eye ... I opened the door ...

and was in the act of fleeing." But as he started towards the rear of the car, he heard a volley of shots. With that, he drew his revolver to protect himself. He aimed at the other car from behind the Monarch, but didn't fire. Some witnesses said he did fire, others said he didn't. Perry thought Jackson fired at least once, but there was no forensic evidence or spent casings to prove it. Jackson could see a man lying face down in the street and could tell by the large aerial that the other car was a police cruiser. As Suchan put the car into first gear and it began moving forward, Jackson jumped in.

"Christ! That was a cruiser," he said. "Let's get out of here!" Suchan gunned the motor and they roared away, through a red light, east on College.

Perry blacked out, and next remembers someone shaking him and asking if he was all right. He looked up to see the black Monarch going east on College. Reaching for the police radio, he gasped into the mike: "Two gunmen ... College/Lansdowne ... ambulance ... hurry...." It has never been firmly established, but it's believed that Perry was not armed, having left his service revolver in his desk at College Street police headquarters.

Laura Price was behind the police cruiser and witnessed the shooting. When the Monarch drove off she left her car and went to Tong's aid. "He was lying face down with one arm under his head," she said. Truck driver William Fawcett ran to her side to help. Price said Tong "motioned with his finger for me to bend down closer, and when I did so, he spelled out a name and I spelled it to the truck driver. He also gave me an address on Wright Avenue."

Price leaned in even closer to Tong. "Who did it?" she asked. "Bank robbers," he replied. The name he had spelled out, she said, was Steve Suchan. How did Tong know it was Suchan, who had only a minor record for passing bad cheques? Either Mary Mitchell had given him the name or, through his informants, Tong was finally closing in on Suchan. Since Tong didn't mention Jackson's name, he either didn't get a good look at him or didn't recognize him.

The information that Tong gave Laura Price was on a slip of paper in Fawcett's shirt pocket, but Fawcett thought it was the injured policeman's own name and address. When ambulances and other police arrived, Fawcett continued his deliveries. But when he called to check in with his office later, he was told the name of the downed officer was Tong. "It was then I realized that he had been trying to give some information, so I immediately called the police, and turned the slip of paper over to the officer who arrived."

Another witness to the shooting, Charles Waddell, said he heard a shot and saw Tong "crumple and fall" to the street. "That shot came from the driver of the car," he said. "Then there was a black revolver thrust out the window of the car" and three more shots were fired at the police car. He also saw Jackson jump from the Monarch and point a gun at the police car. "I did not see him fire," he said. "But he turned and looked squarely towards me. Then he ran back and jumped into the car and it pulled away." He and other witnesses said Jackson was wearing a dark "winter weight" overcoat and a grey fedora.

Suchan and Jackson knew they had to dump the black Monarch as quickly as possible. The police would be swarming after them in minutes. They continued east on College Street for four blocks and then turned right on Sheridan Avenue. Crossing Dundas, they continued south until they spotted a taxi parked on the street. Suchan parked down the street from the taxi, and he and Jackson walked back and got in.

"Twenty-seven Sorauren," said Suchan.

The taxi pulled up at the side entrance to his parents' house, and the driver was told to wait. Inside, Suchan telephoned Anna Camero and told her to call the police immediately and tell them her car had been stolen. "But why, what's going on?" she asked.

"Just do it," said Suchan. "It's better if you don't know."

Suchan would say later, "I knew if she didn't phone she would be in a heap of trouble."

Suchan and Jackson quickly left the Lesso house for the waiting taxi, Suchan carrying his briefcase loaded with weapons and ammunition. They slipped into the back seat, and the taxi headed south on Sorauren.

It was unheard of – policemen didn't get shot down on the streets of Toronto in broad daylight. But it was true. The public was outraged, and the newspapers unleashed a frenzy of coverage. Tong was fighting for his life at Toronto General Hospital and if he survived he would probably be paralysed. The story was fluid, and over the next two days every possible angle would be covered as the newspapers – the *Telegram* and the *Star* in particular – looked for scoops that would win the circulation battle. As the story unfolded, both papers used massive banner headlines and filled page after page with photos, maps, and diagrams.

THE TELEGRAM

GUNMEN FIRE FROM CAR SHOOT TWO DETECTIVES

TORONTO DAILY STAR

2 DETECTIVES SHOT IN GUN FIGHT

TORONTO OFFICER SHOT AS POLICE CHASE TRIO THOUGHT BANK ROBBERS

HOME AND SPORT EDITION

NOMINATE PEARSON, ST. LAURENT FOR NOBEL PRIZE

BACKED BY 56 M.P.'S BEVAN DEFIES ATTLEE LABOR SPLIT WIDE OPEN

Toronto historian Mike Filey says that until Tong was shot, "it was almost kind of a *WOW!* story, rather than these were really bad people. But after the policeman was shot, people said, 'Whoa! this isn't as much fun as we thought it was.' "

Mayor Lamport, frustrated by all the unsolved bank robberies, could barely contain his fury over the shooting of the two police officers – *his* officers. He called it a "reign of terror" and said the city would put up a reward for the gunmen. He also demanded registration of all guns in the city as a deterrent, and said he was sending wires to the presidents of all the banks with branches in Toronto urging them to post armed guards in bulletproof observation bulkheads as a deterrent to bank robbers. Lamport and Chief of Police Harold

Chisholm said one thousand policemen were combing the city in search of the suspects.

Jack Webster, then a uniformed officer, said that Toronto policemen of all ranks were willing to work seven days a week, without any remuneration, to get the men who shot Tong and Perry. "It wasn't long before the wanted posters were out. There weren't enough detectives to check out every tip, so they used uniformed men to make sure every one was checked out. The shootings had a traumatic effect on police officers. I was thinking, it could be me, or it could be any one of us. We've got to get this gang out of existence."

Detective Jack Gillespie was at home with his pregnant wife, doing some painting around the house, when he heard about the shootings on the radio. He lived on St. Helens Avenue about a block-and-a-half north of the Lansdowne and College intersection. "I ran all the way down there, but both Tong and Perry had been taken to the hospital by ambulance. Then I went right in to work."

The Toronto police wasted little time issuing the names and descriptions of the suspects. Tong had provided Suchan's name and address to civilian witnesses at the scene, and he did the same when two police detectives arrived before the ambulance. Barely conscious, Tong again whispered the information to them: "It was Steve Suchan, 190 Wright Avenue." The detectives discovered that Tong's right hand, doubled beneath him, was touching the handle of his police revolver, which was half out of his overcoat pocket. Police investigators speculated later that Tong was probably going for his gun and trying to turn away when he saw Suchan raise his revolver.

In his hospital room that night Tong was breathing with the aid of an oxygen mask. As he drifted in and out of consciousness, his long-time friend, Inspector of Detectives John Nimmo, held up several photographs in front of him and asked: "Who did this to you?"

"That's him," whispered Tong when Nimmo held up a photo Steve Suchan.

Anna Camero was so nervous after Suchan's telephone call that she had to get Betty Huluk to dial the police number for her. "I got someone on the line, and then Anna reported her car stolen," said

Huluk. Police scouring the area in the vicinity of the shooting found Camero's car on Sheridan Avenue less than thirty minutes after Suchan and Jackson abandoned it. A woman looking out the window of her house had seen two men leave the parked car and enter a cab. All city and suburban cab drivers were ordered by police to furnish them with their run sheets.

With the information from Tong, Sergeant of Detectives William Bolton searched Anna Camero's house a short time after she reported her car stolen. He found a receipt for the $200 CPR Express Money Order that Camero's mother had sent to Victor J. Lenoff at the Montreal address. And behind a haversack hanging on a nail in the rear sun porch, Bolton discovered twenty-two .45 calibre bullets wrapped in a handkerchief. Stuffed under the chesterfield in the living room, police found the metal target and two air pistols. And in the basement they found the torso and plaster head that Suchan and Jackson had used for target shooting.

Also found in the house was a light-blue sport jacket. Inside was a label: "Madison Tailored Clothes – made to measure in Toronto, Canada, for Mr. Jackson, on May 11, 1951." Police would soon learn that "Mr. Jackson" was in fact Lennie Jackson, arrested by Eddie Tong on July 30 and wanted for several bank robberies and for escaping from the Don Jail with Edwin Alonzo Boyd.

Anna Camero and Betty Huluk were taken to police headquarters, where they were interviewed for several hours. Detective Jack Gillespie showed them a photo of Steve Suchan. They said they knew him all right – he was the father of Camero's youngest daughter, but his name wasn't Suchan, it was Val Lesso. With that information, police with guns drawn raided the Sorauren Avenue rooming house owned by Suchan's parents. Joseph Lesso was still away in Florida, enjoying his vacation courtesy of Boyd and Willie Jackson. From Elizabeth Lesso and other roomers, it was learned that Suchan and been there twice that day, before *and* after the shooting. Before the shooting he had changed from a windbreaker to an overcoat, which lends credence to the theory that he and Jackson were planning to rob a bank that day: it would have been much easier for them to conceal a revolver in an overcoat. And what reason would Suchan have to change from his windbreaker if he were merely driving Jackson to the bus station? After the shooting, he probably switched to a different overcoat, because witnesses could have provided police with a description of his clothing.

While the police were at the Lesso rooming house, a woman came to the door asking for Val Lesso. When told he wasn't around, she asked to speak to his mother. Detective-Sergeant Charlie Cook questioned the woman and discovered she was Jane Blahut of 474 Roncesvalles Avenue. It was an interesting address – the same address where Eddie Tong and Jack Gillespie arrested Lennie Jackson in July. Frank Watson had also been known to live there. Cook accompanied the woman to the residence, where he discovered photographs of Lennie Jackson and a woman companion taken at a nightclub. The woman was later identified as his wife, the former Ann Roberts. Cook also discovered that Jane Blahut was in fact Lennie Jackson's other sister. (Mary Mitchell would be picked up for questioning later.) Blahut was arrested on a vagrancy charge – a catch-all charge used by police in those days to hold suspects for short periods.

After they put the pieces together, the detectives for the first time made the connection between Suchan and Lennie Jackson. They also knew Suchan's real name and, from the CPR receipt, his Montreal address and alias – Victor J. Lenoff. And now they knew that Lennie Jackson had grown a moustache, was wearing black horn-rimmed glasses, and used the alias Fred Wilson.

Soon after, photographs and descriptions of the wanted men were distributed to airports, train stations, bus depots, and border crossings. The police, who were meticulously checking hotels and rooming houses, now knew exactly who they were looking for. All law enforcement agencies were notified, including the RCMP and the FBI, and descriptions were sent out to all newspapers and radio stations.

Police learned of Suchan's penchant for fine restaurants, and the next day the *Telegram* reported, "Suchan is known as a glutton for food, and throughout the afternoon, restaurants in the west end and downtown areas were fine-combed by police."

By late Thursday, Chief Chisholm had announced that warrants had been issued for the arrests of Suchan and Jackson for the attempted murder of Eddie Tong. "We are hoping fervently the warrant will not have to be changed to one of murder," he said.

Jane Blahut, Anna Camero, and Betty Huluk were held in police cells overnight, and on Friday the newspapers made a meal of them. In a long article in the *Telegram* by Norm Johnston and Doug Creighton,[22] the three women were described as well-dressed. "Jane Blahut, a faded blonde, had on a smart fur coat and wore rhinestone earrings." Anna Camero was "a pretty blonde" who wore "a black coat trimmed with white fur and carried white gloves." Betty Huluk "appeared in a well-cut fur coat."

Bail was set at $1,000 for each of the women. Betty Huluk was mortified by the whole experience. Soon after, she left her room on Wright Avenue and moved back home with her mother near Brantford, Ontario.

While the police were closing in on Suchan and Jackson, Eddie Tong continued to fight for his life at Toronto General Hospital. By Friday morning his condition was slightly improved, but doctors said he was still far too weak to be operated on. The bullet was still lodged near his shoulder-blade, and he hadn't been told that if he did survive he would probably never walk again. At the nursing station on the second floor of the Private Patients' Pavilion where his room was located, the phone rang constantly as well-wishers called to ask how Tong was doing. "Condition fair – no change…. Condition fair – no change…." The message would be repeated hundreds of times over the next few days.

"There's nothing much we can do now," one doctor told a reporter. "He is in such a state of shock, we can't even move him. He was hit by only one bullet, but it touched both lungs." To keep Tong alive, doctors gave him numerous transfusions, and there was an overwhelming response from his colleagues when a police radio call went out for blood donors.

Detective Roy Perry was operated on for a badly fractured arm. Police said that only one bullet, not two as first reported, had hit the officer in the arm. The heavy bullet had split in two when it struck the windshield, and both sections smashed into Perry's raised forearm.

Perry was taken to St. Joseph's Hospital after the shooting but insisted on being moved to Toronto General to be near his partner.

Tong's family – his wife Evelyn, thirteen-year-old son Raymond, and twenty-one-year-old daughter Margaret – were at the hospital Friday morning hoping to see him. With them was Alexandrine Gibb, a reporter for the *Star* who had been assigned to cover the story from a woman's point of view. She had known Tong for some time and had arranged to tag along with the family when they went to the hospital. Gibb's job was to write a touching, emotional account of what she saw. It just happened to be young Raymond's thirteenth birthday, which added a bittersweet element to the story.

A nurse met them at the door of the room and said she had just given Tong "a hypo" and didn't think he should be disturbed.

"I want to do whatever is best for him," said Mrs. Tong. "I'll do whatever you say. We'll come back later." As they turned to leave, Tong called out to his wife to come in.

"He's heard you and he wants you," said the nurse. "You'd better come in." Gibb's account of the meeting appeared in the *Star* that day:

> The family entered quickly. A smile trembled on the wife's lips. She looked at her husband in the high bed, strangely wan and weak. "How do you feel dear?" she asked.
>
> Detective Tong managed a chuckle. It was feeble, but it was there. "I feel fine today and so do all the hoodlums," he said.
>
> "When are you going to get better so we can celebrate Raymond's birthday?" Mrs. Tong asked. "He's 13 today, you know."
>
> "Yes I know he is," her husband said. "I remembered that. We'll have his party yet."
>
> And now there was a moistness filming Mrs. Tong's eyes. "We'll get another cake, too," she murmured. Her husband smiled and closed his eyes.
>
> "How are you getting on?" he asked. "I worried about you being there alone."
>
> Mrs. Tong found a quip from somewhere. "I was all right," she said. "I had a girlfriend of yours with me."

"Oh, did you?" the detective said. "Who was she?"

"Alex Gibb of the Star," Mrs. Tong said.

"Good for her," Det. Tong said. "That's fine." He grinned, closed his eyes again and the only sound was his breathing.

"I think he's going to sleep now," the nurse whispered.

"Yes," the wounded man whispered, "I'm awfully tired."

Mrs. Tong, Margaret, and Raymond tiptoed from the room. The women dabbed at their eyes with handkerchiefs.

Not to be outdone, the *Telegram* did its own "tiptoeing" around Tong's hospital room, and Herbert Biggs found this way to end an account of Tong identifying Suchan's picture:

Skilled hands replaced the oxygen mask on his face as he took up again the fight to stay alive.

A Telegram reporter tiptoed into the room. Tong's eyes were open under the mask and the reporter murmured a word of greeting and a hasty wish for "good luck." And Tong, one of the best-liked officers on the force, gave a flicker of his eyelids – a flicker of recognition.

After consulting with Chief Chisholm, Mayor Lamport announced a $2,000 reward for information leading to the capture and conviction of Tong's assailants. "If the people will co-operate, we'll end this reign of terror," he told reporters at City Hall. "Everybody knows when somebody suspicious moves into their boarding house or neighbourhood, and it is not mean or cowardly to report it. If they report it, they may save the life of a man like Tong … one of the finest officers on the force. We're going to keep Toronto a decent city. We'll welcome decent citizens, but we don't want the other kind and we're going to make war on them. We're going to catch these fellows and we'll punish them."

Ed and Dorreen Boyd were at the movies on Thursday when Eddie Tong and Roy Perry were being ambushed. They were walking down a back alley from their Spadina Road rooming house when they saw their friend Florence Lamb hanging out washing behind her house. Dorreen says Flo and Frank Lamb "never gave a thought about Ed being a bank robber."

"Do you want to go to the show?" she hollered to Florence.

"Yeah, just a minute, I'll be right there."

They went to see *Another Man's Poison*, a 1951 British film starring Bette Davis, who played a man-hungry novelist opposite her real-life husband, Gary Merrill. When they came out of the movie they saw the headlines on a nearby newsstand.

Boyd fished in his pocket and purchased both papers. The story said two gunmen were being sought, but gave no names. Boyd's instincts told him it was Suchan and Jackson. They had told him the day before that they "had taken some weapons and ammunition out to a gravel pit, halfway to Niagara Falls, and they were practising shooting, which I didn't think was a good thing to be doing. They even practised with their machine guns."

Dorreen could see that Boyd was upset. He knew it would mean a lot more heat, just when it was becoming safer to move around in public. "What are we going to do?" asked Dorreen.

"We're not going to do anything but lay low," said Boyd.

The next day he was furious when he saw his picture on the front pages, just where he didn't want to be. Suchan and Jackson had been identified as the gunmen who shot Tong and Perry, and police were telling reporters they were probably on their way to meet Boyd to rob a bank when Tong pulled them over. "Police think Edwin Alonzo Boyd, 37, the 'master bank robber' … was in an automobile on a side street and aided Jackson and Suchan to escape after they abandoned their car," said the *Star*.

The *Telegram* went with the same theme, saying police "hope also to catch in their dragnet Edwin Alonzo Boyd, wanted for armed bank holdups and jailbreaking. Police say Suchan and Jackson were en route to hold up a bank, where they would rendezvous with Boyd … Then Boyd, police believe, met the gunmen in a side street and drove them away in a second car."

Boyd was angry at Suchan and Jackson for not taking more precautions against being spotted by police. "After a robbery they acted like they were royalty. They figured they were beyond any possibility of being caught. They knew the police pretty well, and the police are victims of routine. Until then, the police really hadn't done too much. They weren't all like Tong or Payne. Tong was a guy that if he decided he wanted to get someone, he would latch right on to them until he finally caught them. If you were robbing banks, you couldn't stay in the same city as Tong. So he went after Lennie Jackson, but he wasn't too interested in Suchan, and Suchan was the guy who shot him."

Boyd had no sympathy for Suchan, but he felt badly for Jackson. "Suchan was a real pain. He was so filled with his own importance. He figured when he was tied in with Len, he was in the upper class – a big-time mobster. Len was pretty good. He seemed to have his life figured out. But he got tied in with Suchan." Boyd believes that Suchan's cockiness and womanizing led to Lennie's downfall.

Ambush

hile Toronto police were launching "the most intensive man-hunt in the city's history," Steve Suchan and Lennie Jackson left the Lessos' rooming house on Sorauren Avenue and took their waiting taxi to Queen and Roncesvalles, where they boarded a westbound streetcar. They got off at Long Branch, the end of the line, and from there took a bus along the Lakeshore Highway to Port Credit on the western outskirts of Toronto. About 2:30 Thursday afternoon they went to the office of Port Credit Taxi on Stavebank Road.

"How much for a cab to Oakville?" asked Suchan.

Driver John Rundle conferred with his partner, Ernest Manera.

"Three dollars," said Rundle.

"That sounds fair," said Suchan.

Manera would remember the man as "pimply and kind of sweating in the face." And he noticed that he was carrying a briefcase and was wearing a light brown coat and a fedora. The next day, when Manera looked at the front page of *The Globe and Mail*, he would learn that the man's name was Steve Suchan. Rundle drove the two men to the railway station in Oakville, pulling up just as the eastbound train, for Toronto and beyond, left the platform.

Taxi driver William Bowles was on Spruce Street heading towards the Oakville station when two men flagged him down and asked him to take them to Bronte, halfway between Oakville and Burlington. When they reached Bronte, Bowles asked where they wanted to be dropped off.

"Take us to the hotel," said one of them.

"There is no hotel in Bronte," said Bowles.

"Well, take us to the bus station."

They told Bowles they had missed their train connection, but later changed their story, saying they had had car trouble. He dropped them at a roadside lunch counter and grocery store that doubled as a bus station. Beside it was a small taxi stand. Taxi driver Sidney Plummer was having a coffee at the lunch counter when Suchan tapped on the window and motioned to the cab in front. Plummer came out to the street.

"What's the fare to Burlington?" asked Suchan.

"Two dollars," replied Plummer. One of the men paid him, and they got in the cab. In Burlington, Plummer dropped them at the bus station on the north side of Highway 2 opposite the Aylmer Canning Factory.

About 3:45 that afternoon, George Seaton, owner of DeLuxe Taxi Company, was sitting in his office on Brant Street in Burlington when one of his drivers pulled up with two male passengers who had flagged him down on the street. The driver told his boss the men wanted to go to the Royal Connaught Hotel in Hamilton. Seaton had a rule that he personally checked all long-distance fares to make certain they were capable of paying. He studied the men. Both were wearing topcoats and fedoras and one of them was carrying a briefcase. He thought they might be salesmen and approved the run to Hamilton.

It was still daylight when they were dropped off in Hamilton. "We thought the best thing we could do was to get off the street," Suchan would say later. "It was broad daylight and we were both jittery and panicky. There was a show across the street from the Royal Connaught and we went in there until nightfall."

After the movie they went to the hotel, where Lennie Jackson spent sixty cents to send a telegram to his wife in Montreal: DARLING, WILL BE IN LATER THAN EXPECTED. LOVE, FRED. The telegram was sent at 8:53 p.m. A short time later, Jackson hot-wired a car and the two men drove to Montreal, arriving on Friday morning.

Ann Jackson hadn't seen her husband in more than two days; that was the longest they had been apart in their two-month marriage. She had received his telegram Friday morning, but she was still worried about him. News of the shooting of the Toronto policemen had been on the radio the day before, and she wondered if Lennie might be involved.

Not knowing when her husband would be returning, Ann Jackson left her basement apartment on Lincoln Avenue on Friday around 11:30 a.m. She planned to spend the day window-shopping, and pick up a few groceries on her way home. While she was out, she bought a copy of the *Toronto Star* and read that her husband and Steve Suchan were wanted for shooting Tong and Perry. "I did not recognize the name of Suchan," she said in a statement to police later. "I had never heard of this name before." But she saw the address – 190 Wright Avenue – and read that the car used in the shooting belonged to Anna Camero. That was a name she knew, and she realized then that Steve Suchan was probably Val Lesso. She did not bring the newspaper back to the apartment.

Lennie arrived at the apartment shortly after noon. He immediately shaved off his moustache and threw his horn-rimmed glasses into the trash. When Ann returned in late afternoon, Lennie didn't say where he had been or who he had been with, and she didn't ask. He seemed pleased when she told him he looked handsome without his moustache. She didn't mention the newspaper or Steve Suchan.

"I heard about the shooting of Detective Tong," she said. "Do you know if he died?"

"He's still alive," said Lennie.

"That's good, because it would be murder if he died."

Lennie was silent. It was obvious he didn't want to talk about it. But at 6 p.m. they heard the radio newscast name Lennie Jackson and Steve Suchan as the shooters of Perry and Tong, whose condition remained critical.

"Well, he should never have approached them," said Lennie sullenly. Ann thought *them* was a reference to the men in the car Tong had stopped, but "it was not specifically an admission from my husband that he was one of the men."

Seven minutes before Lennie and Ann Jackson tuned in to the 6 p.m. news broadcast, Toronto police were issuing a description of Suchan's car. Dolph Payne's credo – a car was always involved – was validated once again. Camero's neighbours on Wright Avenue had reported seeing a car with Quebec plates in front of the house from time to time. And when the name Victor J. Lenhoff was passed on to Montreal Police, they reported back that a 1951 dark-coloured Chrysler sedan, with the Quebec licence plate 324–385, was registered under that name. Police in Ontario and Quebec were on the lookout for the car. However, other information, gleaned from the receipt for the $200 that Anna Camero's mother had wired to Suchan, would prove even more important – the address of Suchan's Montreal apartment on Côte des Neiges.

When Suchan arrived back in the apartment on Friday afternoon, he decided to sell his Chrysler for sorely needed cash. He changed overcoats and armed himself with weapons and ammunition from his briefcase. In a holster on the left side of his belt he was carrying the revolver he had used to shoot Tong and Perry – the .455 Smith & Wesson for which he had traded his violin. A smaller right-side holster held a .30 calibre automatic Mauser pistol with a ten-round clip. Under his belt, in front, he stuffed a seven-shot .45 Colt automatic, and in various pockets he secreted four extra clips – two for the Mauser and two for the Colt – and a dozen or so loose rounds for the .455. As heavily armed as he was, the weapons on his person were small change compared to the stash in the suitcase in the trunk of his Chrysler.

Suchan tried three or four car dealers before settling on one, who wrote him a cheque for $1,800 for the Chrysler. He removed a large, heavy suitcase from the trunk, and the dealer agreed to hold it for him until he returned to pick it up.

The Croydon Apartments at 3455 Côte des Neiges was by 1950s standards a luxury building. A doorman was always on duty, and there was a lobby with an ivy-covered fountain, much greenery, and a lot of marble. The building also boasted an upscale street-level restaurant where Suchan ate most of his meals when he was in town. He tipped well, was always quiet and polite, and had a hearty appetite. The restaurant's cashier, described in the *Telegram* as "shapely Cecile," said she was surprised to learn Suchan was just twenty-four. "He looked older, and he's much better looking than the picture of him in the paper."

Suchan's three-room apartment, No. 330, was on the third floor of the eight-storey building. Inspector Alex McCathie of the Toronto police had notified the Montreal police of the address, and around 6 p.m., while Suchan was out selling his car, a team of seven detectives from the Montreal Police Department's Special Squad arrived at his building. Entering through the garage, they took the stairs to the third floor and, using a key provided by the manager's office, entered Suchan's apartment with guns drawn. The suspect wasn't there, but when they searched the rooms, they found Suchan's tan briefcase in a front closet. In it were six spent casings from the bullets he had fired at Tong and Perry, an automatic pistol, two holsters, and an array of ammunition.

Detective Captain Langpré was in charge of the operation, and when he discovered Suchan wasn't there, he assigned four of his men to conceal themselves in the apartment in case Suchan returned. Langpré and the other two detectives would search for Suchan's Chrysler. As they were leaving, Langpré hesitated. "Was the bathroom light on?" he asked. The officers agreed the bedroom and living room lights were on when they arrived, but they couldn't remember about the bathroom. They decided to turn the light off, and arranged a signal – five slow knocks – that Langpré and the others would use if they should return to the apartment.

Two of the detectives, George Poirier and Maurice Bilodeau, stayed out of sight in the bedroom, while Albert Dauphin and George Coté hid behind a half-closed door in the darkened kitchen off the living room. It was decided that if Suchan entered the apartment, Dauphin would confront him first.

Suchan, unaware that the receipt for the $200 from Anna Camero had brought the police to his Montreal doorstep, sauntered into the restaurant below his apartment. He had dumped his car and had the $1,800 cheque in his wallet. That would keep him going for a while. But now he was hungry. He was on a first-name basis with his waiter, Maurice. Suchan studied the menu, but couldn't decide.

"What would you like to eat?" asked Maurice.

"I'm not sure," said Suchan. "Everything looks good."

"May I recommend the lobster," said Maurice. "It's very good tonight."

"Yes, today is Friday. I'll have the lobster."

Reporter George Brimmell would write in the *Telegram* the next day: "Steve Suchan had a big lobster dinner – as well as two loaded 45's – under his belt when he walked into a police ambush in his posh apartment last night."

Suchan left the restaurant shortly after 9:30 p.m. and took the elevator to his apartment. Dauphin and the other detectives had been waiting silently for more than three and a half hours when they heard a noise at the door. It wasn't the five-knock signal from Captain Langpré – it was a key being turned in the lock. Dauphin held his breath and pulled his .38 service revolver from its holster. He heard the door close and peered into the lighted hallway. He had memorized the face in the photo from the Toronto police. A man came into the light from the entranceway. The size was right. Then he saw the face. Suchan.

Suchan turned away from the kitchen, distracted by a suitcase sitting in the hall. He thought he had left it in the closet. "I thought there might be someone in the apartment," Suchan said later. "That was not unusual because the janitor and any of the managers had access to the apartment. They could come in any time they wished."

Suchan was in the middle of the living room when he thought he heard a noise behind him. His right hand reached for the .455 Smith & Wesson in his left holster as he wheeled to face Dauphin, who had stepped out of the kitchen. Suchan's heavy revolver was at a forty-five degree angle, almost level with his chin, from the momentum of his draw. "His gun was too high to shoot," said Dauphin. "Mine was at the hip. He appeared to hesitate with the revolver still pointed upwards. I shot first – in the region of the heart about the middle of the chest."

He fired a second shot that struck Suchan in the stomach. That shot turned Suchan sideways. "He was still holding his revolver in his hand," said Dauphin, "so I shot his arm to disarm him, and then he crumbled to the floor."

Dauphin's first shot had hit an inch below Suchan's heart. The second had caught his lower abdomen, exiting his hip at the back, and the third had smashed his left hand. Suchan was still holding his revolver when he fell to the floor on his right side. He tried to raise it to fire, but he was too weak and it fell heavily to the floor. In court he would deny ever drawing his gun.

"Okay George!" shouted Dauphin as he kicked the revolver out of Suchan's reach. His partner, George Poirier, came out of the bedroom and picked up the revolver, handing it to Dauphin. Poirier removed the Mauser from Suchan's right-side holster and the .45 Colt from the his waistband. Suchan was on his side, and Detective Coté "moved over to him as he lay there and turned him on his back." One of the detectives called for an ambulance. Suchan was conscious. "You guys are poor shots," he sneered. "Why don't you finish me? What are you waiting for? No one will know the difference."

"We want to keep you alive for the Toronto police," said Dauphin. "You won't be shooting any more cops."

Suchan was silent for a moment. "How did you find us?" he asked. No one replied.

The ambulance was instructed to pull up to the rear entrance to the building without sirens, so as not to tip off Boyd or Jackson if they happened to be in the vicinity. The police continued to stake out the apartment until early the next morning. Suchan tried to walk to the ambulance but had to be placed on a stretcher before he reached the elevator. He was taken to Queen Elizabeth Hospital under armed guard, his ankle manacled to the bed. "We've got to watch this man carefully," said one of the police guards. "He's husky and in good condition, and if he ever got hold of our guns, he'd try to shoot his way out of here."

Suchan was operated on early Saturday morning. He told the surgeon, Dr. John Hayward, that he wished the police had killed him. "I'd be better off dead," he said. "That sergeant is a lousy shot. If I had been able to get my guns out, I wouldn't have missed like he did." Strange bravado, thought Hayward, coming from a man who was about to have a bullet removed from an inch below his heart.

Dr. Hayward said that Suchan wasn't in any danger, that he'd been taken off oxygen and was in excellent physical shape. When Suchan went in for X-rays, the doctors were surprised to discover another bullet. It was in the lower section of his right chest, and it had been there for some time. The wound caused by the bullet had been healed for several months. Suchan offered no explanation. The Toronto police would later conclude that Suchan had been shot while fleeing from the Bank of Commerce robbery in Bradford the previous July. OPP Constable Reg Wilson had fired several times at the getaway vehicle. At the time, he thought he might have hit one of the robbers.

On Saturday morning the Montreal police found Suchan's Chrysler on the used car lot. When they opened the suitcase he had left with the dealer, they found two Thompson sub-machine-guns, two revolvers, and more than a thousand rounds of ammunition. This discovery made them very nervous, and they quietly put out a shoot-to-kill order to all their officers in the continuing hunt for Boyd and Jackson.

The Toronto and Montreal police withheld the news of Suchan's capture for two or three hours while officers conducted a series of raids in and around Montreal, working on tips that did not pan out. By the morning both the *Star* and the *Telegram* had the story and reporters were flooding into Montreal. Once again there was blanket coverage.

All of the Toronto dailies followed the practice of dashing off first-person articles, complete with by-lines, for police officers involved in major crime stories. Reporters would do a quick interview and write a first-person story, often embellished, with the policeman's name attached to it.

Jocko Thomas, the *Star*'s senior crime reporter at the time, says that "a lot of the Boyd Gang exploits got these giant headlines because of this competition for circulation, but it was complete excitement – twenty-four hours a day. There was always something going on. And don't forget, a very good policeman – a good man – was shot in cold blood. He didn't even have time to get his gun out. There was great outrage and great pressure on the police to catch these guys."

Page 1 of Saturday's *Telegram* ran a photo of Suchan on a stretcher on his way to the hospital. The paper also did a bit of self-promotion, running a three-column photo of Dolph Payne and Detectives Kenneth Craven and Doug Chapman studying wire photos of Suchan in the *Telegram* office with police reporter Tom Williams. And reporter Herbert Biggs had another of his death-watch stories from Eddie Tong's hospital room, reporting that Tong's condition had worsened:

Mrs. Tong who yesterday was smiling and seemingly confident her husband would live, was quiet and sad-faced, and
maybe a little bitter…. Her eyes are anxious but there are no
tears as she draws a damp cloth across his forehead.

Tong's eyes are shut tight. He breathes with difficulty. His
breathing, sounding almost like groans, strikes terror into the
heart of his wife.

At the top of page 2 there were three large head shots of Suchan,
Jackson, and Boyd. Above the photos of Jackson and Boyd, in heavy
black type, was the word **HUNTED**. Above Suchan's photo, in the
same type, was the word **CAUGHT**. There was also a large **X** crossed
through Suchan's face.

In its Friday late edition, the *Star* had run a photo of Jackson
touched up by one of its artists to include horn-rimmed glasses and
a moustache. On Saturday, at the bottom of page 1, they ran the
photo again, quoting the wounded Roy Perry exclaiming, "That's
him to a 'T'." The *Star* proudly announced that when police officials
learned of Perry's reaction "they decided to use the Star picture in
the manhunt for Jackson."

Also on Saturday's page 1, the *Star* ran photos of Suchan under
police guard in hospital, an exterior shot of his apartment building,
and a photo of Detective Dauphin, who was given a by-line for a "first
person" account of the shoot-out under this two-column headline:
'WHY DIDN'T YOU FINISH ME?' / WOUNDED SUCHAN / ASKS MONTREAL
POLICE. And there was a short item about Mayor Allan Lamport
calling for a day of prayer for Tong's recovery. "I am appealing to all
churches to offer special prayers tomorrow for the recovery of the
gallant police officer who is fighting for his life…."

The morning after Suchan was shot, Jack Gillespie was at home
when a call came from work. "Get packed," he was told, "you're going
out of town for a few days."

"Where am I going?"

"Bill Thompson will pick you up, and he'll tell you."

Thompson was a sergeant of detectives and Gillespie's partner at
the time. Thompson told him they were going to the airport for a

flight to Montreal. Flying with them was the *Star*'s Jocko Thomas. Gillespie, a white-knuckle flier, couldn't wait to land. They wanted him in Montreal because he was one of the few officers who knew Tough Lennie Jackson by sight. He and Thompson were met by Montreal police and booked into the Laurentian Hotel. Montreal newspapers got word of Gillespie's arrival, and his photo was in the papers the next day. At a hastily arranged press conference he said he was there to capture Lennie Jackson.

Lennie and Ann Jackson had not ventured from their single-room Lincoln Avenue basement apartment, and it wasn't until 2 p.m. Saturday that they heard on the radio that Steve Suchan had been shot down and arrested at his apartment, just over a block away. Ann wept when she heard the news, realizing the police might come for her husband any minute. Lennie became despondent.

"Val was only a kid," he said, pacing the room. "Let's get out of here for a while." They got into the Oldsmobile, drove around the city for an hour or so, took in an early movie, and returned to the apartment after dark. Everything seemed normal, but Lennie was feeling smothered. He knew his options were quickly dwindling.

"I should sell the car and give you the money," he said.

"But what about you?"

"I'll get out of here. I'll just go away."

"Do you think you would have a better chance on your own?" asked Ann.

"There's not much chance either way," he sighed.

"Well, I want to stay with you."

Lennie was touched by his wife's loyalty. They had a baby on the way. He had to pull himself together and think things through.

"The first thing is to get some money," he said. "That means selling the car." He knew they had to move quickly, and he sent Ann up to see their friend Sidney Backman. She arranged for Backman to come to the apartment on Monday morning to discuss the car with Lennie.

All day Sunday they stayed in the apartment. Lennie loaded his .32-20 calibre Colt revolver and a P-38 automatic pistol and kept them on the floor beside his chair with a supply of ammunition.

On Saturday, caretaker Henri Côté went to the apartment of Fred Wilson (he knew Jackson by that alias) and asked if could borrow a bed for his father-in-law, who was visiting for the weekend. While he was in the apartment, Côté noticed that Wilson had shaved off his moustache and was no longer wearing glasses. He also noticed that there were no blankets on the beds, and that three suitcases were lined up between them. Jackson helped him remove one of the beds.

Sidney Backman arrived at Jackson's apartment as promised on Monday morning and said he would do what he could to sell the Oldsmobile. He left with the keys, promising to return on Wednesday. Ann went out for Monday's newspapers, and Lennie became more despondent when he saw Jack Gillespie's photo and read of the detective vowing to get him. He sat in his chair with his revolver tucked into his pants and the automatic pistol in the briefcase beside him, and hoped Sidney Backman showed up before Gillespie.

On Sunday night, Henri Coté and his wife, Laurette, were reading the *Gazette* when they saw photos of a man who bore a striking resemblance to Fred Wilson. But the name on the photos wasn't Fred Wilson, it was Lennie Jackson. They also recognized another photo in the newspaper – Steve Suchan. Laurette Coté had twice seen Suchan visit Wilson's apartment, which was at the bottom of the stairs at the front of the building. The Côtés had a three-room apartment towards the rear of the basement. Their kitchen shared a common wall with the Wilsons' apartment.

The story in the *Gazette* mentioned that a reward was being offered for Jackson's capture. Henri Côté telephoned the police, and for good measure stopped in at No. 10 Police Station on his way to work the next morning. He had the newspaper in hand and said Jackson was definitely the man living in the apartment next to his.

On Tuesday afternoon, Ann Jackson saw a man go past their door to Côté's apartment. She sensed something was wrong and went up the stairs to the front door of the building. Laurette Côté came up the stairs carrying her six-month-old baby, but her visitor wasn't with her. Ann presumed that the visitor had left by the back door, but she was becoming more suspicious. She returned to the apartment. Her suspicions were well founded. The man she had seen was a detective who had told Henri Côté to get his wife and child upstairs.

"I think something's wrong," Ann said to Lennie. They kept very quiet, and a few minutes later heard what they thought were footsteps, as if someone was creeping down the stairs. They knew none of the regular tenants walked so softly. What they were hearing was Gillespie and Sergeant of Detectives Leo Murray of the Montreal force coming quietly down the stairs with two other officers. All were wearing twenty-five-pound bullet-proof vests. They came to the bottom of the stairs, which was exactly opposite No. 15 – Jackson's apartment. "Leo Murray and myself turned to the left of the apartment and walked about ten feet to a small side hall," said Gillespie. "The other two Montreal officers turned to the right at the landing and went to the small kitchen at the opposite end of the hall."

It was shortly after 5 p.m. on Tuesday, March 11. While Gillespie and the others were taking up their positions, Detective Thompson was outside with more than a dozen men armed with automatic weapons and tear gas. They covered the building's rear entrance and Jackson's window, which was somewhat obscured by a foot of snow on the ground.

Inside the apartment, Ann went to the window and saw a man standing there. She turned to her husband. "They are here, Leonard," she said. Jackson's jaw tightened. He put on his overcoat and fedora, and with a gun in each hand went to the door.

Gillespie was worried about what might be waiting for him in No. 15. "I was a poor shot," he said, "and Lennie was in there with a revolver and an automatic. We also knew he had sub-machine-guns, but we didn't know that he hadn't found time to assemble them." Gillespie was thinking about his next move when he heard the lock click on the door. "I waited a second and I heard the lock click again," he said, "and then I saw the door opening out to the hall towards me." He tiptoed to the door, grabbed the handle, and yanked it towards him with his left hand. In his right hand was his .38 service revolver. Jackson had jumped back from the door. "When I got the door open, I saw Jackson standing about eight to ten feet away. I recognized him immediately. I knew from his eyes he was going to shoot." Jackson would say later he didn't recognize Gillespie in that instant.

Gillespie said Jackson made a remark that he couldn't make out. "Then he fired and I fired back. I fired six shots, and he was firing at me." To this day, Gillespie can't figure out how Jackson missed him. At the time, the detective weighed about 220 pounds and stood a shade over six feet, filling the doorway. Gillespie's bulky bullet-proof vest was obvious, and perhaps Jackson decided to shoot for his head, a more difficult target.

Jackson wasn't as lucky as Gillespie. Four of the detective's six bullets found their mark – one in the abdomen, two in the left arm, and one in the right hand. "I wasn't aiming, I was just firing," said Gillespie. "Wyatt Earp couldn't do better than that." He continued firing until he realized his gun was empty. "Then I jumped out of the way as Lennie kept firing. Behind me the plaster wall was chewed up all over the place and the door was all splintered." One of those splinters had caught the corner of Gillespie's eye. "I figured I'd been shot. I was wearing a red tie that day, and I looked down and I'm panicking. All I can see is this red on the front of my shirt, and I figure, Holy Geez, I'm bleeding to death."

As soon as Gillespie jumped back, the two officers in the kitchen began blazing away at the doorway while officers outside fired tear gas through the small window and opened up with machine guns. They even had a Bren gun on a tripod available to them.

Ann Jackson was hysterical. She could see that the first detective had hit Lennie in the stomach. Her husband was holding the wound with his left hand as he continued firing with his right. "Don't shoot anymore!" she screamed.

Henri Côté, not wanting to miss any of the action, had decided to stay in his apartment next to Jackson's. "I could hear Jackson moving around in the room as if he were trying to change his position to fool the cops shooting from outside," he told a reporter later. Jackson was moving between the window and the door, firing to keep the police back. The noise of the gunfight was deafening, with glassware shattering and bullets ripping into plaster and wood. Then Côté heard the tear gas smashing through the window, followed by Lennie coughing and retching, and Ann crying hysterically. Côté's eyes began to burn as the gas seeped into his kitchen.

Lennie had dropped the automatic pistol when his left arm was hit, and now he was firing only the revolver, using his right hand to shoot and reload. Ann was still screaming, and when the tear gas canister came through the window, Lennie grabbed her and pushed her under the bed. "Stay down there out of the line of fire!" he shouted.

Gillespie was back with Detective Murray in the small side hall to the left of the apartment. "The only way out was to go by the apartment door," he said. "We were trapped in there." And there was so much noise and confusion, the policemen didn't know if Jackson was firing the tommy guns or not. Gillespie does not like to think about what might have happened if they had been assembled.

When he ducked away from the door, Gillespie tried to grab Murray's service revolver, but Murray refused to give it to him. "Get back here you crazy bugger," said Murray. "If Jackson doesn't get you, our own men will."

Gillespie had got to know Murray over the previous three days, and the two men liked each other. "He was a real potato-faced Irishman and a real good Catholic," said Gillespie. He realized he'd been lucky and that Murray was right. The smell of tear gas was getting stronger, and the best strategy was to wait Jackson out. "You know, Leo," said Gillespie, "my old man used to be King Willy on the twelfth of July, and if he knew I died with a Catholic, he'd turn over in his grave." Murray laughed and shook his head as the bullets continued to fly.

Inside the apartment, Lennie Jackson was a wild man. He was out of the line of fire from the window, but he couldn't stop the tear gas. "Tabernac!" he screamed. "Tabernac! Come and get me!" The gas was becoming unbearable, and his wife continued to scream and plead with him to stop shooting.

"I want you alive!" she screamed. "Please stop shooting! Let me take the guns out!" Lennie, by now covered in blood, ignored her and continued loading and firing, using only his right hand.

"Stop shooting!" cried Ann. "Think of the baby!"

At the mention of their baby, Lennie suddenly stopped. He turned to his wife, his face calm. "Okay," he said quietly, dropping his revolver to the floor.

"Don't shoot any more!" he hollered. "I give up! I give up! My wife is coming out with the guns!" The gun battle had lasted thirty minutes. Outside, two hundred Montreal policemen had been called out to control the crowd, which had swelled to several hundred as the gun battle dragged on. Estimates of the number of rounds fired by Jackson and the police ranged from two hundred to five hundred.

Ann Jackson, wearing a blood-splattered white bed jacket, emerged from the apartment, her eyes streaming tears from the gas. One gun was dangling from each hand. "Walk towards us and drop them on the floor," ordered Gillespie. "Now kick them over here and get behind us." She followed his instructions.

"Okay Lennie!" said Gillespie in a loud voice. "Come out with your hands up!" Because of his wounds, Lennie didn't raise his arms. "Get them up!" ordered Gillespie. He complied slowly, and the detective saw blood pouring from his wounds. "Oh God, he was bleeding all over, and his wife had his blood all over her," recalls Gillespie.

"Hello, John," said Lennie, who always used Gillespie's given name. "I saw your fat ugly puss in the paper. I'm glad I didn't hit you."

"You're not half as glad as I am," said Gillespie.

"Did I hit any cops?"

"No."

"That's good. I was hoping I didn't hurt anybody."

"Have you gone insane?" asked Gillespie.

"I don't know," said Lennie, looking thoughtful. "Look after my wife, will you, John?"

"I'll make sure she's treated well."

"You know, I would not have given up if it hadn't been for her."

Before he was handcuffed, Lennie put his arm around Ann and kissed her gently on the lips three times, transferring more of his blood to her bed jacket. Then he was handcuffed and led to a police car by Thompson and Gillespie. Before getting into the back seat between the two detectives, he yelled out to the crowd, "I know who tipped off the police! Boyd will be back to get them!" He knew it wasn't true, but it added to the drama. It frightened Henri Côté enough that he sent his wife into hiding.

As they drove to the hospital, Lennie turned to Gillespie. "How did you catch on to us, John?"

"A little bird told me," said Gillespie.

"It wasn't the telegram I sent from Hamilton, was it?"

"Could be," said Gillespie, who hadn't known about the telegram. Jackson and Thompson didn't know each other, and after Gillespie introduced them, Thompson asked Lennie if he knew where Boyd was. "I don't know," said Lennie. Thompson could see that Jackson was quickly fading from loss of blood, and didn't pursue it.

Jackson had lived up to his reputation as "Tough Lennie," holding off a small army of cops for half an hour and walking to the police car after being shot four times, but the trauma and loss of blood sent him into shock. "He sort of passed out in the police car," says Gillespie.

Jackson was taken to an emergency treatment centre for immediate attention and then transferred to Montreal General on Dorchester Street, where he was stabilized with blood transfusions and where his wounds were assessed. The bullet he took to the abdomen had missed all vital organs and had not damaged any major nerves or blood vessels. It had lodged near his spine. The wound was cleaned, and the bullet was left inside. The bullet to his right hand had broken two bones, but done no nerve damage. The two bullets that struck his left forearm had done considerable nerve and muscle damage, and surgery was required.

Four armed policemen stood guard over Jackson in the hospital. Gillespie was in the recovery room on Wednesday after Lennie's operation. When he came to, he saw the detective standing there.

"Hello John," said Lennie softly.

"How are you doin', Lennie?"

"John, when I was out I had the most beautiful, beautiful dream."

"What was it about?"

"You wouldn't understand."

In several conversations at the hospital over the next few days, Gillespie said Jackson talked about many personal things, including religion. "I'm an Anglican – Church of England," said Lennie.

"Well, so am I," said Gillespie. "What the hell are we doing trying to kill each other?" Lennie was silent for a few moments.

"You know, John, ever since I lost my foot, I don't really care very much about things any more."

The next day Lennie's mood was upbeat, and at one point he turned to Gillespie with a slight smile and announced, "I'll get out again, John."

"Aw come on, Lennie, don't give me that baloney."

"I'll get out again," he repeated.

"Don't tell me I have to go through all of this again."

"No. Don't worry, John, you won't have to go through this again."

Although Gillespie could never forgive Jackson for his part in the shooting of Eddie Tong, he found him personable and could understand Ann Jackson's devotion to him. "He had a lot of good qualities and she saw that in him," said Gillespie. "And he liked what he saw in her. She was not a classic beauty, but she was attractive and she knew how to dress. She was very soft-spoken. A real lady. I don't know about anything else, but I do know that Ann Jackson really loved her husband."

The shooting and capture of Lennie Jackson was devastating news for his family in Niagara Falls. His mother, Lillian Jackson, sobbed during an interview with a reporter the day after the shooting. She said she was sorry for her son and his new wife. "I haven't any idea what got into him," she said. "He was a pretty good boy. Yes, he was a very good boy."

TORONTO DAILY STAR

THE WEATHER

WEDNESDAY, MARCH 12, 1952—34 PAGES

3c PER COPY, 18c PER WEEK

3 OF 200 SHOTS HIT JACKSON
BOYD SAW POLICE CARS, FLED

| Tip-off Janitor's Wife Flees Afraid of Boyd Vengeance | HOME AND SPORT EDITION | Prefer 'Ike' to Taft, Give Truman Stinging Rebuk |

The newspaper coverage of Lennie Jackson's capture was even more extensive than that of Suchan's. All three Toronto dailies had banner headlines and pages and pages of photos. Jocko Thomas wrote in the *Star* that police had fully expected to find Boyd with Jackson but "Boyd is reported to have seen the police cars and fled." Page 3 of the Wednesday, March 12, edition of the *Star* was completely filled with photographs – nine in all: Lennie in his hospital bed; Ann drinking milk from a pint bottle after the shoot-out; Montreal police with Lennie's arsenal of weapons, including two machine guns; a bullet-riddled wall in the apartment; the smashed window; a blood-splattered sink; a bullet-proof vest used by the police; and a shot of the massive crowd that was looking on as Lennie entered the police cruiser with Gillespie.

One of the stories reported, falsely, that Jackson had used his wife as a shield during the gun battle. "The newspapers all said Lennie used Ann as a shield when he came out," says Gillespie. "But that's just not true. He would never do anything like that. He wasn't that type. He was too much of a man."

In Montreal, the papers ran photos of Edwin Alonzo Boyd, and witnesses came forward reporting that they had seen him at Jackson's apartment and at the restaurant below Suchan's apartment.

The police assumed that Boyd was in the Montreal area, and carried out several more raids in locations around the city, including a nightclub in the suburb of Lachine, a farmhouse twelve miles away, and the Boulevard Hotel across the river from Montreal in LaPrairie. Their assumption was bolstered when police found Boyd's fingerprints

in Suchan's apartment. Several others prints would later be identified as those of Dorreen Boyd and Mary Mitchell. The prints were
found on Pyrex bowls, a quart bottle of Dow beer, a drinking glass,
and bottles of Coca-Cola, skin lotion, and Heinz ketchup.
According to Boyd, those prints were from visits to the apartment
before Tong and Perry were gunned down.

Gillespie held a faint hope that in their hospital conversations,
Lennie Jackson might give him a clue as to Boyd's whereabouts.
Eventually he popped the question: "Where's the leader of the gang,
Lennie?"

"What leader?"

"You know who I mean – Boyd."

"Leader my fanny," said Lennie, who never cursed or used foul
language.

"Where is he?" persisted Gillespie.

"Oh, he's hundreds of miles away from here."

Gillespie said Lennie would talk about anything "except criminal
activity or fellow criminals. The only thing we got out of him was
about the telegram he sent from Hamilton. And he only told us that
because he thought we already knew about it and he wanted to know
how we tracked him down."

A Real Payne

E dwin Alonzo Boyd drew some solace from newspaper stories about the police tearing around Quebec searching for him; at the same time, he knew his situation was precarious. He was now Canada's most dangerous and most wanted criminal. He remained in Toronto, hunkered down in his Spadina Road rooming house, venturing out only at night and never to a well-lighted place like a restaurant or grocery store.

Meanwhile, Sergeant of Detectives Adolphus Payne, trusting his instincts, was certain his quarry had not left Toronto. Payne didn't have a stable of informants but he did spend a lot of time thinking, trying to figure out what he would do in Boyd's place. He had interrogated Boyd for many hours, and now he studied his notes, searching for insights. Although Boyd had hooked up with others for his recent robberies, Payne had a strong sense that he was a loner who knew Toronto well and knew how to disguise himself.

Payne decided that if he was going to get Boyd it would have to be through people close to him – family. He and his young partner, twenty-four-year-old Detective Ken Craven, concentrated on Boyd's wife, Dorreen, and his brother Norman. They discovered that Dorreen Boyd had left the Pickering house, telling neighbours she was returning to England. But the twins were in boarding school and Anthony was on a farm north of Toronto. Payne and Craven also learned that on March 7, the day Suchan was shot in Montreal, Norman Boyd had quit his job as a surveyor with the City of Toronto, declaring that he was leaving for California. "I was thinking of getting out of the country," says Norman. "There was just too much going on and I figured that if I stayed around, it would cause me more trouble than it was worth."

Payne believed that Dorreen and Norman were both still in Toronto, helping Ed Boyd elude the police dragnet. Until Tong and Perry were shot, Boyd had been feeling more secure as the publicity over his escape and the robberies diminished with time. But the shooting of the policemen dramatically increased police pressure and media scrutiny. Payne reasoned it would take careful planning to spirit Boyd out of town, or into deep cover with a new identity. That would take some time, and that time would provide Payne with the opportunity to do his own sleuthing and planning. Once again, he trusted his credo: There had to be a car involved.

A check of provincial records disclosed that Norman Boyd had been the registered owner of a 1949 Austin sedan, cream-coloured, licence plate 85-F-37, but on January 26, 1952, he had transferred ownership to Dorreen Mary Frances Boyd, Old Rose Bank Road, South Rose Bank, R.R.#3, Pickering, Ontario.

Payne had his car. Now to find it. He believed that if Dorreen or Norman, or both, were planning to leave town they would try to sell the Austin. And even if they decided to stay in Toronto, they would want to sell it because it could lead police to them.

Beginning the night after Tong was shot, Payne and Craven studied the For Sale ads in the classified sections of all of the Toronto newspapers. On Monday, March 10, they hit pay dirt: "'49 Austin, radio, new tires and battery, best offer." Disguising his voice, Payne called the number in the ad and asked about the car. The conversation was brief, but he ascertained that the man he was speaking to was Norman Boyd. Payne had a plan ready and immediately put it into action: he contacted Harold Jukes, a young, fresh-faced undercover officer in the Morality Division. Jukes did not meet the department's height requirement and had made it onto the force by sheer determination – he undertook a regime of stretching exercises, attempting to increase his height. He would never reach the height requirement, but the department was impressed with his determination and allowed him to join up as a constable. Because of his height and youthful appearance, Jukes was used as an undercover agent – most policemen were six feet or over, so he didn't look like a copper.

Jukes and a police department clerk, Patricia Prior, met in Payne's office, where Payne outlined his plan and created a cover story for the couple. Jukes then called and made an appointment to see the car. Norman Boyd was living at 96 London Street in a house owned by the sister of Glover Boyd's second wife. At noon the next day, Jukes and Prior, posing as Mr. and Mrs. Harold McCarten, were met at the house by Norman, who showed them the Austin. The couple acted keen to purchase the car, but as Payne had instructed, they made an offer slightly below the asking price. Norman was anxious to get rid of the car and accepted the offer, but when he produced the registration, Dorreen Boyd was listed as the owner, just as Payne had told Jukes and Prior to expect.

The couple feigned great concern, as Payne had coached them to do. They told Norman that the bailiff had repossessed their last car because the person they bought it from wasn't the registered owner. They couldn't go through that heartbreaking and expensive experience again. And their lawyer had told them that in any future deal, they had to make sure the registered owner signed a release in their presence. Norman Boyd said that the registered owner was his sister-in-law, and that he didn't know if he could contact her but he would try. He asked for Jukes' telephone number. Jukes gave him his brother's phone number, and he and Prior left, still gushing about the Austin. Dolph Payne, hiding behind a fence down the street, had watched the whole thing.

Jukes was at his brother's house when Norman Boyd called late in the afternoon. He said the registered owner would be at the London Street house in two hours and would provide Jukes with a written clearance.

In his report later, Jukes wrote that he arrived alone at the London Street address "about 7:30 P.M. on Tuesday March 11 and obtained a receipt for a $10 deposit on the auto and a lien clearance note, both signed by Norman and Dorreen Boyd." Jukes would return in a few days with the balance of the money. After Jukes left, Payne staked out the house from his hiding place behind the fence. Ken

Craven was parked in a cruiser a short distance away, waiting for a flashlight signal from his partner.

About 8:30 p.m. on Tuesday, Norman and Dorreen came out of the house and drove off in the Austin. Payne signalled Craven, who picked him up, and they followed without headlights. The Austin went west on London Street and then north for three blocks on Manning Avenue.

"Pull over before the intersection," Payne told his partner when the car ahead turned right at Olive Avenue. Payne got out of the cruiser and ran to the intersection. He looked around the corner and saw the Austin parked half-way up the block. It sat there for four or five minutes before pulling out and continuing east. Payne waved to Craven, who picked him up at the corner.

"Stay with them," said Payne. "They're just ahead."

"What happened?" asked Craven.

"They pulled over to see if anyone was following them."

"How did you know they were going to do that?"

"Just a feeling," said Payne. "We'll have to check at every turn to make sure they're not waiting for us."

Travelling at no more than twenty miles an hour, the Austin took a circuitous route north around Upper Canada College. After taking several more side streets and stopping twice, the car headed south and stopped on Heath Street West, about a block from Yonge Street. Payne and Craven stayed well back and timed the stop at four minutes, after which the Austin drove slowly ahead, stopping again just short of Yonge.

"Both Norman and Dorreen Boyd walked back west and entered No. 42 Heath St. West where they remained for half an hour," wrote Payne in his report later. The house was three storeys with apartments on each level and another in the basement. It was in a quiet, upscale neighbourhood of solid brick and stone houses on tree-lined streets. After leaving the house, Norman and Dorreen walked east on Heath, past their auto, to Yonge. Craven remained in the cruiser, out of sight in a circular driveway down the street, while Payne followed them on foot. "They remained standing in a doorway on Yonge Street for some minutes and then returned to their Austin car," he wrote.

The detectives took note of the Heath Street address and continued their surveillance, following the Austin to a laneway running off Maplewood Avenue near Bathurst and St. Clair. "Upon entering the lane, the lights of their auto were turned off," reported Payne. "And they proceeded south to a garage at the rear of 86 Kenwood. They both left the auto, entered the garage, and after about ten minutes, they got back into their auto and proceeded south on the lane, with the lights out."

From the garage, the detectives followed the Austin south on Bathurst Street nine blocks to Wells Street, where it turned east and followed several side streets to Spadina Road, just north of Bloor Street. "Both left the auto, and walked over to the east side of Spadina, then south to Bloor Street where they turned around and walked back north to No. 19 Spadina Road," reported Payne. He and Craven didn't realize it then, but they had discovered the rooming house hideout that Edwin Alonzo Boyd had been using for several weeks. Dorreen and Norman entered No. 19 by the side door.

The detectives had been watching the building from their car for about twenty minutes when Norman Boyd came out and returned alone to the Austin. "He drove in a direct manner to his home at 96 London St.," wrote Payne, "at considerably greater speed" than he had earlier in the evening.

It was after 11 p.m. by the time Craven and Payne called it a night. Their doggedness had paid off: they had located possible hideouts on London Street, Spadina Road, and Heath Street, and there was the garage behind Kenwood. They could raid them all, but if Boyd happened to be out, or at some location they didn't know about, they would miss him and he would be alerted. It made more sense to wait until they were certain Boyd was at one of the addresses. The Austin, although using side streets, had travelled fairly direct routes to the garage and to the Spadina Road rooming house, but the run to the Heath Street West apartment building had been much more devious, and Payne and Craven concluded that was where Boyd would eventually turn up.

Ann Jackson was being held in Montreal as a material witness. On Thursday the police persuaded her to broadcast an appeal for Boyd to surrender. In a sob-choked voice over radio station CJAD, she told Boyd, "I just wouldn't want any more shooting. The others – Steve and Leonard – have been badly shot up. Don't let it happen to you." But she told reporters after the broadcast that she had delivered it as a gesture of co-operation to the police and didn't think it would make a difference. "One thing I know," she said, "if the tables were turned and Len or Steve were in Boyd's place, they wouldn't fall for a thing like that. Some of the boys would rather die anyway than serve a long time inside – that's the thing that frightens them more than shooting it out."

There was no response to Ann Jackson's plea, and by Friday the Montreal police, after combing the city for Boyd, had begun to suspect he had left the city.

Also on Friday, the *Telegram* ran a story stating that Dorreen Boyd had disappeared from her Pickering home. The police, meanwhile, were not letting on that they knew her whereabouts. Witnesses had told police that just before her disappearance, Mrs. Boyd was suddenly "in the chips" and had been seen driving a new car.

Payne and Craven checked out the house at 42 Heath Street West. It was owned by a young lawyer, George Stoddard, who lived with his wife on the second floor and rented out the rest of the house. The Stoddards were about to leave for a Mexican vacation and had decided to rent out their apartment in their absence. Norman and Dorreen Boyd had passed themselves off as a Mr. and Mrs. Hall. Gail Ostroski, who managed the building and lived in the basement apartment with her 18-month-old son, was told by Mrs. Stoddard "that Mr. Hall was a very quiet nice chap – a writer – and he wouldn't be holding any loud parties or anything like that." And Mr. Hall also said he had been a missionary in Cuba and that his brother would be staying with them for a while. The Stoddards would be leaving Friday, and the "Halls" would be moving into the furnished apartment that night.

Rooms on the third floor of the house were rented by Norman Keefer, Harry Thomas, and Frank Raby. Keefer, a civil servant, had been introduced to Mr. and Mrs. Hall earlier in the week. "I would have put him down as a retiring type of Englishman," Keefer would say later. "He had practically nothing to say when we were introduced.

Nor did the woman I was told was his wife."

Mr. and Mrs. F.B. Poucher, who lived on the first floor of the building, were in Florida on vacation. Mr. Poucher was an executive with National Trust Company.

When Payne and Craven revealed that Mr. and Mrs. Hall were Edwin Alonzo Boyd's wife and brother, Stoddard feared that his building would be shot up and his other tenants injured. The police department had to post a bond covering any damages before Stoddard would agree to co-operate.[23]

Allan Lamport says that the police were aided by a woman who lived across the street from the house. "We couldn't have policemen going in and out of houses around there. Anybody could tell a policeman or a detective miles away." The woman watched the house "night and day," reporting by telephone to Payne and Craven. "The police commission gave the woman a remembrance tray for her work in observing," says Lamport.

On Friday morning, Payne persuaded another neighbour, a Bell Telephone manager, to let the police use his front living room to stake out the house next door. They waited in the house all day and into the evening. Then, shortly after 9 p.m., Norman Boyd pulled up in the Austin. The policemen watched as he made several trips into the house, carrying luggage and clothing. He was so quiet that other residents in the house didn't even know he'd been there. He left, but returned again before 10 p.m. With the aid of overhead street lights, Payne and Craven could see the silhouettes of two passengers in the Austin. Norman Boyd left the car and walked into the house. The lights came on in the second-floor apartment. Norman returned to the car and opened the door for Dorreen Boyd, and the two of them entered the house. When Norman returned to the street once again, the door to the Austin opened and another man got out. He was wearing a topcoat and a fedora and looked to be about the right build for Edwin Boyd. As he started up the walk to the house, Payne got a glimpse of his face and knew it was Boyd. He noticed he was carrying a bulging briefcase. The Boyd brothers disappeared into the house, and Payne breathed a sigh of relief.

In the basement apartment, Gail Ostroski noticed that the Halls "were very quiet and went upstairs without making a sound. We didn't even get a look at them. Mrs. Stoddard told us they would be very quiet, and I remember thinking how right she was."

Recalling that night, Boyd says that before entering the apartment "I looked around and didn't see anyone watching, so I went across the street and into the house. Of course I didn't know that the cops were in the house next door. I shouldn't have trusted anybody else. I was the only one left, and the police were circling around me. When Norm and Dorreen put that car up for sale, it did me in. If I had been sensible I would have gone north on Yonge Street and rented a hotel room. That Heath Street thing was for the birds. It was too wide open, and I was tired. I hadn't been getting as much sleep as I needed. I was making all the mistakes in the book. I should have stayed away from my family. I should have known the police would be watching them."

Once Boyd was inside the house, Payne called his boss, Inspector Archie McCathie, chief of detectives, who was primed to have his men rush in and subdue Boyd with heavy firepower. Payne objected strongly. His widow, Helen Payne, says "Dolph told his superiors he was in charge of the case and no one was going in until they were certain the Boyds were asleep."

"If we go in now, there'll be a big shoot-out," Payne told McCathie. Payne was aware that both Suchan and Jackson had carried briefcases crammed with weapons before they were shot down, and he was certain Boyd's briefcase also contained a small arsenal. "It was quite a big satchel," he told Helen later.

By midnight, more than fifty heavily armed officers had the house surrounded, but Payne would not be budged. He and Craven would go in first, but not until *he* was ready.

"Dolph and Craven were apprehensive," says Helen Payne. "Dolph phoned me around midnight to let me know that Boyd was there and what they had planned to do. I had a pretty restless night. Before I went to bed, I got down on my knees and prayed that he'd be all right. I think I managed to get some sleep."

The day before, Payne had removed the chain lock from the back door at 42 Heath and had an extra key made. He would enter that door, and Craven would come through the front door a few minutes later. Payne at the time was forty-three, almost twenty years older than Craven. "Craven was a lot younger, and Dolph didn't want him to get hurt," says Helen Payne.

Between them, Payne and Craven had one bullet-proof vest and a heavy blue-steel riot shield.

"We'll toss for the vest," said Payne. Craven won the toss.

To satisfy McCathie, Payne had agreed to a plan whereby McCathie would telephone Boyd at 6 a.m., tell him he was surrounded, and demand that he surrender. But Payne had no intention of following the plan. He thought it would end in disaster because Boyd would have read about police shoot-to-kill orders, even though no such order had been issued by the Toronto department.

Payne's concern was well-founded. In the apartment with Boyd was a stamped envelope with a letter addressed to the *Toronto Daily Star*. He had planned to mail it the next day. The letter stated that Toronto detectives "would go to any length to obtain convictions. They will do their utmost, with the full approval of higher officers to keep their weaknesses covered. They will use an order of 'shoot to kill' rather than intelligent directed efforts so well known in Britain's Scotland Yard." The sometimes rambling letter said that from now on the initiative would remain with him. "Death has always been a friend to me and I will meet it face to face. So keep out of my way and avoid bloodshed. Death means nothing to me when I am fighting for my family. Start seeing me in your every shadow. Start guarding your families … they are your weakness, for I am no longer a respecter of persons."

As proof that the letter was genuine, Boyd dipped his fingers in ink and pressed them to the bottom of the page. "My fingerprints are on this paper," he wrote. "This will prove I'm not kidding."

About 5:50 a.m. on Saturday, ten minutes before McCathie was to make the call to Boyd, Payne and Craven made their move. Payne, with the shield in front of him and his .38 revolver in hand, used the key to enter the back door and started up the staircase with two men behind him, one carrying a shotgun. There were no landings. The stairs went directly to the door of Boyd's second-floor apartment.

Helen Payne laughs when she thinks of her husband creeping up the stairs. "He was not a dainty man by any means. He was about six feet, over two hundred. He never came in the house without me hearing him, so I don't know how he got up those stairs quietly."

Payne opened the door to Boyd's floor and entered the hallway, which ran the full length of the apartment to the front. He had studied the layout and knew that Boyd could be in one of three rooms. He thought Boyd must have heard them by now, and decided on a new approach: he would announce himself. Boyd knew him, and perhaps he would decide not to shoot it out. It was a gamble, but Payne felt it was the best strategy. He charged through the first door. "Boyd – it's Payne!" he said in a loud voice. The room was empty. He ran to the second door, again shouting the warning as he opened it. He thought the room was empty, but Norman Boyd was asleep under the covers on a bed in the corner. Payne rushed to the last door. "Boyd – it's Payne!" he hollered as he entered. "Boyd – it's Payne!"

Dorreen says she and her husband had pushed two single beds together and were sleeping soundly when she was awakened by Payne's shouting. "I didn't hear him coming before that. Everything was in turmoil, our nerves were on edge. Ed always woke up early, but we had stayed up talking for a while and didn't get to sleep until after midnight." She sat up as Ed, foggy with sleep, was just beginning to rouse himself. "Payne is here," she said. Just then Payne came through the door and ran straight for Boyd, pinning him to the bed with the shield and holding his revolver to his head. "It's Payne!" he said. "You sonofabitch, if you grab your gun I'll blow your head off!"

Dorreen says Payne "looked so silly" when he came through the door. "I look up and there he is with a shield with a gun over the top. I laughed but I didn't think it was funny, just nerves I guess. I thought, oh they don't know Ed at all. He wasn't Billy the Kid, he would never have shot Payne." But Payne had reason to be cautious – just a reach away at Boyd's bedside was his open briefcase with five fully loaded handguns, arranged with handles up for instant access.

Payne handcuffed Boyd as the room suddenly filled with policemen. In the next room, Norman Boyd, still groggy with sleep, was also being handcuffed.

The arrest of Edwin Alonzo Boyd by Adolphus Payne was a

defining, and much discussed, moment in the Boyd Gang saga. Dolph Payne would always insist that Boyd could have shot him. Boyd's memory of that moment is that he woke up with a gun at his head. Helen Payne says that Dolph told her Boyd "was just coming awake," with Dorreen trying to wake him up, when Payne came through the door. "That's what Dolph told me. I suppose they were dazed. And once Dolph was on top of Boyd, he couldn't get up."

Jocko Thomas: "The way I heard it from Dolph Payne, Boyd wouldn't have had much of a chance to use his guns. I think Payne had his gun right up to Boyd's temple."

Jack Webster: "From the number of weapons that Boyd had access to at that time, he could have shot Payne dead. But he didn't, and Adolphus Payne was forever grateful for this. Through his long career, he had been in a lot of cases involving violence, but I had many hours of conversation with him and he'd become very emotional when he talked about the moment he entered that room and said, 'Boyd – it's Payne. Boyd – it's Payne,' and Boyd didn't shoot him. That remained with Payne right up until the end of his life."

Payne once wrote down his thoughts of that moment: "At Boyd's bedside, within inches of his hand was the brief case full of money, on top of which were five loaded guns. No doubt to shoot it out with me would endanger his own life, nevertheless that course was open. I am sure that it was not because he was scared of me that he didn't shoot, because, quite the contrary, he was very calm, which is more than I could say for myself at that moment."

Jocko Thomas missed Boyd's capture. He was still in Montreal covering Suchan and Jackson and the search for Boyd in that city. He flew back to Toronto when he learned of the arrest. The main *Star* story on Boyd's capture was written by Frank Teskey, the paper's accomplished two-way man (photographer-reporter), who was often called out to cover police stories at night and in the early hours of the morning. The lead on Teskey's story was typical of the journalism of the day: "The climax of the greatest police manhunt in Canada's crime history was written without a shot today when Edwin Alonzo Boyd, last of a trio of desperate gunmen, looked up from his bed in a Heath St. W. apartment into the muzzle of a police revolver."

What will never be known is whether Boyd would have tried to shoot it out if he had been fully awake when Payne entered the house. He might have trusted Payne not to "shoot to kill", but judging by the letter Boyd wrote to the *Star*, that trust would not have extended

to others. He would have known there was no chance for escape, but if he thought they were trying to kill him he probably would have tried to take as many of them with him as he could.

In a *Star* story later that day, Boyd's other brother, Gordon, who lived in Lindsay, Ontario, was quoted as saying that a Toronto policeman had warned Dorreen Boyd to have her husband give himself up to a newspaper or to his lawyer. "He told her if the detectives got word first, they'd come in and shoot him down."

Gordon Boyd also told the *Star* he was relieved that his brother had been captured without a shoot-out. "I expected he would shoot it out. I wouldn't want to go to jail for twenty years. I'd rather shoot it out."

Gordon was worried about his younger brother, Norman. "I told Norman to stay away from him. Talking on the telephone is different, but he should have stayed away." Gordon didn't know where his older brother was during the hunt. "I kind of figured he was in Toronto, but I didn't know anything about the Heath Street place. He'd have been much better off if he'd stayed in the Don Jail. He would have had a good defense and I'm sure he would have got off."

He said Ed Boyd was not a criminal type, "but he's pretty smart. We all have a little larceny in our souls. We go to church on Sunday and beat it out of the others on Monday. But he's not a vicious type."

Mayor Lamport had instructed Chief John Chisholm that he was to be contacted the minute Boyd was captured, and that they were to wait until he arrived at the scene before bringing Boyd out. Translation: he wanted his picture taken and some of the credit for nabbing the notorious gunman. Besides, as chairman of the police commission, he had as much right to be there as anyone.

Lamport lived on St. Clair Avenue, a few minutes' drive away. He had told his driver to remain in the area and to be ready at a moment's notice. The mayor was asleep when Inspector John Nimmo called shortly after 6 a.m. "You better get over here, we've made the contact," said Nimmo.

"I'll be there in twenty minutes," said Lamport. As he was putting on his shirt and tie, the telephone rang again. It was *Telegram* reporter Doug Creighton. The newspapers had been tipped off about Boyd's arrest, but Creighton was in Hamilton.

"I was following a Boyd lead that somebody had phoned in to the office," says Creighton. "I didn't want to go to Hamilton because I was certain from a friend of mine on the police force that he was in Toronto. But the paper sent me to Hamilton anyway, and then they phoned up panic-stricken when they got Boyd on Heath Street."

Creighton was most concerned that the *Telegram* have a photographer at the scene to record Boyd's capture. "I called Lampy and pleaded with him," says Creighton. "They [the police] had called him to say they'd wait for him, and the mayor decided to have some breakfast."

"Doug Creighton phoned me, and I said 'I'll hold it up for you,' and I did somewhat," says Lamport. Creighton didn't make it back from Hamilton in time, but *Telegram* reporter Derm Dunworthy and photographer Russell Cooper were there to witness Boyd being brought out of the house. Creighton managed a one-on-one interview with Boyd at police headquarters later that morning.

Lamport, carefully dressed in a suit and tie, but unshaven, arrived on Heath Street to find the street blocked off by police cars. Reporters and photographers were arriving en masse about the same time. Lamport was so excited he could barely contain himself. He jumped from the car and headed quickly for No. 42. "It all moved under a run," he says. "There was no walking."

In the second-floor apartment, meanwhile, Dorreen Boyd was fuming. She was in her pyjamas (Chinese yellow silk) surrounded by a roomful of men. "There were eight or nine bloomin' guys in one room," she says. "Payne said 'get dressed', but I wasn't about to change in front of a roomful of cops. I was very upset."

"My wife's not getting dressed until you put a blanket in front of her," said Boyd. Inspector McCathie had arrived, and he held up a blanket but was looking over it.

"You can look the other way," said Boyd.

Dorreen now laughs at the memory. "He did turn away," she says. Ed Boyd was also allowed to change. He put on a shirt, tie, and sports jacket.

When police checked Boyd's briefcase they found $23,329 in cash. Another $639 was in his wallet. Norman Boyd had $1,608 in a wallet and two envelopes, and in Dorreen Boyd's wallet there was $100.81.

The fully loaded guns found in the briefcase included two .38 calibre Smith & Wesson revolvers, one 7.35 mm Beretta automatic pistol, one 9 mm Luger automatic pistol, and one .455 calibre Smith & Wesson revolver. The .38 calibre revolvers had been stolen from banks at Pickering and the Bank of Toronto on Kingston Road. The Luger had been stolen from the auto of a Guelph man in 1942. It isn't known how Boyd acquired it.

When Boyd's clothing was searched, red and black pepper was found in almost every pocket. "The pepper was a precaution he took in the event a police officer stopped and questioned him," Payne wrote later. "If the officer recognized him or was about to establish his identity, he would toss the pepper in his eyes to make good his escape, rather than resort to the use of a gun." To Payne, the pepper was further evidence that Boyd did not want to shoot anyone.

"When I was on the run I always carried pepper in my pocket in case anybody got too close," says Boyd. "I could just give them an eyeful of pepper and take off. I don't know whether it would have worked or not, but the police thought it was quite an idea and they passed it on to the newspaper people, who made a big deal out of it. I'd like to have thrown a handful in the mayor's face. Wouldn't *that* have been nice. When they took me down to the veranda to get the pictures taken, the mayor was so excited he was hopping from foot to foot. He had a habit of doing that. When he got excited he was always jumping around."

There was a carnival atmosphere by the time the Boyds were brought down the narrow staircase. Neighbours had awakened stunned to a street filled with policemen, reporters, and photographers. Later they brought out chairs, and some of them served coffee to the policemen when they realized they had been up all night.

Lamport went into the house just as the Boyds were being brought downstairs. He wanted to be seen coming out the door with Boyd and the police. The reporters and photographers moved in, cameras clicking and bulbs flashing as Boyd appeared in the doorway with the mayor and the police. With all the attention, Boyd's spirits seemed to lift.

"I didn't think it would take something like this to meet your worship," he said, nodding to Lamport. "Shall I smile?"

"With the trouble you're in, you'd better not," said Lamport. "You can be thankful you're alive. You're in the land of a fine police force."

"Yes," said Boyd, glancing at Payne, "you fellows did a fine job."

At 8 a.m., Inspector John Nimmo telephoned Eddie Tong's wife to tell her Boyd had been captured. "My husband is avenged at last," she said. "I couldn't rest until all those men were taken in. I am so glad the police have been successful but I am terribly worried because my husband was not too well yesterday. He moaned all day and it made me afraid. If only he would get better everything would be wonderful."

The *Star*'s Alexandrine Gibb reported from Tong's hospital room at Toronto General that he had managed a weak smile when told of Boyd's capture.

Later that morning, Dorreen Boyd appeared before Magistrate G.A. Thorburn on a charge of conspiracy to rob and was remanded in custody to March 21. Norman Boyd was also remanded on a similar charge.

Edwin Alonzo Boyd did not appear in court that day. He was with Dolph Payne and Ken Craven. There were matters to discuss, loose ends to tie up.

Answered Prayers

Detectives Payne and Craven transported Edwin Alonzo Boyd to No. 11 Station at London and Markham Streets. He was given the standard police caution, and once he learned that some of the bills found in his briefcase had been marked, he quickly admitted to the March 4 robbery of the Bank of Montreal at College and Manning. He refused to identify the other two hold-up men. At noon, Boyd took Payne and Craven to a garage at the rear of 294 Euclid, where he had hidden the stolen 1948 Chevrolet coupe used in the robbery.

Later, the detectives went to the garage in the laneway behind Kenwood Avenue, where the Austin had led them the night they tailed Dorreen and Norman Boyd. Inside, they found the 1951 grey Nash sedan that Ed Boyd had purchased under the name Charles Hunter. The licence plates on the car had been stolen. Three other sets of stolen plates were found under the Nash's rear seat.

In the glove compartment was the owner's manual for the Nash. Thumbing through it a few days later, Payne noticed the numbers 5, 6, and 0 pencilled in on succeeding pages along with a telephone number that checked out to a rooming house on Logan Avenue. Further investigation revealed that Joseph W. Jackson had rented a room at the house shortly after the March 4 robbery. He had left there following Boyd's arrest and had not returned. In a search of Jackson's room they found a motor vehicle ownership permit listing one of the stolen sets of licence markers found in Boyd's Nash. A background check revealed that Joseph Jackson was the brother of William R. Jackson, now in Kingston after escaping the Don Jail with Boyd.

Provincial records disclosed that Joseph Jackson had purchased three motor vehicles since the March 4 robbery, and his latest registration listed a Jarvis Street address as his residence. The house was placed under police surveillance.

Ontario's new Deputy Minister of Reform Institutions, Col. Hedley Basher, appeared at the Don Jail in person to discuss the security measures to be used for Ed Boyd. The jail governor, Thomas Brand, whom he had chosen to run the Don after Boyd's first escape, said that Boyd would be going to No. 9 Hospital on the jail's second level. Basher went with him to inspect the cell. No. 9 had not been used as a hospital or infirmary for many years, but the name had stuck. It now housed the death cells, so named because of their proximity to the gallows. No. 9 Hospital was a row of four cells with a corridor in front. Beyond the corridor, through an iron grille gate, was a narrow antechamber about twelve feet long. The entrance to the antechamber was through a solid, oversized oak door.

In Basher's days as governor, the four cells had been one large cell. He had ordered the installation of the antechamber after a guard had been viciously attacked by an inmate. "Up to that time there had been no separation," Basher explained to Brand. "The guard was in the room with the man." High on the east wall of the corridor in front of the cells, Basher noticed a window that could be opened inward to provide ventilation. Beyond the glass was a set of double-bars – the only such set at the Don. They were seen as necessary because outside the window it was only a short drop to the top of a partitioning wall that led to the jail's outer wall. As he studied the window, Basher noticed the raised weld scars where the original bars had been repaired after Frank McCullough sawed his way out in 1919.

For added security, the ceiling and dividing walls of the four-cell block were made of metal. Only the floors were made of wood. And the front grilles and cell doors were of steel fabricated by the J.J. Taylor Safe Company. Beyond the oak door was a landing, another steel grille, and three or four steps leading to the other eighteen cells on No. 9 Corridor. When the oak door was open, a guard sitting on the landing outside No. 9 Hospital had a full view of the corridor in front of the cells and a partial view of the cells themselves.

Basher noticed a screened air shaft on the ten-foot ceiling of the corridor in front of the four cells. As an additional security measure, he instructed Brand to have a microphone installed behind the screen. Wire would run from the microphone to a speaker in Brand's office on the main floor. Boyd was a dangerous criminal and Basher wanted him watched continuously.

As Basher and Brand were inspecting the cells, they were told that Boyd had arrived at the jail. They ended their discussion and went down to watch him being processed. After Boyd was issued his prison denims, a guard escorted him to Brand's office. After a stern warning from Brand about following the rules and behaving, Boyd asked if he could have something to read in his cell.

"I wouldn't give you anything to read if you were to stay in here for the next fifty years," said Brand. Boyd realized then that he would be paying the consequences for his escape four months earlier and for being associated with the men who had shot down a policeman. "I guess I'm sunk," he thought.

He was despondent when he entered his assigned cell, which was second from the corridor entrance. From behind the bars of his cell door he could see the double-barred window directly ahead high on the east wall. To his left was the stone wall at the end of the corridor; to his right, through the grille and the open oak door, sat a guard. This was to be his world – for how long, he didn't know. A couple of days later a workman arrived to install a microphone behind the screen in the ceiling air vent. He said he was making plumbing and electrical repairs, but Boyd knew differently.

Boyd was feeling guilty that his wife and brother had been incarcerated because of his crimes. Thoughts of suicide crossed his mind, but were quickly dispelled. As he lay on his bed contemplating his life, and the predicament he found himself in, he began thinking about "all the stuff in the Bible I'd been brought up to believe in."

Then he decided to fast and meditate. He wasn't allowed to eat in the mess hall with the other prisoners, and when his meals were brought to his cell, he flushed them down the toilet. Two days after his arrival, he received a letter from Dorreen. Writing from her cell, she said she was feeling helpless, depressed, and hopeless. On March 19, Boyd replied:

My darling wife:

It hurts me more to see you in this trouble than it could possibly bother me about myself. You and our family are the sufferers. If only you had done what I asked and stayed away from me. Anyway, even if I have nothing else to offer, you have my deepest love which has always been the most solid asset in our marriage. As you say we have pulled through worse messes than this. The little cell I have here is not bad although it is a bit lonesome. Nobody is allowed near me so I have lots of time to think, which I have always enjoyed anyway. Some of the greatest men in history did their best work in prison. So you see there is no need for you to worry about me. Let us pray that you and Norm are able to leave soon and I also pray that you will receive some help to make a living instead of having snobs refuse you a job because of me. Darling, don't let anything get your spirits down. I'm sure that with all of us pulling hard together, we'll get through the rapids with only wet skin. Now do you feel better?

All my love and a barrel full of kisses.

Eddie xxxxxxx

With Boyd facing a long penitentiary term, it's difficult to imagine what "worse messes than this" he was writing about. All letters coming into or going out of the Don were read by the administration, and Brand would have seen Dorreen's letter and Boyd's response.

Boyd continued fasting and meditating and began "visualizing." He began to see himself outside the prison, taking walks on streets he knew, visiting shops and houses. For hours he stared at a matchstick on the floor, attempting to move it by force of will. It didn't work, but he felt his powers of concentration growing. He desperately wanted reading material and decided to focus all of his mental energies on that. "I thought maybe I could get what I wanted if I visualized it," says Boyd. "So I visualized myself leaving my cell, walking down the steel stairs, and stopping in front of the steel gate where the superintendent[24] was at his desk." He visualized their conversation:

"What do you want?" asked Brand.

"I want a book to read."

"Well go back to your cell, and I'll think about it."

Perhaps because he was fasting, the visualization was very real to him, and he repeated the mental exercise for the next three days. On the fourth day, as he lay on his back in bed with his eyes closed and his hands clasped behind his head, he heard the clank of the grille being opened and looked up to see Brand standing there, with a book and some pamphlets in his hand.

"Can I talk to you?" asked Brand.

"Certainly."

"I brought you up a couple of books to read."

He handed Boyd a couple of Rosicrucian pamphlets and the Bible. "I was amazed," says Boyd. "I thought, geez this visualizing and self-hypnosis really works."

He wasn't interested in the pamphlets but was immediately engrossed in the Bible. "The more I read it, the more it became a part of me. And when I started thinking about something, the text from the Bible that fitted in would shoot into my mind." Now, in addition to visualizing, he began praying – hoping a Higher Power would help him find a way out of his situation.

While Boyd was praying for a way out, Jack Gillespie was in Montreal preparing to bring Lennie Jackson in. Jackson was released from hospital on March 21, six days after Boyd's capture. Although Jackson's wounds were healing well, his arms were still immobile; one was in a cast, the other in a splint.

Gillespie and Jackson sat together on the plane to Toronto, and the detective said later that it was a pleasant flight. There was no personal animosity between the two men, though Gillespie has always believed that Lennie wanted to kill him in the gunfight, and that he had survived only "by sheer luck." On the plane, Gillespie described a hypothetical scenario to Jackson: "What if you just came out of a bank. You're standing there in a doorway with a sub-machine-gun under your gabardine topcoat, and I happen to drive up in a uniform car. What would you do?" Lennie rolled his eyes, shook his head, and didn't say a word. "Aw, come on, Lennie," said Gillespie. Jackson smiled slightly but kept silent.

Mug shots of Elizabeth and Joseph Lesso, parents of Steve Suchan.
Mug shot of Mary Mitchell (right), sister of Leonard Jackson and occasional
informant to Edmund Tong. (Toronto Police Museum)

Funeral cortege for
Sergeant of Detectives
Edmund Tong
passes honour guard
on Danforth Avenue.
(Toronto Telegram/
Toronto Sun)

Detective Jack Gillespie returns wounded
Lennie Jackson to Toronto on Trans Canada
Airway's flight from Montreal.
(Toronto Telegram/Toronto Sun)

Jack Webster, former staff superintendent and now historian at the Metropolitan Toronto Police Museum and Discovery Centre. He walked the beat with Edwin Boyd's policeman father, Glover Boyd. (Brian Vallée)

Crime reporter Gwyn "Jocko" Thomas, who won three National Newspaper Awards, covered the Boyd Gang for the Toronto Star. (Toronto Star)

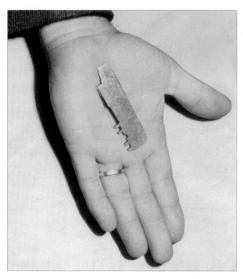

Key fashioned by Edwin Alonzo Boyd and used to open the gang's cells. (Toronto Star)

Oak door and row of cells in No. 9 Hospital at the Don Jail. Steve Suchan and Lennie Jackson stood on the table (foreground) and held a pillow over a microphone while Boyd and Willie Jackson sawed the window bars. (Toronto Police Museum)

Photo of the Don Jail 9 showing escape route during the Gang's second break-out, September 1952. In fact, the labelled window was opened, but not smashed. (Toronto Telegram/Toronto Sun)

Reward poster distributed by Ontario Provincial Police after the Boyd Gang's second escape from the Don Jail. (Toronto Police Museum)

North York barn where Boyd Gang was captured without a fight. (Toronto Star)

*Boyd and Willie Jackson being escorted from the North York jail by
Constable Ernie Southern (white shirt) and Detective Bert Trotter (fedora),
who were in on the capture the night before.* (Toronto Telegram/Toronto Sun)

Dorreen Boyd reads a letter from Edwin Boyd written in the Don Jail after his recapture in a North York barn in September 1952.
(Toronto Telegram/Toronto Sun)

Edwin Alonzo Boyd going to court handcuffed to Sergeant of Detectives Dolph Payne. (Toronto Star)

Steve Suchan (second from left) and Lennie Jackson handcuffed together as they arrive at the City Hall courtroom to face murder charges in September 1952.
(Toronto Telegram/Toronto Sun)

Willie "the Clown" Jackson with cigar after he was sentenced to a long term in Kingston Penitentiary. Also sentenced were his brother Joe Jackson (left) and Allister Gibson. (Toronto Telegram/Toronto Sun)

Ann Jackson with eight-week-old Michael in October 1952, while her husband, Lennie, was in the death cells at the Don Jail. Lennie was refused permission to see his son because prison officials thought it would be too hard on him. (Toronto Star)

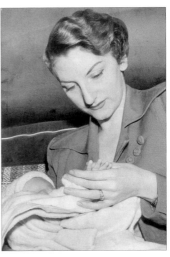

Boyd (second from left) and Willie Jackson (rear) mug for photographers as a police paddy wagon whisks them off to Kingston Penitentiary after their trials. (Toronto Telegram/ Toronto Sun)

Cover of promotional package for 1983 docudrama on Edwin Alonzo Boyd. (Toronto Police Museum)

Dorreen Boyd in her apartment near Toronto in 1996. (Toronto Star)

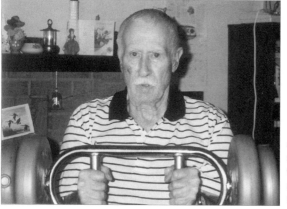

Edwin Alonzo Boyd, now 83, lifting weights in his home in British Columbia. (Brian Vallée)

"He was quite capable of killing any policeman who tried to capture him," says Gillespie.

Less than half an hour after he was booked into the Don Jail, Jackson's shoes and his artificial foot were sent by Brand for examination under a fluoroscope at the Medical Arts Building, at Bloor Street and Avenue Road. In a barely visible slit in the boot extension that covered the calf, two used hacksaw blades were discovered – one full ten-inch blade, and a second broken blade about eight inches long. Jail administrators had been unsuccessfully lobbying the City of Toronto for a fluoroscope at the Don. The discovery of the blades bolstered their position. The blades used in the November escape had come from the same boot, and if the city had spent $900 for a second-hand fluoroscope, Tong and Perry might not have been shot.

When Jackson arrived at the jail, he was assigned to the Debtor's Room, so called because it had been used in the jail's earliest days to incarcerate people who didn't pay their bills. Because Jackson couldn't look after himself, another inmate was assigned to attend his personal needs – to wash his face and help him use the toilet, and so on. The Debtor's Room was directly above No. 9 Hospital, where Boyd was. Brand was worried about the two notorious inmates "being one over the top of the other," and after ten days he moved Jackson to a cell in No. 3 Hospital, "the only available place I had for him."

At 12:23 a.m. on Sunday, March 23, seventeen days after being shot down by Steve Suchan, Sergeant of Detectives Edmund Tong died when a massive blood clot from his paralysed legs moved to his heart. His wife and children were rushed to the hospital in a police cruiser. Evelyn Tong had expected her husband to survive. She had already been planning a rehabilitation program and was thinking of selling their Doncrest Avenue home and moving to a bungalow so that Eddie would be able to get around in a wheelchair. Evelyn had become engaged to Eddie when she was sixteen and had followed him to Canada five years later to become his wife. Now he was gone. "It never should have happened to him," she said. "He was a good man and never hurt anyone in his life."

The *Telegram*'s Doug Creighton wrote that "to those who didn't know Tong, he was a tough cop. But underneath he was as long on kindness as he was on courage. Since the shooting which touched off the largest manhunt in the city's history, the police department switchboard has been flooded with calls from citizens, even criminals he had arrested, asking about his condition and wishing him well." A *Star* editorial said Tong was "a fearless officer and never hesitated in the performance of his duty because of danger to himself. The Toronto force will be poorer without him."

There had been hope that Tong might survive, but he was in and out of a coma for several days. In a lucid period, ten hours before he died, he was able to grasp that Suchan, Jackson, and finally Boyd had been captured. "They're all in the bag," his friend Inspector John Nimmo told him. Tong responded with a taut grin and a murmured "good." Doctors at Toronto General said Tong had survived for seventeen days "on courage alone." An autopsy confirmed that if he had survived, he would never have walked again.

Attorney General Dana Porter paid tribute to Tong in the Ontario legislature: "His cases and arrests read like a rogue's gallery, with almost every prominent criminal listed. Murders, holdups, shootings, big robberies – Tong got them all. He cultivated underworld contacts and was known by criminals everywhere. Though many criminals feared and hated him, others admired and respected him. For Eddie Tong was fair. He never lost his head or used bad judgment. He was kind and considerate to those who deserved it. He was hard and tough with others – those who usually ended up in Kingston Penitentiary."

One of the few visitors who saw Tong in the hours before he died was Jocko Thomas. "I wasn't there to interview him," recalls Thomas. "He couldn't talk or anything, but I got right close to him and whispered in his ear, 'Eddie, it's Jocko.' He did make a little twitch of one finger, but that's all he could do. He was still alive, but he was comatose."

On Tuesday night at a Danforth Avenue funeral parlour, Evelyn Tong was composed as she received friends and officials who came to pay their respects. Tong's body was moved to the Church of the

Nativity on Monarch Park Avenue. On Wednesday morning, light snow was falling as 250 mourners filled the small church for the funeral service. Hundreds of others stood outside listening to the proceedings over loudspeakers set up by the police department.

It was one of the largest funerals the city had ever seen for one of its policemen, with officers and contingents from many parts of Canada participating. Also on hand were dozens of dignitaries, from the province, the city, and other municipalities. Chief John Chisholm led the procession on foot east along the Danforth to Woodbine Avenue. Between Coxwell Avenue and Woodbine the marchers broke off and formed an honour guard as the hearse and Tong's family passed slowly by. Scores of onlookers lined the Danforth sidewalks as more than one hundred vehicles, led by a motorcycle escort, followed the hearse to Pine Hills Cemetery off Kennedy Road. After a short graveside ceremony, Rev. A.R. Beverley, Anglican Bishop of Toronto, spoke a few words of condolence to Mrs. Tong and her children, and Mayor Lamport, who had cut short his Florida vacation, shook hands with them.

When the news of Tong's death reached Lennie Jackson in the Don Jail he was silent, but his eyes registered concern, and he was sullen for a few days, realizing he would now be facing a charge of first-degree murder – a capital offence.

In Montreal, *Toronto Star* reporter Powell Smily went to the fifth floor of the Queen Elizabeth Hospital to see how Steve Suchan was reacting to the news. There was an armed policeman posted outside his room. Smily could see Suchan sitting in an easy chair, and a second policeman in a chair next to him. "He looked pale, but well on the road to recovery," wrote Smily.

The guard motioned to Smily to move away from the door out of earshot. "He still talks about wishing he'd been killed," said the guard. "But I guess he was meant to be saved for something besides bullets."

Detective-Sergeant Lucien Goulet, in charge of the guard detail, arrived while Smily was speaking with the guard. "What did Suchan say when he heard Tong had died?" asked the reporter.

"He didn't say anything," replied Goulet, "because he doesn't know about it. He gets no papers and has no radio, and we're under strict orders to see that no one tells him. In fact, he's allowed no visitors, not even his mother."

"Aren't you going to tell him about Detective Tong?" asked Smily.

"No, we're not," said Goulet. "If he found out, he'd probably try to make a break for it, and we don't want any more shooting. Even now, when he doesn't know anything about Tong, we have to keep an eye on him all the time. We have three shifts of guards doing eight hours each shift. Sometimes Suchan lies in bed, and you'd think he was dead to the world. But he often isn't asleep. He's just pretending to be, in case we let up and give him a chance to grab one of our guns. No sir – we don't want him to know about Tong's death until he's out of the hospital and safely behind bars."

Dorreen Boyd spent two weeks in the Don Jail before she was released. They had been holding her as a material witness. "They had nothing to hold me on," she recalls. "You can't be charged with harbouring your own husband."

While she was in the Don, Dolph Payne and Detective Charlie Cook "every second or third day" took her out of the jail for lunch. "I think they were looking for Joe Jackson and his brother-in-law, Allister Gibson. I wasn't going to tell them anything."

At the Heath Street apartment, besides the cash and the weapons, police had found several stiletto knives, hundreds of rounds of ammunition inside several wool socks, an electric cattle prod, several pieces of new luggage, and some of Dorreen's clothing and other personal items, including a box of Tampax. Upon her release from the Don Jail, Dorreen Boyd wanted her things back, but mostly she was concerned about her box of Tampax. Detectives Payne and Cook were there when she arrived to pick up her belongings.

"Well we better look through all this again," said Payne. They had already searched the luggage and other items several times, but Payne was going through it once more to irritate Dorreen. She spoke up when he picked up the box of Tampax.

"Please don't embarrass me," she said.

"Oh, I'm sorry, Mrs. Boyd," said Payne, quickly dropping the box.

She gave police Frank Lamb's address on Ennerdale Road near Eglinton, and her belongings were delivered there. Frank and his wife Flo were buying the house and had agreed to rent the basement and one upstairs room to Dorreen for her and her children. Dorreen telephoned Frank Lamb later in the day.

"Have those suitcases arrived yet?" she asked.

"They've been here about ten minutes," said Lamb.

"Open the blue one," ordered Dorreen.

"For what?"

"Just open it. Is Flo there?"

"No, she's out shopping."

"Well open it," she repeated, "and take out the Tampax."

"What the hell do I want Tampax for?"

"Just see if it's all together. If you look careful, you'll see one that's open."

"I have to do this?" asked Lamb.

"Yes. Yes. There's money for rent in there."

Lamb worked one of the packages open. "Oh yes! It's here, Dorreen."

"Thank God. I was worried the police had found it."

The Tampax held more than $6,000 in $100 bills, which Ed and Dorreen had tightly rolled and inserted in the tampon tubes.

On April 2, 1952, Steve Suchan was returned to Toronto. Ed Boyd was surprised when he was assigned a neighbouring cell in No. 9 Hospital. Suchan wasn't his favourite person, having brought down the police pressure that led to Boyd's arrest. But he could also see that Suchan was very ill from his wounds and he felt sorry for him. By now, Suchan knew about Tong's death and didn't seem to care if he recovered or not. Boyd thought Suchan's presence was a strange way of answering his prayers.

The prison doctor came to the cells twice a day, and after the fifth day told Brand that Suchan was so sick he would have to be hospitalized. He was sent to Toronto General Hospital under round-the-clock armed guard.

With Suchan gone, Boyd realized just how isolated and lonely he was, and despite his access to reading materials, he again fell into a depression. On April 10 his lawyer, F.J. McMahon, wrote to the sheriff, J.D. Conover, who was technically in charge of the jail:

> Due to previous circumstances which are well known, my client is being held under special security conditions in a cell sometimes known as 'The Death Cell'. The Governor of the Jail has at all times been exceptionally considerate to this prisoner and cooperative to myself. He has done all possible to insure the comfort and well being of Boyd and has cooperated in every way in permitting me to interview my client under suitable conditions for the preparation of his defense.
>
> However the Crown has asked for and received remand after remand and indicated in court this morning these remands might well run into months before charges are proceeded with. From my interview with Boyd and from discussions with members of his family who have seen him, I am firmly convinced his present confinement in what well could be referred to as solitary confinement is preying upon his mind and creating a despondency which is neither desirable nor in the best interests of his defense.

McMahon said that if the trial was carried over to the fall, arrangements should be made to treat Boyd as a remanded prisoner "in the sense that he is not held in solitary confinement."

Sheriff Conover wrote to Col. Basher on April 17, enclosing McMahon's letter. The sheriff said he had talked it over with Brand, and although keeping Boyd confined by himself might not be in the best interest of his health, "in view of his past performance, it might be very risky to transfer him to a corridor with other prisoners. The Governor has arranged for Boyd to get an hour's exercise in the yard each day when it is not being used by other prisoners, and as soon as Boyd's associates are physically fit they will be moved in with him so that he will not lack company." In his letter, Conover asked for Basher's advice.

Basher responded the next day: "I believe that it is in the interests of Boyd's own protection that he remain precisely where he is, as there is a definite feeling against him throughout the Institution.... Therefore to place this man in a corridor with other inmates would be inviting a disturbance and probably injury to Boyd. Our limited staff would perhaps be unable to provide the protection which he would need.... we cannot afford to accede to his request, except perhaps allowing him some limited freedom within the confines of No. 9 Hospital."

Basher said later that the letter was largely designed to satisfy McMahon, because they planned to keep Boyd at the Don for an extended period, and if McMahon were aware of that he would have continued agitating. There were some negative feelings towards Boyd because his escape had caused a loss of some privileges and the removal of the much-liked Governor Sanderson, but for McMahon's benefit, Basher probably overstated the depth of those feelings.

The surveillance at Joe Jackson's Jarvis Street address finally paid off for Payne and Craven, and on April 16 they arrested Jackson and his brother-in-law Allister Gibson, who was living at the same address. Both were charged with armed robbery for the March 4 hold-up.

Through evidence gathered during the investigation of Joe Jackson, it became evident that his brother William R. Jackson might well be implicated in robberies prior to his arrest on December 18, 1951, in Montreal.

Payne had a busy spring and summer meticulously investigating the Boyd Gang, including all the peripheral players. He conducted a series of identification line-ups at which scores of bank employees and other witnesses tried to pick out the gunmen from the many robberies.

On May 2, 1952, Mary Mitchell and Ann Jackson jointly applied for a restaurant licence at 338 Queen Street West. The licence was granted, but six days later, Payne arrested Mitchell at her restaurant for aiding and abetting Edwin Alonzo Boyd. She was remanded to May 15 on $5,000 bail. Around the same time, Elizabeth and Joseph Lesso were also arrested for harbouring Boyd and Willie Jackson.

On May 14, Willie Jackson was returned to the Don Jail from Kingston Penitentiary to face charges for two hold-ups: the Bank of Toronto at Boustead and Dundas on November 20, 1951, and the

Leaside branch of the Royal Bank ten days later. Jackson was brought down from Kingston by Payne and Detective-Sergeant Charlie Cook.

The next day, Ed and Norman Boyd's request for bail was denied by Magistrate Tupper Bigelow,[25] who said "the charges are so numerous and so serious that I don't consider bail could possibly be granted." In addition to eleven charges of armed robbery, Ed was facing charges of escaping the Don Jail, conspiracy to rob, and possession of an offensive weapon, as well as two charges of car theft. Norman was facing charges of aiding and abetting his brother's escape, two charges of armed robbery, and a charge of conspiracy to rob.

That afternoon, Steve Suchan and Lennie Jackson were officially remanded on first-degree murder charges in the death of Eddie Tong.

Preliminary hearings for some of the gang began in June. Ed and Norman Boyd, Joe and Willie Jackson, and Allister Gibson were ordered held in jail and committed to trial in September. Mary Mitchell and the Lessos were released on bail. They too would go to trial in September.

Edwin Alonzo Boyd couldn't believe his eyes when Willie Jackson was brought to No. 9 Hospital and lodged next to him in the vacant cell next to the grille gate. The boisterous Willie would certainly break the monotony. And with another brain at work, who knew what possibilities lay ahead? Boyd was ecstatic – his prayers were being answered.

Keyed Up

Boyd soon had Willie Jackson reading the Bible and trying self-hypnosis and visualization. They even had limited success trying to read each other's minds. They decided to pray for deliverance from the Don Jail. "Nothing happened for a couple of weeks," remembers Boyd, "and then Willie suggested we might be directing our prayers to the wrong place."

"Why would God want to help us escape from jail?" asked Willie. "We should be praying to Satan."

At first Boyd thought it was a silly idea, but eventually he decided it had some merit. "You can see how I was always open to suggestion in those days," laughs Boyd. "So I thought, well, I might as well try it." But how does one pray to the Devil? "The same way as you pray to anyone," says Boyd. "You just pray – pray to get out."

While Willie and Ed were praying to the Devil, Lennie Jackson was engaged in a more down-to-earth plan over in No. 3 Hospital. The broken bones in his right hand were healing and some of the strength and feeling was returning to his left hand, although he let on to the prison doctor that he wasn't doing too well. Except for the inmate sent in to help him from time to time, Jackson was usually alone in his cell with the wooden door closed. Sometimes there was a guard posted on the landing outside the door, but there wasn't the manpower to keep Jackson under continual surveillance, and besides – the administration believed – it would be a while before he recovered from his wounds. Not much of an escape threat there.

Jackson was a quick judge of people, and he liked what he saw when he met guard James Morrison, a thirty-year-old Scottish immigrant on the job just three or four months. Morrison was unmarried and lived with his father in a rooming house on Rose Avenue near Parliament and Wellesley. Jackson soon engaged him in conversation and discovered that Morrison was unhappy in Canada. By their third or fourth meeting they were like old friends. Morrison was from Glasgow, and Jackson had been there during the war when he was with the merchant navy. They talked about a couple of pubs and hotels they both had been to. Morrison became nostalgic.

"I don't like it over here," he said. "I want to get enough money to get back to Glasgow. That's where I belong." Jackson knew that a guard at the Don Jail started at about $2,200 a year. After rent, food, and a few beers every week, there wasn't a lot left for travel.

"There are ways and means of getting money," said Jackson.

"And how is that?" asked Morrison.

"There are people on the outside who pay for things."

"What things?"

"Someone on the outside will be in contact," said Jackson.

A few days later, Morrison was approached by Jackson's underworld mentor, Frank Watson. Watson gave the guard $20 and asked him to smuggle in a couple of chocolate bars for Jackson. Morrison agreed and made the delivery. Later he received $100 in twenties through the mail from Watson. The bills were counterfeit, said Watson, but "it's good stuff … better than real dough."

"He told me it was 'queer' money," Morrison said later. "I didn't want to take a chance, so I burned it."

About two weeks later, Watson gave Morrison hacksaw blades to take to Jackson. Morrison delivered the blades along with a wrench Jackson needed to remove the screen over the window in his cell. Jackson had long studied the window and knew he would have to cut out one vertical bar and one cross-bar to create a large enough opening to pull himself through. His cell was on the second storey, and he would have to tear his sheets and blankets into strips to fashion a rope to lower himself to the boiler-room service yard below. Once in the yard, he would have to find a way to either climb the eighteen-foot wall, or force the padlock on the gate through which coal was delivered to the boilers. With proper planning, he could get outside help with the delivery gate.

Jackson used the wrench to loosen and remove the square-headed screws holding the screen in place, and then began sawing the bars, first lubricating the blade with soap as Boyd and Willie Jackson had done in the November escape. He was still weak from his wounds, and the work was slow and painful, but the bars were soft and each day he could see progress. Probably, he never worked more than half an hour at a time before leaving the saw blades out of sight on the windowsill, camouflaging the cuts in the bars with a mixture of soap and dirt, and replacing the screen. His cell was often searched, but no tools were ever found. Because the screen was in place, the guards never gave the bars more than cursory look. By their logic, if the screen was in place the bars couldn't be touched, especially by an inmate who needed help shaving, washing, and going to the toilet.

It's likely Jackson hid the wrench in his cast or splint, or perhaps Morrison took it in and out of the cell for him. Another guard twice saw Morrison arrive at work early, go up to Jackson's cell, and speak to him through the slot in the door.

By late July, Jackson had sawed through the top of the vertical bar and was almost through the two cuts on the crossbar, leaving just a fraction of an inch to hold the bar in place. It would take only minutes to finish those cuts and remove the bar. The only major work left was the cut to the bottom of the vertical bar. By July 30 he had started on that cut. He would be ready to make his break in a matter of days. Frank Watson would arrange for him to be picked up outside the jail, and Morrison had agreed to smuggle in a gun just before the escape.

But on July 31, police picked up Frank Watson on suspicion of bank robbery, and in his pocket they found an envelope with the name James Morrison on it. Police ran a check on the name and found there was a James Morrison working as a guard at the Don Jail.

On August 1, shortly after 7 a.m., Morrison was arrested as he started his shift at the Don. He was interrogated at the jail by the governor, Thomas Brand, and by Inspector John Nimmo of the Toronto police. Morrison was charged with aiding and abetting a prisoner to escape. He confessed to giving Jackson a screwdriver, although none was ever found. He didn't mention the wrench and said he had given the saw blades to Ann Jackson. She denied it. Governor Brand had implemented strict visiting procedures for members of the Boyd Gang: they could meet only clergy or their lawyers in private; all visits from family or friends were one-to-one, with a guard in the room beside them and another posted at the door outside; and inmates were thoroughly searched after the visits. It would have been impossible for Ann Jackson to pass her husband the saw blades. The blades and the wrench had to come from Morrison.

Morrison was arraigned and remanded in custody until August 8. Police spirited him to a cell "somewhere out of the city" for his own protection and because Brand didn't want him in the Don, where he was familiar with security procedures. He would later be sentenced to two years in jail.

With the arrest of Morrison, the guards were all over Lennie Jackson's cell. Every crack in the wall and every split and joint in the wooden floor were checked with a high-strength magnet, but nothing was found. At that time they didn't realize that Jackson had access to a wrench; they also missed the saw blades on the outer windowsill, once again concluding that the bars could not have been touched since the screen was in place. Brand had a night light installed in the cell, and ordered that two flat steel bars be secured horizontally across the window screen. He also had Jackson strip-searched, and had his clothing sent to his office, where Brand himself checked it. "We did not find a thing in No. 3 Hospital, or on Jackson's person or clothing," Brand would tell a Royal Commission later in the year.

Brand did not stop at searching Jackson's cell and person: he again sent the inmate's artificial foot and his shoes for a fluoroscopic examination. The results were negative. Convinced that blades or tools must be buried in the exercise yard, Brand asked the army to lend him a mine detector, as well as two experienced operators to run it. With Brand supervising, two army technicians began scanning the yard at 10 p.m. on August 4. By first light the next day, they had found only a shoe horn, a tin cup, and a pair of pliers. In frustration, Brand decided his only option was to move Jackson out of No. 3 Hospital.

Steve Suchan had been returned to his cell in No. 9 Hospital in June after two months at the Toronto General. Now three of the cells were occupied and only cell No. 4 – the one next to the wall beside Suchan – was still empty. But when Governor Brand had Lennie Jackson moved in, all the cells were filled – and the Boyd Gang was back together.

Brand believed that No. 9 Hospital was the most secure area in the prison, and thus the best possible location for the Boyd Gang while they awaited their trials, which were scheduled for mid-September. He knew that Suchan and Leonard Jackson were escape risks, since they were facing capital murder charges and would possibly be hanged. And Boyd and Willie Jackson had already escaped once and were facing long prison terms.

No. 9 Hospital was considered almost escape-proof because each night the four inmates were locked into their individual cells. And even if they should somehow manage to get out of their cells, the corridor in front was secured by the locked grille gate and the window had a double set of bars. And beyond the corridor there was the antechamber with the oak door, which was manned by a guard on the landing when it was open.

Besides all the physical barriers, there was the microphone in the ceiling, which picked up even the slightest sounds coming from the cells. On one of his visits to Brand's office that summer, Basher was impressed as they listened to the sounds coming over the microphone from No. 9 Hospital. Except for the voices, the sounds were completely foreign to Basher, but Brand knew the source of each one.

"Now what's that sound?" Basher would ask.

"Oh, that's somebody drawing off a cup of water," Brand would say. He had purposely installed the microphone and speaker while Boyd was present, describing it as "a psychological weapon."

Under ideal circumstances, there would have been guards posted at No. 9 Hospital between the oak door and the grille gate twenty-four hours a day. But Brand had the whole jail to worry about and simply didn't have the manpower for continuous observation of the Boyd Gang. Also, the Boyd Gang had been reunited at the peak of the vacation season, when a number of guards were taking their summer holidays.

Brand ordered that the oak door remain open at all times except during meal parade, when other prisoners went through No. 9 corridor on their way to the dining room. He wanted it closed then so that Boyd and the others couldn't receive contraband or pass messages. With the oak door open the rest of the time, the guard on the landing in front of No. 9 Hospital had a full view of the corridor in front of the four cells. And he could also see into the front portion of the first cell – Willie Jackson's. Willie often stood at the door of his cell joking with the guard on duty.

There had been a general tightening of security under Brand. He had eliminated bowling in the corridors because it had been used as a ruse to distract the guards while Boyd and Willie Jackson were sawing bars. He had abolished the playing of quoits in the exercise yard because it was thought that outsiders might insert a saw blade into a rubber-hose ring and toss it over the wall. And the blankets covering the card tables in the corridors had been ordered removed because it was thought they could be used to subdue a guard.

Brand had also installed an alarm system that would sound in the radio room of police headquarters on College Street, bringing fifty officers to the jail within minutes. Switches for the system were located in Brand's office, at his residence, and in the jail's main rotunda. Brand was just as worried about criminals breaking into the Don or his home in an effort to free their friends, as he was about escapes from the inside.

Also, Brand had an officer patrolling the grounds outside the walls throughout the night. Two or three times a night a scout car from the Toronto Police Department would check with the guard, who duly reported the police visits in his notebook.

In late summer, as the trial date for the Boyd Gang neared, Brand was approached by Inspector Charlie Greenwood, who was in charge of No. 8 Police Station on Pape Avenue just north of Queen Street East. The Don Jail fell within the boundaries of his division, and he offered to station two policemen at the rear of the jail to improve security at night. Brand was delighted with the offer. As a further precaution, Brand agreed to block off the rear laneway running between the jail and Riverdale Isolation Hospital. The lane was on jail property, but the public had been using it as a short-cut to Broadview

Avenue. The two police officers assigned by Greenwood would ensure that barricades installed at both ends of the lane were not breached.

The Boyd Gang at first were fed in their cells, but Brand thought it was risky to have a guard carry the food in to each of them. And when the guard returned to the landing, the angle was such that he couldn't observe them eating. Brand worried that the eating utensils might be used for some nefarious purpose. He decided to set up a table with benches in the narrow corridor in front of the cells. All four men could now be watched as they ate, and the table could be used for playing cards as well.

"So all of a sudden, there we are – the four of us," says Boyd. "And the next thing you know, the superintendent lets us walk up and down in front of the cells all day, and they give us a table and benches and a deck of cards and a pencil to keep score."

At first the four men had to exercise in their tiny corridor, and for security reasons they were issued felt slippers with thin soles instead of the regulation prison boots. In August, however, Brand decided that they would be taken to the jail's exercise yard for an hour a day, except Sundays. But they would not be allowed to exercise with the other inmates. And to keep them off balance, they never knew what time of day they would be taken out to the yard. It could be early or late morning, or early or late afternoon. For Boyd, Suchan, and the Jacksons it was a relief to get out of the corridor. For Brand, it was an opportunity to have each of their cells thoroughly searched each day.

Since they were now using the exercise yard, Boyd and the others were issued boots, but their slippers were not taken from them. Lennie Jackson had special socks without heels to wear over his stump, but his prosthesis had been confiscated, and Boyd doesn't remember if he was allowed to wear it during the daily exercise period. "I don't recall if he used his artificial foot in the yard or if he rigged up something else," says Boyd. "I know he didn't have it in his cell." The men were handcuffed together in pairs for the daily walk around the bull-ring – the cement path circling the perimeter of the exercise yard. Boyd was usually paired with Willie, and Suchan with Lennie.

A lot more than handcuffs bound Steve Suchan and Lennie Jackson together. They had known each other longer than the others, they were both facing capital murder charges, and they had both been gunned down by police in Montreal. Suchan had lived with Lennie's sister, and they were both recent first-time fathers (Ann Jackson had given birth to a son on August 10, 1952). Lennie treated Suchan like a kid brother, and apparently bore no grudge against him for his impulsive act of violence, which might soon leave both of them dangling at the end of a rope.

As soon as Willie and the others arrived in the cells at No. 9 Hospital, Boyd warned them that their conversations were being monitored by the overhead microphone. They realized it was a two-way system when somebody inadvertently hit the wrong switch and a short conversation from Brand's office was piped into the cells. On another occasion Brand's voice came through the speaker: "Suchan, your lawyer will be in to see you this afternoon."

Life in No. 9 Hospital had improved considerably for Boyd since he first arrived in mid-March. From being alone and depressed with zero privileges, he now had three relatively congenial cellmates, with Willie always providing the entertainment. His cell was unlocked from 7:30 a.m. to 8 p.m. He had unlimited reading material. He could wander in and out of his cell into the small corridor at will. He was allowed a full hour of exercise in the yard every day but Sunday. And his meals were delivered to his cell, which spared him from the assembly-line feedings that other inmates had to face three times a day.

Most of the guards treated Boyd and the others with cautious deference. Two or three were downright friendly. The guards were only human, after all. To them, besides being dangerous criminals, the Boyd Gang members were also celebrities. Wasn't the whole country talking about them? And weren't the guards' friends fascinated and impressed when it slipped out that they saw the infamous inmates just about every day – actually *spoke* with them?

Guard Murray Clarke treated the members of the Boyd Gang in a civil manner, but as far as he was concerned they were criminals just like all the rest, and he didn't trust them. He had been a guard at the

Don for eight years, and before that a policeman in Britain for eight years. His first conversation with Ed Boyd came after a thorough search of the four cells in No. 9 Hospital while the inmates were out for their daily exercise. Clarke had stood on their beds while searching the cells.

"Do you wear size nine boots?" asked Boyd on his return from the yard.

"Yes I do," said Clarke.

"Then you are the man who has been searching our beds."

"No. I don't search your beds."

"Well you left your footprints on top of the blankets. You have no respect for our beds."

Clarke stayed off their beds after that, and Boyd became more friendly. "Where do you live?" asked Boyd one day.

"In the east end of Toronto near the Nash plant," said Clarke.

Boyd smiled. "Well they make good cars, the Nash people do. I know because I own one. I drove it back and forth to Montreal a few times with no problems at all."

Clarke knew Suchan best of all because he had been one of the three men assigned to guard him while he was recovering from his wounds at Toronto General. And when Suchan had visitors at the Don it was usually Clarke who accompanied him to the visitors' room. Suchan felt comfortable with Clarke, despite Clarke's businesslike approach to his job. When Suchan arrived back at the Don after attending a prolonged line-up session at police headquarters, Clarke was waiting to escort him to his cell.

"Where were you?" asked Clarke.

"A police line-up," said Suchan.

"What was the reason for that?"

"Well, they fingered me for a bank hold-up."

"And is it true?" smiled Clarke.

"Well it might be."

"What are you going to do with all the money from these hold-ups?"

"Do you want some of it?" asked Suchan, his voice suddenly serious.

"Yeah, sure I do." said Clarke.

"Could you use $5,000? You'd get it in twenties, tens, and fives."

"Certainly I could use it."

"You'll have to do something for it."

"What would you like done for $5,000?"

What Suchan wanted was for Clarke to spirit him out to the service yard in one of the jail's oversized garbage pails.

"Well, are you interested?" asked Suchan.

"No, $5,000 doesn't interest me," said Clarke. "Not the kind of money you handle."

Clarke reported Suchan's bribery attempt to Brand. Nothing much could be done about it, but it became a running joke between Suchan and the guard. Clarke certainly wasn't humourless, and he particularly enjoyed the antics and jokes of Willie Jackson.

Boyd continued to read his Bible and other religious books and pamphlets, which were supplied to him by a visiting clergyman. He had decided to change his life, and he was looking for spiritual guidance. But he was also keeping his options open, and he and Willie Jackson continued praying to the Devil.

"I just took things day by day," says Boyd. "I would fast for a while and meditate, but not as much as before."

He and the others were also studying their situation. Lennie Jackson wanted out, and Boyd was prepared to help him. He felt he owed him, since Lennie had provided the saw blades for the first escape and was now in a tight situation. "I would have gone straight if I had not felt obligated to help these guys," says Boyd. "I know now I shouldn't have helped them. I didn't care what happened to Suchan, but I thought Len deserved a chance to get out of there."

The four inmates were quick to see that there was a major gap in the security measures in place against them. From about 5 a.m. to 7 a.m. the oak door leading to their corridor was shut and locked and the guards simply disappeared. The deputy warden and others would tell the Royal Commission that because the jail was short-staffed, the guards had to leave their post to start breakfast and to rouse whatever prisoners had to get ready for morning court appearances. The police department had a patrol at the jail at 6:45 a.m., ready to transport the prisoners to police cells in the court building.

The guards were so busy that the inmates going to court were expected to make their way to the first-floor marshalling point without an escort. When there were no guards on the landing at No. 9 Hospital, the oak door was kept locked to prevent passing prisoners from communicating with the Boyd Gang.

All of this was news to Brand, according to his testimony before the Royal Commission. He said it did not require the services of all the men on duty to prepare the prisoners for court and get breakfast started. Further, if the oak door was closed between 5 a.m. and 7 a.m., "they were not carrying out my orders, because my orders were definite. There was no reason for their not having a man on that door." Brand's testimony was disputed by others, who said that locking the oak door had always been the practice and that Brand must have been aware of it.

Having a two-hour "safe period" wasn't much good to the Boyd Gang if they couldn't get out of their cells to get at the bars. And if they did get out of the cells, they would need saw blades to cut through the bars. This time they couldn't depend on Lennie Jackson's artificial foot. There wasn't much they could do. The visits by close friends and family were monitored too closely, and there was no access to other prisoners who might have been ready to help them. It seemed hopeless, but Boyd and Willie Jackson continued praying to the Devil.

One day Willie returned from a visit with his court-appointed lawyer. He approached Boyd with a big smile. He couldn't say much in the corridor with the microphone overhead, but in the exercise yard he revealed his good news. Willie said that the lawyer had told him he wasn't optimistic about Willie's chances in court, but he was willing to help him get out of jail – for a fee. Willie quickly agreed that the lawyer would be paid $10,000 from the gang's first two bank robberies once they escaped. The lawyer, who is still alive, vehemently denies that any such discussion took place.

Boyd couldn't believe what he was hearing. Their prayers to the Devil were working. Meetings between lawyers and their clients were considered privileged, and the guards stood outside the door of the visitors' room while they occurred. Boyd says that Willie brought him a small piece of flat steel and a file, which Willie told him came from the lawyer. Boyd planned to fashion a key from the piece of metal.

Boyd's cell was littered with religious books and pamphlets, and when the guards and turnkeys conducted searches, they paid more attention to Lennie Jackson's and Suchan's cells. For some time Boyd had studied his cell looking for a perfect hiding place. He found it in the wooden base of the toilet at the back of his cell. He was able to loosen a small piece of board in the base, and discovered a tiny hollow behind it. He slipped the steel strip and the file into the hollow and replaced the board. The base of a toilet wasn't a guard's favourite place to search.

Over the next few days Boyd and the others stole glimpses at the key the guards used to open their cells in the morning and lock them in at night. Studying the key gave Boyd a general idea of its shape and notches, but it wasn't enough that he could begin filing. Willie Jackson came up with the answer. One night, as guard Murray Clarke was preparing to lock them in their cells, Willie grabbed the key attached to the ring on Clarke's belt. "Let me lock Suchan in," laughed Willie. "Just for fun."

"Come on Willie, you know I can't allow you to do that," said Clarke. Willie released the key, laughed, and went into his cell. The moment Clarke left the corridor, Willie opened his hand. He had held the key so tightly the marks were still there. Grabbing a pencil, Willie held his hand up and quickly reproduced the exact shape of the key on the metal wall. Now that he had a pattern to work from, Boyd began shaping a key from the piece of steel, hiding it and the file at the base of the toilet when he wasn't working on it.

The sound of Boyd filing was barely audible, but without covering noise, the microphone would pick it up. While he worked, the toilet was flushed more than usual and conversations were more animated. Sometimes there were prolonged manufactured arguments.

It wasn't long before Boyd was ready to try the replica key. To allow them access to a toilet, one of the cells was left open each day while the four inmates were in the corridor. The other three cells were locked until the prisoners were returned to their cells for the night. While the others distracted the guard, Boyd inserted the key into the lock on the door of the open cell. When he turned it, the bolt slid out smoothly. Boyd was elated, but when he turned the key back to the original position, the bolt didn't budge. He tried again and again but it didn't move. "You could get it out, but you couldn't get it back in," recalls Boyd with a chuckle. He removed the key. Willie Jackson was frantic. "He didn't know what to do," says Boyd.

The guard who had let them out of their cells went off shift at 3 p.m. His replacement saw the bolt sticking out from the lock when he arrived to lock them into their cells for the night.

"What the hell's going on here?" he asked.

"I guess the guy this morning turned the key the wrong way when he took it out," shrugged Boyd. The guard accepted the explanation without comment and locked the men in their cells.

The next morning, as they were being let out of their cells, Boyd and Willie studied the jailer's key to see where they had gone wrong. Both of them saw it at once. The operative parts of the key were its four teeth. What they had missed was a tiny notch between the second and third teeth. "There was this little indentation, about a sixteenth of an inch or so," says Boyd. "It didn't take long to shape that out, and then it was perfect." Perfect indeed. The next time he tried the key, the bolt slid in and out effortlessly, and just as important, it barely made a sound.

Now the prisoners in No. 9 Hospital could, at will, let themselves in and out of their cells. They turned their attention to the bars. Boyd says Willie told him that the lawyer readily supplied a hacksaw blade to Willie, which he worked into the waistband of his denim trousers.

Boyd was delighted with the saw blade. "It was a new type of material that seemed to get sharper as you used it. I had never seen anything like that." The blade was too long for the hollow at the base of Boyd's toilet, but there were plenty of hiding places in the cracks of the corridor's ninety-year-old hardwood floor. Boyd chose a deep but narrow crack in front of Lennie's cell close to the back stone wall. The guards barely glanced at the floor during their searches. They were more interested in the inmates' cells.

Boyd's strategy was for him and Willie to work on the bars for no more than half an hour, between 5:30 and 6 a.m., except Fridays and Saturdays when there was no court and the guards didn't have to assemble prisoners for the police transport.

After the oak door was shut in the mornings, Boyd would wait a few moments and then reach through the bars and slowly and silently turn the key to open his cell door. The microphone was a constant worry, and they knew it would have to be neutralized before they could saw the bars. Their solution was to quietly move the table directly under the vent screen covering the microphone. Suchan and Lennie Jackson then climbed onto the table and took turns holding a pillow over the screen. Boyd and Willie Jackson moved one of the two benches to the top of the radiator, to use as a platform while they were sawing. They used the other bench as a step to get to the first bench.

Boyd plugged the sink in his cell to soften part of a bar of prison-issue red carbolic soap in a couple of inches of water. Using the soap as a lubricant, he began sawing the first bar under the faint glow of the dim ceiling bulb in the adjoining antechamber. In the first escape, only one bar had had to be removed. But these were double-bars, so at least two would have to come out. What they didn't realize was that the crossbars were lower than the one in their previous escape. That meant the hole would be smaller.

After each sawing session, Boyd would rub a mixture of soap and dirt into the cuts and run his hands up and down the bars to give them a uniform appearance. He was always amazed at how well the camouflage worked. "You would never know the bars had been touched," he says.

They had started by sawing one of the outer bars first. It was difficult to get good leverage, and Boyd realized that even with the improved blade it was going to take several days to cut through the two bars. Their time was running out. It was late August, and they were scheduled to go to court on September 15. By the time they were ready for the final cuts to the two bars, the weekend was upon them. Saturday would be their worst day. They knew that the cells would be searched while they were out in the exercise yard, and there was always the chance that an overzealous guard would discover the cuts in the bars. They returned to their cells with great trepidation, but everything was normal. They were relieved that there was no exercise period on Sunday. With the four of them sitting at their table and the oak door open all day, the guards barely glanced at the bars.

At 5:45 the next morning, with a few firm passes of the saw blade, Boyd completed the cuts through the two bars. As the bars came free he handed them down to Willie. Standing on the radiator, Boyd began to pull himself through the narrow opening. His head and torso went through, but not his hips. Twisting and struggling for several minutes, he realized it was impossible. His hips were stuck, and Willie had to pull him back inside. Boyd was the smallest of the foursome, but Willie gave it a try anyway. He too was thwarted.

"We have to cut two more bars," groaned Boyd.

They had no other choice. Suchan and Jackson were deflated as they watched the two smaller men struggle unsuccessfully to get through the bars. It would be another several days, and their days were running out. In the meantime, the cut bars would be held in place only with soap. The slightest nudge from a guard and the game would be over. Boyd fitted the bars back into place and smoothed the surfaces with his hands. It was impossible to tell they'd been tampered with.

Boyd felt badly for Lennie and Suchan, but he thought the fact that he couldn't get through the bars was a sign that he shouldn't be going with them. He decided he would help the others get out but would stay behind himself. Lennie tried to talk him out of it. "They'll blame you anyway," he said.

"I'll just tell them I was asleep and didn't see a thing," said Boyd.

"They won't buy it."

But Boyd relished the idea of helping the others escape, locking the empty cells, locking himself in his cell, and watching the reaction of the guards and turnkeys. He and Willie were back sawing the bars the next morning. Two more heart-stopping weekends, including Labour Day, would pass before they were ready to complete their last cuts and remove the bars.

Guard John McNulty reported for night shift duty shortly before 11 p.m. on Sunday, September 7. In the rotunda he joined the deputy governor, Alexander Noble, and together they picked up

their keys and headed for No. 9 Hospital. They arrived at the landing at exactly 11:10. The oak door was open, and Noble unlocked
the grille gate and entered the corridor in front of the four cells.
McNulty followed him in and went to the back wall to punch the
clock that recorded his visit. Noble tried each of the cell doors to
make sure they were secure while McNulty played the beam of his
flashlight over each bed. "They had blankets over them, but their
heads were visible," he would later tell the Royal Commission. "As
far as we knew they were sleeping."

He said they opened the hinged window and flashed the light over
the bars. Nothing seemed amiss. McNulty was asked whether he or
Noble "took hold of the bars at all."

"They were too high," said McNulty. "You couldn't climb on a
table and make lots of noise to try the bars at that time of the night.
You would have them cat-howling." They didn't want to disturb the
prisoners. That disturbed the Royal Commission.

McNulty, like many of the guards, probably thought checking the
bars any more closely was redundant. The men were locked in their
cells right in front of him. They couldn't get at the bars, so what was
the point of checking them?

McNulty spent much of the night on the landing outside the open
oak door. He said the cells were checked and the clock punched several more times, until the oak door was closed and locked at 4:45 a.m.

A few minutes later, Boyd was out of his cell listening at the grille
gate. When he was satisfied McNulty was gone, he opened the other
cells. Suchan climbed up on the table and held the pillow over the
microphone while Boyd finished sawing the bars and Lennie prepared
his stump for the ordeal ahead. He pulled on two pair of heelless
socks, wrapped strips of newspaper around them, and fitted his
enamel drinking cup over top. It wasn't snug enough so he added
more strips of paper. When the cup felt secure, he folded the socks
down over the cup to attach it more securely. Meanwhile, Boyd had
removed the two bars he had cut two weeks before and passed them to
Willie, who placed one under his pillow and one on the floor. Within
a few minutes, Boyd had cut through the other two bars. Willie put
one on the radiator, and decided to keep the other for protection.

Finally, for the second time in two weeks, they were ready to go. Boyd easily pulled himself through the opening, grabbed one of the intact bars, and swung himself over a couple of feet to the wall dividing the jail cemetery from the service yard. Even with the extra bars cut out, the opening was just over nine inches by thirteen inches. It was a tight fit for Suchan, but he managed to wriggle his way through. Boyd helped each of them to the wall. They were lying flat on top of the wall ahead of him. He stared back at the window, debating whether to return to his cell. It was still dark and nearly 50°F. The air smelled fresh with a touch of fall. "I think there's a guard out there," one of them whispered.

Boyd hesitated for a moment. *To hell with it, I'm going*, he decided. Climbing over the others, he lay flat on the wall and crawled commando-style to the junction with the main wall, which overlooked the lane behind the jail. Peering over the wall, he spotted a policeman patrolling between the jail and Riverdale Isolation Hospital. He signalled to the others to stay low. "We didn't know about the policeman until we got up there," says Boyd. "I was lying flat with the other guys behind me and we couldn't get off the wall as long as he was standing there."

Five minutes went by, then ten, then fifteen. Dawn was beginning to break. If they didn't get off the wall soon they would be spotted easily. "Just then somebody opened the door at the side of the hospital," recalls Boyd. "And the policeman went in for a cup of coffee or something."

Boyd signalled to the others, then moved to the main wall and slid back three of four feet to give them room to swing their legs down the side of the wall. Willie went first. It was eighteen feet from the top of the wall to the ground. He hung by his hands for a moment and then let go, landing with a muffled thump. Lennie Jackson was next. As he swung his legs over, the cup covering his stump clanged against the top of the wall and bounced to the ground. Nobody moved for a few seconds. When no guards or policemen appeared, Willie picked up the cup. Then Lennie dropped to the ground, followed by Suchan and Boyd.

Fallout

eorge Hutchinson, a guard at the Don for sixteen years, arrived
for work at five minutes to seven on Monday, September 8. Following his usual routine, he picked up the keys for No. 9 Hospital.

"That was the most important spot," Hutchinson would tell the
Royal Commission later, "and I liked to get that over with first. I had
one key for the wooden door, one for the grille gate, and one that fit
all four cells to let them out for the day." It was Hutchinson who had
twice reported seeing guard James Morrison arrive early for his shift
and stop at Lennie Jackson's cell in No. 3 Hospital.

On this day, Hutchinson walked up the steel stairs to the second
level, met his partner from No. 10 Corridor, and proceeded to the
landing in front of No. 9 Hospital. They unlocked the oak door and
entered the antechamber. As he was unlocking the grille gate,
Hutchinson happened to glance up. He saw the open window and a
space between the bars that wasn't supposed to be there. They entered
the corridor and saw that all four cells were empty.

Hutchinson noticed that the table "was pulled underneath the microphone and there was a pillow on top of it. And one of the benches
was at the base of the radiator and the other one on top." He found
one of the severed bars on the bench on top of the radiator, another
on the floor, and a third under William Jackson's pillow. The fourth
bar was missing.

In Boyd's cell, the guards discovered that the sink was plugged and
that a bar of red carbolic soap "was lying in about an inch of water.
Just enough to soften it." Hutchinson also noticed that the prisoners
had left behind their felt slippers and that Lennie Jackson's enamel
drinking cup was missing.

Dawn was just breaking when he hurried to the rotunda office to report the escape to W.J. Woodside, the day shift's chief turnkey, who had replaced the deputy governor, Alex Noble, just minutes earlier. Hutchinson and Woodside checked the jail's cemetery but saw nothing.

Guard Murray Clarke was also on the day shift that day. He had arrived before Hutchinson but was assigned to a different part of the jail. Just before 7 a.m. he noticed Hutchinson hurrying down to the rotunda "very agitated, with a serious look on his face." Hutchinson told Clarke that Boyd, Suchan, and the Jacksons were gone. They had escaped.

Clarke ran to the guard at the front door and got the keys for the arms rack in the governor's office. He loaded a rifle and a revolver and ran outside to the rear of the jail, where he told one of the patrolling policemen that the Boyd Gang had escaped. Two police cruisers arrived within minutes. "Seeing the jail was properly secured from the outside, I handed my rifle to another guard and gave the revolver to the man on the door," said Clarke. A team of detectives arrived from police headquarters, and Clarke accompanied them to No. 9 Hospital.

Thomas Brand was shaving when the alarm buzzer sounded at his residence across from the jail at 7 a.m. He dressed quickly and was at the jail in five minutes. "The police were there before I got there," he said. "The building was filled with them by the time I arrived."

Brand joined the detectives looking for clues in No. 9 Hospital and ordered Woodside to conduct a thorough search of the building. There was considerable confusion and milling about as a result of the escape and the prisoners had not been given their breakfast. Brand told his guards to leave the investigation to the police and concentrate on the operation of the jail. The prisoner's parade to breakfast was soon under way.

Brand accompanied Detective-Sergeant Bill Bolton in a search of the large vacant attic above No. 9 Hospital. They found nothing. As they came down the stairs to the second floor, they heard several people shouting that the prisoners were on the roof of the jail. More policemen had arrived, and they quickly ringed the jail. Some of them climbed nearby telephone poles to get a better view of the roof.

Jocko Thomas remembers being called out to cover the escape. "When I got there, the cops were ringed around the jail and the prisoners were yelling at them through the bars. The fire department had sent aerial trucks, and cops were at the top of the tall ladders, sweeping the roof with spotlights. The two sentries stationed outside the jail ... insisted that no one could have got by them without being seen."[26]

At one point Thomas was standing beside Chief Inspector Robert Anderson from the police department when an inmate yelled out a window, "Hey you flatfeet, they're gone!"

Anderson turned to Thomas. "You know, Jocko, I think that guy's right."

Both prison officials and the police thought Boyd and the others must still be in the jail, because they were certain that the opening in the escape window was too small for the gang to go through. "Then one of the sentries remembered hearing a flock of roosting starlings suddenly take off around five o'clock in the morning," says Thomas. "Well, they finally realized the prisoners flew away with them."

Brand and Police Inspector John Nimmo drove out to the Peel County Jail to reinterview former jail guard James Morrison, who had been arrested for trying to help Lennie Jackson escape earlier in the summer. Morrison had nothing new to tell them. Brand returned to the Don about 2 p.m. and was told that his boss, Col. Hedley Basher, wanted to see him at Queen's Park for a conference with ministry and law enforcement officials.

At the conference it was decided that Basher's department would hold an immediate inquiry. Brand and all of his officers who were on duty at the time of the escape were ordered to attend. The inquiry began at 5 p.m. that afternoon and did not conclude until the following morning at 9 a.m. Six hours later, Brand was summoned to Basher's office and told that he and seven of his officers, including Alex Noble, had been suspended immediately with pay, pending a Royal Commission investigation of the escape. In the meantime, officers from the Ontario Provincial Police would take over the guards' duties. At the Royal Commission, which would begin only nine days after the escape, Basher would do his best to distance himself from Brand, the man he had hand-picked to take over as governor after Boyd and the Jacksons escaped the first time. Basher would stay on as deputy minister until 1959.

Mayor Allan Lamport and his police chief, John Chisholm, were both out of town at the time of the escape. Chisholm flew back to Toronto from a convention in Winnipeg as soon as he learned of the escape. Lamport rushed to the city from his cottage on Lake Simcoe. He made a brief visit to the Don on Tuesday morning, after which he spoke to reporters waiting outside. He referred to the guards as "morons" and railed against Brand without naming him. "Who in blazes was such a fool to put them in one cell block?" he asked. "The men were allowed to eat together, sleep together, and were practically given club car privileges."

Lamport estimated that the Boyd Gang had so far cost taxpayers $1 million "in apprehending them, caring for them after their arrest, and bringing them to trial. There have been thousands of man-hours consumed at great cost. It's pretty shabby treatment for our police who have done all they can and are let down like this."

While Brand and his men were under attack from all sides, the minister of reform institutions, Major John Foote, said that the two Toronto policemen assigned to watch the rear of the jail "were definitely on the job." Why then, asked a reporter, had they not seen the four fugitives? "That's something I can't answer," replied Foote. But the Boyd gang had the answer: they had been lucky. If the policeman on duty had been waved into the hospital for a cup of coffee fifteen minutes earlier, he would have been back on patrol in time to catch them coming off the wall.

The coverage of the Boyd Gang's escape from the Don Jail was unprecedented in the history of Toronto journalism, garnering more attention than Tong's shooting, the Montreal shoot-outs, and Boyd's capture on Heath Street.

Every story and picture on the first three pages of Monday's *Star* was about the escape, and the three-line headline took up one-third of page 1.

TORONTO DAILY STAR

40TH YEAR   MONDAY, SEPTEMBER 8, 1952   42 PAGES   5¢ PER COPY, 30¢ PER WEEK

THE WEATHER

BOYD, SUCHAN, 2 JACKSONS SAW WAY OUT OF DON JAIL POLICE TOLD SHOOT TO KILL

Find 4 Death Row Keys
Say Should Only be Two

HOME EDITION

Don't Even Know When
Boyd, Pals Escaped–Police

The lead on the main *Star* story was written by Thomas:

> Edwin Alonzo Boyd, master bank robber, and three members
> of his gang, regarded as the most desperate criminals ever
> locked in the Don Jail, have sawed their way out and every
> policeman in Ontario was alerted for the hunt today, with
> orders of "shoot to kill."

In another of the page 1 stories in the *Star*, Eddie Tong's tearful
widow was quoted as saying the escape was "a disgrace to the city."
Her husband had warned his superiors "and the jail warden to watch
them before the first escape was made. They didn't listen then, and
they're not listening now. My husband said extra guards should be
put on Jackson and Boyd. If they had listened to my husband the first
time, he would still be living."

Monday's *Telegram* ran the main story on page 1, with the rest of
the space taken up by three-column pictures of the gang members
under this headline:

BOYD, KILLER PALS LOOSE/POLICE 'SHOOT ON
SIGHT'/HUSBAND "WON'T BE TAKEN ALIVE" – MRS. BOYD

A few days before the escape, *Telegram* reporter Tom Williams
took a copy of a note written by Boyd to handwriting analyst Anne

Shaw. Williams' story appeared on one of the inside pages on Monday. Shaw said of Boyd: "He has pride and is level-headed. He has strong intuitive reasoning and a strong tendency toward literary ability. He is a cautious individual thinker and does not leave things half done…. He can't be told anything … knows it all, and spurns advice. He allowed his abilities for good to be sidetracked. He is selfish and self-centered and considers only himself. And the police better keep a close eye on him…. He may be in jail now but his brain is always working. He is a clever man."

So clever, reported the *Star*, that Boyd was able to con a number of clergymen who visited him at the Don before his second escape:

> Edwin Alonzo Boyd is a master actor as well as a master bank robber, detectives said today.
>
> He has been the centre of attraction to a large number of clergymen who came to the jail to visit him, and, according to some of them who spoke with police, he had convinced them of his sincerity to reform.
>
> He was said to be "ready to take his medicine," hoping for a term of 20 to 25 years, and earnestly praying he would not receive a life sentence, which he had been told he would likely receive for his 11 bank robberies.
>
> Boyd is said to have prayed with some of the pastors who visited him. One mentioned him in his sermon as being a criminal likely to reform his ways.
>
> In letters to his wife from the cell, Boyd spoke religiously, telling her he had seen the evil of his ways. "I have accepted the Lord," Boyd wrote in one letter.

The hunt for circulation was as intense as the hunt for the escaped prisoners, and by Tuesday the headlines were even larger. The big news of the day was the announcement by Premier Leslie Frost that a royal commission, headed by Judge Ian Macdonell, would convene immediately to look into the escape, and that Brand, Noble, and six guards had been suspended. It was also announced that the province, the City of Toronto, and the Canadian Bankers' Association were offering rewards totalling $26,000 for the capture of the Boyd Gang.

The *Telegram* ran a huge banner line above the nameplate and a second headline below.

8 JAILERS OUT

THE TELEGRAM

77TH YEAR   40 PAGES   TORONTO, TUESDAY, SEPTEMBER 9, 1952   PRICE 5 CENTS

PREMIER FROST ORDERS ROYAL INQUIRY AT DON

Below the second headline was a five-column photograph of Dorreen Boyd holding a copy of the *Telegram* with her husband prominently displayed. The photo was there to promote an exclusive in-depth interview with Dorreen by reporter Dorothy Howarth. The story filled most of page 3. Dorreen said she would always remain loyal to her husband. "If it had been murder or rape I might feel differently, but Ed never hurt anybody, only the banks and they're heavily insured. They don't lose anything."

Of the reward offer, she told Howarth: "I wouldn't give him up for a million. You know what it's like when you love a man." Dorreen reminisced about her childhood in England and talked about how she had met Ed and how they were both dispatch riders during the war. During the interview she pulled a photo of her husband from her wallet. "He looks like Errol Flynn, doesn't he?" Yes, Howarth told her readers, "Edwin Boyd certainly does look like the famous movie actor – a handsome, dashing young fellow and a devil-may-care gleam in his clear eyes that look straight out of the picture at you."

Dorreen confided to Howarth that Boyd had told her after his

THE WEATHER

TORONTO DAILY STAR

60TH YEAR   TUESDAY, SEPTEMBER 9, 1952—50 PAGES   5c PER COPY, 30c PER WEEK

REBUKE HEAD, SUSPEND DEPUTY
REPORT 2 GUARDS TO BE FIRED

JAIL NIGHT HEAD TOLD   **HOME AND SPORT EDITION**   *Bought Peroxide, Make-up*
OF NOISES, TESTIFIES   *Girl Sure Man Was Boyd*
TOOK NO PRECAUTIONS   BOUGHT PEROXIDE

first escape that there was no sense in stealing two or three hundred dollars at a time, "you might as well make it big." She said the only gambling Ed did was with his own life.

"He even took me to a show in Toronto one night. We passed right by a policeman phoning his girl in the lobby. But Ed never batted an eyelash, just said to the cashier 'two tickets please' and walked right into the show. You can't say he hasn't got guts, maybe he doesn't use them the right way, but he certainly has them."

Dorreen warmly described the previous Christmas she and Ed and the children had spent together at the Sunnyside Motor Hotel. "The only thing we didn't manage was a Christmas tree. In the evening Ed and I went to the Famous Door and had supper there. It was nice but we both had the feeling we might be recognized at any minute and that didn't make us feel very comfortable." She also recounted New Year's Eve when Ed bought champagne. "It wasn't the best New Year's we ever spent, but we both had high hopes for the future."

A few days after New Year's, Ed drove Dorreen and the children to Niagara Falls for the weekend. "We stayed in a motel near the Rainbow Bridge. For those few short days at Niagara it seemed as though we were a normal family again. It didn't last long. Early in March Eddie Tong was shot."

They went into hiding after the shooting, but living in one room (on Spadina Road) was difficult for both of them, and that was when they decided to move to the Heath Street apartment. Dorreen confirmed that her husband had no contact with Suchan or Lennie Jackson from the time of the shooting until they were re-united in the Don Jail.

Dorreen said it was her fault her husband was captured. "Norman said I was to go to his place because ... the car was in my name.... Ed said ... it was a police trap and to be careful. I said I didn't think it was a trap."

The night of the capture Dorreen suggested to Ed that he take a leisurely bath. "He said that he was too tired and there would be plenty of time in the morning. He never did get that bath. Perhaps he will be able to have one now that he's out again."

Dorreen knew it was wrong, but was glad her husband was free again. "The only regret I have is the effect this is having on the children. The other kids tease them so much. After all, it's not their fault, is it?"

If the Boyd Gang had been looking for maximum publicity, they couldn't have chosen a better day to escape: that very evening, the Canadian Broadcasting Corporation began regular television service in Toronto on CBLT Channel 9. The three-hour package began at 7:15 p.m. and included an address by Prime Minister Louis St. Laurent. But fugitives Edwin Alonzo Boyd, Steve Suchan, and Leonard and Willie Jackson upstaged the opening program: they were the first to appear on air as CBLT televised police photographs of them at regular intervals all afternoon and early evening. And on the first CBC News Magazine program at 7:30 that evening, Lorne Greene – referred to affectionately by his colleagues as "the voice of doom" – led off with an item about the escape: "This is Lorne Greene. Our first story – the story of a manhunt." Over clips of the Don Jail, a police dispatcher, motorcycle policemen streaming out of police headquarters, and policemen arming themselves with rifles, he said that the fugitives were desperate and that, as two thousand policemen went after them, "the unofficial word was 'shoot to kill.' "

On the Sunday following the escape, Mayor Lamport used the new medium to ask for the public's help in capturing the Boyd

Gang: "I plead with all citizens for their co-operation. Your efforts may be the means for saving a lot of lives by bringing to trial these four desperadoes who escaped from the Don Jail."

The story of the escape made the front pages of most newspapers in the country. But it was Torontonians who expressed the most anger and disgust. It was *their* policemen who had been shot down in the streets. It was *their* banks that were being routinely robbed. And it was *their* jail that had twice allowed the culprits responsible to escape. Editorial writers and columnists reflected the public anger and frustration. *Globe and Mail* columnist Frank Tumpane wrote two days after the escape: "How many innocent lives will be lost this time through the bungling incompetence and stupidity that permits desperate men to treat the Don Jail as if it were a sardine can?" He joined the chorus of those calling for a new jail and a shake-up in the Don's administration: "The time has come for a change. The vermin are crawling over the walls and they are the kind of vermin whose bite is poisonous."

Only the *Peterborough Examiner* showed any sympathy for Governor Brand and the guards: "When the birds have flown, public condemnation and loss of employment is their reward. But when the birds are all safely in their cages, who ever thinks to give the jailer a kindly word? Every job has its peculiar difficulties, but that of being a jailer seems to us to be especially unfortunate."

In *From Police Headquarters*, Jocko Thomas writes that there was obvious and considerable public interest in the Boyd Gang and the upcoming Tong murder trial, "but we turned the escape into an even greater sensation than it was." The reason, he says, was the ongoing circulation war between the *Star* and the *Telegram*. "For the first few days after the breakout, the two papers seemed to be locked in a contest to see which could print the biggest headline.... By the end of the week however, the public was sick of it and Hindmarsh [the *Star*'s president] ordered us to lay off unless we had something real to report."[27]

Hindmarsh may have been feeling complacent, because just a month before the Boyd Gang's escape from the Don, his nemesis and greatest antagonist, George McCullagh, who had vowed to "knock that shitrag [the *Star*] right off its pedestal," died of a heart attack. But the man McCullagh had picked to run the *Telegram*, John Bassett, was just as determined as McCullagh to win the circulation war against the *Star*. Hindmarsh would not be complacent for long.

30
Manhunt

For the second time in ten months, Edwin Alonzo Boyd and Leonard and Willie Jackson were on the move up the Don Valley. But this flight to freedom would be markedly different: this time there was a fourth man – Steve Suchan. And instead of going over the wall at 5 p.m., they had gone over at 5 a.m. And instead of a $500 reward for their capture, it was $26,000. And instead of a couple of dozen policemen looking for them, there were more than two thousand, fully armed and ready to shoot. And this time Leonard Jackson was wearing a tin cup over his stump instead of his prosthesis.

In the first escape, it was three hours before the guards discovered they were gone; this time it was two hours. Since the first escape was at night, they were able to leave the valley and melt into the city after covering no more than half a mile in the bush. This time, the sun broke the horizon just about the time the escape was discovered, and because police were flooding the city and closely watching the gang's families and associates, they would have to stay in the bush for miles as they worked their way north. The first escape had been on an unseasonably cold, dull day, with light snow. This time the weather was in their favour: the temperature was 50°F. when they came off the wall and would reach 70°F by early afternoon.

But the warm weather was not fortuitous for Lennie Jackson. As soon as the fugitives skirted Riverdale Hospital and headed into the bush, Lennie knew he was in trouble. It was as if someone had sliced open a strong onion and held it under his nose. He had for most of his life suffered from hay fever and asthma, a condition so serious it had led to his hospitalization for two months in England during the war. Lennie dreaded late summer and early fall – the peak of the rag-weed season. Ragweed pollen was the most prevalent cause of hay fever and related allergies, and now, as he moved into the bush near the Don River, the pollen-filled air instantly inflamed the mucous membranes in his eyes and nose. He was miserable as his nose dripped incessantly and tears flowed from his swollen, itchy eyes. His breathing was laboured, and he knew there would be no respite as long as he was in the bush.

As Boyd, Suchan, and the Jacksons worked their way north, stay-ing out of sight but following the railway tracks, there was chaos around the Don Jail. With so many police vehicles and fire trucks converging from 7 a.m. onwards, traffic was badly snarled along Broadview and Gerrard near the jail. And on north Yonge Street traffic was also at a standstill as all northbound vehicles were halted and searched at a police roadblock.

As soon as the police realized the fugitives were not in the Don Jail, they launched an intensive manhunt throughout the city and beyond. Every OPP cruiser was radioed a description of the four men. The same information was sent to RCMP offices across the country, and to the Montreal and Quebec Provincial Police. Photographs and fingerprints of the gang followed by air mail.

By 9:20 a.m. Monday, the FBI and U.S. and Canadian immigra-tion offices had been notified of the escape and sent descriptions of the men. By 10 a.m. police photos and descriptions were in the hands of Norman DePoe, editor of *News Round-Up*; he would broadcast them on CBC Television at half-hour intervals. Two Toronto detectives and two OPP inspectors were staking out Malton Airport.[28] Three more officers were stationed at the Island Airport, and others were keeping watch on the cable ferry running between the Toronto waterfront and the airport. Police marine units patrolled the waterfront.

There was plenty of wild speculation in the media, some of it attributed to police sources. One story suggested that a $28,000 bank robbery at Roncesvalles and Howard Park Avenue, three days before the escape, had been committed by associates of the gang to help them get out of Toronto.

On Monday morning, as the four fugitives stayed low and moved north through the bush and ravines of the Don Valley, the Fall Assizes for York County got under way, although without the star players. Crown attorney William O. Gibson presented indictments to the grand jury against Suchan, Leonard Jackson, and Boyd. The jury was considering indictments against Boyd for armed robbery and related charges, and against Jackson and Suchan for murder. Willie Jackson had been indicted earlier and was to be tried with Boyd. Gibson expressed hope that the gang would be caught in time to go to trial as scheduled on September 15. The case against Lennie Jackson's associate, Frank Watson, was among a total of twenty brought before the grand jury at the assizes. Watson was charged with bribing jail guard James Morrison and possession of counterfeit money.

The extensive publicity and the prospect of a reward for the capture of the Boyd Gang – dead or alive – turned the trickle of tips into a deluge. The reports came to police from all over the country, and nearly all were checked out.

Whitby poultry farmer Roy Larsen didn't wait for the police. On Monday night he was sitting at home by the fire listening to radio reports of the Boyd Gang's escape when he heard loud squawking from his chicken run. He grabbed his .22 and went out to his yard, where he saw a trespasser limping rapidly in the direction of the fence. He fired into the ground three times, but the man ran faster. Larsen thought it must be Lennie Jackson. His fourth shot struck the man in the buttocks. "The blast caught the intruder in the seat of the pants," reported *The Globe and Mail* the next day. "The intruder jumped, howled, clutched at the tender spot and fell writhing to the ground. Municipal police responded and took the culprit away." The "culprit" was a mental patient who had escaped from a nearby hospital.

Two days after the Boyd Gang's escape, a constable on all-night surveillance at the home of Suchan's parents at 27 Sorauren Avenue brought seven police cruisers to the scene around 7 a.m. when he shouted into his radio, "I just saw a man enter Suchan's house."

Uniformed police ringed the house with guns drawn as Inspector Bert Mace and several detectives went to the door, where a bewildered factory worker explained that he was a roomer at the house and had just returned from the night shift. And that night, acting on tips from the public, police raided hotels on Yonge Street, Queen Street East, and Jarvis Street, with no results. "You've got to follow up each of those tips, no matter how crazy they may seem," Inspector Mace told a reporter. He suggested that the gang was probably trying to reach Vancouver, where they could catch a ship for the Orient or Australia.

Although detectives close to the case believed the Boyd Gang was still in Toronto, they were convinced the four would eventually split up and leave town. But they also feared the gang would need cash to finance their getaway. For that reason, every bank in Greater Toronto was placed under police watch and a flying squad was placed on standby in case a robbery alarm came in from any part of the city.

By Wednesday, three days after the escape, police had staged raids in Montreal, Winnipeg, Fort William, Windsor, Welland, Stratford, and North Bay. In the Cochrane area of Northern Ontario where Suchan grew up, police set up roadblocks and checked every car entering and leaving the district. Police were also watching Boyd's relatives in Gravenhurst. As a result of tips from the public, roadblocks also went up in Quebec and British Columbia, where many suspects were detained for questioning. In Havelock, northeast of

Peterborough, four male tourists where surrounded by thirty police officers at a motel after a tip that they were the Boyd Gang. "It's too bad to shock them like that, but we can't take any chances," said one of the officers on the raid.

Also on Wednesday, the OPP issued its official Wanted poster advertising the $26,000 reward. All four fugitives were shown and described. Boyd was back on top of Canada's most wanted list – a position he had relinquished after his capture in March.

On Thursday, September 11, Dorreen Boyd was back in the newspapers in a big way when she appealed to her husband to surrender:

> My Dearest Eddie,
> Am I asking too much of you under the circumstances to give yourself up? If to anyone, to me, or to the men both you and I know would give you a fair deal. I have thought this over so much in the past three days, and knowing me as your devoted wife, I'll wait for you no matter what the outcome may be. God willing we will have the privilege of growing old together. This is all I ask of you, and remember always I love you.

The letter ran in all three Toronto dailies, along with Dorreen's picture. The next day Dorreen, her children in tow, showed up at Toronto radio station CKEY and sent a similar appeal over the air-waves. This time her plea was underlined with another from the children: "We miss you daddy, please come home." The station was flooded with callers, half of them expressing outrage that she was exploiting her children, the other half expressing sympathy for her plight.

In the week following the escape, police in Toronto and its sub-urbs conducted raid after raid on former hang-outs and haunts of the gang members and their associates. By Friday the police were still on high alert, but they had quietly returned to normal hours. At the time of the escape, all time off had been cancelled or delayed as all officers, including those on traffic and desk duties, had been called out.

By week's end the police were becoming increasingly frustrated.

There had been hundreds of leads and dozens of raids, but not a whiff of the gang's whereabouts. "Everybody thinks they've seem them," complained Sergeant of Detectives Bill Matthews, "but nobody we've talked to really has seen them."

For Boyd the escape was an anniversary of sorts: he had robbed his first bank three years earlier almost to the day. Even the weather was the same. Whisky had messed up his plans on that day, and only luck had saved him from being shot or captured. Now he was wondering if that luck would hold.

The run for freedom up the Don Valley wasn't exactly aimless. The Boyd Gang had a destination – a hideout where they could lie low for a few days to consider their next move. Boyd says that Willie had directions to an abandoned farm in North York and had arranged for a cache of food and supplies to be left there. The Don Valley of the early 1950s was largely undeveloped. There was no Ontario Science Centre; no Inn on the Park; no Donalda Golf and Country Club; no Flemingdon Park Golf Club; no North York General Hospital; and, most significantly, no expressway running through the heart of the valley. It was mostly dense bushland broken only by the Don River and the ribbon of railway tracks.

Canadian National Railways constable Francis John Goodenough was patrolling in Leaside about 9 p.m. Monday when he spotted a man in the shoulder-high grass in the northeast corner of the CNR yards near a patch of small gardens maintained by some of the men who worked in the railway shops. The shop men had asked the officer to check their plots that night because somebody had been stealing their vegetables. Goodenough's CNR flashlight was broken, and he was using one that he kept in his car. It didn't throw much light, and he could barely see the figure in the grass. He drew his revolver. "Hold it right there!" he shouted. But the man dropped down in the grass out of sight.

"I ran over to him and when I did so, he started running away from me," Goodenough would tell the Royal Commission a few weeks later. "I had a gun on him and I warned him I would shoot if he didn't stop." But the CNR had strict rules about its men firing their weapons. "We are cautioned quite a lot about shooting at a person unless he tries to shoot at you." Goodenough eventually lost sight of the man in the darkness.

Boyd's memories of the escape up the Don Valley are somewhat blurred, but he thinks it was one of the Jacksons who ran from the CNR. Worrying that the railway cop might bring in reinforcements from the city, the gang moved quickly north again, still following the railway tracks. They made it to a point about half a mile south of present-day Eglinton Avenue, where they slept overnight in the bush. "We found a dense growth of trees where there were no paths, and just curled up and went to sleep," says Boyd. "We were lucky it wasn't winter."

Early Tuesday morning the Boyd Gang was on the move again. "We never crossed any main roads or highways until after dark, so we wouldn't be spotted," says Boyd. "We were just trying to keep out of sight in the daytime. And at night we went out grubbing for food in gardens and farms. We ate so bloody many onions that we could barely stand to talk to each other."

On Tuesday night after darkness fell, they crossed Sheppard Avenue and slept in a woodlot in farm country west of Leslie Street. Either they had been given the wrong directions or they had simply got lost; in either case, they had overshot by a mile or so the abandoned farm where the food cache was supposed to be. "I don't remember why we didn't get there," says Boyd. "We just kept moving north."

When they awoke in the woodlot on Wednesday morning they were pleased to discover that the adjacent barn and farmhouse had been abandoned. Known locally as the Doner Farm, it had been vacant since July 5. The farm was on the west side of Leslie Street, a mile north of Sheppard Avenue. The farmhouse was set well back from the street at the end of a long driveway. And well back from the house was a large barn beyond which, to the west, was a woodlot and a deep ravine. The Don River and the CNR line ran through the property, and there was an "at your own risk" sign posted where the tracks crossed the driveway leading to the house. Boyd thought it was an ideal spot to hop a freight heading west. At the time the Boyd Gang arrived at the farm, the driveway was being torn up by crews digging a massive trench for an oil pipeline. The trench was parallel to the railway line. Dump trucks, bulldozers, backhoes, and other heavy equipment were at the site.

Having a construction crew so close to the farm was a mixed blessing for the Boyd Gang. With the driveway impassable, no cars could suddenly approach the farm, but with so many workers in the area, the risk of discovery was greater. Boyd and the others decided they would stay out of sight in the woods during the day and sleep in the barn at night. The barn, with its rough stone base, was "banked" – built into the side of a hill – with the main doors opening directly to the loft. Below the loft was the stable, its entrance facing south.

The farmhouse had fallen victim to young vandals. It had been peppered with gunfire. "We tried to sleep in the house," says Boyd, "but the windows were all broken or shot up and it was dirty compared to the barn, and probably not as safe." The house was in the open, and for anyone looking west from Leslie Street there was cleared land all the way to the wooded lot behind the barn. Any of the gang coming out from behind the barn in daylight would be visible all the way from Leslie Street.

On Thursday as darkness approached, Steve Suchan left the others. He returned early the next morning with a bundle of clothes, an artificial foot for Lennie Jackson, a large supply of ammunition, and three automatic pistols – a Luger, a Canadian Army-type Browning, and a Walther P-38. There were plenty of clothes, but they were too large for Boyd and Willie Jackson, who opted to keep wearing their denims. Suchan didn't talk about where he went for the guns and clothes. Boyd assumes Suchan walked to Yonge and Sheppard and called one of his or Lennie's underworld contacts from a pay phone. "Some of his cronies probably picked him up and dropped him off the next morning with the clothes and guns, and a new foot for Lennie," says Boyd. "He was probably on the other [west] side of the valley. Lennie would have told him who to contact to get his foot."

For food, the gang raided neighbouring farms at night, stealing corn, potatoes, onions, carrots, and apples, all of which they ate raw. Taking a page from his days riding the rods with Red the Barber, Boyd decided to have a cooked meal for a change. "One night we went deep into the bush and lit a fire to cook the vegetables," he says. "It didn't work too well, everything was half-burned or half-cooked, but it kept us from starving."

By Friday they were ready to gamble. They had about $45 in cash between them and decided to send Willie Jackson out to buy some food. He was the least known of the four men, and he was willing to give it a try. His hair had started to recede a bit, and to change his appearance Boyd shaved it back further, leaving him bald on top at the front.

Willie cut through the bush, emerging on Sheppard Avenue west of the farm. It was about two miles from there to Yonge Street. He had covered about a quarter of a mile when he heard a car coming. He decided to test his luck. He turned and stuck out his thumb. A pleasant, middle-aged woman was driving the car. She pulled over. Willie, with his broad, engaging grin, had a ride. He turned on the charm and entertained her with his wit. When she dropped him at Yonge and Sheppard he went into the Magazine Depot and bought cigarettes, soap, and razor blades. Glancing casually at the newspaper rack, he picked up information about the continuing manhunt, the suspension of the guards and governor at the Don Jail, and the appointing of a royal commission.

Willie was gaining confidence. He walked around a bit, enjoying the feel of a city sidewalk for the first time in nine months. Then he went into an IGA store just two blocks south of the North York police station. He bought three loaves of bread, two quarts of milk, sausage, cold cuts, cheese, two large cans of pork and beans, a couple of boxes of cookies, and a box of salt that might make the raw vegetables more palatable.

"Nobody recognized me," he would brag later. "The clerks were nice to me. They even told me about that terrible Boyd Gang hiding in some richly furnished house."

Willie was given a hero's welcome when he returned to the barn with the groceries and cigarettes. Never had food tasted so good to them.

Another of the myths about the Boyd Gang is that Lennie Jackson left the others to visit his wife and month-old son and to pick up another artificial foot. But Boyd says that the gang stayed together until they reached the barn, and "Lennie was too sick to go any-where." Ann Jackson and her child were staying in Apartment 7 at 6 Howard Street with Lennie's half-brother Sammy Stone, recently released from Kingston Penitentiary. Dolph Payne and Charlie Cook had the apartment under observation "for some hours" from the moment they learned of the jail break. Once Payne was con-vinced Lennie was not showing up and that Ann hadn't heard from him, he went to the apartment and interviewed her. Ann Jackson told him the same thing she would tell reporters later: "I didn't know a thing about the escape. I hope they don't catch him. I don't know if I'll ever see him again, but I hope so."

Farmers near the Doner Farm were soon aware that outsiders or transients were hanging around the barn. Most of them didn't think much of it at first – they knew that abandoned farms attracted hobos and transients. They'd seen it before.

Robert Trimble, 49, from the nearby village of Oriole, went to the Doner farm on Thursday or Friday about 5 p.m. to remove some old wire from the property. He had been hired to manage the prop-erty, which was now used by other farmers as pasture for their cows. While Trimble was there, he noticed a man sitting by the railway track in front of the house. He thought the man might be one of the workers pushing the oil pipeline through the farm. He would learn later the man he saw was Steve Suchan.

At about 10:30 a.m. on Saturday, September 13, Trimble and his brother Howard, who farmed nearby, were back on the property to repair a fence when they saw another man come out of the barn car-rying hay and walking towards the house. He realized later the man was Boyd.

A Toronto junk dealer, known in the Oriole area as Stephenson, had spoken with the men and later told Robert Trimble they were "very nice guys." They had helped him load his truck with scrap metal he was removing from the property. With that reassurance, Trimble didn't pay much more attention. "I saw them going towards the old house on the farm, but nobody was living there, and it wasn't any of my business."

Another Trimble brother, John, who lived three farms to the south, discovered that his potato patch had been raided. And on Monday, September 15, his dog had howled all night and strained towards the barn with its hair standing on end. "We get used to bums around here," he said. "We figured the men around that house would just stay here one night to catch onto the train that rides through the property."

Catching the train was exactly what Boyd was thinking about, and to this day he regrets not hopping one heading west or north. He can't understand why he ignored his own instincts. They had been too long in the same place. Perhaps he was clinging to his Hollywood ideal of what a gang was supposed to be. Perhaps this time Suchan and Lennie Jackson might not run off with their women, leaving him and Willie in the lurch. Or perhaps he simply felt sorry for Lennie. "Even without his foot Lennie moved pretty good up the Don Valley," says Boyd. "He never let anything slow him down. But he was suffering terribly from hay fever and asthma and he seemed like a beaten man. He was never the same after he was shot up in Montreal."

Boyd thinks back to those days in the barn. His eyes are intense and he shakes his head. He can't find an answer. "I don't know why I stayed there with them," he says finally. "If I had been smart, I would have been in a boxcar heading north or west. I just never got around to it, and in no time at all it was too late."

31

Trapped

Scarborough police constable Andrew Ouellette was on patrol alone at 10:30 a.m. on Tuesday, September 16, 1952. Ouellette, a native of Quebec, was considered an observant and diligent officer. A few weeks earlier, he and a partner had nabbed a gang of five safe-crackers. On this day he noticed a black 1951 Ford parked opposite the Gleneagle Hotel on the Lansing cut-off in Markham Township north of Highway 7. What drew his attention to the car was the rear licence plate, which had been bent up, concealing the numbers. As Ouellette approached the Ford to investigate, a man standing beside the car jumped in and drove off to the west at a high rate of speed.

As Ouellette sped after the Ford, he noticed there were two other men in the car. The chase continued for three miles at speeds reaching ninety miles an hour. Ouellette fired two warning shots. When the Ford didn't slow down, he fired four more shots, emptying his revolver. As the chase continued along the Brooks Sideroad, Ouellette tried to get his cruiser alongside the Ford. He was within ten feet when a man in the rear seat rolled down the window and fired four bullets, which ripped into the cruiser. Two of the bullets popped holes through the windshield on the passenger side.

"There was no doubt that the man was shooting to kill," Scarborough Police Inspector Harold Adamson[29] said later. "He was aiming directly at the constable. One bullet passed within four inches of his head."

The road was in poor condition, and as Ouellette swerved to avoid further shots he lost control of the cruiser, which went off the road, through a ditch, and into a tree. He radioed for help and was taken to hospital with internal injuries.

Ouellette's call set in motion a chain of events that would have dire consequences for the Boyd Gang. After more than a week of fruitless searching, police pressure had begun to slacken, and many senior officers believed the gang had split up and moved out of the area. Now police were convinced Ouellette had flushed out the gang. Within minutes the area was flooded with cruisers from the Scarborough Police Department and an all-out search had been launched.

When word got out that the fugitives were in farm country northeast of Toronto, police officers from across the region, including the OPP, descended on the area by the hundreds. The Toronto police rushed out as many officers as they could spare, but held back enough men to keep an eye on the city's banks because, as the *Star* reported, "they thought it might be a Boyd trick" to divert police so that he and his gang could rob a bank without interference. In downtown courtrooms, several cases were quickly adjourned to allow any police officers who were there to testify to join the manhunt. As a precaution against the gang doubling back into Toronto, roadblocks were set up on north Yonge Street, Avenue Road, Bathurst Street, and the Lakeshore at the Humber River.

Over the next six hours police would closely search eight square miles of farms, woodlands, and sideroads northeast of Toronto. Ontario Hydro offered the use of one of its helicopters, and police sergeant George Long, armed with a heavy automatic rifle, climbed aboard it at Malton Airport and used a short-wave walkie-talkie to stay in contact with cruisers on the ground.

The Boyd Gang had no access to a radio or newspapers and so had no way of knowing that a manhunt, more concentrated than that of the first day of their escape, was under way not more than a couple of miles away.

Early Tuesday afternoon, police officers involved in the search came upon a cache of food on the ledge of a pump house at an abandoned farm less than a mile south of the Doner farm. The police decided to leave the food as bait. Detective Frank Cater, who had arrested Boyd in his panel truck after the bungled robbery with Gault in October 1951, was assigned with another officer to stake out the farm.

Cater was at police headquarters on College Street as weapons were being distributed for the manhunt. He left for his assignment armed with a machine-gun, a shotgun, his service revolver, and a 9 mm Luger from his personal gun collection. "When the hunt was on for Boyd, I got permission from the inspector to carry the Luger with me as an extra precaution," says Cater, now retired and living in Burlington. While he was on the police force he belonged to a revolver club and won several marksmanship trophies.

"Frank Cater was a gun nut," laughs Jack Webster. "We used to joke around the department that if Cater was having a shower and you tried to sneak up on him, by the time you pulled the curtain back he'd have you covered with three guns. He always had a gun strapped to his ankle, one in the small of his back, and another in his shoulder holster."

Cater wasn't too pleased about concealing his cruiser and lugging all his weaponry into a field to watch a box of groceries. "The upper echelon figured that we should lay there in the high grass and wait for the buggers to come and get their food," he says. "We lay there and lay there for hours."

Meanwhile, in the woods beyond the Doner barn, the Boyd Gang was feeling miserable and restless. The weather had cooled a bit and there had been some light rain earlier in the day. Lennie Jackson could barely breathe after nine days without respite from his hay fever and asthma. Willie Jackson had eaten too many cookies and had a toothache. And Suchan and Boyd wanted to get moving again. The four fugitives talked it over and decided they would leave the next morning. Maybe they would hop a freight train and head north and then west. "We'd had enough of the dirty barn," says Boyd. "We were ready to make a break. Lennie was in agony all the time. Another day and we would have been far away from North York."

They knew they had been seen. They'd even talked to the scrap collector and to one of the workmen from the pipeline project. And just the day before, they'd had an unexpected visitor. They had been lying in the loft when they heard someone approaching the barn.

They grabbed their weapons and through cracks in floor looked down into the stable. A man walked in, glanced around, and stretched out in the hay. Above him the four men didn't make a sound as he unbuttoned his trousers and proceeded to masturbate. When he was finished, and wandered out of the barn, Boyd and the others, like adolescent schoolboys, could barely suppress their laughter. "It was one of the funniest things we'd ever seen," says Boyd. "Willie nearly busted a gut trying to keep from laughing out loud."

When farmer Howard Trimble first told his brother John about the men living at the barn on the Doner farm, John jokingly suggested they might be the Boyd Gang.

"Don't be silly," said Howard.

John Trimble worked as a farmhand on an immense estate owned by Col. W.E. Phillips, a Toronto industrialist. The estate was not far from the Doner farm. Col. Phillips' superintendent, and sometimes chauffeur, was Maurice Doyle. While Doyle was having lunch at his Sheppard Avenue East home on Tuesday, he heard on the radio about the Boyd Gang being suspected in a shoot-out with a Scarborough policeman. Not all that far away, he thought. After lunch, while working on the estate, Doyle had a chance meeting with John Trimble. They talked about the shooting incident, and Trimble mentioned the men at the Doner farm.

"My brother Robert has seen some tramps hanging around the barn," said Trimble. "Stephenson, the junk dealer, was taking some scrap from there and these fellows helped him load it. My brother looked in the barn and he saw hay piled up where they had apparently been sleeping. One of them was a big fellow, and Robert saw him sitting on the veranda at the house smoking a cigarette. But they seem to be away during the daytime." Trimble also told Doyle about his missing vegetables and how his dog had howled half the night.

"*Our* dogs were raising quite a fuss for about an hour during the night too," said Doyle.

The suspicious men on the Doner farm and the shooting that morning were enough for Doyle. At 5:30 p.m. he telephoned

Sergeant Edward Dagleish of the North York Police Department. The two men had known each other for years. Doyle told him about the tramps at the barn. "I was thinking of taking my rifle and checking out the barn myself," said Doyle.

"No, I wouldn't do that, Maurice," said Dagleish. "I'll send our boys over."

The day shift was just ending, and Dagleish decided to wait until Detective Bert Trotter came in about 5:50. "Do you know where the old Doner farm is?" asked Dagleish when Trotter arrived.

"No I don't."

"Well wait for Richardson and go out there with him," said Dagleish. "He knows the area." Sergeant of Detectives Maurice Richardson arrived a few minutes later.

About 4 p.m. Tuesday afternoon, twenty-four-year-old Evan Taylor and nineteen-year-old Elgin Rohrer were hauling a truckload of dirt from the pipeline excavation towards a dumping spot near the Doner farm. It was raining lightly. They were driving along the right-of-way beside the railway tracks. At the top of the hill above the farm, they stopped the truck when they saw a man lying on the ground about thirty yards from the barn. The man stood up and waved or signalled and a second man appeared from behind the barn. "We continued down the hill to where we were dumping our load, and the man who had come out of the barn came down to where we stopped," Taylor told police later. "He was very pale, and was wearing a black rubber raincoat and another coat under it." The man was Steve Suchan.

"Hello," said Taylor.

"How are you today?" asked Suchan. "Pretty slippery since the rain." Taylor nodded agreement. Suchan walked off to the side of the road, picked up some clothing that was lying on the ground, and returned to the barn.

"I've seen his face before," said Taylor to his partner. "I bet it's that gang."

"That's what struck me," said Rohrer.

The men worked a while longer and then asked their boss if they could drive over to the village of Oriole to phone the police with their suspicions. The boss agreed, and a few minutes later they were in the village. They discussed the men in the barn over Cokes at a lunch counter, and then Taylor called the North York police from a telephone booth outside. He described the location of the farm in relation to the pipeline project. He told the police he was suspicious of the men because their skin was pale, as if they hadn't been out-doors for a long time. And he wondered why they were hanging around a deserted barn.

Detectives Richardson and Trotter were still at the North York sta-tion when Evan Taylor's call came in at 5:30, but the dispatcher real-ized the barn was the same one Doyle was talking about and felt no need to pass on the information: the detectives were headed there anyway. At 6:20 there was a third call, this one from Gordon Beauchamp, the proprietor of the lunch counter in Oriole. Beauchamp's mother, who worked at the lunch counter, had over-heard Rohrer and Taylor discussing the barn, and told her son. While Taylor was on the phone to police, Beauchamp asked Rohrer what was going on. Rohrer mentioned the suspicious men but was pur-posely vague when Beauchamp asked about the location of the barn.

Richardson and Trotter stopped by the lunch counter on their way to the Doner farm, but quickly realized that Beauchamp had no idea where the barn was. He told them it was somewhere on Don Mills Road. (Beauchamp's later claim that his tip to the police had led to the capture of the Boyd Gang received extensive coverage in the newspapers, but his petition for the $26,000 reward was rejected. Instead, $11,000 would go to Maurice Doyle, $4,500 to John Trimble, $4,000 each to Evan Taylor and Elgin Rohrer, and $2,500 to Robert Trimble, even though he had told the attorney general's office to "give it to Doyle. He has a girl that has infantile paralysis and needs the money. I earn my money with my hands and am quite content that way.")

After leaving Beauchamp's lunch counter in Oriole, Richardson and Trotter continued to the Doner farm. When they made the turn to the laneway off Leslie Street they were confronted with the impassable trench. A four-man bulldozer crew was working the site.

One of them asked the policemen where they were going.

"We're going over to the barn," said Richardson.

"Well, we can fill the hole in so you can drive over."

"No, it's all right," said Richardson. "We'll just walk in."

"Be careful, you might run into the Boyd Gang," said one of the men in jest.

"Sure thing," laughed Richardson.

They had to walk about two hundred yards to the farmhouse, which they determined was deserted. A boy was playing in an adjoining field as they approached the barn, and Richardson went over to the fence to question him. Trotter meanwhile went up the ramp to the main doors of the barn, which were at the rear facing the wooded lot. He leaned forward and peered through a crack in the door. Inside he saw one man standing with his back to him and two others crouched or lying in the hay. With his .38 in hand, Trotter opened the door, walked in, and whistled for his partner.

Richardson had left the boy and was about to open the back door to the stable on the lower level when he heard his partner whistle. He ran up the ramp to see Trotter with his gun levelled at Edwin Alonzo Boyd, "Tough Lennie" Jackson, and Willie "the Clown" Jackson.

"We didn't hear a thing," says Boyd. "We didn't hear anybody approaching, and we didn't hear anybody down below. Then suddenly this guy came in the front door with a gun on us. They caught us by surprise. That was it."

"I held a gun on them until Richardson joined me and then we led them outside," Trotter said later. "The two Jacksons were lying down. Both of them had guns, but neither made a move for them. Boyd didn't have a gun. I'm not underestimating that they were desperate men. It was just that we caught them completely by surprise."

Richardson told the *Star* later: "We just happened to catch them bedding down for the night. They were spreading out some raincoats on the barn floor."

Boyd, Suchan and the Jacksons had established the routine of taking turns keeping watch whenever they were in the barn before dark. "It was Lennie's turn," says Boyd. "He was supposed to be looking out through the cracks in the wall, but he was in agony and wasn't watching. You can't blame him, we didn't really expect anybody to come in like that. We had already eaten and Suchan was out getting apples for our dessert."

Boyd says if they had known about the morning shoot-out and the renewed manhunt they would have hid in the wooded lot or started moving north in the bush. "We were unaware that the police were around. I was relaxed waiting for darkness."

At first Boyd told the police officers that he and the Jacksons were vagrants who had dropped off a passing freight train to spend the night in the abandoned barn.

"What's your name?" asked Richardson.

"West," said Boyd. The policemen knew better.

Richardson reached down and felt Lennie Jackson's lower leg. It was wooden, and that convinced the officers there had been no mistake. When the three fugitives were searched, one gun was found in Lennie Jackson's coat, which he had been lying on, and another was found in the hay beside Willie Jackson. Although Boyd didn't have a gun, about thirty rounds of ammunition were found in his pockets. In all, ninety-seven rounds were found among the three men.

Trotter and Richardson looked around for Suchan, but there was no sign of him. While Trotter kept Boyd and the Jacksons covered with his revolver, Richardson ran to the cruiser and radioed for help.

Richardson's call was momentous. He had the Boyd Gang in a barn on Leslie Street. "Attention all cars," said the Toronto police dispatcher from headquarters on College Street. "North York police require assistance.... " He went on to give the precise location of the barn, and scores of squad cars from all over the city rushed to the scene. Reporters monitoring the police radio also heard the call, and ran to their cars. Editors called out every available reporter and photographer.

North York police constable Ernie Southern was with a search team checking a barn on Steeles Avenue when he heard the call. "Richardson shouted over the police radio that he had Boyd in a barn on Leslie Street," said Southern. "And I called to the boys in the other four cars and we raced to the scene."

When Southern arrived he saw Richardson's cruiser on the laneway near the railway tracks. He and the others left their cars and ran towards the barn. They got as far as the farmhouse when they saw Trotter and Richardson escorting Boyd and the two Jacksons from the barn. The prisoners were taken to the clutch of police cars and were handcuffed together and to North York constable Ray Geno.

"There's still one more around somewhere – Suchan," said Richardson. He ordered Southern and constables Bill Adams and Havre Lowe to search for him. Southern was aware that it was Suchan's bullet that killed Eddie Tong.

Steve Suchan was unaware of the drama that had just taken place when he returned to the barn with a supply of apples. The others weren't there, but that wasn't unusual – they were probably wandering around outside somewhere. Boyd says that because of the way the barn was situated, with the main doors out of sight of Leslie Street and the laneway leading to the farm, Suchan wouldn't have seen them and all the police cars beyond the railway tracks. "If he had seen what was going on he would have taken off," says Boyd.

Instead, Suchan made himself comfortable in the hay and waited for the others. Outside the barn, constables Adams and Lowe headed for the stable door at the back, while Southern, as Trotter had done, walked up the ramp to the main doors. With gun drawn, he entered to find Suchan facing away from him in a kneeling position on the floor. He had probably heard Adams and Lowe entering below and thought it was Boyd and the Jacksons. Suchan heard a noise behind him and turned to face Southern's revolver aimed at his chest.

"What's up?" asked Suchan.

"One move and you've had it," said Southern.

"It's okay – I give up," said Suchan, raising his hands above his head. His fully loaded P-38 was tucked in his belt on the left side, but he made no move for it. Memories of the Montreal shoot-out and of his long and painful convalescence were no doubt still fresh in his mind.

Lowe and Adams were standing in the stable below with guns drawn. Southern ordered Suchan to jump the ten feet or so from the loft to the hay below. Suchan complied, and Lowe removed the automatic pistol from Suchan's belt. "The safety catch was off," said Lowe later, "but he didn't try to go for it." The three officers led Suchan over to the others in the laneway beyond the railway tracks.

The newspaper accounts of the capture of the Boyd Gang varied wildly, and inaccurate versions of the story have persisted ever since. One bit of mythology has it that Suchan was in the rafters of the barn all along and could have shot the police officers at any time. Another – the "*click ... click ... click*" version – has it that Suchan tried to shoot the officers from the rafters but his gun misfired. It seems inconceivable that after hearing the first "click" a police officer wouldn't have turned and fired at him, but the myth persists.

In a search of the Boyd Gang's hideout, police found one whole and two partial loaves of bread, one can of pork and beans, a few stunted carrots, a dozen or so green apples, a box of salt, an empty cookie box, a bar of soap, a razor with extra blades, two pairs of brown trousers, two raincoats, and two ties. And among them, the four had a bit of pocket change and $25 in bills.

What would have happened if Richardson and Trotter had been able to drive right up to the barn on that day? No doubt Boyd and the others would have heard them. But would there have been a shoot-out? Boyd says the first option would have been to get out of the barn and into the bush before they were spotted. And if they were spotted? "We'd probably have started firing at them – not to hit them, but to scare them away – and then try and get away ourselves."

And what if they were cornered in the barn, but had time to reach their weapons? "I know Len would have used his gun," says Boyd. "His willingness to shoot it out in Montreal indicated what he thought about going to jail. And Suchan probably would have shot it out too. He was a guy that just thrived on having weapons. Willie didn't give a damn if he was caught or not. He did a lot of narcotics in prison, and he had a captive audience for his jokes." Boyd says that he himself would not have shot it out unless he thought somebody was trying to kill him. "I was never someone to shoot it out," he says. "If you do get away, it just brings more heat."

Detective Frank Cater had been in the tall grass staking out the food cache at the abandoned barn south of the Doner farm when word came that the Boyd Gang had been spotted. He ran for his cruiser and locked the machine-gun in the trunk, and he and his partner roared off to Leslie Street.

There were already several North York police cars in the laneway as they pulled up. Cater had his Luger out of his pocket, but he saw Boyd and the two Jacksons already in handcuffs standing beside the North York police cruiser. Boyd recognized Cater and noticed the Luger, which was much like the one Cater had confiscated from him eleven months earlier.

"Hey!" said Boyd. "You got my bloody Luger."

"Like hell I do," said Cater. "This is my own Luger."

Boyd laughed.

Suchan had just arrived near the cars with Constable Southern, and Cater noticed that the prisoner had not been handcuffed. "I gave them my cuffs to put on him," says Cater. "They were my own. They were a standard cuff, but the key was a different shape. Mine was a solid key, while the others had a hollow stem." Standard police keys wouldn't work in Cater's cuffs.

Boyd and the two Jacksons, still handcuffed to Constable Ray Geno, were bundled into the back seat of a Toronto police car driven by Detective Jack Crilly. Beside Crilly in the front seat, with his gun drawn, was a young North York constable, Charles Doyle. He was looking back with his revolver trained on the prisoners. It was obvious to him that Lennie Jackson was in bad shape.

"Go ahead," said Lennie. "Why don't you just shoot me in the head and get it over with."

"One false move and you'll get it," said Doyle.

Detective Crilly, now seventy-six, remembers that young Doyle was "very nervous" and that Willie Jackson was taunting him.

"You couldn't shoot anybody," said Willie. "You don't have the guts."

"Willie put his nose right up to the gun," says Crilly.

Boyd, trained in the proper handling of guns, did not like the idea of a nervous cop aiming at him over the seat with his finger on the trigger. "I remember this policeman was in uniform in the front seat," says Boyd. "He was all shook up and ready to shoot us. He turned around quick and pointed the gun at us. And I got mad." Boyd didn't understand the need for the gun. They were in handcuffs and they weren't going anywhere.

"Don't point that thing at us, you're going to accidentally shoot somebody." said Boyd. "Don't you know anything about guns?"

"Just don't shoot me," said Detective Crilly.

Boyd says the young officer was agitated, but he put the gun away.

Suchan was placed in another cruiser, handcuffed to a North York officer. Detective Cater's cruiser was facing the wrong way, and it took some time to turn it around with all the congestion. Police cars, reporters, photographers, and interested onlookers continued to pour into the area. "They took off with Suchan and we tried to follow," says Cater. "We were maybe two hundred yards behind, but cars started coming in from sideroads all over the place and they got to the station nearly an hour before we did. It was unbelievable. The capture must have gone over the radio right away because you couldn't move up there. It was just clogged with cars."

Cater realized that until he arrived at the North York police station with his key, they would be unable to remove Suchan's handcuffs. Then he thought about Eddie Tong lying in the street with a bullet in his chest and Suchan's problem didn't bother him a bit.

By the time the cruiser with Boyd and the Jacksons arrived at the North York police station, at Princess Avenue and Yonge Street in Willowdale, hundreds of people had gathered for a glimpse of the notorious foursome. The cruiser made it to the basement garage and the door was closed behind it.

Detective Trotter removed the cuffs from Boyd and the Jacksons while Detective Crilly searched them. In one of Boyd's pockets he found the home-made key.

"That's probably the key for the cells in the Don Jail," said Trotter. Boyd and the two Jacksons just smiled. The cruiser carrying Suchan arrived soon after, but it would be a while longer before Cater arrived to remove his handcuffs.

Meanwhile, the growing crowd outside was in a festive mood. Maurice Richardson, who retired as a police inspector in 1976, has vivid memories of the station that day. "It was already in an uproar when we got back there from the farm. When I got there, all the people that I knew in North York were there. It was chaos with all the media and all the people. As a matter of fact they had to bring officers up from the city to put a cordon around the station, so people couldn't get at the windows." Across the street, the Hydro helicopter caused a stir when it landed in the lot beside the community hall.

Shortly after 7 p.m., Mayor Allan Lamport's limousine, with a motorcycle escort, came to a screeching halt in front of the North York police station. Looking dapper with his pearl-grey fedora tilted low on his forehead, Lamport was quick to point out to the horde of reporters that he had arrived before Toronto Police Chief John Chisholm: "I beat the chief to the draw." He reminded them he had also been "in on the kill" when Boyd was captured on Heath Street six months earlier. To some, the mayor was like a big game hunter posing with his kill after a hunt. He needed photographs because his trophies were headed for prison rather than the wall of a recreation room.

As reporters bombarded police officials with questions about the capture, Lamport was in a corner getting the names of the officers involved in the capture. The mayor could barely contain himself as he posed with Chisholm and Inspector of Detectives Alex McCathie. "My God, chief," shouted Lamport, "wouldn't this just make you cry. I'm so happy."

Then Lamport, Chisholm, and McCathie headed for the basement cells for a chat with the Boyd Gang. The three cells were in a guarded room with a heavy steel door and grate. Boyd was in the first cell, Suchan and Willie Jackson in the second, and Leonard Jackson in the third. The prisoners had received sandwiches and coffee, and except for Lennie were in good spirits.

Ever since the capture the police had been questioning the gang about the morning shoot-out in Scarborough. Over and over they denied any involvement. When McCathie or Chisholm asked about it again in the cells, Boyd said, "I'm telling you rightly, we weren't in on it and don't know anything about it."

Reporters outside could hear Lamport lecturing the prisoners. "You can't beat society this way," he said.

"But remember," said Boyd, "we didn't shoot anybody. We didn't hurt anyone."

"Don't worry, you'll get fair treatment," said Lamport.

In conversation with Lennie Jackson, the mayor asked: "Wasn't the pressure pretty tough?"

"It certainly was," said Lennie. "I wish they'd got me. I wish it was tonight." Jackson told the mayor that it wasn't until two weeks before the break that they were able to talk Boyd into leaving the Don Jail with them.

Outside the jail, the crowd had swollen so much that traffic was blocked on Yonge Street. Uniformed officers and detectives from North York and Toronto continued to patrol the grounds of the station, some of them still carrying machine-guns and shotguns. The crowd was in a raucous mood, and many – mostly teenagers – began chanting, "We want Boyd! We want Boyd!" Inside, Boyd could hear the chanting. He smiled, and winked at one of the detectives guarding him.

Lamport remembers well the night of the capture. "I went up to North York to see them right away. They were very respectful to me. They knew damn well I meant business. They were a hell of a bunch of good-looking men. They looked more like bank managers or company executives, but they tried to make money the easy way. Unfortunately that's not the way it turns out. They always get caught. They outsmart themselves. I don't know why they took those girls along. They were getting away with so much, they got careless. Boyd was too smart for his own good."

Boyd's take on Lamport is that "he just wanted publicity. He wasn't too interested in us. He was interested in the pictures. He used every device he could to get his picture in the paper."

At an impromptu press conference after his meeting with the prisoners, Lamport said the capture had been a disheartening experience for the gang. "They're a bunch of whipped lambs tonight, and I rubbed it in. Leonard Jackson is about ready to throw in the sponge."

Jocko Thomas was among the reporters who had arrived at the North York jail. For the first time he found that the newspapers were facing serious competition from television. "We thought that television was being given a little too much leeway by the police. They were anxious to get the television reporter in there to set up his cameras and photograph Boyd behind the bars. They were let in first. We had to wait our turn."

Thomas found that none of the four prisoners had much to say. "It was really just a photo opportunity for the papers to take a picture of the reporter talking to Boyd or the Jacksons and Suchan behind bars."

The next day the *Telegram* described Lennie in his cell: "Leonard Jackson, furthest from the door, looked like a wild man, and now and then let out a loud laugh. His woolly hair was in disarray. He was suffering badly from asthma."

A doctor was called in to look at Lennie, who was still wheezing and struggling for breath. The doctor gave him some pills. Thomas says that although Lennie Jackson wasn't well, "he was quite cocky. That was his natural manner. He was what was known as a cop-hater. Boyd would not be a cop-hater because his father was a policeman." Boyd, in contrast, seemed relaxed.

From behind his cell door Boyd asked a reporter, "Do you have a good car?"

The puzzled reporter said he did. A late model.

"Do you keep it filled with gas?" asked Boyd.

"Yes."

"That's fine. Keep it that way. I'll need it to get out of Kingston next year."

Boyd's comments were the grist for more headlines the next day. The papers gave him celebrity treatment as the circulation war turned white-hot again. All of the papers ran huge headlines and dozens of photos and stories about the capture. One entire page in the *Telegram* was filled with a portrait-style photograph of Boyd staring out pensively from behind the bars of his cell. Possibly, the *Telegram* was playing one-upmanship with the *Star*, which had run a similar photo of Boyd that filled all but the bottom two inches of a page.

While the Boyd Gang was being held in the modern cells in North York, workers were labouring through the night to make their old cells at the Don Jail "Boyd-proof," in the words of one jail official. The bars in the window they had escaped through were replaced with new, saw-resistant ones from Taylor's Safe Works. And instead of regular jail guards, a special squad of seven OPP officers – including a sergeant and a corporal – were to guard the four prisoners round the clock – the first time in the history of the jail that police were brought in for day-and-night guard duty.

As soon as word of the capture got out, hundreds gathered at the Don Jail hoping for a glimpse of the gang. The crowd finally began to disperse after 11 p.m. when a police inspector told them they would not be returned from North York until morning.

The Globe and Mail

Sunny
High Here 75

Where to Find It

109th Year. No. 32,063. ● ● ● ● TORONTO, WEDNESDAY, SEPTEMBER 17, 1952. 5 Cents Per Copy 30 PAGES

Cringe Before 2 Detectives

NAB BOYD GANG

TORONTO DAILY STAR

THE WEATHER

WEDNESDAY, SEPTEMBER 17, 1952–56 PAGES 5c PER COPY 30c PER WEEK

'SAW MY WAY OUT AGAIN'-BOYD BOAST REBUILD DON CELLS

On Trial

There were no thoughts of escape when the Boyd Gang returned to the same cells they had sawed their way out of eight days earlier. Now they had new bars and twenty-four-hour armed guards. In addition, Reform Institutions Minister John Foote said that "all privileges will be taken away from these men. They will not be allowed newspapers or magazines, and there will be no more card-playing."

All the Boyd Gang trials, including those of its peripheral members, began on September 22, in the third-floor courtrooms of the City Hall building on Queen Street West. Suchan and Leonard Jackson went on trial in Supreme Court before Mr. Justice James McRuer, while Boyd and the others appeared in County Court before Judge Robert Forsyth. The gang was transported between the courts and the Don Jail in heavily armed police convoys. They entered the building's inner courtyard off Albert Street and from there were escorted in manacles to the basement cells. When the court convened, they were taken up the elevator to the courtrooms while dozens of police officers armed with shotguns lined the corridors.

All of the trials would be over in less than three weeks, during which the newspapers were again flooded with Boyd Gang stories and photos. "In those days production was much faster," says Jocko Thomas. "I'd send something over from the courts at City Hall at one o'clock and it would be in the paper by the time I picked it up at two o'clock. Pneumatic tubes ran under the street from City Hall right down to the *Star* office at 80 King Street West. The *Telegram* had the same thing. You put your stories in little containers and shoved them into the tube in the press room. City Hall and court stories occupied quite a bit of the newspaper space in those days."

For the duration of the trials, the Toronto Police Department kept the Don Jail under heavy guard. Inspector Charlie Greenwood was in charge of the police detail. Jack Webster was working in the traffic division at the time, and it was from traffic that Greenwood got most of his manpower. Greenwood was a notorious disciplinarian and was feared by most officers on the force. Problem officers were transferred to Greenwood's No. 8 Station for discipline. "That was before the Police Association had any real power," says Webster. "It didn't matter where you lived in the city, you would be sent to No. 8 at Queen and Pape. The first thing Greenwood did was put you on nights for three straight months."

Webster says he and other officers hated duty at the Don. "It was so boring. You just stood around all the time." Each night during the trials, about forty officers ringed the jail. Webster smoked in those days and Greenwood, a nonsmoker, didn't allow his men to smoke while on duty.

One cold and rainy night, Webster had just lit a cigarette when Greenwood's voice boomed out of the darkness: "Put that out!" Webster was surprised to see him. "It wasn't unusual to have a patrol sergeant come around when you were working," he says. "But not an inspector in the middle of the night."

"What's your name?" asked Greenwood.

"Webster, sir."

"Do you know who I am?"

"Inspector Greenwood."

"Well, put that down in your book – visit from Inspector Greenwood, 3:10 a.m."

"You son of a bitch," Webster mumbled under his breath as Greenwood walked away. Webster was relieved when Greenwood didn't take further action.

As the trials got under way, Edwin Boyd, who had originally decided to plead not guilty to all charges, changed his mind after he was found guilty in the $49,270 Leaside robbery. He knew the evidence against him was overwhelming on most of the remaining charges.

He pleaded guilty to eight of the bank robberies and related car thefts, and to one charge of attempted bank robbery.

That left two charges still pending – the $4,300 robbery of the Dundas–Roncesvalles branch of the Bank of Toronto, and the $10,000 robbery of the Birchcliff branch of the same bank. The eyewitness identification of Boyd in the Dundas–Roncesvalles robbery was questionable and he was found not guilty, and the Crown decided not to proceed on the Birchcliff charge, since the other accused, Steve Suchan, was facing capital murder charges.

After Boyd pleaded guilty, Sergeant of Detectives Dolph Payne went into the witness box and gave Judge Forsyth a detailed account of how Boyd had planned and carried out the robberies, using stolen getaway vehicles. But all of his comments about Boyd weren't negative. "He's a very safe man with a gun," said the detective. "And he has less respect for his own life than for the lives of the people he robs or the police." Payne said Boyd had been fired on many times, but had returned fire only once – when he shot over the head of the bank manager who fired at him during the aborted Imperial Bank robbery, at Fairlawn and Avenue Road on October 11, 1950.

"Boyd had great opportunities to fire on me, but never did," said Payne, who was so overcome with emotion as he started to recall the Heath Street capture that he could not continue. A recess was called, and Payne explained later that he believed he owed his life to Boyd because Boyd could have shot him during the capture in the apartment.

During the two and a half weeks of the trials, Jack Webster one day was assigned to the holding cells in the basement of City Hall. As he stood outside Boyd's cell he remembered his early days on the police force when he worked with Glover Boyd, who used to brag about his son overseas in the army.

"You know, I knew your father," said Webster.

"Did you?"

"Yes, I walked the beat with him in Parkdale – No. 6 Station."

Webster said Boyd found the information interesting and they talked a while longer.

"You know," said Webster, "your father was very proud of you."

"Well he should still be proud of me," said Boyd with a slight smile. "My picture's been on the front page of every newspaper in Canada."

Webster said Boyd made the comment "in sort of a facetious way."

Boyd knew he was facing a long prison term, but what troubled him most was the fate of his brother Norman, who was facing two charges of armed robbery and one charge of harbouring. He felt responsible for his brother's legal problems.

On Friday, September 26, Norman Boyd was found guilty of harbouring. On Monday morning he was back in court to face armed robbery charges for the $46,270 hold-up of the Leaside Royal Bank. In one of the few moments of levity at the series of Boyd Gang trials, Norman Boyd said he had lent his Austin to Dorreen Boyd.

"But that car was registered in her name," said the Crown counsel.

"It was her car in name only," said Norman. He said he had switched it to Dorreen Boyd's name because after he lent her the car she had received numerous tickets for driving the wrong way on one-way streets.

"I thought she might as well pay the tickets herself," he said. His comments brought laughter in the courtroom. Edwin Boyd smiled broadly in the dock and glanced at his wife, who also smiled.

Norman and Edwin Boyd and Willie Jackson were all found guilty of the robbery. Norman was stunned by the verdict. He had been doing survey work with the City of Toronto's sewer department that day – even his boss had testified to that. But he had been convicted, and still faced one more charge of armed robbery. After his experience with the jury in the first case, he decided to be tried by judge alone. The charge stemmed from the robbery of the Dominion Bank on Sheppard Avenue East in September 1951.

At the trial, Norman testified that while questioning him about the robbery, Dolph Payne took him into a room, slapped his face and said, "You're the man we're looking for." And on the same day, he said, Payne had banged a belt on the table beside him and said, "Okay, we'll make you talk." Payne denied the allegations on the witness stand.

But Norman Boyd stands by the allegation that Payne struck and threatened him. "That was normal police practice," he says. "I think anybody who was arrested went through the same kind of thing. That's the way they got their evidence. You might call it torture, you might not. I guess it's a matter of opinion."

Judge Forsyth said that the case against Norman Boyd in the Dominion Bank robbery was difficult. There was conflicting evidence that raised some doubt, "and the benefit of the doubt must be given to the accused." By acquitting, Judge Forsyth may have been redressing the injustice of the jury decision in Norman's earlier armed robbery trial.

Thursday, October 16, was a crisp, sunny day with light winds. The Boyd Gang had been recaptured exactly one month before. It was the day of reckoning for Edwin Alonzo Boyd, Willie "the Clown" Jackson, and the six others with connections to the Boyd Gang, including Boyd's brother Norman, Steve Suchan's parents, Willie Jackson's brother and brother-in-law, and Leonard Jackson's sister, Mary Mitchell.

All eight faced Judge Robert Forsyth in the General Sessions Court at City Hall. The first to be sentenced were Joseph and Elizabeth Lesso, parents of Steve Suchan, who were charged with harbouring Edwin Boyd and Willie Jackson after their first escape. Joseph Lesso had been held in custody and was brought up from the cells. His wife had been free on bail. At the sentencing hearing, Crown counsel A.O. Klein said that Joseph Lesso had been convicted of beating his wife three years earlier, but explained he was suffering from mental illness at the time.

The defence counsel, Lou Herman, said that Joseph Lesso was "in a desperate position" with his son facing the death penalty for the murder of Eddie Tong, and that Lesso's harbouring of Boyd was a case of "overindulgence as regards his son." Lesso, he said, had been forced to take out a second mortgage on his house to help pay for his son's defence, and if he drew a jail term he would lose his home. Lesso had been in custody for thirty-nine days and, said Herman, "that is surely punishment enough and would serve all the ends of justice."

Elizabeth Lesso's lawyer was Lou Herman's brother, Carl. He said that his client had a four-year-old son at home and asked for a suspended sentence. It she were sent to jail, there would be no one at home to look after the boy.

Judge Forsyth was not swayed. He sentenced Joseph Lesso to nine months in jail, and Elizabeth Lesso to six months indeterminate, meaning she could be released at any time on good behaviour.

Twenty-eight-year-old Mary Mitchell, composed and stylishly dressed, was next to appear before Forsyth. She was also charged with harbouring Boyd and Willie Jackson after their escape from the Don. Crown counsel Klein said she had no previous criminal record until the conviction for harbouring Edwin Boyd, "a very dangerous man."

The defence lawyer, Frank Nasso, said that Mitchell's "primary interest" had been Steve Suchan and not Edwin Boyd, even though she had harboured him in her Montreal apartment and at the Sunnyside Motor Hotel, where she had arranged rooms for him. "She should be sentenced apart from all the others," said Nasso. And in sentencing her "no consideration should be given to what the others have done." He said she had quit Suchan's company in February 1952 and had done nothing to help Boyd after that. Nasso asked for a suspended sentence; instead Judge Forsyth sentenced Mitchell to six months indeterminate – the same as Elizabeth Lesso.

Next to be brought into Forsyth's courtroom were Edwin and Norman Boyd, Willie and Joseph Jackson, and Allister Gibson. They were shackled to detectives and to each other, and there was barely room in the prisoner's box for all of them. Boyd managed a wan smile to Dorreen as he was brought into the courtroom.

Each of the five men was dealt with in turn by the court. Gibson had been found guilty of the $24,000 Bank of Montreal robbery at College and Manning on March 4, 1952. He had been paid $1,000 for the job. His lawyer said his client was truly repentant, and except for a conviction for break and entry in 1944, he had never been in trouble until the bank robbery. Forsyth sentenced Gibson to eight years in penitentiary.

Joseph Jackson, convicted in the same robbery, was sentenced to ten years. His lawyer said he was "easily led."

Norman Boyd, found guilty of armed robbery in the Leaside hold-up of November 30, 1951, had no previous record, and the jury had recommended leniency. Lawyer Fred McMahon, who represented both Boyds, said Norman had studied engineering for two years after the war and had a solid employment record. McMahon added that there was "a very strong brothers' affection" between the Boyds, and that it was affection rather than any criminal intent that had led to the harbouring. Also, he said, Dorreen Boyd had asked for his assistance and he had given it; thus Norman had been helping her rather than helping his brother escape police.

Forty-five years later, Norman Boyd is philosophical about the harbouring conviction. "His wife came along and asked me if I could find Ed a place to stay," he says. "When you get a request like that, from someone so close to you, it's pretty hard to say no. You just do whatever you can. In this case, it didn't work out."

Forsyth sentenced Norman to three years for the armed robbery and nine months for harbouring his brother after the first escape from the Don Jail. McMahon launched an immediate appeal of Norman Boyd's armed robbery conviction, and it was overturned by the Court of Appeal four months later. Norman is still bitter at the justice system over that conviction. "The appeal court quashed it entirely," he says. "The jury automatically believed all the stuff in the newspapers. But the appeal court said it was an impossibility – it couldn't have happened. All the witnesses said four people took part in the robbery, and here we've got five people charged."

The appeal court also could not understand how the jury could have convicted Norman Boyd after his boss testified that he was working with him at the time of the robbery. "If your name was Boyd, you were automatically guilty," says Norman. "That's the way juries think."

Then it was William Jackson's turn before Judge Forsyth. His lawyer said his client was "prepared to take his punishment," and emphasized that there had been no shooting in the robberies in which he participated. If Willie Jackson was prepared to take his punishment, Judge Forsyth was ready to dish it out. He sentenced Jackson to twenty years concurrent for each of the two November 1951 armed robberies. The twenty years, however, was in addition to the seven years he was already serving for his previous crimes. Jackson was also sentenced to two years concurrent for each of his escapes from the Don Jail.

Edwin Alonzo Boyd was the last to be sentenced by Judge Forsyth. McMahon made an eloquent appeal for leniency, saying that Boyd had spent more than five years "as a fine, outstanding soldier" in the Second World War, and had fought bravely until his discharge in early 1945. "As far as I have been able to find out, he is an introvert, a deep thinker," said McMahon. "He takes things to heart. When he was a teenager, his mother died and this sorrow crowded all else out of his mind. Later his father remarried and this weighed heavily on him." He said that Boyd's police record from his days riding the rails had been held against him when he sought work after the war.

"He became frustrated, and the record shows what happened," said McMahon. "He has been made out to be a super colossus of crime, but the record doesn't show that."

In the prisoners' dock, shackled to the others, Boyd nervously ran his tongue over his lips and leaned over to whisper something to his brother. "I beg that he be left a ray of hope," said McMahon. "He has a deep affection for his wife, the twins, and his oldest boy. As he is a deep thinker, I submit that the loss of these loved ones will torture him more than the actual sentence of confinement. There is nothing so desolate as a human being without hope."

Judge Forsyth turned to Boyd, whose jaw tightened as the sentence was solemnly pronounced: eight life terms, one for each of the banks he was convicted of robbing; ten years for the bungled robbery attempt in which he fired in the direction of the bank manager; four years for each of two auto thefts; two years for each of the escapes from the Don Jail; and five years for each of two counts of jail breaking. In all, he received eight life terms, plus thirty-two years. The sentences were concurrent, however, and the speculation in the press was that he would serve twenty years, perhaps less depending on his conduct in Kingston.

Dorreen Boyd was sitting in the front row of the courtroom about fifteen feet from her husband. Beside her was her friend Florence Lamb. Dorreen, hatless and wearing a scarlet coat, had been tense as she waited for the verdict. Sometimes her eyes were closed, and she continually clasped and unclasped her hands.

When the life sentences were passed on her husband, Dorreen gasped and rose to her feet. Her friend fainted, and Dorreen went to her aid. "Are you all right, Flo? Are you all right?" The woman came around. Tears streamed down Dorreen's face as Boyd and the other prisoners were taken from the dock. She moved to the railing, put her arms around her husband, and kissed his cheek. Inspector John Nimmo rushed across the courtroom and pulled Dorreen away from her husband.

Dorreen rejoined Florence Lamb, and they sat in stunned silence for a moment. Several well-wishers approached and said they thought Boyd's sentence was too harsh. One man, who said he knew Ed's father, asked if Glover Boyd had been in the courtroom. "I have not heard from the family at all," said Dorreen, "and at no time have any members of his family been in court as spectators." (Glover Boyd did appear as a character witness for Norman Boyd.)

Dorreen left City Hall through the side door. "When they sentenced Ed, they sentenced me to life too," she told *Telegram* reporter Dorothy Howarth.

Boyd and the other prisoners were taken through the gauntlet of armed officers, down the elevators past the basement holding cells, and out to the courtyard to face the throng of reporters and photographers. The page 1 newspaper photos that night and the next morning belied the fact that Boyd and Willie Jackson had just been given such heavy sentences. Boyd's Hollywood grin was in place, and Jackson, his fedora at a rakish tilt, was positively effusive as he puffed on a large cigar clenched between his teeth. The cigar was courtesy of Inspector John Nimmo, who had promised it to Willie when the trial ended. Both Willie's hands were in cuffs, and he used his tongue to roll the cigar around his mouth, much to the amusement of the media. Willie and his cigar of course made the front pages. Willie had told Dolph Payne that whatever sentence he received, he would serve it standing on his head. "You're going to have an awful flat head," said Payne.

Dorreen Boyd arrived home at her basement apartment at the Lambs' at 1:30 p.m. She immediately telephoned the prison and set up an appointment to visit her husband late in the afternoon. "I told him I would bring up the children to the best of my ability," she told a reporter after the visit. "I'm not going to bring up my children to hate their father. When they're older I'll tell them of the wrong and how he paid for it."

Dorreen said her husband was in a cheerful mood and didn't talk about the stiff sentence. "He told me he is going to study hard while he is in Kingston and further his education."

At 6 a.m. the next morning, one year and one day after he was first arrested by Toronto police, Boyd was spirited out of the Don Jail in a blue patrol wagon with a motorcycle escort. With him were Willie and Joseph Jackson. As the van's rear door closed Boyd shouted, "Give us a blanket. It's cold in here."

The night before, Boyd had signed a waiver stating that he did not plan to appeal his life term. He also signed statements providing the details of his two escapes. But he did not disclose the source of the hacksaw blades, or of the file and piece of steel he used to make the key for the cells in the second escape. The information about the escapes would be passed on to the Royal Commission studying the jail breaks.

The security surrounding Boyd's removal from the Don Jail was unprecedented, but Col. Hedley Basher was nervous whenever Boyd was around and didn't want another embarrassment. The usual practice was to transfer prisoners to Kingston by train, but Boyd rated special attention. Two officers from the morality squad, William Harris and Harry Long, sat in the rear of the van with the prisoners, and in front with the driver were two sub-machine-guns. Inspector Nimmo, who co-ordinated the operation with Sheriff J.D. Conover, kept the transfer secret until the convoy was well on its way. Meanwhile, Kingston police set up barriers on roads leading to the penitentiary, and all traffic was diverted.

While the gates of Kingston Penitentiary were closing behind Edwin Alonzo Boyd and William R. Jackson, Leonard Jackson and Steve Suchan were awaiting their fate in the cells of No. 9 Hospital – sometimes called the Death Cells.

Dead Men Walking

A young boy, a wanderer from home for seven months, sits between two tramps in a railway yard and drinks in with blue-eyed astonishment the story of how easy is the life of the pilferer and housebreaker, and how ample the rewards. The boy snaps at the shining lure they cast before him, and the robber's trade and evil become the good of fifteen-year-old Frank McCullough.

———

Three men struggle at desperate grips in a livery stable. Nearby stands a buggy with a few paltry yards of stolen cloth. Suddenly from among the writhing figures two shots flash out in the semi-darkness and Frank Williams, aged 24, guardian of the lives and property of his fellow-citizens, falls, and the blood froth on his lips tells that he has sealed his pledged service with his life.

———

Throwing away a smoking revolver, a tall figure runs through the open door to the street, and the mark of Cain is on Frank McCullough.

———

"Our father which art in heaven …" The words of the greatest prayer human lips have ever repeated, are now used as the stopwatch of the hangman. The prayer is broken by a jarring clash, and the falling figure at the rope's end is Frank McCullough.

That melodramatic language, typical for newspapers of the period, was the lead in a *Toronto Telegram* story describing the hanging death of Frank McCullough, twenty-seven, at 8:15 a.m. on Friday, June 13, 1919.

Seven months earlier, McCullough had shot and killed Detective Frank Williams of the Toronto Police Department. Williams had approached McCullough to arrest him for selling stolen fur-lined coats. McCullough was convicted of capital murder and sentenced to hang. But he sawed his way out of his Don Jail death cell and enjoyed three weeks of freedom before he was recaptured and hanged.

There are several uncanny parallels and coincidences in the Frank McCullough and Boyd Gang cases:

- Both Sergeant of Detectives Edmund Tong and Detective Frank Williams were shot in daylight in the city's downtown.
- McCullough, in 1919, sawed his way out of the same window that the Boyd Gang would escape through in 1952.
- Col. G. Hedley Basher was called in to take over the Don after McCullough's escape, and was called in to take over *again* after the Boyd Gang's first escape.
- After McCullough was recaptured he befriended Detective Bart Cronin, just as Leonard Jackson befriended Jack Gillespie. "Who squealed on me?" McCullough asked Cronin several times. "A little bird told me," replied Cronin. More than three decades later, Lennie Jackson asked a similar question of Gillespie. Gillespie's reply: "A little bird told me."
- A prominent lawyer, Thomas C. Robinette, tried to save Frank McCullough from the gallows. Thirty-three years later, Robinette's son, J.J. Robinette, tried to save Steve Suchan from the same fate.

John Josiah Robinette, "perhaps the greatest lawyer this country will ever see,"[30] had quietly earned a reputation among litigation lawyers for his thorough and articulate arguments before the Ontario Court of Appeal. But his reputation was publicly and firmly established in 1947 when he won a new trial for twenty-five-year-old Evelyn Dick, who had been convicted of murdering her husband and sentenced to hang. The public and media interest in the case was as intense as it would be with the Boyd Gang, and when Robinette convinced a jury to acquit Evelyn Dick at her second trial, the lawyer's reputation was further enhanced.

Robinette later described the aftermath in Jack Batten's 1982 book, *In Court:* "When the trial ended, the front page of the *Star* carried a double red banner, 'EVELYN ACQUITTED.' Nobody needed to be told what that meant. I've never seen a case for such sensation, and overnight, I went from being an academic lawyer to being a criminal lawyer."[31]

Seven weeks after her acquittal, Dick was charged with manslaughter when the body of her seven-month-old son was discovered encased in concrete. Even Robinette couldn't save her this time. She was sentenced to life, but was released after eleven years.

Five years after the Dick case, Robinette was working late in his office one night when a cleaning lady told him her son was in trouble and needed help. The woman was Elizabeth Lesso, and her son was Steve Suchan. Robinette thought Lesso to be hard-working and decent. He later told Jack Batten, "She was such a nice woman that I couldn't say anything except that I'd help her."

The day after their capture in the North York barn, Steve Suchan and Leonard Jackson were taken directly from the North York jail to the holding cells beneath Toronto City Hall. At 2:15 p.m. on September 17 they were brought before Chief Justice James McRuer of the Ontario Supreme Court and arraigned on capital murder charges in the death of Edmund Tong. The trial was set to open a week later, but Robinette asked for more time to prepare his defence. Besides, the court was told, Leonard Jackson didn't even have a lawyer. But Justice McRuer had already solved that problem: he had cornered up-and-coming lawyer Arthur C. Maloney and asked if he would mind taking the case. Maloney already had a reputation as a brilliant defence lawyer but wasn't sure about handling a major murder trial. He decided it would be unwise to turn down the Chief Justice, and besides, by accepting the assignment he would get to work with the distinguished Robinette. Leonard Jackson agreed to McRuer's choice of counsel.

The *Telegram* described the upcoming court case as "one of the biggest legal battles of the century" and described Robinette, forty-five, and Maloney, thirty-two, as "two of Ontario's best-known legal brains." Robinette, said the article, was regarded by his peers "as one of the top lawyers – criminal or civil – in Canada." And Maloney's views on abolishing capital punishment were internationally respected. "Capital punishment is brutal and outmoded," he had often stated. "It is not morally justified and not necessary."

Robinette and Maloney suffered their first setback in the case when McRuer refused to delay the trial. It would go ahead on schedule September 22, leaving them just a week to prepare.

For Robinette and Maloney the strategy was clear. There was no dispute that Suchan and Jackson were in Anna Camero's Monarch when Suchan's bullets hit Eddie Tong and Roy Perry. To save their clients from the gallows, they would have to convince the jury that there was no conspiracy between Suchan and Jackson to resist arrest by potentially lethal means, and that when Suchan fired, he didn't see Tong and didn't know it was a police car. The lawyers knew their clients had no chance of walking free; they were after a verdict of manslaughter.

Their opponent was a tough veteran Crown attorney, William O. Gibson, considered one of the best in Ontario. He methodically laid out the Crown's case, presenting expert medical and forensic evidence that connected Suchan and Jackson to the shooting and describing the wounds to Tong and Perry. One of the worst moments for the defence was Justice McRuer's decision to allow in as Crown evidence the mannequins from Anna Camero's basement, which Suchan and Jackson had used for target practice. Robinette and Maloney had argued that the mannequins were irrelevant and that introducing them would be prejudicial to their clients. Some of the jurors gasped when they saw the plaster head, and the chest portion of the papier mâché torso, riddled with holes from the air pistol pellets. It wasn't difficult for the jurors to conclude that those shooting at the targets were decent marksmen. If Suchan was a decent marksman, how could some of his shots have hit the cruiser's windshield in the area of Roy Perry's head when he was supposedly aiming at the car's engine a few feet away?

It took one week and forty-three witnesses for Gibson to lay out the Crown's case. On Monday, September 29, the defence began its case, with Robinette and Maloney calling just one witness each – Suchan and Jackson. Suchan was first, and after a brief outline of his background, Robinette quickly led him to the crucial part of his testimony – the shooting of Edmund Tong. As Suchan told his story, Justice McRuer sometimes interjected with his own "clarifying" questions.

Suchan claimed in court that he thought the man yelling at him to pull over was the angry driver or passenger of a car he had cut off in traffic a few minutes earlier.

SUCHAN:	I assumed this was the car that was trying to crowd me over and, well, I had Len in the car. I got panicky I guess.
McRUER:	You mean Leonard Jackson?
SUCHAN:	Yes.
ROBINETTE:	Would you explain that, or what you mean by that?
SUCHAN:	At the time Len was hotter than a firecracker.
McRUER:	What do you mean by that?
SUCHAN:	He was wanted. He escaped jail.... I didn't want to be discovered with him. I couldn't risk any investigation, because my connection with Boyd would be found out.... It would have been discovered that I harboured Boyd.
ROBINETTE:	Were you thinking of Jackson's position at all?
SUCHAN:	No, I was not.
ROBINETTE:	Whose position were you thinking of?
SUCHAN:	I was thinking of myself.

ROBINETTE:	Now, what did you do?
SUCHAN:	I thought this car was trying to crowd me over on the sidewalk. I reached for my gun and I threw a shot back in the direction of the hood.
ROBINETTE:	What was your purpose?
SUCHAN:	The purpose was strictly to damage the engine of the car and get away from there.

During Gibson's cross-examination of Suchan, Justice McRuer again interjected, asking why Suchan did not call the police since Jackson was a wanted man. "I've never been a stool pigeon in my life," said Suchan.

"You consider that would be a stool pigeon, if one knows a man has escaped from custody and a good citizen sees him and tells the police where to go to get him?" asked McRuer.

"I think they have various other lines to find where a man is. I have never been an informer and I did not intend to start being one."

Both Robinette and Maloney felt that Suchan was a credible witness and had survived, relatively unscathed, the questioning from both Gibson and Justice McRuer. The questions had been tough, but Suchan had not given the Crown the answers he wanted. Suchan said he was looking out for himself and did not have a compact or understanding with Jackson that they would protect each other – with violence if necessary. And Suchan had stuck to his story – he had fired to cripple the car, and had not seen Tong approaching when he fired the shot that caused Tong's death.

But Lennie Jackson read it differently. He thought that to cover for him, Suchan had taken a lot of heat. And Jackson wasn't a man who would tolerate others taking heat for him. He didn't seem to fully grasp the tightrope that he and Suchan had to walk to raise enough doubts in the minds of the jurors about the Crown's conspiracy theory.

Maloney wasn't sure if his client should testify, but Jackson insisted. He was called to the stand at 11:40 a.m. In his testimony in chief, Jackson said that as the Monarch pulled over he saw a figure approaching "through the corner of my left eye." Because he was wanted, he opened the door to run away.

MALONEY:	You got out of the car, and what did you say was your plan?
JACKSON:	To flee.... As I got out of the car, I started towards the back and I heard a volley of shots.
MALONEY:	After hearing the volley of shots, what if anything did you do?
JACKSON:	I had a gun and I pulled it out to protect myself.
MALONEY:	Did you at any time that day fire that gun?
JACKSON:	No sir.
MALONEY:	When you were at the back of the car and had your gun out, what, if anything, did you see?
JACKSON:	I seen a man lying face down.

Jackson said he knew Tong, but didn't know it was him lying on the street that day because he couldn't see his face. And he didn't realize the car was a police cruiser until he looked up and saw the radio aerial. Jackson's defence was that he didn't fire his revolver, wasn't aware Suchan was carrying a gun, and had not entered a pact with Suchan to resist arrest. He did admit that he was prepared to take violent action to avoid capture, and would have shot at the police – though not to kill. He said he wasn't expecting Suchan to help him avoid capture, and therefore there was no conspiracy, and Tong's death was not a joint act by him and Suchan.

Jackson's testimony in chief went relatively well, but under intensive cross-examination by Gibson, with "clarifying" questions thrown in by Justice McRuer, Jackson became visibly agitated.

JACKSON: Sir, the reason I carried the gun was to not be
                apprehended, to assist me in escaping appre-
                hension, not to use the gun but to help....

MCRUER: ... Just a moment. Did you have it loaded?

JACKSON: Yes, sir, I did.

MCRUER: Did you need to have it loaded just to assist
                you in escaping without using it?

JACKSON: Yes sir.

MCRUER: You thought you should have it loaded to
                assist you in escaping?

JACKSON: Yes, sir.

MCRUER: Without using it. Is that your answer?

JACKSON: Yes sir.

Jackson told Gibson that in Montreal he had been prepared to fire
his automatic pistol "to assist me to escape if possible." He said he did-
n't recognize Jack Gillespie when the door to the apartment was
opened.

"But when the door was opened, there is the man – you fired?"
asked Gibson.

"The firing was approximately simultaneous," said Jackson, who
also testified he would not have given up in the Montreal shoot-out
if it had not been for his wife. Jackson also told Gibson that Suchan
had no choice but to help him.

"In the rules of your society, he could not refuse to, could he?"
asked Gibson.

"Not after once, sir," said Jackson.

After Gibson's cross-examination, Justice McRuer had more questions.

MCRUER: I want to understand a little more of what

you mean with reference to the purpose
that you had in mind when you armed
yourself with a loaded revolver. Was it a
revolver or a pistol?

JACKSON: A revolver, sir ... 32-20.

McRUER: That is a revolver that will cause death?

JACKSON: Yes, sir.

McRUER: No doubt about that?

JACKSON: That is right, sir.

McRUER: What was your purpose in arming yourself
with a loaded revolver?

JACKSON: To aid me in attempting to flee if I was
apprehended.

McRUER: ... You would fire it to assist you in
attempting to flee if you were apprehended
– was that the purpose?

JACKSON: Not to kill, sir.

McRUER: I am saying to fire it?

JACKSON: Yes, sir.

McRUER: So it is perfectly fair and perfectly clear, is
it, that as you went out and got into that car
and drove to the corner of Lansdowne and
College, you were armed with a loaded
revolver, having in your mind that you
would fire it if necessary in an effort to
assist you in escaping lawful apprehension.

JACKSON: Yes, sir.

Jackson's testimony under cross-examination had given Gibson all he needed to prove his conspiracy theory.

"I was shattered," Maloney later told Jack Batten. "I listened to Jackson and I knew he had thrown in the sponge. He virtually admitted that he knew Suchan was carrying a gun, that it was loaded, and that he knew Suchan would use it to shoot anybody who tried to stop the pair of them." Maloney later asked Jackson why he had given such self-incriminating evidence.

"If those bastards, that judge and that prosecutor, want me this bad, hell, I'm gonna give myself to them," said Jackson. He could see Maloney was upset. "I let you down, didn't I?"

"You didn't let me down," Maloney told him. "You let yourself down."[32]

After the lunch break, Robinette and Maloney gave their summations to the jury, hoping to salvage what had been lost through Lennie Jackson's damning testimony. Robinette in his thirty-five-minute address reiterated the theme he had established with Suchan on the stand – there was no common intent to kill Tong, he didn't see Tong when he fired, and he fired to disable the car and not to hurt anyone. "If after all the evidence, you are not certain, you must find him guilty of the lesser charge [manslaughter]."

In an unusual move, probably in desperation, Robinette became somewhat melodramatic when he suggested that a higher force had intervened to save Suchan's life in the Montreal shoot-out.

Maloney followed with a forty-minute address, telling the jury that Jackson did not fire his revolver and had nothing to do with Suchan's actions that led to Tong's death. The lawyer said Jackson "will not walk from this courtroom a free man, but he does deserve to live."

In an effective opening, Crown attorney Gibson scorned Robinette's contention of a higher power intervening to save Suchan. He said he had been working on the Tong case for months and months and "today is the first time I've heard it said that the case involved divine intervention."

In the crisp, thirty-minute address that followed, he reviewed the facts of the case and said that both Suchan and Jackson had practised their shooting skills with air pistols in Anna Camero's basement. He said that Roy Perry probably saved his own life when his raised arm took a bullet. "Otherwise he would have received a bullet in the same place as the marks on the dressmaker's dummy – in the head."

In his charge to the jury, Justice McRuer said, "If you feel these two men had formed a common intention to resist lawful apprehension by use of firearms, and one of the two fired a fatal shot, it does not matter which one fired the shot – both are guilty of murder or manslaughter."

The jury retired at 5:55 p.m. and returned with a verdict less than two hours later. Both were found guilty of murder. Jackson and Suchan stood impassive as the verdict was read.

Addressing the jurors, McRuer said, "I cannot see how you could have arrived at any other verdict upon the evidence, but I know it is always difficult for jurymen who sit in judgement on their fellow men to arrive at this solemn verdict."

McRuer displayed rare emotion as he sentenced Suchan and Jackson, in turn, immediately following the verdict. In a quavering voice he said, "You shall be taken to the place from where you came and there kept in close detention until the 16th of December, 1952, and thence you shall be taken to the place of execution, and there be hanged by the neck until you are dead. May God have mercy on your soul."

Robinette turned to Maloney as they sat side by side at the defence table. "My God, I've never heard those words before," he said.

After Suchan and Jackson were removed to the Don Jail, Boyd and Willie Jackson, whose trials were ongoing, were taken to different cells. No. 9 Hospital was now truly the Death Cell. Willie Jackson and Boyd would never see Lennie Jackson or Suchan again.

Ann Jackson heard the verdict over the radio and collapsed in shock. "It's a life for a life, I understand that," she said in an interview a few weeks later. "But two lives for one seems too many to take. I don't see that he should hang for something he didn't do. Lennie isn't guilty."

Ann also attacked the newspapers for repeating the lie that Lennie had used her as a shield in the Montreal shoot-out. "I came out of the apartment away ahead of my husband," she said. "Lennie was well behind me. All my friends were upset by those stories. Lennie isn't a coward."

Robinette and Maloney immediately filed appeals of the death sentence, but their last hopes for clemency died on Friday, December 12, when Mr. Justice J.W. Estey of the Supreme Court of Canada decided there were no legal questions of sufficient importance to justify a full hearing before the Supreme Court.

In the two and a half months until their executions, Steve Suchan and Leonard Jackson gradually turned to religion for solace. Elizabeth Lesso had asked Robinette if her son could see a Roman Catholic priest. Robinette, who was not Catholic, asked Maloney to help. Maloney recommended the Reverend John Kelly[33] from St. Michael's College in Toronto. Father Kelly became a daily visitor to the Don Jail to see the condemned men. Suchan renewed his lost faith, and Jackson, half-Jewish and raised an Anglican, became a convert to Catholicism – with his mother's permission.

There were other visitors besides Father Kelly. Suchan's mother had been released from jail and came to visit her son, as did Anna Camero, who talked about their child, now eleven months old. Ann Jackson visited Lennie as often as she was allowed.

Although Ann had given up hope of a reprieve for her husband, she continued to speak out publicly on his behalf. "They're not hanging him – they're murdering him," she told the *Telegram* two days before the execution. "No lawyer could have saved him. No one on earth could have saved him. As soon as the police caught him, they decided he was guilty – long before the trial."

She predicted that her husband would go bravely to his death. "These stories about a man at the end always being scared and hollering and being dragged to the gallows – I've been expecting them. But Leonard isn't that sort of man. He's brave. He always has been and he always will be. He'll go like a man."

Leonard and Ann had agreed to name their son Michael. "Leonard said the boy would have two strikes against him if I named our son after him," she said. "He does look like Leonard. His eyes are blue now, but I hope they change so they're dark like Leonard's."

Robinette visited Suchan for the last time on the afternoon of December 15. Suchan had written a final letter in Slovak to his mother, and he translated it for Robinette. In it he urged her to be strong for his four-year-old brother. "Keep your head up, and look people straight in the face, because they are no better than you are. Straight from my heart, I love you Momma. And my small brother a million times. Please forgive me, Momma, for bringing you so much sorrow. Bye, bye, Mother dear." Robinette was in tears when he left the cell. Suchan had come to believe that he had been spared in Montreal to allow him time to prepare his soul for death.

Robinette would, like Maloney, become a crusader against the death penalty. Ten years later, two others would be hanged back-to-back in the Don Jail. No one has been executed in Canada since then.

The temperature hovered just above freezing as three or four hundred protesters gathered outside the Don Jail at midnight. Swirling winds and light snow made it seem colder. Cars crawled past the jail, bumper to bumper. Inside, Suchan and Jackson appeared calm after spending three hours in prayer and meditation with Father Kelly. Jackson's request to wear his prosthesis was turned down, and he was forced to walk to the gallows on his stump.

Father Kelly administered the last rites to the men, and each shook his hand before the hangman placed black hoods over their heads. The priest prayed as Suchan and Jackson stood back to back on the trapdoors. The hangman pulled the lever at 12:14 a.m., and they dropped through the trapdoors. They were pronounced dead at 1 a.m. on December 16.

Ann Jackson and Elizabeth Lesso had arranged for the bodies to be removed to cemeteries outside the prison for burial. They did not want their loved ones to be buried in the jail cemetery.

Edwin Alonzo Boyd had been in Kingston Penitentiary for two months when Lennie Jackson and Steve Suchan were hanged in the

Don Jail. It seemed to him unfair that Lennie should hang for Suchan's rash act, but he also thought Lennie should have known enough to stay away from Suchan.

The back-to-back hangings added to the myth and lore of the Boyd Gang, which thanks to the media had surpassed all others for notoriety in the annals of Canadian crime. But had it really been much of a gang at all? When Boyd thought about it, he had only robbed two banks with Lennie Jackson, and three with Suchan. He had escaped from the Don Jail twice with Lennie and once with Suchan. But other than the eight days they had spent together as fugitives after the second escape, the gang hadn't spent much time together at all. It certainly wasn't like the gangs he had seen in the movies.

As Boyd pondered the years of incarceration facing him in Kingston, he could not know that the myth of the Boyd Gang would survive Leonard Jackson and Steve Suchan.

34
Kingston

Edwin Alonzo Boyd entered Kingston Penitentiary with clear resolve – to improve his education, study religion, and be left alone to serve his time. Being left alone would not be as easy as it seemed; he soon realized that his notoriety had made him a hero to much of the inmate population. He would have to work at being a loner.

Boyd was prisoner No. 1760, and home was a small cell with a fold-down metal bed, a fold-down table, a shelf, a sink, and a toilet. He didn't know how many years he would be behind bars, and on his mind was the wife and three children he had left behind in Toronto. The twins were nine years old and Anthony twelve when Boyd went into Kingston. He wondered how old they would be when he got out.

The cell blocks in the 117-year-old penitentiary were like spokes in a great wheel, fanning out from the hub of the main dome. At the dome's centre, on a platform of polished wood, was the bell that would dictate Boyd's daily life for as long as he was in Kingston. "Everything had to be done by the bell," he recalls. "You woke up by the bell, you went to work by the bell, you went to your meals by the bell … I think it was used deliberately to get the guys all riled up." At 6:45 a.m. the bell would ring three times, the sound penetrating every block, range, and cell, and another day would begin.

In his best-selling book *Go Boy*, long-time Kingston inmate Roger Caron describes the bell as a symbol of oppression and regimentation to the inmates: "The bell was actually the golden cow for the prison staff. They all gathered around it.… You lived and breathed by the bell. It drove people literally crazy. In June 1959, the bell rang in the dome. This guy came charging completely across from 'A' Block like a mad enraged bull and butted the bell with his head. I don't know what happened to him, but they took him away on a stretcher."

Boyd says mental breakdowns were not uncommon. "Every once in a while there are guys going off the beam around you – smashing up their cells, breaking their toilets, and knocking the sinks off the wall. You hear it. You see the water coming down – sometimes into your cell. These things are just part of living in a cloistered atmosphere where you don't really want to be. You've got to keep your own counsel and keep your mind occupied so you don't go over the edge and turn into a moron. So I constantly read books."

Boyd's arrival at Kingston Penitentiary could have been like old-home week if he hadn't been so intent on keeping to himself. His old partner, Howard Gault, was there serving time for the robberies he had committed with Boyd. But Gault and Boyd didn't care if they ever saw each other again. Fellow gang members Willie and Joe Jackson were also there, along with their brother-in-law Allister Gibson. Boyd says Gibson didn't belong in Kingston, and the administration apparently agreed, because Gibson was soon transferred to Joyceville, a prison for less-hardened inmates about twelve miles away.

Among the others that Boyd knew in Kingston were Lennie Jackson's mentor Frank Watson and Lennie's half-brother Sammy Stone, who had arrived back in the prison about the same time as Boyd went in. This time Stone had been convicted of possession of more than one hundred heroin capsules. Watson was in for twelve years for trying to bribe prison guard James Morrison and for possession of counterfeit money.

When Stone put the word out that Willie Jackson and Boyd were somehow responsible for the deaths of Lennie Jackson and Suchan, Boyd thought he had to put Sammy straight.

"Look, you're climbing up the wrong tree," said Boyd when the two met in the yard.

"Well how come you and Willie are in here, and they were hanged?" asked Stone.

"Because they messed up," said Boyd. "They killed a policeman.

We had nothing to do with it. So Willie and I are in here serving time, and they're dead."

Sammy was thoughtful for a moment. "Yeah, I guess you're right," he said. "I flew off the handle there."

"We're just in here trying to do our time, same as you are." said Boyd.

In his first interview with a penitentiary counsellor, Boyd said that although he was a good athlete, he had no interest in the sports programs for inmates. He wanted to concentrate on reading and studying. He did not brag about his past criminal activities, and said that the first half of his life had been a miserable failure. When he talked about studying religion, the counsellor warned Boyd that he might be greatly scorned and misunderstood by other inmates. Boyd said he was aware of that, but "if a man has a purpose, there is nothing that will shake him from it."

Boyd was assigned to work in the canvas shop making straight-jackets and mailbags. His instructor reported that "he is not mixing with other inmates, but he's doing the work of two ordinary men."

Ten months later, Boyd was still at work in the canvas shop. By then, prison staff believed his interest in religion was sincere, noting that he was maintaining his self-imposed isolation. "He seldom bothers with other prisoners, but will give his opinion if asked," said one report.

Boyd says his first three years were the most difficult because he was looked up to as a "big shot" after all the media attention over his criminal exploits, and when he rejected those inmates who curried his favour, there was some resentment against him. Boyd kept himself in peak physical condition with a rigorous exercise and weight-lifting program. He had been in Kingston just over a year when two inmates came at him from opposite directions in the exercise yard. Boyd was always watchful and had been wondering when someone would "test" him. One of the inmates was of medium build, and the other was stocky and much taller than Boyd. When they lunged at him, he kicked the heavier inmate in the testicles while simultaneously grabbing the other by the wrist, flipping him and sending him sprawling in the dirt. The smaller of the two brushed himself off but kept his distance. The other, quite pale, was on his knees holding his crotch. Boyd stepped back, eyeing the two men. "You guys know my reputation," he said, his voice calm and measured. "You know the training I've had in the army. You know I've taught karate and judo. So you just think about what's going to happen if you try to push me around again. I don't bother anyone, and I want to be left alone. You had better understand that."

The men didn't say a word as Boyd turned and walked away. A guard had witnessed the incident, but decided not to intervene. "In no time, everybody in the joint heard about what had happened," says Boyd. "From then on, nobody ever bothered me again."

In 1955 he announced that his official religion was no longer Church of England. He now considered himself a Seventh-day Adventist. Despite his apparently sincere interest in religion, Boyd was kept under close scrutiny because of his notoriety and his reputation as an escape artist. "For the first three or four years in Kingston I was never anywhere where there wasn't a guard," he says. "At night a guard was even posted outside my cell. I guess because of the breakouts at the Don Jail they figured they had to keep an eye on me."

The media had often compared Boyd to Red Ryan and Mickey MacDonald, both of whom had escaped from Kingston. Ryan went over the wall on September 10, 1923. He was serving twenty-five years for armed robbery when he escaped with four others after setting fire to the stable adjacent to the east wall. Ryan, who was wounded, was captured in a blazing gun battle with police in Minneapolis three months later. He was suspected in a series of bank robberies. Ryan received thirty lashes and a life sentence when he returned to Canada. He was a manipulator, and convinced many clergy, politicians, and some reporters that he had reformed. He even had a visit in prison from Prime Minister R.B. Bennett, who declared that the convict was reformed. Ryan was released on parole in July 1935. Ten months later he was shot dead while attempting to rob a bank in Sarnia. He killed a policeman in the shoot-out.

On August 17, 1947, Nicholas Minnelli, Ulysses Lauzon, and Mickey MacDonald sawed their way out of their cells, climbed up to the attic, and escaped over the wall. Minnelli was recaptured a year later after being stopped for drunk driving in San Francisco. Lauzon was found murdered in the United States, and MacDonald was never heard from again. MacDonald and Boyd had ping-ponged as the No. 1 most wanted criminal in Canada: when Boyd was out of jail, he was No. 1, when he was in jail, MacDonald was back on top.

In 1954, two pieces of hacksaw blade, obtained from one of the workshops, were found in a search of Boyd's cell and he was sent to solitary confinement for ten days. His religious zeal apparently wasn't sufficient to quell the desire to escape.

And he made a second attempt after he was turned down for parole in the late 1950s. "I just got fed up waiting for them to do something about me, so I started sawing the bars," he says. The bars were in an office used to interview and counsel prisoners. The office was one of three in a row near a dormitory Boyd had been assigned to. Through an inmate he trusted, he was able to get several short pieces of hacksaw blade. Using a flat piece of steel as a screwdriver, he unscrewed the plate over the lock on the office door. It was an ordinary lock with three or four tumblers that moved up and down when a key was inserted. "I left the front tumbler and threw away the others," says Boyd. He could then quickly pick the lock with a nail or a needle and enter the office. The single tumbler would fall into place and the door would lock behind him. For a month he worked on the bars of the office window.

"I would do that in the evening in the winter time," says Boyd. "It got dark early. The guys were watching TV, and the guards weren't really watching the guys. I'd slip away and lock myself in the office and saw the bars. I had to work from the lights on the wall outside which was only about fifteen feet away."

As he had done in the Don Jail, Boyd used soap mixed with dirt to hide the cuts in the bars. "You had to rub the dirty soap on all the bars to make sure they all looked alike," he says. "Several times when I was inside sawing, a guard would try the door. If they had come with a key, I would have been sunk. They couldn't see into the office because the glass in the door was frosted for privacy when the inmates were being interviewed."

Boyd says that not all of the guard towers were manned at Kingston. His plan was to drop to the prison yard once the bars were cut and make his way to the base of one of the unmanned towers under cover of darkness. "You could attach a rock to a rope and catch it on the guard tower railing, or you could ease your way up the wall at the corner and go over the top," he says. "I was in good enough shape to do that."

But his plan was foiled when one of the guards decided to check the bars of the office window. "They didn't bother for months, and then all of a sudden one of them decided to tap the bars with a hammer and he found the saw cuts."

Those two incidents would be the only blemishes on Boyd's otherwise perfect record in prison. By January 1960, his good behaviour had earned him 814 days of remission from his sentence. After five years in the canvas shop, he had moved on to the machine shop, where he became a welder. "Boyd has conducted himself surprisingly well," said one report. "He was well thought of by the officers in the canvas department, and the officers in the welding shop where he now works, report that he is doing exceptionally well there."

During this time Dorreen Boyd's visits to the prison dropped from once every two months to once or twice a year. She had been moving from apartment to apartment and job to job as she tried to raise the children on her own. It became easier as they grew older and found employment.

By 1960 Boyd was in group therapy. His therapist felt that Boyd had not achieved much insight into the reasons for his behaviour and had made up his own mind about what was wrong with him. Boyd told them his "confused thinking" always seemed to place him in the position where he had to be the leader "directing and bossing others." He saw this as a form of compensation for his lack of education or trade.

"He is not afraid of returning to Toronto because he feels the police there are not hostile to him and that he has many friends on the police force," reported the counsellor. "He is relying too strongly on assistance from outside rather than making the necessary efforts himself."

Therapy disclosed that Boyd wanted to prove to himself that he was stronger than the police (who subconsciously represented his father). He wanted to outsmart the police, but was not interested in harming anyone.

Boyd's second application for parole was denied on July 15, 1960. Soon after, Dorreen wrote to Pierre Berton, then a columnist and associate editor of the *Toronto Star,* saying that her husband had reformed and that there was no need to keep him in prison. His family had suffered, and they needed him. She added that his parole had been rejected only because of public opinion, and she was asking Berton to write something in his column to help the situation. She also said that Boyd's relatives "through all the long years have not so much as phoned me to ask me how we are and if we are with or without bread."

Berton contacted the parole board and asked about the status of Boyd's case. He was told that the case was under review and would come up again automatically in two years. Boyd had made a lot of progress, and there was a good chance he would be paroled in 1962, although this sentiment was not conveyed to him.

A parole analyst said in his report to the parole board: "This is the most notorious inmate in Kingston Penitentiary and possibly in any prison across the country.... During his incarceration, Boyd has given no cause for criticism. He has continuously rejected the adulation and preferred treatment from the inmate population which could easily have been his and indeed which was offered to him by reason of his notoriety."

Prison psychiatrist George D. Scott said of Boyd: "This man's future does not seem to be unusually concerning. He is an intelligent man who understands clearly his role in society when he returns, and with his insight and relatively long sentence, he is not likely to offend. It would be my opinion that there is no psychiatric problem within this man which would interfere with his rehabilitation to society."

But Boyd's imminent parole was placed suddenly in jeopardy when at 1:30 a.m. on November 24, 1961, prison guard William Wentworth was stabbed to death in Dormitory C, where Boyd had

been living with forty-one other inmates. The dormitory was supposed to hold soon-to-be-released prisoners as a way of resocializ-
ing them in a group setting. For reasons never made clear, the
prison had also assigned a number of dangerous troublemakers to
that dorm. The prisoners had the run of the place, and it was no
secret that there was extensive use of drugs and homebrew, and that
some of the inmates had home-made weapons.

Wentworth, alone and unarmed, was making the rounds in the
dorm when he was jumped from behind in one of the washrooms
and a knife was driven into the back of his neck. He was stabbed ten
more times as he struggled and screamed for help, before bleeding
to death on the floor. Wentworth left behind a wife, a ten-year-old
son, and a fifteen-year-old daughter. (The son, Michael, killed himself in 1996, saying in a suicide note that he had never recovered
from the pain of his father's death. His sister Daphne has fought for
years to get answers about her father's death.)

Boyd and the other prisoners were awakened by the struggle and
the screams. Most thought it was a fight between two inmates and
stayed out of it. Boyd's bed was near the washroom, and he says he
looked up to see inmate Ralph Cochrane coming out of the washroom, naked and covered with blood. Two or three of Cochrane's
friends helped him to the shower to clean up, while another cleaned
up the washroom. Boyd and the others looked into the washroom
and saw Wentworth on the floor. "There was blood everywhere,"
says Boyd, "but right away there was a guy in there with a mop and
a bucket cleaning it up."

Boyd and two other lifers found themselves in a difficult situation
when the parole board announced that no one in the dorm would be
granted parole until Wentworth's killer was found. And there would
be no parole-for-testimony deals. Boyd and at least two other
inmates told the prison administration privately that Cochrane was
the killer. But they would never testify in court as long as they were
behind bars "because someone might come up and stick a knife in
you from behind."

As it turned out, the Wentworth murder case would not go to
court for more than thirty years. Prison officials and police decided

there wasn't enough evidence for a conviction. At the time of the murder, Ralph Cochrane was thirty-four. He would be almost twice that age, in June 1994, when he appeared in a Kingston courtroom to face a murder charge for Wentworth's killing.

With no resolution of the case in sight, the ban on parole for C-dorm inmates was lifted. Boyd was granted parole on September 24, 1962, and was released on October 1, two days before the announced date, to avoid the intense media pressure that had been building since news of his parole was leaked.

The Parole Board issued a press release stating that the secrecy in Boyd's case was a departure from usual procedure but was necessary because of the unusual circumstances and his high profile. "It is hoped that he will not be hampered in carrying out the terms of his parole by undue publicity."

The media ignored the board's plea. On the night of October 1, Dorreen Boyd called the penitentiary to complain that her house was surrounded by reporters and that it was "floodlighted" as everyone waited for Boyd to show up. Boyd did not show up at Dorreen's, nor did he call. Instead, he took a motel room in Scarborough and waited for the media pressure to subside. But it didn't, and with the approval of his parole officer he called a press conference to get the inevitable over with.

The newspapers and other media gave extensive coverage to Boyd's return to society and continued to badger him after the press conference. Daniel Coughlan, head of Ontario Parole Services, who was in overall charge of Boyd's case, said there shouldn't have been a press conference, even though Boyd's parole supervisor had approved it. Boyd was confused.

Boyd already knew that Dorreen was with another man. He says he attempted to reconcile with Dorreen but failed. He wrote to D.M. McLean, regional director of penitentiaries for Ontario, to thank him for his help, and added: "Also, my good wife packed me in favour of another man, so I'm on my own and can put in full time on homework." Boyd had signed on for an eighteen-month government retraining course at the Adult Retraining Centre on Jones Avenue. He would be paid $6 a day, for a five-day school week.

Boyd rented an apartment and invited the twins to come and live with him. It didn't work out. His son Robin, then nineteen, "was very hostile, and he wouldn't do a damn thing that I asked him to do. They were both kind of standoffish. They didn't really know me, you see. So I decided to move out, and when I did, Dorreen moved in, and I didn't have much to do with them after that."

Boyd was living at a house on Page Street on December 13, 1962, when Dorreen and a male friend, Kenneth Caustan, arrived and smashed the front door. Boyd called the police. Dorreen said she was trying to retrieve some clothes. Police arrested her and her friend for being drunk. They were held in jail overnight and pleaded guilty in court the next day. Dorreen was fined $10, and Caustan $25.

Boyd moved to an apartment nearby on Clinton Street. At school he had met sixteen-year-old Adele K., who came from an abusive background that Boyd says he related to because of his own upbringing. He found Adele easy to talk to and wanted to help her. In spite of the innuendo that followed, he insists that his relationship with the girl was never more than platonic.

By now Boyd knew he was being followed almost constantly, and thought the authorities might be planning to pick him up. Boyd says Coughlan didn't try to help him: "All he did was tell me I was going back in again if I didn't toe the line." Boyd believes the Ontario Probation Service wasn't qualified to handle a parole lifer like him, because they usually supervised only those serving sentences of two years less a day in provincial jails. He says Coughlan tried to browbeat him from the first moment they met.

"He had been an Anglican priest and he didn't like the religion I was in," recalls Boyd. "He ordered me not to go to the Seventh-day Adventist Church. I guess he was afraid that there would be a lot of bad publicity if I was ever in trouble. He wasn't taking any chances and he had the police following me everywhere. If I went into a restaurant for a hot dog or something, they would be looking through the window, and when I looked up they would dash off to one side."

Boyd says he was called into Coughlan's Queen's Park office one day for an encounter he would never forget. "Coughlan got into a real rage and he said, 'Look, I used to be a boxer, and I could wipe the floor with you in no time at all.' He said, 'If I ever catch you not doing what I tell you, you're going to be in trouble.' " Boyd says the pressures on him at that point were so great that "I would have been better off in Kingston because nobody would bother me there." Coughlan's harangue brought Boyd to the verge of tears, and after he left the office, all of his old resentments towards authority began to surface.

"I'd always been like that," he says. "When somebody started pushing me, I would do the opposite to what they wanted. Coughlan didn't know how to handle me, and he wasn't going to take any chances, so he overdid it the other way."

Boyd might have overdone it too. He had started to think about robbing banks again and had even obtained a .22 rifle, which he modified by cutting off the stock. Then he thought it over and decided it would be foolish to attempt another robbery. "I knew that if I did it, I would be in for another twenty-five years. I realized I had to get rid of the gun, so I took it down to the ravine near Bloor Street on the other side of Bathurst. I cut it into pieces and threw it in the bushes."

By mid-December, Boyd was not co-operating and was expressing increased hostility towards his parole officer and parole conditions. And he continued to see Adele. She was his friend, and nobody was going to tell him not to see her.

At 8:30 p.m. on February 5, 1963, Boyd was arrested at the City Wide Telephone Answering Service, on Bloor Street. Adele worked there, and he was waiting to meet her after her shift.

Boyd was escorted to the Don Jail. A search warrant was obtained for his room at 353 Clinton Street, but nothing was found. The next day Boyd was brought before Magistrate R.C. Taylor, who signed the warrant of committal suspending his parole and ordering him held in jail.

Parole Board representative R.S. Beames met with Boyd on February 12. Boyd was remorseful that his parole hadn't worked out, and agreed that next time it would be better if he went some-where else to live secretly. "I asked if this would not work a hardship on him because of his family and relatives," wrote Beames later. "He replied that it wouldn't because he has now lost all interest in all of them, and this includes his three children, which he now maintains are not his, but were fathered by other men." Boyd also complained to Beames about Coughlan's conduct.

Boyd was sent back to Kingston, then to Joyceville, and finally back to Kingston. In all, he would remain in prison for four more years before being released again on October 30, 1966. It was decided to send him out to British Columbia with a new identity. And this time a special condition was attached to his parole: he was ordered "not to communicate with the press and/or other mass media without the express consent of his supervisor." He left Kingston with $217 in his pocket.

Epilogue

After he left Kingston, Edwin Alonzo Boyd held a variety of odd jobs until he found full-time work driving disabled adults to and from craft workshops in a small van. At night he worked as an instructor at a driving school. He bought an eight-year-old Nash for $175. After he was settled in, he was visited by his brother Gordon, a safety co-ordinator with Union Carbide, who was in British Columbia on business. Later, Boyd's oldest son moved out to B.C. with his wife and three-year-old daughter.

Boyd identified with the handicapped and seemed to enjoy his work. It was while driving that he met Marjorie,[34] a physically handicapped woman in her late thirties. "He was very nice, and very good about helping people," recalls Marjorie, whose disability gradually affected her ability to walk, and today keeps her bedridden most of the time. When they began dating, Marjorie was shocked when Boyd revealed his true identity, but it didn't change her opinion of him. She kept the truth from most of her family, whom she describes as "straight-laced." Boyd and Marjorie soon fell in love, and in May 1970, after Boyd's divorce from Dorreen was final, he and Marjorie married at the Seventh-day Adventist Church. Boyd's parole officer was his best man. Included among the guests was the RCMP officer he was reporting to as a condition of his parole. Boyd bought a Ford van, and he and Marjorie took a three-month trip across the country, visiting relatives along the way.

Boyd was content and happy with his new life and new identity, but the media weren't ready to leave him alone. *Toronto Star* reporter Earl McRae set out to locate Boyd shortly after the first anniversary of his parole. McRae, identifying himself as Dr. Lloyd Rickner of the National Parole Service, telephoned Boyd's brothers and sister, his father, and Dorreen Boyd. He used same approach in each call, stating that the board was concerned because Boyd had not reported to his parole officer for over three weeks. From the responses he got from relatives, McRae was able to piece together that Boyd was in B.C., and that so was his oldest son. He called the son with the same story and was told that Boyd had visited "the previous weekend."

It was only *after* the calls that Dorreen and Boyd's son realized something was amiss. The son called Boyd's parole officer, and Dorreen called the National Parole Service in Ottawa. The parole officer alerted Boyd that a newspaper reporter would probably try to contact him.

At 1 p.m. on November 22, Boyd called his parole officer from a senior citizens' home where he was picking up a wheelchair patient. "I have a *Toronto Star* reporter in my bus, what do I do?" asked Boyd. He was told to drive to, and park near, the RCMP detachment. Boyd was there within ten minutes. McRae was taken into the RCMP office and grilled about impersonating a parole board doctor. McRae initially told police he was there with the blessing of the board, but he backtracked when Boyd's parole supervisor came in. McRae said he had trailed Boyd for two days before revealing his true identity, and that he had enough material for a story, but wanted to top it off with an interview with Boyd.

Earlier, McRae had showed up at Boyd's work place saying he was from the local newspaper and was there to do a story on the craft school. He took pictures, which Boyd tried to avoid being in, but McRae snapped one while Boyd was moving away. It later appeared in the *Star*. The Parole Board later contacted the *Star*'s management to complain about "unethical, illegal methods used by their reporter to track down the story." The RCMP in B.C. felt there was sufficient evidence to lay impersonation charges against McRae under the Criminal Code, but did not proceed.

Boyd left his job and took another one driving children to a Seventh-day Adventist day school. Later he bought an old Chev thirty-six-passenger bus and converted it to a mobile home. He and Marjorie came east again to Ottawa for the marriage of Marjorie's niece.

In 1976, Boyd, Marjorie, and Marjorie's close friend, Pearl,[35] who was handicapped from polio, moved into a house specially built to accommodate the women's wheelchairs. Pearl says she liked Boyd from the moment she met him. "He was very friendly, very talkative, outgoing – a little pushy," she says. "He was fun and a nice person. And he was a good thinker – he talked about everything under the sun. He was good to everybody, and very energetic. He was always wanting to help people. We got on darn well."

The three have lived together ever since. Boyd runs errands, buys the groceries, cooks, and helps home care workers look after the women. On most mornings Boyd sits beside Marjorie's bed and reads to her. "I try to read to her every morning because she likes to be involved in what's going on."

Boyd says he tries to do the best he can to look after his wife and Pearl. "That's my philosophy, and I couldn't possibly change it, because I can't think of anything that would be better. I enjoy what I'm doing and I love the two ladies. We get along fine. We talk to each other."

It seems somewhat incongruous that the once dashing bank robber with the flashing smile, in his eighty-fourth year, has spent most of the last twenty-five years caring for his invalid wife and her friend. He continues to exercise and lift weights, and seems content, although there is a certain longing in his intense eyes, which Marjorie and Pearl describe as "Paul Newman blue."

Does Boyd ever think about robbing banks? "If I set my mind to it, I could go out and do all the silly things I used to do, but what good would it do? It would hurt Marjorie. It would hurt Pearl. I'd lose this house, and we all love this place. I couldn't possibly bring myself to even think of robbing a bank, let alone doing it."

In 1976, with the approval of the parole board and Boyd's cooperation, Marjorie Lamb and Barry Pearson wrote a book about the Boyd Gang. Six years later, the book was turned into a CTV documentary drama, *The Life and Times of Edwin Alonzo Boyd*, with Gordon Pinsent playing Boyd and narrating the story. The movie has been shown across the country numerous times since its first release.

In 1988 there was an offbeat musical about the women connected to the gang. Called *Girls in The Gang*, it opened at the Factory Theatre in Toronto.

And in 1994, Boyd was back in the headlines when Kingston police re-opened the Wentworth murder case and convinced Boyd and several other former C-dorm inmates to testify against Ralph Cochrane. Boyd testified at the preliminary hearing, after which Cochrane was ordered to stand trial. But the case didn't proceed. The murder charge was stayed when defence lawyers produced evidence that Cochrane had in fact been charged with murder in 1961, even though he had never been informed of the charge. Cochrane has always denied killing Wentworth. The judge ruled that it would be a breach of Cochrane's constitutional right to a speedy and fair trial if he were to be tried more than thirty years after the initial charge was laid.

(Cochrane, a habitual bank robber, has spent much of his life behind bars, much of it in solitary confinement because of the suspicion that he was responsible for Wentworth's death. He once went to court to win his release from solitary, which a judge described as "cruel and unusual" punishment.)

Willie "the Clown" Jackson was released on parole from Kingston about the same time as Boyd, after serving fourteen years. For a time he worked as a caretaker at a Cabbagetown church, where he often entertained youngsters with his jokes and his impressive repertoire of "crime does not pay" stories. The clergyman who employed Willie was asked by the *Star*'s George Gamester if he thought Willie was truly reformed. "Oh yes," he said. "Except he says it's still tough when he walks into a bank to resist the temptation to yell: 'Stick 'em up!' "

In 1973, Willie moved to British Columbia and eventually looked up Boyd. By then Willie was living with a woman and they had two children. Willie and his family stayed with Boyd, Marjorie, and Pearl for about four months before finding their own apartment.

Willie helped Boyd pour cement for a large front patio that would make it easier for Marjorie and Pearl's wheelchairs. Willie eventually found a good job as a janitor and maintenance man. "They liked him, because he was a good worker," says Boyd. "He'd do his work and ask them if there was anything else he could do. He was an easy-going guy."

Willie's biggest problem was that he drank too much, says Boyd. "When he was drunk, he'd say the wrong things all the time. If we were out somewhere, say to one of the stores on the main street, he would get out and pee on the side of the van. Marjorie didn't think that was a good idea." Willie died five or six years ago. "I guess he was just worn out," says Boyd. "I don't know."

Dorreen Boyd had also moved out west. "I had a friend then. An excellent chef. We used to go to different resorts where he cooked and I waited tables." After their relationship ended – he often beat her when he was drunk – she moved back to Ontario for a while, then back to B.C. again. She married another man, but they eventually separated, and she returned to Ontario, where she now lives quietly in her own apartment in a community east of Toronto.

Of her life with Edwin Alonzo Boyd, Dorreen says: "I'm glad I met him. We had good times and bad times, but I still love him."

Robin Christopher Boyd, one of the twins, died of AIDS on March 7, 1991. "I didn't even know he was sick," says Dorreen. "It hit me like a ton of bricks. I knew he was gay, but he didn't want me to know he had AIDS. Her son's name is on a monument for AIDS victims on Church Street in Toronto. Robin had a brief run-in with the law: In 1975 he was convicted of robbing a Safeway store of $20,000 and sentenced to two years less a day.

Dorreen stays in touch with her oldest son Anthony. Her daughter has a successful business career in the Toronto area and they see each other from time to time.

After Norman Boyd was released from the Guelph Reformatory he had trouble finding a job because of all the Boyd Gang publicity. But through the efforts and influence of his lawyer, Goldwin Arthur Martin, and former Toronto mayor Robert Saunders, Norman was hired by Ontario Hydro, where he spent a long and satisfying career. He and his wife raised two daughters.

At seventy-five Norman still has his flying licence, and he had his own plane, a Cessna 150, until 1994. "Once you get the flying bug, it's pretty hard to get over it."

Glover Boyd died in 1984, just a few days short of his ninety-fourth birthday. He had continued to live in Wiarton, Ontario, and married a third time after Minnie died. He and his third wife made several trips to visit Edwin in British Columbia.

"He was trying to get closer to me," says Boyd, "but it never really worked. Maybe because of my frame of mind, or my way of looking at things. I just wanted information. I didn't want to do anything to bring us together. He wasn't the kind of father that I wanted to get close to. He had spent all those years wasting my life and my time and my talent. I missed out because I was really talented. I could sing. I could play musical instruments. I was good at sports. If he had treated me right and given me the approval that I needed, I would have been successful as a musician or whatever. I would have been fine. I never would have been robbing banks."

Life was not kind to some of the others with connections to the Boyd Gang. Ann Jackson remarried after Lennie's death. Michael, her son by Lennie, was adopted by his stepfather but kept the Jackson surname. Michael Jackson, now forty-five, runs a successful landscaping business in Calgary. He says his stepfather became his legal guardian after his mother became an alcoholic and the marriage ended.

Michael remembers his mother showing up at the house when he was nine or ten and living in Pickering. "She would grab me and take me away for a week. All of a sudden we'd be in Toronto, over around Sunnyside and Lansdowne. Her friends would all be drunk and my guardian would come and pull me out of there. It was real skid row." He said his mother often suffered physical abuse at the hands of the men she was with.

In 1967, Michael was fifteen when his stepfather came home one day and said without sentiment: "Your mother is dead. She died three days ago. She was buried today." Ann Jackson was forty. She had cirrhosis of the liver.

"I probably last saw her when I was twelve," says Michael. "She was beat up as well at that time. Her life was tragic, but one lady said to me, 'Maybe her death was like a mercy killing, and she died early in life rather than suffering for a long time.' "

Shortly after Michael Jackson moved to western Canada in 1976, someone sent him a copy of a book[36] about the Boyd Gang that repeated the erroneous newspaper accounts of the Montreal shoot-out. "When I read that Tough Lennie used his wife as a shield, right then – boom – I closed that book. I visualized that, and I was disgusted because, as a kid, I saw my mother beaten up." He didn't want to know anything more about his father. But several years later, when he learned that the book's account of the incident was false, he renewed his quest to know his father. That quest continues to this day, and he is working on a book about his father. He says that one of the late Arthur Maloney's former law partners told him that Lennie did not die in vain, because his death lead to the abolition of capital punishment in 1976.

Lennie's Jackson's sister, Mary Mitchell, died of a brain tumour in the early 1960s. Michael Jackson says Mitchell betrayed his father by giving information to Eddie Tong about Anna Camero's Monarch. "She brought my father down," he says. "Her own brother. In letters she wrote to Lennie in jail, she says 'You probably don't want to talk to me.' Why do you think that was?"

The Boyd Gang case helped the careers of many Toronto police officers, whose profiles were raised considerably by the intense media coverage. One was Jack Gillespie, who died in Toronto in May 1997. His obituary in the *Star* was written by Jocko Thomas.

The headline read: JACK GILLESPIE HELPED NAB BOYD GANG.

Thomas also wrote the obituary for Adolphus "Dolph" Payne, who died in 1981. "He became a national hero for breaking up the notorious Boyd Gang of bank robbers in 1952," wrote Thomas.

Three years before Payne died, Boyd went to visit him at his Port Hope home. "Payne always had a sort of grudging respect for Boyd," says Jack Webster. "He didn't like him because he was a bank robber, but as a man he respected the unwritten code of honour that seemed to be out there. And I think that Edwin Boyd respected Payne."

Payne's feelings for Boyd were not shared by his widow, Helen Payne. "I didn't want him there," she says. "I wasn't afraid of him, but I just didn't like him because I knew all the trouble he had caused. He was a con man."

The era of the newspaper battles that helped create the Boyd Gang is gone, but the memories linger. Val Sears, who worked for the *Telegram* at the height of the circulation war with the *Star* during the Boyd Gang era, was once quoted as saying: "The *Telegram* was one paper that came with the garbage already wrapped." In his book *Hello Sweetheart ... Get Me Rewrite*, Sears amended that quote: "I lied. It wasn't garbage. It was the fragrant leavings of contemporary history. It was the refuse of a battle between the *Star* and the *Tely* that consumed 10 years of our lives, some of our loves, all of our skill. And oh what a lovely war."

Doug MacFarlane, hired from the *The Globe and Mail* as the *Telegram*'s city editor, described the period as "great, exciting days. In my lifetime there was never a period to match those whoop-de-do years. We didn't hurt anybody. We may have embellished. We may have stretched. But there was always a hard kernel of fact there."[37]

Newspaper readers revelled in Boyd's exploits. They had the satisfaction of participating vicariously in the action. They were even pulling for him, for to be successful in their eyes, Boyd had to get away with it – for a time at least. Besides, the banks were loaded, so who cared if they lost a few thousand here or there? But the death of Eddie Tong spoiled it for most. It was no longer a game: it was time for punishment.

Boyd was ultimately caught and imprisoned for many years; even so, robbing banks was the most success he ever had, and all the publicity that went with it made him famous.

One of his favourite movies was *White Heat*, starring James Cagney in his last great gangster role. The movie came out in 1949, the year that Boyd robbed his first bank. Cagney plays a vicious, psychopathic killer with a mother obsession. In the movie Cagney goes berserk in a prison mess hall when he learns of his mother's death. The movie ends with him trapped and wounded on top of a gas storage tank, which explodes under him as he yells, "I made it, Mom! Top of the World!"

Boyd wasn't looking for that kind of a fiery end. And he doesn't want to go back to robbing banks, but subconsciously he may feel cheated that he can't today walk into the public spotlight and declare "I did that! That was me!" In the end, Boyd, who craved approval and recognition, paid for his crimes not just with fourteen years in prison, but with a life sentence of relative obscurity.

Notes

CHAPTER 1

[1]Tom Graham left the Toronto Police Department to go into the hardware business. Years later he was back in law enforcement as chairman of the Ontario Police Commission.

CHAPTER 2

[2]Bee Street was later changed to Cosburn Avenue.

CHAPTER 3

[3]The centre, at 107 Cedarvale Avenue, celebrated its ninetieth anniversary in 1997.
[4]Marjorie Lamb and Barry Pearson, *The Boyd Gang*, pp. 8–9.

CHAPTER 4

[5]A pseudonym. Ed Boyd doesn't remember his name.
[6]Pauline Kael, *5001 Nights at the Movies*, p. 221.

CHAPTER 5

[7]Parole was then called ticket-of-leave.

CHAPTER 6

[8]Templeton later became an agnostic, and a successful fiction and non-fiction author, newspaper and magazine editor, and television news public affairs director.

CHAPTER 8

[9]Lamb and Pearson, *The Boyd Gang*, p. 16.

CHAPTER 10

[10]John D. (Jack) Webster was staff superintendent when he retired from the Toronto police force in 1988. He is now a historian with the Metropolitan Toronto Police Museum and Discovery Centre.

CHAPTER 11
[11]Lamb and Pearson, *The Boyd Gang*, p. 19.

CHAPTER 12
[12]Jocko Thomas, *From Police Headquarters*, p. 122.
[13]Val Sears, *Hello Sweetheart ... Get Me Re-Write*, p. 17.
[14]Carlos Baker, *Ernest Hemingway: A Life Story*, p. 157.
[15]Val Sears, *Hello Sweetheart ... Get Me Re-Write*, p. 18.

CHAPTER 14
[16]Decades later, the Ontario government purchased land for an airport at Pickering, but after much public opposition the project was mothballed.

CHAPTER 15
[17]After his retirement from the Toronto Police Department, Cater moved to Port Elgin, Ontario, where he was mayor from 1980 to 1985.
[18]Jocko Thomas, *From Police Headquarters*, p. 22.

CHAPTER 16
[19]Eric Arthur, *Toronto: No Mean City*, 1964, pp. 140–141.

CHAPTER 17
[20]The dictionary definition of *Tong* is 'association' or 'secret society.'

CHAPTER 23
[21]Lamb and Pearson, *The Boyd Gang*, p. 104.

CHAPTER 24
[22]Creighton went on to be a founder and publisher of the *Toronto Sun* after the Telegram folded in 1971.

CHAPTER 26
[23]Douglas Creighton, *Sunburned*, p. 31.

CHAPTER 27

[24]Boyd always used "superintendent" instead of "governor."

[25]Tupper Bigelow was a Sherlock Holmes authority and buff who donated his extensive collection on the fabled detective to the Metropolitan Toronto Reference Library.

CHAPTER 29

[26]Jocko Thomas, *From Police Headquarters*, p. 128.

[27]Jocko Thomas, *From Police Headquarters*, p. 129.

CHAPTER 30

[28]Malton Airport is now Lester B. Pearson International Airport.

CHAPTER 31

[29]Harold Adamson later became chief of the Metropolitan Toronto Police Department.

CHAPTER 33

[30]Ontario Chief Justice Roy McMurtry, *Maclean's*, December 2, 1996, p. 85.

[31]Jack Batten, *In Court*, p. 137.

[32]Jack Batten, *In Court*, p. 147.

[33]Father Kelly later became president of St. Michael's College.

EPILOGUE

[34]Surname not used for reasons of anonymity.

[35]Surname not used for purposes of anonymity.

[36]Lamb and Pearson, *The Boyd Gang*.

[37]Val Sears, *Hello Sweetheart ... Get Me Re-Write*, pp. 38–39.

Sources

The dialogue in this book was recreated as accurately as possible from statements to police, court transcripts, Royal Commission transcripts, first-person recollections of those still alive, and newspaper accounts of events.

The newspapers themselves were, of course, a part of the story, and coverage of the Boyd Gang saga by the three major Toronto newspapers of the day was rich in detail and captured the flavour of the time. I thank the dozens of reporters and editors, many of them now deceased, who brought the stories to life in such colourful fashion.

Other sources are listed in the Notes.

Index

A

Adams, Bill, 302, 303

Adamson, Harold, 294

Adele K., 344, 345

Aldershot (England), 54-56, 67, 68

Allard, Edward, 178

Anderson, Robert, 274

Atkinson, Joseph E., 81

B

Backman, Sidney, 172, 216, 217

Baldwin, Allan, 117

Banks:

  Bank of Commerce, 88, 90, 91, 99, 132-135, 137, 153, 165, 213

  Bank of Montreal, 4, 5, 79, 84, 85, 97, 105, 133, 180, 191, 242, 315

  Bank of Toronto, 80, 159–161, 176, 177, 186, 187, 240, 253, 312

  Dominion Bank, 92, 95, 100, 106, 108, 136, 313, 314

  Imperial Bank, 95, 164

  Royal Bank of Canada, 134, 161, 167, 168, 176, 254

Barron, Harry, 136

Barry, Richard, 92

Basher, Col. G. Hedley, 118, 119, 128, 184, 185, 243, 244, 252, 253, 259, 274, 275, 319, 322

Bassett, John, 82, 282

Batten, Jack, 323, 330

Beams, R.S., 345

Beauchamp, Gordon, 299

Bebe, Mrs. Fred, 161

Bennett, Alfred, 148, 150

Bennett, R. B., 39, 338

Berton, Pierre, 341

Beverley, Rev. A.R., 249

Bigelow, Tupper, 254

Biggs, Herbert, 203, 214

Bilodeau, Maurice, 211

Black, Georgina, 87

Blahut, Jane, 200, 201

Bleuthner, Ernest, 161

Bolton, William, 199, 273

Bowles, William, 206, 207

Bowmanville, 112

Boyce, William Harry, 95

Boyd, Alonzo (Lon), 10, 12, 26,

Boyd, Anthony, 61, 62, 75, 157, 175, 226, 351

Boyd, Dorreen Mary (Thompson), 56-62, 65, 67-70, 72, 73, 75, 76, 79, 80, 90, 91, 94, 102, 105, 146, 156, 157, 175, 189, 191, 203, 204, 225–233, 235, 236, 238, 239, 241, 242, 244, 245, 250, 251, 278–280, 287, 313, 316, 318, 319, 340, 341, 343, 344, 347, 348, 351

Boyd, Edwin Alonzo, 2, 10-50, 52-56, 58-70, 72-114, 119, 120, 123, 124, 128, 133, 134, 138-144, 146-151, 154-165, 168-184, 187-189, 191-194, 203-205, 213, 215, 221, 224-227, 230–248; 251–280, 283–285, 287-293; 295-297; 300–308, 310–320, 331, 333–355

Boyd, Edwin Alonzo Jr., 61

Boyd, (Edwin) Glover, 10-13, 16-18, 24-29, 33, 38, 46, 48-50, 69-72, 75, 146, 175, 312, 318, 341, 352

Boyd, Eleanor (McCallum), 11-15, 17, 18, 26, 27

Boyd Gang, 2, 100, 139, 159, 161, 165, 167, 178, 186, 187, 214, 236, 253, 254, 259–262, 265, 275, 277, 281, 285, 286, 288–290, 292, 295, 297, 299–301, 304, 306, 309, 310, 322, 334, 351–353

Boyd, Gordon, 13, 25, 26, 37, 38, 48, 54, 74, 76, 238, 347

Boyd, Irene, 13, 18, 48

Boyd, Minerva (Minnie), 27-29, 48, 69, 75

Boyd, Norman, 13, 15, 25, 26, 48, 54, 74, 76, 100-103, 156, 163, 226–233, 235, 238, 239, 241, 242, 245, 254, 280, 313–316, 318, 351, 352

Boyd, Oswald, 12

Boyd, Robin, 344, 351

Boyd, twins, 65, 69, 75, 175, 344

Bracebridge, 10

Bradford, 135, 137, 138, 213

Brand, Thomas Woodward, 184, 243–247, 251, 252, 257–260, 273, 275, 277, 281

Branston, Brian, 159

Brantford, 201

Brimmell, George, 211

Bronte, 206

Brown, Alfred, 92

Brunet, Tony, 136

Buffalo, 179, 185

Burlington, 109, 206, 207, 296

Burwash (prison farm), 123, 184

Butler, Helen, 101

Butt, Helen, 132, 133

C

Cabbagetown, 139

Cagney, James, 1, 40, 179, 355

Calgary, 32, 33, 36, 37, 40, 42, 47

Camero, Anna (Bosnich), 153, 154, 161, 168, 175, 178, 179, 188–193, 196, 198, 199, 201, 208, 209, 330, 332

Camp Borden, 135

Campeau, Bette, 162

Canadian Broadcasting Corporation (CBC), 1, 280, 284

Canadian National Exhibition (C.N.E.), 3, 18, 52, 70, 71, 73, 128, 129, 187

Canning, Robert, 117

Care, Fred, 86, 89, 90

Carnegie, Dale, 53

Caron, Roger, 335

Caskie, Cecil, 89

Cater, Frank, 109-111, 295, 296, 304–306

Caulfield, Samuel, 49

Caustan, Kenneth, 344

Chambers, Robert, 177

Chapman, Doug, 214

Chisholm, John, 166, 186, 198, 200, 203, 238, 249, 275, 306

Church, William, 87, 88

Churches:

Church of England, 222, 338

Church of the Nativity, 248, 249

Faith Tabernacle, 17

St. Brigid's Catholic, 19

St. James the Apostle Anglican, 174

Seventh-day Adventist, 338, 344

Clarke, Murray, 262–264, 266, 273

Clement, John, 131

Cochrane, 152, 286

Cochrane, Ralph, 342, 343, 349

Colborne, 133, 153

Constantine, George, 117

Conover, J.D., 252, 319

Cook, Charlie, 200, 250, 254, 292

Cooper, Russell, 239

Copes, Maynard Elroy, 159

Coté, George, 211, 212

Coté, Henri, 189, 217–219, 222

Coté, Laurette, 189, 217

Coté, Turpo, 139

Coughlan, Daniel, 343-346

Cranfield, William, 6-8, 83

Craven, Ken, 114, 214, 226–234, 241, 242, 253

Creighton, Doug, 201, 238, 239, 248

Crilly, Jack, 304, 305

Crockford, Oliver E., 17

Cronin, Bart, 322

Crooked Creek, 112

D

Dagleish, Edward, 298

Dauphin, Albert, 211

Davidson, Ruth, 101

Davis, Bette, 204

Dempsey, D. A., 98

Depoe, Norman, 284

Dick, Evelyn, 322, 323

Don Jail, 1, 114-116, 119-123, 138-146, 150, 156, 159, 161, 164, 173, 175, 184, 185, 238, 242–247, 249–254, 260, 275, 276, 280, 281, 284, 305, 307, 309, 317, 319, 322, 331, 333, 334, 339, 345

Don River, 284, 289

Don Valley, 22, 29, 30, 89, 126, 149, 283, 285, 288, 289

Doner (farm), 289, 292, 295–299, 304

Doyle, Charles, 304, 305
Doyle, Maurice, 297, 299
Dunworthy, Derm, 239

E

Edmonton, 32, 43
Edmundston, 174
Elwood, George, 4-9, 97
Empey, Joyce, 5, 6, 85, 98, 99
Estey, J.W., 332

F

Factory Theatre, 350
Fawcett, William, 195
Filey, Mike, 165, 197
Films:
Another Man's Poison, 204
The Golddiggers of 1933, 39
The Gunfighter, 95
Kind Hearts and Coronets, 95
Tight Little Island,v95
Typhoon, 47
White Heat, 355
Winchester '73, 95
Finlay, Mrs. Murray, 177
Florida, 170, 191
Foote, John, 275, 310
Forgie, David, 177
Fort Saskatchewan, 32
Fort William, 286
48th Highlanders, 129
Forsyth, Robert, 314-317
Foster, Dawn, 107

French, Jean, 155

G

Gamester, George, 350
Gault, Howard Ferguson, 99-101, 104-111, 113, 114, 120, 156–159, 296, 336
Geno, Ray, 302, 304
Gibb, Alexandrine, 202, 203, 241
Gibson, Allister, 180-182, 250, 253, 254, 315, 316, 336
Gibson, Richard, 109
Gibson, William O., 285, 324, 326–330
Gillespie, John "Jack", 124, 125, 127, 137, 138, 157, 188, 198, 200, 215-225, 246, 247, 322, 328, 353, 354
Gipp, Fred, 93
The Globe And Mail, 81, 82, 94, 206, 281, 285, 354
Goodenough, Francis, John, 288, 289
Goodfellow, John, 108
Gordon, Lamont, 187
Goulet, Lucien, 249
Gravenhurst, 10, 286
Green, Kenneth, 117
Greene, Lorne, 1, 78, 280
Greenwood, Charlie, 260, 311
Guelph, 240
Guelph Reformatory, 118, 120, 121, 139, 184, 185, 351
Guinane, Mary Helen, 92

H

Halifax, 53, 68

Hamilton, 207, 222, 225, 238, 239

Hardy, Russell, 139

Harris, William, 319

Harriston, 187

Havelock, 286

Hayward, Dr. John, 213

Head, Audrey, 98

Hemingway, Ernest, 81, 82

Herman, Carl, 315

Herman, Lou, 314

Hill, George, 154

Hindmarsh, Harry C., 81, 82, 281

Hockley, Albert, 162

Holiday Tavern, 125, 131

Holmes, Gilbert, 139

Horseshoe Tavern, 125-127, 131, 132, 134, 192

Howarth, Dorothy, 278, 318

Huluk, Betty, 153, 190, 192, 198, 199, 201

Humber River, 295

Hume, Christopher, 116

Hunter, John, 57

Hunter, Kate, 57, 58, 62, 65, 68, 73

Huntsville, 10

Hutchinson, George, 272

I

Innes, John, 166

J

Jackson, Ann (Roberts), 131-134, 136-138, 145, 146, 150, 154, 155, 168, 172-174, 179, 189, 190, 200, 207-209, 216-220, 223, 230, 253, 258, 262, 292, 331-333, 352

Jackson, Leonard "Tough Lennie", 127-134, 136-151, 154, 155, 159–163, 168, 172–174, 176, 179, 180, 181, 184, 188-196, 199-201, 204-209, 213, 215-225, 231, 233, 236, 246-249, 254-259, 261, 262, 264-274, 276, 280, 283-285, 289, 290, 292, 293, 296, 300-308, 310, 314, 322-334, 353

Jackson, Joseph, 176-178, 180, 181, 183, 187, 242, 250, 253, 254, 315, 319, 336

Jackson, William R. "Willie (the Clown)", 138-141, 144, 147-151, 154, 155, 157, 159-163, 168-170, 172, 173, 176, 180, 184, 191, 199, 242, 253-255, 257, 259-262. 264-271, 273, 280, 283-285, 288-291, 293, 296, 297, 300-306, 313-320, 350, 351

Jackson, Lillian, 127, 128, 223

Jackson, Michael, 332, 352, 353

Jamieson, Adelene, 107

Jarvis, Charlie, 116

Johnson, Norm, 201

Joyceville, 336, 346

Jukes, Harold, 227, 228

K

Kapuskasing, 137

Keefer, Norman, 231

Keeler, W.W., 106

Kelly, Rev. John, 332, 333

Kelvington, 34, 35

Kilworthy, 10, 14

Kindness, George B., 152, 153

King Edward Hotel, 153, 178

Kingston, 156, 319, 343

Kingston Penitentiary, 117, 119, 120, 136, 138, 140, 144, 173, 179, 242, 253, 308, 318, 319, 320, 333-338, 340, 341, 345-347, 350

Kitchener, 33

Kline, A.O., 314, 315

Knox, W.J., 163

L

La Prairie, 224

Lac Seul, 38

Lachine, 224

Lamb, Flo, 76, 204, 251, 318, 319

Lamb, Frank, 76, 156, 176, 204, 251

Lamb, Marjorie, 349

Lamport, Allan, 185-187, 197, 203, 215, 232, 238-241, 249, 275, 280, 306, 307

Langpré, (detective captain), 210

Langstaff (jail farm), 118

Larson, Roy, 285

Lauzon, Ulysses, 338, 339

Leaside, 161, 254, 288

Leigh, Ervin H., 98, 106

Lesso, Elizabeth, 152, 155, 168, 170, 199, 206, 253, 254, 314, 315, 323, 333

Lesso, Joseph, 152, 155, 168–171, 191, 199, 206, 253, 254, 314, 315

Lethbridge, 35

Lindsay, 238

Lombardo, Guy, 3

Long Branch, 206

Long, George, 295

Long Harry, 319

Lorimer, Barry, 109-111, 156

Lowe, Havre, 302, 303

Lowes, John, 161

M

MacDonald, Mickey, 338, 339

Macdonelle, Ian, 277

MacDougall, A.G., 134

Mace, Bert, 286

MacFarlane, Doug, 354

Machesney, Beverley, 177

Maclean, John, 162

Maloney, Arthur C., 323–327, 330–333, 353

Malton Airport, 284, 295

Manera, Ernest, 206

Martin, Goldwin Arthur, 352

Matthews, Bill, 288

McAuliffe, Joseph H., 164

McCallum, Colin, 93

McCallum, Harold, 11, 12, 18, 24, 174, 175

McCathie, Alex, 210, 233, 234, 239, 306

McCullagh, George, 82, 281, 282

McCullough, Frank, 116, 118, 243, 331, 322

McGregor, Irene, 93

McHugh, Patricia, 115

McLean, D.M., 343

McLean, Walter, 107, 108

McMahon, F.J., 252, 253, 316, 317

McNulty, John, 269, 270

McRae, Earl, 347, 348

McRuer, James, 310, 323-326, 328, 329, 331

Medicine Hat, 37

Merrill, Gary, 204

Miller, L. E., 88

Mimico, 128, 156

Minneapolis, 338

Minnelli, Nicholas, 338, 339

Miskiw, John, 93

Mitchell, Mary, 131, 138, 146, 150, 154, 160, 172-179, 188, 189, 193, 200, 225, 253, 254, 314, 315, 353

Moosomin (Jail), 37

Montreal, 156, 160, 168, 172-174, 176, 178-180, 188, 189, 192, 199, 207, 209, 211, 214, 216, 236, 249, 253, 263, 286, 303, 330, 332

The Montreal Gazette, 217

Morrison, James, 255–258, 272, 274, 285, 336

Mount Sinai Hospital, 175

Murray, Leo, 218, 220

Muskoka, 10, 13, 14, 15, 26

Musselman Lake, 134-137

N

Nasso, Frank, 315

Neal, Norman, 117

New York City, 113, 178, 179, 186

Niagara Falls, 128, 130, 131, 174, 204, 223, 279

Nimmo, John, 198, 238, 241, 248, 257, 274, 318

Nipigon, 33

Noble, Alexander, 269, 270, 274, 277

North Bay, 30, 286

North York, 288, 306, 308, 309

Numbers Mob, 2, 136, 141, 164

O

Oakville, 206

O'Kane, Duke, 33-37

Oriole, 292, 293, 299

Oshawa, 23, 155, 156, 190, 192

Orillia, 136, 138

Ostroski, Gail, 231, 232

Ottawa, 38, 39

Ouellette, Andrew, 294, 295

P

Payne, Adolphus "Dolph", 111-114, 120, 156, 182, 188, 205, 209, 214, 226–237, 239-242, 250, 253, 254, 292, 312-314, 319, 354

Payne, Helen (Croft), 112, 113, 233, 234, 236, 354

Pearce, George, 116

Pearson, Barry, 349

Peel County Jail, 274

Perry, Roy, 193-195, 198, 201, 203, 204, 208-210, 215, 225, 227, 324

Peterborough, 287

Peterborough Examiner, 281

Phillips, Jean, 21, 22

Phillips, W.E., 297

Pickering, 102, 132, 133, 141, 156, 189, 226, 227, 231, 240

Pine Hills Cemetery, 249

Pinsent, Gordon, 349

Plummer, Sidney, 207

Poirier, George, 211, 212

Police Departments:
  East York, 89, 167
  Etobicoke, 167
  FBI, 200, 284
  Leaside, 167
  Mimico, 167
  Montreal, 209, 210, 213, 215, 218, 221, 224, 284, 332
  North York, 8, 84, 167, 298, 299, 301, 302, 304, 305, 307
  Ontario Provincial, 8, 89, 135, 284, 309
  Quebec Provincial, 284
  RCMP, 44, 194, 200, 284, 348
  Scarborough, 167, 295
  Toronto, 8, 13, 78, 89, 118, 124, 206, 210, 211, 213, 295, 296, 301, 307, 332
  Weston, 167

Polka Dot Gang, 2, 117, 124

Port Arthur, 30, 34

Port Hope, 112

Porter, Dana, 248

Poucher, Mr. and Mrs. F.B., 232

Price, Laura, 195

Prince Albert, 44, 46

Prior, Patricia, 228

Provost Corps, 55, 64-66, 68

Q

Quebec City, 52, 53

Queen's York Rangers, 52

R

Raby, Frank, 231

Red Hill (England), 59, 60

Regina, 39

Reigate (England), 56, 59, 62

Richardson, Maurice "Moe", 84, 298-303, 306

Richardson, Ruby, 101

Riley, Mary, 132

Riverdale (Isolation Hospital), 149, 271, 283

Robinette, J.J., 322-326, 330-333

Robinette, Thomas C., 322

Rogers, Roy, 171

Rohrer, Elgin, 298, 299

Royal Connaught Hotel, 207

Royal Field Artillery, 11

Royal Canadian Regiment (RCR), 52, 55, 59, 64, 70, 128

Royal Regiment of Canada, 118, 128, 129

Royal Tour, 104, 105, 142

Rudge, Carl, 93

Rundle, John, 206

Rutherford, Max, 133

Ryan, Red, 338

S

St. Joseph's Hospital, 202

St. Laurent, Louis, 280

Salvation Army, 12, 31, 33, 43

San Francisco, 339

Sanderson, Charles, 120-123, 143–145, 184, 185, 253

Sanderson, John, 187

Saskatchewan Penitentiary, 44, 46

Saskatoon, 37, 40, 47

Saunders, Robert, 352

Sauriol, George, 162

Scarborough, 343

Schools (Toronto):
   Earl Beatty Public, 18, 21, 24
   Fern Avenue Public, 192
   Gledhill Public, 16, 17
   Oakwood Collegiate, 52
   Riverdale Technical, 52
   St. Michael's College, 332
   Secord Public, 17
   Upper Canada College, 229
   Vaughn, Collegiate, 159

Scott, George D., 341

Sears, Val, 354

Seaton, George, 207

Shaw, Anne, 277

Shortreed, Neil R., 132, 133

Silver Rail, 125

Sioux Lookout, 38

Skelly, Frank, 107-109

Smily, Powell, 249

Smith, Margaret, 181

Smith, W.H.G., 95, 96

Southern, Ernie, 301-303

Spellman Gang, 116

Spellman, Mac, 116

Starr, Jack, 126

Stavroff, Louis, 136

Stephenson, Mrs. James W., 106

Stewart, Donald, 107-109

Stoddard, George, 231

Stone, Samuel "Sammy", 128, 292, 336, 337

Stratford, 286

Streets (Toronto):
   Avenue Road, 4, 84, 94, 95, 98, 105, 247, 295
   Bathurst Street, 86, 94, 125,

230, 295, 345
Bay Street, 139, 192
Bayview Avenue, 110
Bloor Street, 48, 139, 230, 247, 345
Boustead Avenue, 136, 159, 253
Broadview Avenue, 22, 115, 284
Cedarvale Avenue, 17
Chisholm Avenue, 17, 28
Church Street, 78, 152
Clinton Street, 344, 345
College Street, 83, 111, 114, 124, 127, 137, 177, 180, 182, 186, 193, 195, 196, 198
Cornell Avenue, 177
Coxwell Avenue, 249
Danforth Avenue, 16, 20, 23, 133, 249
Davenport Avenue, 11, 136
Doncrest Avenue, 247
Donlands Avenue, 88
Don Mills Road, 88, 89, 299
Don Roadway, 149
Dovercourt Road, 136, 177
Dufferin Street, 92, 117
Dunblaine Avenue, 7
Dundas Street, 78, 159, 180, 193, 196, 253
Dupont Avenue, 112, 117
Eglinton Avenue, 73, 74, 77, 86, 90, 102, 117, 251, 289
Elm Road, 4, 8
Ennerdale Road, 251
Euclid Avenue, 180, 182, 242

Fairlawn Avenue, 95, 105
Felbrigg Avenue, 8, 9
Gerrard Street, 115, 154, 284
Glebemount Avenue, 18-20
Glencairn Avenue, 92, 93
Haddington Avenue, 7, 105
Harbord Street, 156
Harris Avenue, 16, 20
Heath Street, 229-231, 233, 236, 238, 239, 250, 280, 306
Howard Park Avenue, 49, 284
Howard Street, 292
Humberside Avenue, 150
Jarvis Street, 180, 243, 253, 286
Jones Avenue, 343
Kennedy Road, 249
Kenwood Avenue, 230, 242
King Street, 112
Kingston Road, 23, 176, 177, 186, 240
Laird Drive, 161
Lakeshore Boulevard, 174, 295
Lansdowne Avenue, 193, 195, 198
Lawrence Avenue, 94, 105-109, 158, 180
Leslie Street, 289, 290, 299, 301, 302, 304
Logan Avenue, 242
London Street, 156, 229, 230, 242
Lumsden Avenue, 133

MacPherson Avenue, 165

Madison Avenue, 158

Main Street, 16, 48

Manning Avenue, 181, 229, 242

Maplewood Avenue, 230

Marchmount Road, 11

Marion Street, 152

Markham Street, 242

McCaul Street, 127

Monarch Park Avenue, 249

O'Connor Drive, 87-89

Old Orchard Grove, 4

Olive Avenue, 229

Ossington Avenue, 11

Page Street, 344

Parliament Street, 154, 256

Pottery Road, 164

Queen Street, 131, 136, 157, 175, 253, 286

Queen's Park Crescent, 111

Roncesvalles Avenue, 136, 137, 165, 175, 193, 200, 284

Rose Avenue, 256

Rosedale Valley Road, 149

Roxborough Street, 48, 49

St. Clair Avenue, 87, 89, 230, 238

St. Helens Avenue, 198

Sandra Road, 87, 88

Sherbourne Street, 139

Sheppard Avenue, 100, 109, 289-291, 297

Sheridan Avenue, 196, 199

Sorauren Avenue, 152, 155, 157, 167, 168, 196, 206, 285

Spadina Avenue, 126, 152

Spadina Road, 226, 230

Steeles Avenue, 301

Swanwick Avenue, 16

Walmer Road, 164

Warden Avenue, 177

Wells Street, 230

Winchester Avenue, 150

Woodbine Avenue, 20, 23, 133, 249

Wright Avenue, 153, 165, 175, 193, 195, 198, 201, 208, 209

Yarmouth Gardens, 48

Yonge Street, 11, 48, 73, 74, 77, 92, 100, 105, 106, 108, 109, 112, 125, 158, 180, 229, 233, 284, 286, 290, 291, 295, 307

York Mills Road, 110

Suchan, Steve ("Val" Lesso, Victor J. Lenhoff), 135, 146, 149, 152-154, 157, 159, 160, 167-180, 187-196, 198-201, 203-217, 225, 226, 231, 233, 236, 247- 251, 254, 258, 259, 261-264, 266, 273, 280, 283–285, 290, 292, 293,

296, 298, 300-306, 308, 310, 314, 315, 320, 330-334

Sudbury, 99

Sunnyside, 71, 112, 165

Sunnyside Motor Hotel, 175

Swift Current, 174

T

Tavignot, Charles, 165

Taylor, Evan, 298, 299

Taylor, R.C., 345

Templeton, Charles, 48

Teskey, Frank, 236

Thomas, Gwyn "Jocko", 82-84, 111, 126, 159, 165, 214, 216, 224, 236, 248, 274, 281, 308, 310, 353

Thomas, Harry, 231

Thomas, William, 115

Thompson, Joan, 58, 67

Thompson, William "Bill", 215, 216, 218, 221, 222

Thorburn, G.A., 241

Thornton, 28

Tong, Edmund "Eddie", 124-127, 136-138, 186-189, 192-205, 208-210, 214, 215, 223, 225, 227, 241, 247-251, 254, 275, 276, 279, 302, 305, 314, 322-327, 330, 353, 355

Tong, Evelyn, 202, 203, 215, 247, 249

Tong, Margaret, 202, 203

Tong, Raymond, 202, 203

Toronto City Hall, 323

Toronto General Hospital, 197, 201, 202, 241, 248, 251, 258

Toronto Island airport, 284

Toronto Star, 1, 81-83, 90, 94, 98, 116, 165, 181, 197, 202, 204, 208, 213-216, 224, 234, 236-238, 241, 248, 249, 275-277, 279, 308, 310, 323, 341, 348, 353

Toronto Telegram, 1, 81-82, 83, 90, 94, 134, 137, 151, 162, 165, 181, 197, 200, 201, 203, 204, 213, 214, 231, 237, 238, 248, 276, 278, 308, 310, 321, 323, 332, 354

Toronto Transit Commission (TTC), 22, 73-77, 97, 185

Trimble, Howard, 292, 297

Trimble, John, 293, 297, 299

Trimble, Robert, 292, 293, 299

Trotter, Bert, 298-303, 305

Tumpane, Frank, 281

U

Underwood, Bill, 49, 175

Upritchard, Marie, 181

V

Valcartier, 52, 53

Vancouver, 38, 47, 286

Victoria Industrial School, 128

Virgin, R. J., 133

W

Waddell, Charles, 196

Walker, J. D., 19

Walter, A.G., 21

Wasaga Beach, 113

Watson, Frank, 127, 136-138, 257, 285, 336

Webster, Jack, 70-72, 166, 186, 198, 236, 296, 311, 312, 354

Weisman, Waldimar, 177

Welland, 286

Wentworth, William, 341–343

Wentworth, Michael, 343

Wentworth, Daphne (Jenkins), 342

Whitby, 23

Wiarton, 146

Williams, Frank, 321, 322

Williams, Tom, 214, 276

Wilson, George, 96, 106

Wilson, Reg, 135, 136, 213

Windsor, 131, 286

Winnipeg, 31, 35, 36, 40

Woodbridge, 134, 135

Woodside, W.J., 273

Y

YMCA, 18-22, 31

Young, Cecil J., 161